SIX AUSTRALIAN BATTLEFIELDS

SIX AUSTRALIAN BATTLEFIELDS

THE BLACK RESISTANCE TO INVASION AND THE WHITE STRUGGLE AGAINST COLONIAL OPPRESSION

AL GRASSBY AND MARJI HILL

ANGUS & ROBERTSON PUBLISHERS

ANGUS & ROBERTSON PUBLISHERS

Unit 4, Eden Park, 31 Waterloo Road, North Ryde, NSW, Australia 2113, and 16 Golden Square, London W1R 4BN, United Kingdom

First published in Australia by Angus & Roberston Publishers in 1988

National Library of Australia Cataloguing-in-publication data.

Grassby, A. J. (Albert Jaime), 1926–
Six Australian battlefields.

Bibliography.
Includes index.
ISBN 0 207 15595 X.

1. Battles - Australia - History. [2.] Aborigines, Australian - Government relations. 3. Australia - History 4. Australia - Race relations. I. Hill, Marji. II. Title.

994

The illustration on page 3 is reproduced by permission of the publishers from E. J. Brandl, Australian Aboriginal Paintings in Western and Central Arnhem Land, *Australian Institute of Aboriginal Studies, Canberra, 1973.*

Maps by Winifred Mumford

Typeset in 11/13 pt. Goudy Oldstyle by Midland Typesetters
Printed in Australia by Globe Press

To Lionel Keith Murphy,
one of Australia's finest

CONTENTS

PREFACE

I have wanted to write this book ever since I discovered, as a fifteen-year-old cadet journalist with the *Dartmouth and South Hams Chronicle* in South Devon, England, that the Battle of the Eureka Stockade had an importance and significance never acknowledged in Australia. Browsing through old files of that newspaper I found the issue of January 1855 and discovered that Eureka had pushed the Crimean War off the front page because it was seen for what it was, a bid for independence. While the people of England and indeed the world knew about it, Australians were being taught that the continent had been settled peacefully, that there was no "conquest", no blood spilt on Australian soil, and that Australian history began with Captain Cook.

The partnership of which this book is the result was based on a desire to refute these pernicious myths—a passion shared by Marji Hill whose scholarship is demonstrated in her various publications, which deal mainly with the first Australians, and in her effort to help to correct the misconceptions that have existed in the vast majority of texts about them. As a painter, too, her art is rooted in Australian history, the themes paralleling those of this book. Together we embarked on this enterprise and this is what we say about it.

Six Australian Battlefields seeks to redress the situation where part of the complete history of Australia has been either suppressed or distorted, to demonstrate that Australia was not *terra nullius* when Captain Cook took possession of half the continent for the King of England, that Cook, far from being the first European navigator to come, was in fact one of the last. It places Australia and its history in the context of over 40,000 years of the oldest continuing civilisation on earth, a civilisation, highly developed and attuned to the particular Australian environment, of a people who Pope Paul VI described as a "special people among all mankind".

In fact Australia was far from unpeopled and its invasion and settlement by Europeans far from peaceful. Within a year of the arrival of the First Fleet the original people of Australia began a fierce resistance. For over 100 years the struggle took the form of guerilla warfare against the invasion forces. These were spearheaded by the British marines and followed up by twenty-seven British regiments and associated units which served as an army of occupation until 1870. When the British Army then left for England a network of armed auxiliaries in the form of colonial volunteers, mounted police and black police took over their duties. This book is a testament to the war that was waged. The specific battles—the two in the Sydney region at Hawkesbury (1795) and Parramatta (1797), Vinegar Hill (1804), Bathurst (1824), Pinjarra (1834), Eureka (1854) and Battle Mountain (1884) in north Queensland—are placed in the context of that Hundred Years War.

These battles were not only between the original Australians and the invaders but also between the oppressed and their oppressors. During the 100 years it was not only Black Australians who fought oppression but the Irish, Germans, Italians, Greeks, North Americans from USA and Canada, Jews, Chinese, English, Scots, Welsh and others.

For Black Australians the war has continued into the 1980s, pens and protests replacing guns in the struggle for basic rights that have yet to be recognised.

Six Australian Battlefields is written from a definite ideological position. It has been truly said that history belongs to the victors: it is they who tell it as they want it to be remembered; it is their heroes who are honoured and commemorated; the monuments are to their triumphs. This book is a chronicle of the struggle against overwhelming odds. It speaks for those defeated in battle and those who will never yield even should injustice last another 200 years.

We have drawn on a wide variety of written sources—sometimes primary source material and sometimes secondary and tertiary data. Considerable primary research had already been done by the time we commenced our own. People such as Henry Reynolds, Noel Loos, Michael Christie, Neville Green, R. E. M. Armstrong, T. Salisbury and P. J. Gresser, James Symes and Manning Clark have already made significant contributions to exposing the other side of Australian history. As the extensive documentation shows the evidence clearly is there, but in most cases the material is in specialist historical accounts or in documents that are either out of print or not readily accessible to the general public.

In this account, written not as a specialised academic treatise but for all people, we have interpreted the evidence and woven it into a story to communicate to all Australians some of the truths that have been suppressed over the years.

ACKNOWLEDGEMENTS

Generous assistance and support for this project has come from many people.

The first acknowledgement must go to Jan Bradley who took over as editor at a particularly challenging time and displayed an erudition and a knowledge of Australian history which was invaluable.

Two who have been very close to the project and who have watched its development are Doreen Hill and Alex Barlow. Doreen Hill spent many long hours working as an unofficial research assistant gathering data in the Library of the Australian Institute of Aboriginal Studies and then in the Mitchell Library in Sydney. Alex Barlow was always there to offer critical advice and comment, providing a valuable sounding board for ideas; in the final stages he gave much-needed and painstaking editorial assistance. We thank them both.

Our sincere appreciation goes to the Australian Institute of Aboriginal Studies in Canberra who provided the project with an institutional base. The Institute made an office available for the duration of the research and writing. We thank the principal of the Institute, Warwick Dix, and his deputy, Colin Bourke, for this invaluable support. Our thanks go too to all the staff members who assisted us in various ways, particularly those in the library who eased our access to the research materials.

Other people have helped in a variety of ways. Barbara Ledger read the manuscript and provided useful editorial comment. Ken Colbung arranged our visit to Pinjarra. Oscar Little took us over the battle site of Pinjarra. John Barclay proved an excellent navigator through Sydney traffic on our trip to Vinegar Hill and was always there with his encouragement and support of the book from beginning to the end. The Irish Ambassador HE Sir Joseph Small provided useful books. Sr Angela of the Franciscan Missionaries of Mary gave much needed assistance in

Mount Isa. Margaret Major and Arthur Petersen came to the rescue and drove us to Battle Mountain. John Suttor welcomed us to Brucedale and escorted us to view Windradyne's memorial.

We are appreciative of the support provided by the British High Commissioner HE Sir John Leahy, June Bauer, Erna Valetti, May Phillips, Kieran O'Connor, Peter Stanley, Clare Dunn, Nan Lyons, Henry Reynolds, Mount Isa City Council, Parramatta City Council, Blacktown City Council and the Richmond Shire Council.

Last and not least we would like to thank our families and close friends who bore with us throughout the "magnificent obsession".

1. *INVASION*

The unknown and unnamed fifth continent now known as Australia was the last to be recognised as part of the world by other continents. When Australia lay beyond the ken of the overwhelming majority of humankind, Asia, Europe, Africa and the Americas had long been known to each other, had shared common experiences, leadership, cultural and language links, which spanned both time and distance. These links had been forged by a series of world empires. The first transnational empire, that of Alexander the Great in the fourth century BC, was followed by the Roman Empire which set the scene for the next 2000 years. The Portuguese, the Spaniards, the Dutch, French and English, who expanded to become the "British", followed them in quick and dramatic succession. The epicentre of the oriental world was China. The Celestial Kingdom spanned 4000 years of recorded history, yet it was not until the fifteenth century that this civilisation looked to the south of the globe and the unknown continent.

Here, in fact, was one of the earliest centres of civilisation in the world, which had its beginnings at least 40,000 years ago. The people of the Australian continent were global pioneers in many ways. They were among the first great sea voyagers: between 40,000 and 100,000 thousand years ago the original people had to cross open channels between the islands of South-east Asia and Australia, which, even when the sea levels were low during the ice ages, meant developing craft capable of covering up to eighty kilometres of ocean. They were among the first people on earth to develop a sophisticated technology which gave them implements and weapons of stone, and the first to apply practical aerodynamics, creating the boomerang. They were the first to recognise the dynamics of land conservation, and the first to develop a religious, social and cultural life that recognised the essential bonds between mankind and the land.

In their history they had demonstrated man's ability to reach for the stars in art, in legend and oral history, and in their ceremonial life, which embraced the first ritual expressions ever undertaken in the history of the world. Their cremation and burial ceremonies pointed to a firmly held belief in the afterlife.

By the eighteenth century it is likely that there were nearly a million people, divided into as many as 270 groups, speaking distinctive languages and identifying as social groups which in other continents would command the title of nation, in full and unchallenged sovereignty of what today is called Australia. The people shared a common stock and a basic heritage, yet in many ways, such as language, they were as distinct as the people of Europe. The Australian languages embraced perhaps 700 dialects. Just as there are scores of dialects of English, so the languages of Australia varied within themselves; within the one language, however, there was mutual understanding just as an English-speaking American can be understood by an English-speaking Australian. At the same time major languages such as Pitjantjatjara, Bundjalang, Kamilaroi or Gupapuyŋu are as distinct and different as English, German, Italian, Spanish or French.

In times past, as today among Black Australians following traditional life, monolingualism was unknown. Among the peoples of New South Wales, for example, an encounter with a stranger might lead to the inquiry "Do you speak Kamilaroi?" Whether the person did or did not hardly mattered: they showed themselves to be civilised by acknowledging that they understood the question. Aranda children playing on the banks of the Todd River in Alice Springs today normally know something of several languages before they begin school, a contrast to their white counterparts who generally know only one.

The division of land among Black Australians was according to divine law, a division of greater significance than national boundaries because it could not be altered by conquest, nor bought nor sold. Such a concept had no parallel in English law or for that matter in Roman law, which prevailed in most of Europe, or in the brehon laws of old Ireland. The land belonged to the people and the people to the land, bound in everlasting union. The divine beings who journeyed across the continent at the beginning of the world established the boundaries, the sacred sites, and the religious ceremonies that bound people to their obligations to the land and its conservation.

This tie between the people and the land has its origin in the great heroic sagas of the Dreamtime, which involves not only the past but a timeless eternity subsuming present and future. The ancestral beings emerged from the subterranean or heavenly world and moved over the featureless earth. The places where they first appeared, where they journeyed and where they departed, became the billabongs and rivers,

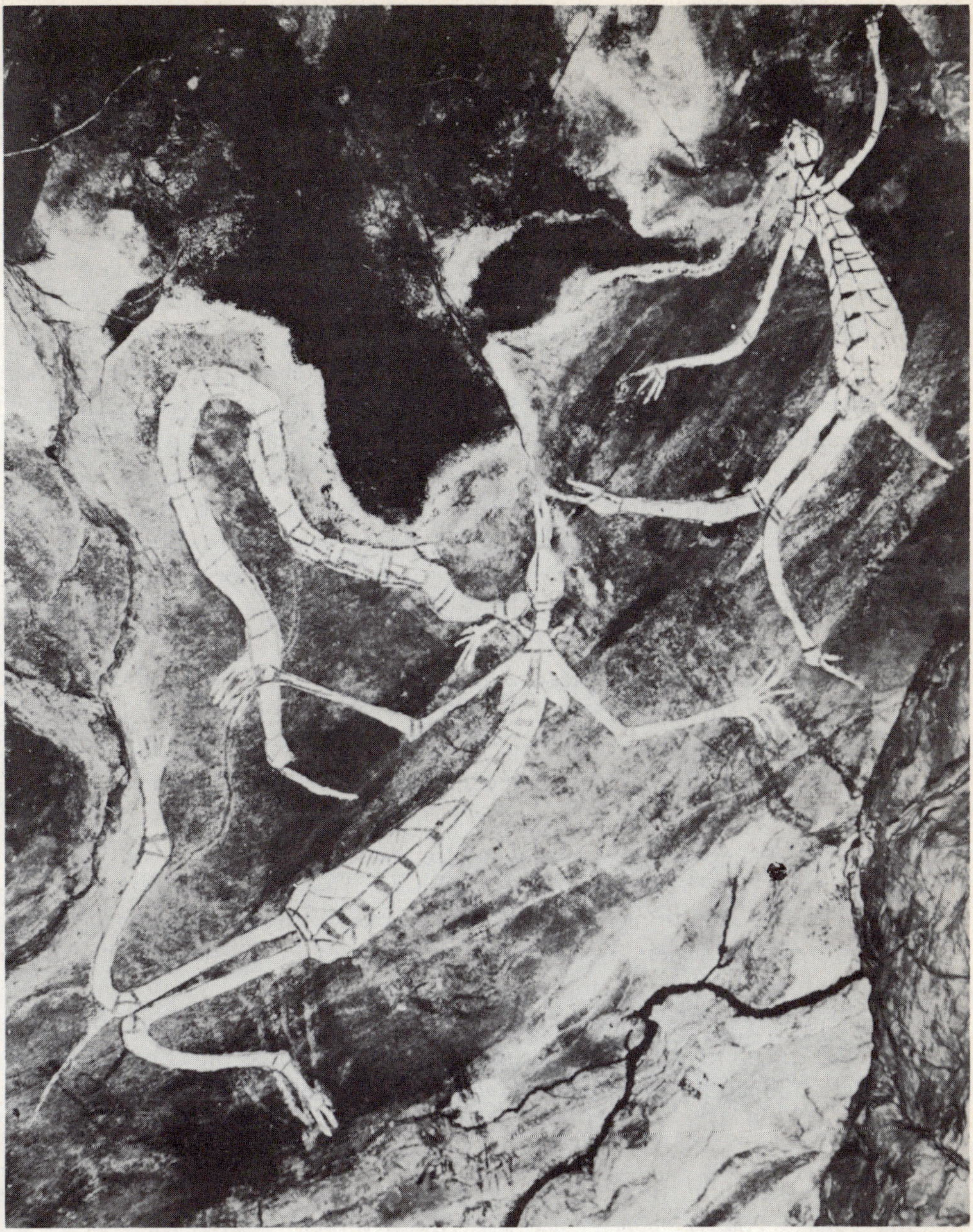

The ancestral beings of the Dreamtime remain a vital force in the present. Two Namorodo spirits and a Rainbow Snake in X-ray style. Rock painting, Cadell River, Northern Territory. AUSTRALIAN INSTITUTE OF ABORIGINAL STUDIES

the rocks, hills and mountains, and all the features of the environment. At the same time the ancestral beings placed in this setting all life, human, animal and plant, in an interconnected system of relationships.

Having created the features of the landscape and the life to populate it, the creators formulated sets of rules for all living things to abide by. This done, they retired—to the sea, or underground, or to the heavens. Yet they never really left the land they created: their hidden presence remains as a vital force, with the power to intervene in the lives of the people they had brought into being.

One of the stories of south-eastern Australia relates to a powerful creative being called Baiame, who shaped this part of the world and created the peoples, plants and animals that live in it. When his work was done he is said to have ascended to the heavens, where he watches events on earth. Baiame returns to earth from time to time, his voice being heard in the whirr of the bullroarer at the bora ground ceremonies when boys are brought to manhood and to an awareness of their history and sacred responsibilities. His name was used in some early translations of the Bible to depict the Father of All as recorded in Genesis.

Among the responsibilities the land demanded were the rituals that recalled and saluted creation, and which ackowledged the continuing presence and suzerainty of the ancestral beings. The rituals and their testament may be described as the eternal title deeds to the land. The people's responsibilities to the land in the spiritual sphere were thus clearly acknowledged, but the economic use of the land was vital to their earthly survival.

The basic operations governing food supplies were the responsibility of family groups. Depending on the nature of the environment they often ranged over lands belonging to other people, but they did so with permission and with respect for the sacred sites of the owners, sharing the food they obtained. The attitude of the people across the continent in relation to land tenure involved reciprocity and sharing. Daily life was regulated by definite rules; the concept of helping each other created in effect a social security system; the weak depended on the strong, the sick on the healthy and the young or old on the middle aged; and help was freely given. The young were regarded as future support, the old as keepers of wisdom.[1] Social order was maintained by rules that governed life from the cradle to beyond the grave. The kinship system ensured every individual a unique position in society, defining everyone's responsibilities to everyone else. Nobody was outside the system; no children could be left orphans, no widows left without support.

Care and planning were used to ensure regular supplies of food and water. In drier regions freshwater springs were turned into wells and covered from the sun's heat. Sufficient seed was left after the harvesting of vegetables, grains and fruit to ensure future crops. Game conservation was ensured by the totemic identification with various species and the application of rules that protected game at breeding time. The propagation of kangaroos, wallabies, wombats and emus was ensured by "firestick farming", burning off to encourage the growth of sweet fresh grass. Food supplies were also maintained through the performance of sacred rituals.

The southern continent was at peace within, apart from sporadic clashes, which were fought ritualistically until the lawmen and elders called a halt and a parley, or from those instances of individual homicide from which no society has ever been free. In comparative terms it also contributed to these Australians' "more affluent" society than that of their counterparts in Europe and Asia. The "success of their way of life can be seen in the fact that they managed to survive so long in so many uncompromising places in which Europeans with their technology can only live with a vast network of external support".[2]

For most of the 40,000 years the peoples of neighbouring New Guinea had been the only outside contact. During the ice ages, when the water levels were low, the two countries were connected by land for many centuries. In New Guinea with its different climate, vegetation and topography, life evolved in a different way and above all its peoples retained their contact with the neighbouring peoples to the north. Domestic animals and plants were introduced and a system of agriculture, practised for 5000 years, was developed. Different types of housing, outrigger canoes and bows and arrows testify to a technology adapted to the New Guinea environment. The peoples of New Guinea, Torres Strait and Cape York, however, intermarried and exchanged cultural values and technology.

In Australia agriculture was not adopted, perhaps because it demanded long hours of labour for the same return that could be secured from firestick farming and careful conservation and husbanding of food and water supplies. Agriculture would also have demanded great changes in both lifestyle and the very rules that governed society.[3]

The thousands of years of contact between the peoples of Australia and New Guinea had been peaceful. It was a pattern which was to be repeated in the contact that was later established between the Australians and the people from Macassar, who enjoyed an essentially friendly relationship for about 200 years.

THE BAIINI

Pre-dating the Macassans and still a mystery to European Australians was the arrival on the shores of north-east Arnhem Land of the Baiini, hailed in verbal histories as the first visitors to the northern coast. Some stories indicate they were of European origin, others suggest they were traders from the East Indies or sea gipsies of Malayan type who were to be found in all parts of the East Indies Archipelago.[4]

They are described as having come by sailing ship, and once they arrived on the shores of Arnhem Land they built houses of stone and ironbark. The women are said to have been light skinned and beautiful with colourful sarongs of many patterns. They planted rice, and the men fished and hunted as the people of northern Australia did then and now. But it is the women who are remembered in many *yirritja* songs, planting rice, cooking, weaving, dyeing their yarn in large pots and decorating the cloth with designs of coloured triangles, fishing, making armbands and necklets, stitching sails and caring for their families.

The Baiini apparently left Australia to return from whence they came, abandoning their houses and rice plantations and leaving only memories of their coming in song and story.[5]

THE MACASSANS

For a period of 200 years to just after the end of the nineteenth century at least 1000 Macassans, more than the total complement of the English First Fleet, came south each year from the Indonesian island of Sulewesi to north Australia, to fish for the sea slug known as trepang, or *bêche-de-mer*. Dried trepang, which was prized in Chinese cuisine, was a major commodity throughout Asia. The Macassans called the Northern Territory coast "Marege", and they also worked along the Kimberley coast of Western Australia, which they called "Kayu Jawa".[6]

This peaceful invasion left Macassar each year as the north-west monsoon began, providing the constant winds needed to avoid being blown off course. They would stay in Australia for approximately five months before heading back in April when the winds changed to the south-east. The Macassans established settlements on sheltered beaches along the coast of Arnhem Land not far from the shallow waters where trepang could be collected. Near their settlements they set up processing plants for the trepang, rows of stone fireplaces which supported the cauldrons in which it was boiled. Some of these still stand, silent monuments to the period.[7] The second stage of processing involved burying the trepang in sand; then it was smoked and packed ready for export to Macassar and the markets of the north. Many Macassans returned year after year, following a family tradition in which Australia was a second home.

The arrival of the first twenty-five tonne Macassan praus provoked tremendous interest, and undoubtedly some panic, among the Arnhem Landers. The praus captured the imagination of artists and they were vividly and accurately recorded; most images show the crew on board, working hard, and some depict interiors showing how the boiling pots and processing equipment were stored. The observers also saw how the prayer man on board called the faithful to prayer with a traditional Arabic chant as all faced Mecca. Each prau carried several dugout canoes and

A visiting Macassan prau recorded on bark.
N. McLEOD, ALEX BARLOW AND MARJI HILL

containers of food and rice for the stay in Australia. A Yirrkala account of their arrival in north Australia as if from outer space paints a contrast with European arrivals some time later.[8]

Two Macassan praus were spotted on the horizon. Hurried counsel was taken and the people of Arnhem Land pulled back, leaving observers in the thick coastal jungle, but two young boys, unaware of the momentous events about to unfold, went out to spear fish in the mangrove swamps. One of the praus anchored in a tidal creek and two young Maccassan boys collected some shellfish and began to hammer them open. The Australian boys heard the noise and saw to their astonishment the two strange boys who were not their people and the praus. Being well versed in the history of their land, they wondered if they might be Baiini returning.

The four young men, overcoming fear and shyness, came forward to meet and talk, but there was no understanding of each other's language. The Macassans persuaded them to come to their camp. They watched the people dancing before going to work, and were examined all over by the Macassan leader or "father" and mobbed by everyone in the camp. They were given food and shown how to smoke the long Malay pipe and finally, with many signs of friendship, were sent home.

The boys were greeted by their families with great excitement. They led a delegation back to the Macassan camp and accepted an offer to work with them, an example followed by many men of the north. The boys who made this first contact learned the Macassan language and became teachers themselves.

This pattern of peaceful contact was repeated again and again along the northern coasts as Macassan settlements with semi-permanent platform houses on bamboo stilts with steeply pointed roofs of woven coconut palm leaves were established.[9] A flourishing trade between the two peoples built up over the two centuries, the people of north Australia exchanging tortoise shell, pearl shell and pearls for tobacco, alcohol, cloth, axes, knives and other items. The huge influx of people every year had a dramatic impact on many aspects of life. The language spoken by the Macassans not only contributed richly to northern Australian languages, but became the lingua franca right along the northern coastline. Even the word now commonly used for Europeans, *balanda*, was an adaptation from the Macassan of the Dutch *Hollander*. Macassan place names have also survived, such as Camburinga at Grays Bay in eastern Arnhem Land, which is derived from Kampong Renggang in Macassar.[10]

As well as trade, language and technology, intermarriage indicates the depth of the contact between the two peoples. The Macassan men were not usually accompanied by women, and some married local women and so were incorporated into the kinship system—the equivalent in

European Australia of acquiring citizenship.

There were some conflicts, usually arguments over women or fairness in trading, but there was no general conflict, no pitched battle. As the years passed relations matured and Macassan fathers and friends took Australians to stay in Macassar, where a quarter of the town was reserved for them. One visitor, Djaladjari from Galiwin' ku (Elcho Island) in north-east Arnhem Land, described his voyages to what he called the mainland of Borneo and Java.[11] He recorded wonderment at the busy port, the easy acceptance of the visitors into the houses of the bosses, surprise at finding a fellow countryman married to a Macassan woman with four sons and four daughters. Nine young men were reported as having decided to stay and work, and there were young women, too, some who were married and others who worked in the town. The governor-general of the Dutch East Indies, on a visit to Macassar in 1824, commented on the distinctive appearance of the well-built black people from the southern continent.[12] In 1876 there were still twenty or so Australians in Macassar and it is a significant commentary on relations between the two people that the captains of industry often accommodated them in their own houses.

The connection between Macassar and north Australia was severed in 1907.[13] English pearling interests had for some time called for the exclusion of the Macassans from what was by then an English colony. Settlements had been established, customs officials suddenly appeared to exact tribute from the visiting fleets, taxes were imposed, policing was enforced and the imposts strangled the Macassan enterprise. That the people of north Australia favoured working and associating with the Macassans rather than with the English fuelled the repeated attempts to exclude them. The fleets were banned by law in 1906, and the last, which arrived in 1907, was warned off by colonial officials. Two hundred years of peaceful relations had been ended.

Prior to and during the period of Macassan contact a series of probes of the Australian continent took place. Of some we have only sketchy knowledge, but the last, and most significant, opened the way for general invasion and occupation, changing the southern continent for all time.

THE CHINESE

It is possible that the first foreign probe to Australian shores was made by the Chinese, who may have landed in what is now Darwin in 1432.[14] Although the Chinese were already great travellers and seafarers, the period of the Ming Dynasty (1368–1644) was the most expansive for China. The admiral Ch'eng Ho assembled a fleet of more than sixty junks and on seven great voyages between 1405 and 1432 visited almost all the regions bordering the Indian Ocean, including East Africa, India, Java and

Sumatra. The Chinese were known to have already reached Timor, where there was a valuable trade in sandalwood.

In 1879 a Chinese statuette from the Ming Dynasty was uncovered in Darwin, then an English outpost only ten years old. A piece of porcelain believed to be of the same era was also found in the Gulf of Carpentaria.[15] While precise dating of these objects is not possible, they could have arrived in Australia during the time of Ch'eng Ho.

The Chinese Empire later turned inwards and never again despatched fleets across the world. The southern continent and its peoples were left undisturbed until the rise of the European world empires of modern times.

THE SPANISH AND PORTUGUESE

While it appears that the Portuguese Captain Cristovão de Mendonça could have led his fleet of caravels down the east coast of Australia in 1522, sailing south as far as today's Warrnambool and mapping the coast as he went, it was a Spanish probe which was to pose the first threat of invasion and settlement.

The first Spanish voyage of exploration and discovery in the southern seas was captained by Alvaro de Mendaña de Neyra, who sailed from Callao in Peru in 1567; he was the first European to sight the Solomon Islands. On a second voyage in 1595 he claimed the Marquesas and Santa Cruz islands for Spain. The pilot on this voyage was Pedro Fernandez de Quiros, sometimes hailed as the Christopher Columbus of the Pacific.

In 1605 Quiros, now an admiral, returned to the Pacific full of inspiration to explore and conquer and with the personal blessing of Pope Clement VIII. After a long hard voyage west from Callao they reached what Quiros first thought to be the great south land, which he claimed in the name of the King of Spain, Phillip III of the House of Austria, and named in his honour Austrialia del Espiritu Santo. He established a settlement, and then discovered he had reached an island in what is now Vanuatu. He sailed back to Acapulco in Mexico and reached Madrid in October 1607, penniless but determined to return to the South Pacific. Seven years later he received authority to assemble a further fleet to establish a permanent settlement, but he died in Panama on the way back in 1615. Not even the site of his grave is known and as the Spanish Empire declined his dream of a Spanish Australia died with him. But the name he had used for the whole region south to the pole, modified to Australia, survived.

Quiros' second-in-command, Luis Vaez de Torres, returned to Spain via Manila. The route he chose was through the strait which today bears his name. An attempted landing at the tip of Cape York was repulsed. The people of Australia, changing their tactic of withdrawal before would-be intruders, attacked with spears and war clubs, as Torres reported on his return to Madrid.[16]

THE DUTCH

In 1606, the same year that Torres sailed into history, Willem Jansz in the *Duyfken* made a probe on behalf of the expanding Dutch Empire. Like Torres he found the people of the north hostile: as the Dutch came ashore on the western side of Cape York the sailors found themselves under heavy attack. Torres failed to record any casualties, but Jansz acknowledged that a number of his sailors were killed in the clash.[17] It was seventeen years before any further Dutch probes were attempted. In 1623 Jan Carstenz fought not one engagement but several[18] while attempting to assess the Gulf of Carpentaria's potential for Holland. The repeated attacks forced him to withdraw completely. He captured a range of weapons, including spears, shields, clubs and sticks, and one Australian, who he took back to Batavia.

The Dutch tried again in 1642–44 when Anthony van Diemen, governor-general of the Dutch East Indies, sent Abel Tasman on two epic voyages of discovery. On the first, Tasman discovered Van Diemen's Land and named it in honour of his sponsor, but he made no contact with the people. The Dutch had a healthy respect for the people of Australia—curse them as miserable barbarians they might, but they acknowledged their ability to defend their land: in the instruction given to Tasman in 1644, when he charted the coast from Cape York west to North-West Cape, he was advised to land with "great caution, circumspection and prudence . . . the Southlands are peopled . . . by rude, wild, fierce barbarians, for which reason you will always have to be well-armed, and to use every prudent precaution".[19]

The only Dutch captain to attempt contact was Willem de Vlamingh, who ordered "sixteen cautious land" surveys on the western Australian coast in 1697,[20] but confronted by his armed party of nearly ninety men the Australians withdrew and avoided all contact for the six weeks of his stay.

One of the last Dutch reports on the people of the north came from the governor-general in Batavia, Martin Van Delft, who in 1705 admitted the strength of the rude and barbarous "islanders"—he had formed the opinion that north Australia was an archipelago.[21] The final report was made in 1756 by Lieutenant J. E. Gonzal, who surveyed Carpentaria. He made many contacts but was respectful and friendly, offering sugar and spirits as gifts. The reward for the northern people not driving them out was to see two of their compatriots kidnapped.

The Dutch finally gave up—the land was too barren, and the people were too tough. The people of Australia had registered their first major victory—any thought of planned invasion was abandoned.

The Chinese, Portuguese, Spaniards and Dutch had probed and explored, but all had failed to mount a permanent presence on the continent. That was to be left to the last wave of invaders from the far horizon. As the Chinese turned inwards on themselves, and the European empires began their steady decline, a new empire based in London was rising.

THE ENGLISH

The occupation of Australia became, in fact, a race between the English and the French, another vigorous people on the imperial ascent. The first recorded English presence in Australia was in 1622, when an English ship, the *Tryal*, was wrecked on rocks just north-west of Monte Bello Islands off the west coast. Forty-six survivors reached Batavia in two small boats. They were followed by the notorious William Dampier, who made two visits to the west in 1688 and 1699. His ambitions to establish an empire of his own came to grief on the twin rocks which defeated the Dutch—harsh land and tough people.

A new chapter in the history of the Australian continent began when Britain decided to challenge the claims of Spain, her rival on land and sea for 200 years. On 26 May 1768 Captain James Cook was selected to search out the southern continent, which the Spaniards had claimed but failed to settle and the Dutch had found but could not settle. The official reason for this armed probe into the Pacific was to observe the transit of Venus from Tahiti and there were scientists on board the *Endeavour* to justify this part of the voyage. After leaving Tahiti in August 1769, Cook sailed south and in October reached New Zealand. He spent until March 1770 charting the coast and making careful observations of the people as he had done in Tahiti, then determined to head west for New Holland, for the Dutch name had long superseded the Spanish Australia. Cook had both Spanish and Portuguese maps, and the course he set should have taken him from New Zealand, already discovered and named by the Dutch, to Van Diemen's Land. It was the great swell of the ocean which carried him instead to the mainland.

On 19 April 1770 Cook reached the east coast of the mainland. He named Point Hicks after the man on board who had first sighted it, then made his way north to Botany Bay, which was already marked in Portuguese on the Dieppe maps as "Coste des Herbaiges".[22]

It was here that the English were first challenged. A group of Eora people observed their coming and a youngster threw a stone at a small boat coming ashore. Cook ordered a musket shot in reply and the people on the beach withdrew. Exploration parties examined the hinterland. Cook was enthusiastic, the deep black soil, the fine timber and what he described as "fine meadow" all went down in his records.[23] He had the name of the ship and the date cut into a tree near the creek from which they drew water. Years later the English First Fleet Marine, Watkin Tench, was to suspect that there had been a major confrontation between the English and the Eora people but that Cook, unlike Torres a century before,

Cook's landing in Botany Bay as depicted almost a century after the event.
NATIONAL LIBRARY OF AUSTRALIA

had ignored it in his log and journal.

Cook raised the anchor and proceeded north until on 22 August 1770 he reached Possession Island off the northern tip of Cape York. Fulfilling the main purpose of his voyage, he hoisted the English flag and took possession of the whole eastern coast from latitude 38° S to Possession Island in the name of King George III. He named the entire eastern half of the continent New South Wales.[24]

As far as Spain was concerned Cook was a trespasser on Spanish territory. The Spanish Minister for the Marine and the Indies, Josef de Galvez, when he learned of Cook's voyage to the South Pacific, instructed the Viceroy of Mexico to arrest him and charge him with infringing the Spanish law of the Indies. Similar instructions were sent to the Viceroy of Peru.[25] Cook successfully eluded capture and the Spanish Council of the Indies recommended in 1779 the establishment of a Spanish colony in Australia or New Guinea. This was to facilitate direct trade between Spain and the Philippines by taking advantage of the new south-western route across the Pacific discovered by Cook. A Spanish navigator named Francisco Maurello attempted this route in 1781 but turned back.

Cook's actions in the South Pacific brought a series of protests by the Spanish Ambassador in London, Bernardo del Campo, between April and December 1789. The establishment of the English colony at Port Jackson in 1788 brought protests by the Spanish government to the courts of Europe. In fact, the establishment of the settlement almost provoked a war with Spain.[26] The Viceroy of Mexico, Conde de Revilla Gigedo, notified the Spanish Minister of War that there were not enough Spanish forces in the south seas to confront the English. The Spanish authorities regarded the Port Jackson settlement as a base from which expeditions could, with impunity, because of distance, make highly damaging raids on Spanish colonies. But Spain's time had passed; the warrants for Cook's arrest were unenforceable and there was no war. Spain had lost her chance to settle Australia with the passing of Quiros. There was to be no second chance in 1789.

The Australians could not have known that the declaration by Cook on Possession Island was to change their lives for all time. Cook's contact with them had been limited and his experience dictated his comments that they were a "timerous inoffensive race" that in no way seemed inclined to cruelty, who could be said to be in the pure state of nature and might appear to some to be the most wretched on earth (a reference to Dampier's slanders) but in reality were far happier than Europeans.[27]

The botanist Joseph Banks largely supported Cook's observations and agreed that the New Hollanders were a distinct people, quite different from those of New Guinea. Cook was a meticulous observer and his reports on the land and people were to be the basis for much future planning, including his suggestion that sheep and cattle would do well on the land. Yet neither Cook nor any of his officers were able to communicate with the New Hollanders. He came and went without knowing anything of their life and culture beyond the material points he recorded.

Cook was killed in 1779 on a voyage to Hawaii. In contrast to Quiros, who is remembered by only one street name (in Canberra) and by a plaque on Vanuatu, Cook is remembered in every town and village in Australia. It was his proclamation, not his discoveries, that made him the benchmark in Australian history.

THE FRENCH

The French had been hard on Cook's heels. Between 1771 and 1828 they sent eight expeditions to Australia to extend their knowledge of the country, the climate, physical features, bird and animal life and above all the people they would confront if they decided to settle. These explorations were not quick and simple surveys. In the last quarter of the eighteenth century France was in a ferment of political and intellectual change and inquiry. Serious attempts were made by learned societies and the cultural departments of the government to seek expert knowledge of the little known world of Australia and the Pacific.[28]

The first two French expeditions were those of St Allouarn, who sailed close to Cape Leeuwin on 18 March 1772 and along the coast to north-west Australia and on to Timor, and Du Fresne, who spent a week in Tasmania from 3 March 1772. La Pérouse arrived in Botany Bay at the same time as Captain Arthur Phillip and the English First Fleet; after sailing from Botany Bay the expedition was lost at sea. D'Entrecasteaux spent April and May 1792 in Tasmania, December near Esperance, and returned to Tasmania in 1793 for another sojourn, which left his name well-remembered on the map today.

Baudin arrived at Cape Leeuwin in May 1801 and followed the coast north to Rottnest and Shark Bay. After sailing to north-west Australia he headed for Timor. In November he returned to Tasmania where he surveyed the south-east and east coasts, Bass Strait and Western Port. He was laid up in Port Jackson for about six months in 1802. Louis de Freycinet in 1818 and 1819, Duperrey in 1824 and D'Urville from 1826 to 1828 also made their mark on the Australian coasts, but their voyages were essentially reconnaissance, one of their priorities being to try to understand the life and ways of the Australian people.

Following this strong display of interest by France in Australia, the French Ambassador to London asked the British Foreign Minister, Lord John Russell, what parts of the Australian coastline the British government considered within their "sphere of influence". Russell drew a pencil outline around the whole coastline and replied in one word—"All".[29] It is interesting to speculate if the Napoleonic Wars had ended in a French victory in 1815 whether Joseph Bonaparte Gulf, Cape Catastrophe and Geographe Channel, which still survive on the map of Australia, would have a French presence today.

Terra Nullius

The great invasion, however, was not French, Dutch or Spanish, but English, and the proclamation of 1770 that led to it was in fact a declaration of war. In accordance with instructions issued to him by the British Admiralty Commissioners in 1768 Cook had taken possession of eastern Australia, yet the instructions also said he was "with the consent of the natives to take possession of convenient situations in the country in the name of the King of Great Britain or if you find the country uninhabited take possession for His Majesty by setting up proper marks and inscriptions as first discoverers and possessors".[30]

Cook made a strange choice of location for his proclamation seizing half the continent, to quote his own words, "in the name of His Majesty King George III". The place was today's Possession Island and his landing was observed by a party which he described as armed like all the other Australians he had seen except for one warrior who had a bow and arrow. To his surprise their landing a little before sunset was not opposed. The people simply withdrew and left him with enough land for his ceremony. Choosing the highest hill he hoisted the English flag, made his proclamation and ordered three volleys to be fired by the armed shore party, which was answered by cannon fire from the ship. Next morning, looking across at the land he had claimed, he noted that the people had returned. A party, mostly women, were picking up shells along the beach; the men were wearing large breastplates of oyster shell.

It was not until later that Cook put in the name he had chosen for King George's new domain. It looks as if he tried "New Whales" first, then "New Wales" and finally, realising there was already a New Wales in Canada, New South Wales.

Despite his professed admiration for the New Hollanders, Cook took their lands as if they did not exist; they became from that moment a shadow people with no rights of any kind to their hearths and homes. This was an application of the dictum of *terra nullius* (land without people); following it no restrictions were recognised on occupation or exploitation. In the 1970s the courts of Australia continued to uphold this view.

Unlike Canada, Australia has no treaties between its original inhabitants and the invaders. John Batman, in 1835 one of the first English settlers in Victoria, attempted to acquire land by treaty, but the governor of the colony, Richard Bourke, declared that all such treaties were void as the British Crown, on the basis of Cook's proclamation, owned the entire continent. The British authorities did have second thoughts about this sweeping expropriation in 1836, when Lord Glenelg, Secretary of

State for the Colonies, instructed Robert Torrens, Chairman of the South Australian Colonising Commission, to negotiate with the people of that area to purchase land. The instructions, however, were ignored by the invaders, who arrived intent on taking what they could.[31]

In some parts of the world invading nations attempted (or were forced) to make agreements that at least partially recognised the rights of those who had been occupied. In New Zealand the Treaty of Waitangi in 1840 granted the Maori chiefs "full exclusive and undisturbed possession of their lands . . . so long as it is their wish and desire to retain the same".[32] In Papua in 1884 the conquering Germans assured the people "your lands will be preserved unto you".[33] In the United States and Canada, after protracted wars with the Indian nations, treaties were signed, peace was maintained and land was guaranteed to the vanquished.

By contrast, the law of England, including English property law, became the law of the Australian colonies on 26 January 1788 when Governor Phillip raised the English flag. Without being consulted or even informed the people of the continent became subject to English law; neither then nor since could they appeal to their own law to justify their claims to their own land. The English view, based on nothing but casual observation, was that the people of New Holland did not have a system of law and did not constitute a sovereign state. The legal fiction that Australia was unoccupied led to a war that lasted well over 100 years, and to the conflict that persists to this day between the conquerors and the conquered.

Cook sailed away to meet his death leaving his flag flying and the legacy of his proclamation. The war that was an inevitable result was postponed for a futher eighteen years, until the recommendation by one of Cook's officers, James Mario Matra, to settle Botany Bay—a recommendation Cook never knew about—was put into effect. The arrival of the invasion forces from England, the First Fleet, on 26 January 1788 was the signal for the wars of resistance to begin.

2. THE ARMY OF OCCUPATION

The seeds of the Hundred Years War were sown when Captain James Cook executed his secret mission for the British Crown, seizing an entire continent, proclaiming it *terra nullius* and dispossessing its people. The instruments of that war, the troops, first came ashore with the First Fleet. After a period in which the people of the continent used their traditional tactic of withdrawing to wait for the departure of the intruders, it must have become apparent that they were here to stay. The people of the Sydney and Hawkesbury regions were the first to go into action against the English armed forces. Their struggle was taken up across the continent as the intruders pushed out in all directions from the original English "Pale".

The ensuing battles engaged the British Army and its colonial auxiliaries from 1788 to 1884. Black Australian casualties in north Australia, above the Tropic of Capricorn, exceeded 10,000, twice the number of white Australians from the same area killed in foreign wars between the outbreak of the Boer War and the end of the Vietnam conflict.[1] Total black casualties were many times more—the death toll in action alone is estimated to be 20,000.[2] The existence of their burial mounds, offering silent testimony to the conflict, was not disclosed by imperial authorities lest the world challenge a claim based on a lie.

Montgomery of Alamein defined war as "a prolonged conflict between rival political groups by force of arms". This statement is further qualified by Clausewitz, who makes the point that wars are undertaken to force an opponent to fulfil one's will in continuation of political policy.[3] Since the century-long conflict in Australia met these conditions, it may fairly be described as having been a war.

The armed forces that held Australia for the British Crown constituted an occupation force; it arrived in 1788 and remained until 1870, when the last garrison sailed back to England. During that time the marines (later the Royal Marines), the New South Wales Corps and twenty-seven regiments served in Australia; the last fourteen years of occupation duties were undertaken by the Royal Artillery. These regiments were reinforced by paramilitary units of colonial police and "loyalist" forces made up of Englishmen and others, who volunteered to serve in defence of His Majesty King George III, in whose name the first thirty years of the war was conducted. Following the death of King George, whose titles gave him suzerainty over not only the United Kingdom of Great Britain but also Ireland and Hanover, the fight was carried on in the names of George IV, William IV and finally Queen Victoria, in whose long reign (1837–1901) resistance was broken and the last battle won.

The Occupation Forces

The responsibility of the occupation forces was to "afford Protection to the Settlers" on the frontiers of white settlement.[4] The marines accompanying the First Fleet numbered 211 complete with drummers,[5] and were commanded by Major Robert Ross. As soon as they had disembarked and unloaded their supplies they built an earth redoubt with two guns to command Sydney Cove at what is now the northern end of Macquarie Place near its junction with Loftus Street. Within three years they had established two more forts—Fort Bennelong (later Fort Macquarie) and Fort Phillip—in Sydney Town, and were also guarding the outlying settlement at Parramatta, where a redoubt was erected in December 1788.

The Marines laid the foundation for the English military occupation and when most of the detachment left to return to England on 18 December 1791 they were described as "as valuable a corps as any in his Majesty's service".[6] They were succeeded by the New South Wales Corps, perhaps the most controversial unit in the history of the British Army, being rivalled only by the auxiliaries known as the "Black and Tans", which saw service in Ireland in the War of Independence 1919–21.

The New South Wales Corps, created specifically for service in the colony, consisted of 300 men plus officers. The Marines were offered a cash incentive to re-enlist in the Corps, their officers being offered promotion in addition; in spite of the privations they had suffered, nearly sixty took up the offer, including Captain Lieutenant George Johnston.[7] The Corps was not a Line regiment but a force permanently resident in the colony; its members received special allowances and could also be rewarded with land seized from the people of the continent. The recruiting officer and first commander, Major Francis Grose, was rewarded with money and honours.

The Corps' first casualties were thirteen men who died on the voyage to New South Wales in 1792. Within weeks of taking over Sydney and

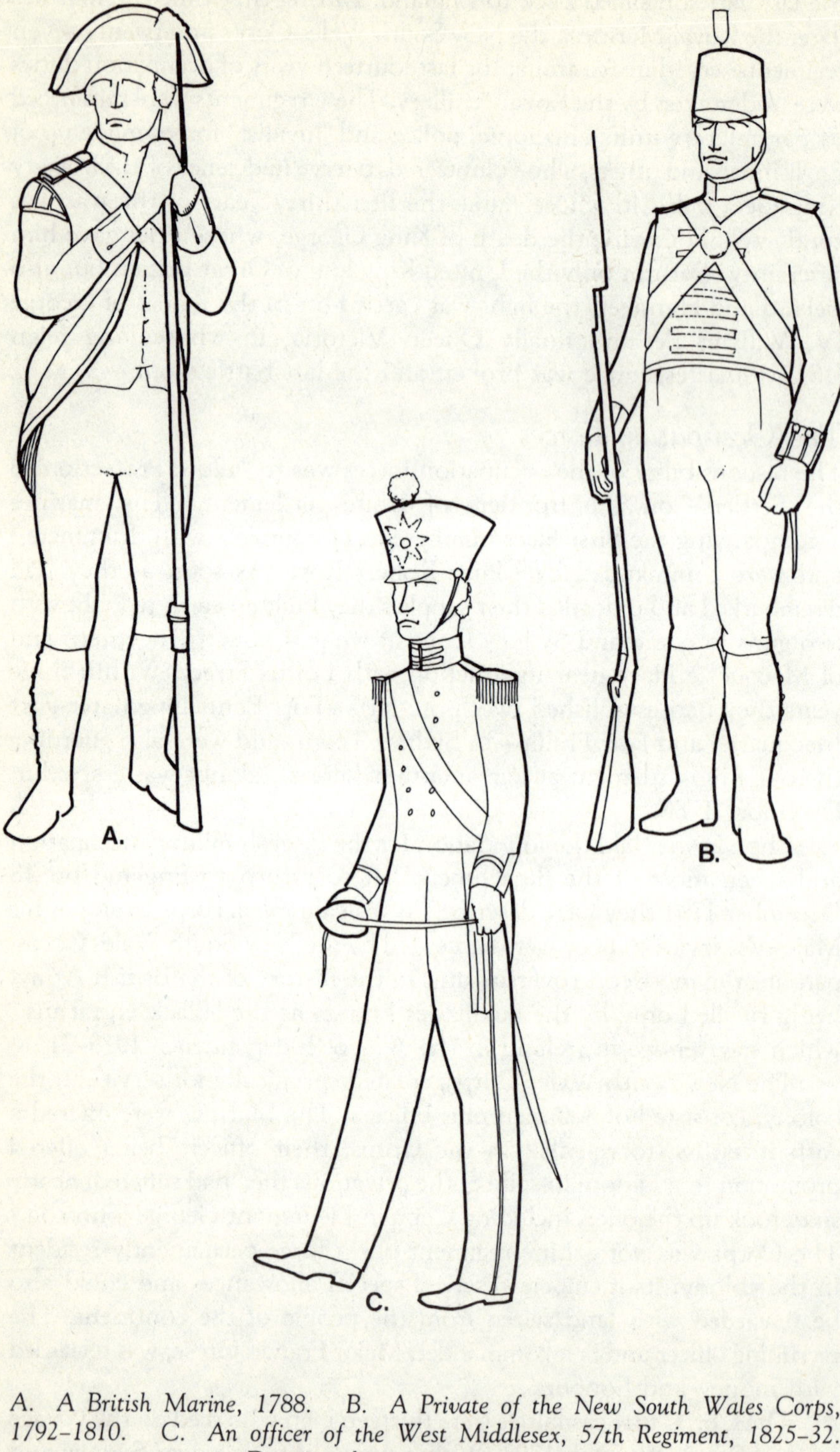

A. *A British Marine, 1788.* B. *A Private of the New South Wales Corps, 1792–1810.* C. *An officer of the West Middlesex, 57th Regiment, 1825–32.*
Drawings by WINIFRED MUMFORD

its forts, the new soldiers were complaining about rations and the fact that they had scarcely shoes to their feet.[8] Both officers and men began almost at once to agitate for free land. Governor Phillip held them at bay, but within two years the soldiers were spending more time in the prisoners' huts, eating, drinking, gambling and taking their women, than in carrying out their military duties.[9]

After Phillip left in December 1792, the military had complete control of the colony until Governor John Hunter arrived in September 1795. Matters went from bad to worse. Riots broke out regularly. In January 1794, after ten soldiers were taken as prisoners to the barracks, a majority of the detachment poured out of the barracks with fixed bayonets in a spontaneous mutiny, taking over the town for five days.[10] The chaplain noted the Corps' record of extortion, despotism and debauchery and their monopoly of trade, in which they exacted up to 1200 per cent profit on some items.[11] Officers compelled their men to receive part of their pay in goods. Captains and lieutenants, who had previously been tailors, tobacconists or pedlars, made their fortunes by extortion and a military gangsterism rarely equalled anywhere. Hunter told their commander, William Paterson, who had been acting governor, that the conduct of the Corps was the most violent and outrageous of any British regiment in history.[12]

Yet the New South Wales Corps, for all its corruption, won three key battles which secured the colony for the British Crown. In 1795 near Richmond Hill they fought and won decisively a pitched battle against the Dharuk people, thus opening the whole of the Hawkesbury to the invaders. They suffered defeat at Toongabbie in 1797 in the face of an Eora attack led by Pemulwuy, but redeemed themselves by totally destroying the strength of the Eora in a subsequent attack on the fortifications at Parramatta. In action against the Irish rebel forces at Vinegar Hill in 1804 the Corps were again victorious, although hardly with honour, as they used the flag of truce to capture and kill the Irish commanders.

Under the command of Major George Johnston, the Corps even turned their guns on Governor William Bligh when he attempted to exercise some restraint on their unbridled corruption. On 26 January 1808 Johnston proclaimed martial law and appointed himself lieutenant governor. In battle array, with muskets cocked and ready, 300 men marched through the settlement to the strains of "The British Grenadiers" and rapidly deployed artillery from the Sydney forts to deal with any resistance.[13] They broke into Government House, arrested the magistrates who had been hearing charges against military officers, and arrested Bligh, who was put on a ship in the harbour to be deported to England.

With the deposition of Bligh, civilian power was annihilated. The garrison ruled supreme for nearly two years. They appointed their own magistrates, tried and of course acquitted their own officers who had faced charges under Bligh and ran the entire colony as a feif for their personal benefit.

The British government despatched Governor Lachlan Macquarie with his own regiment, the 73rd Royal Highlanders, to put down the rebellion and take Sydney back for the Crown. When they arrived in December 1809 there was, in fact, no opposition. The Highlanders took over and the New South Wales Corps embarked for England, never to return. It was converted to a Line regiment, the 102nd, with a career described as "brief and not glorious".[14]

Of the twenty-seven Imperial regiments that served in Australia as occupation forces, almost all saw action before being posted to the colonies. Most were fresh from action against other enemies of England—the French, the Spaniards, the Indians, Maoris and the armies of the then young United States of America—but the British Army saw more action in Australia than in any other British colony with the exception of southern Africa.[15]

General Wellington described his soldiers as the "scum of the earth",[16] but to survive English soldiers had to be tough. They wore a uniform like a deep sea diving suit and carried sixty rounds of ammunition, and a weapon and bayonet 4 feet 6 inches (1.37 metres) long and weighing 11 pounds (5 kilograms). These weapons were muzzle loaders which fired metal balls. It was not until the 1830s that percussion caps came into use, and breach loaders were still a novelty when the last British regiments left in 1870.

British military dispositions were based on regiments 800 strong, divided into ten companies each led by a captain; overall command rested with a lieutenant colonel. The troops spent more time in barracks than in battle, watched as they ate and slept by corporals and drilled by sergeants, their officers comprising a god-like elite only to be addressed on parade.

In nineteenth-century Australia displays of British military and naval power took place frequently. Royal salutes of 21 guns were fired whenever an occasion offered—royal birthdays, swearing in of new governors, and celebrations of highlights of English arms such as Waterloo Day. Parades involved a turnout of entire garrisons augmented by military bands and, as the colonial auxiliaries developed, by mounted police, volunteers and loyalist units. Carefully selected speakers were invited to give addresses of loyalty to England and the Crown and the assembled crowd would be led by the governor or the senior military officer in cheering the sovereign with well-disciplined hurrahs. Such celebrations were carefully planned by the Imperial authorities to rally loyalty to their cause and above all to demonstrate the military and naval might of the Empire as a deterrent to both black freedom fighters and dissident republicans who might dare to challenge the established authority.

The first regiment to arrive in Australia, Macquarie's Royal Highlanders, had served in India for seventeen years. They had fought Haidar Ali and, on two occasions, his son, Tippoo Sahib, leading the columns that broke his power at Seringapatam in 1799. On leaving Australia in 1814 the Royal Highlanders were the first British soldiery to travel through New Guinean waters and to see the coast of New Britain.[17]

They were succeeded by the South Devon Regiment (46th), which also stayed for four years; the Northamptonshire Regiment (48th), which served for seven years; the Buffs (3rd), which spent four years in the colony; and the 2nd Somersetshire or 40th Regiment, which had seen action at the Battle of Waterloo and at the Plains of Abraham in Canada, when the British, under Wolfe, defeated the French once again.

Arriving in New South Wales in 1824, commanded by Colonel Thornton, the 40th Regiment comprised thirty-three officers, forty-one non-commissioned officers and nearly 600 rank and file divided into four companies. They were victorious at the Battle of Bathurst, and also carried out successful punitive attacks in the region which broke the guerilla resistance of the Wiradjuri. After seeing action in the Black War in Tasmania they left for India, but returned to Australia for a second spell of duty in 1852. It was the 40th which snatched victory by surprise at Eureka in 1854. They remained in Australia until 1860, becoming a light cavalry unit to provide armed protection for the tax monies and gold won from the various goldfields in eastern Australia.

One county regiment followed another—the West Middlesex, Dorsetshire, West Suffolk, Leicestershire, King's Own, the West Kent. The Royal North British Fusiliers, 21st Regiment, arrived in 1833 for a six-year stint, during which they served in Tasmania and later at Perth. They took part in the military operations against the Nyungar people which culminated in the Battle of Pinjarra in 1834.

The 12th Regiment, the East Suffolk, arrived in 1854 and stayed for seven years. One of the oldest regiments in the British Army, raised in 1661, it had engaged in almost every major campaign including Monmouth's 1685 Rebellion against the Stuart king James II and the Battle of the Boyne in Ireland in 1690, which sealed the fate of Gaelic Ireland for 300 years.[18] Led by Captains Wise and Pasley under the general command of Captain Thomas (of the 40th Regiment at Eureka), the East Suffolk regiment also played a leading role in suppressing the Eureka revolt. It has never been permitted to claim the honour undoubtedly due to it, however, for a bold and successful operation that frustrated the attempt to found the first republic beneath the Southern Cross.

The 11th North Devon Regiment of Foot was one of the longest serving units in Australia. In the twelve years they were in New South Wales, from 1845 to 1857, they guarded prisoners, protected settlers against attacks by the local people, gave assistance in civil emergencies and were on alert during the Eureka rebellion. They were also involved in a confrontation with the diggers.

Squatter repression of the diggers in Victoria was paralleled in New South Wales, where diggers were also subject to taxation but denied political representation. The first signs of revolt came in January 1853, when nearly 1000 diggers on the Turon goldfield north of Bathurst marched four abreast into Sofala to the sound of fife and drum carrying a banner reading "Australia expects that every man this day will do his duty"—a variation on Nelson's appeal to English patriotism fifty years earlier.[19] The arrival of the North Devons forestalled any military action by the diggers. Many were arrested and put into chain gangs which toiled at musket and bayonet point along the Turon River, treatment which brought condemnation that the troops were used by the "foolish and mongrel Legislative Councilmen of Sydney" to fight at their bidding.[20] The North Devons left Sofala in April to the jeers of the population but remained in reserve in nearby Bathurst in case the diggers rose again.

At the time of the decision to withdraw the British occupation forces from Australia the regiments still in service were the Buckinghamshire, the Royal Irish and the Royal Artillery. It was they who handed over to the local forces, just as the legions of Rome had done 1500 years before when they handed over the defence of Britannia to the Romanised Britons.

The Eureka rebellion, the continuing Maori Wars in New Zealand and rumours that the Russians were coming (Russia having succeeded Spain and France in the lexicon of English bogeymen) led the Imperial authorities, working through their governors and the network of powerful landowners, to seek auxiliary help from each of the colonies to establish volunteer army regiments. Offering grants of fifty acres (twenty-two hectares) as incentive, they were able to recruit during the 1860s over 2000 volunteers in New South Wales, 3600 in Victoria, 200 in Queensland, 2000 in South Australia, 700 in Western Australia and 1200 in Tasmania.[21] Once these colonial forces had been established the British authorities began to negotiate the withdrawal of their garrisons. By 1870 the British regiments had gone home and it was left to the locally raised forces to fight the last pitched battle of the Hundred Years War at Battle Mountain in north Queensland in 1884.

During their time in Australia the Imperial regiments provided not only the occupation forces but also the governors and administrators. The early governors were essentially military dictators. The police were drawn from the military, the courts were military, and soldiers directed the building of roads, forts and public buildings.

Australia was, however, regarded as "the worst country on earth for a soldier",[22] while the 1720 infantrymen and others who were returned as fit for duty in New South Wales on New Year's Day 1838 were described by their own officers "as belonging to 'the least soldier-like and worst conducted' regiment of any of Queen Victoria's Army".[23]

In the 1830s the typical garrison was comprised of three regiments of infantry, some guarding prisoners over a large area, others guarding fortified positions and all contributing to mounted police patrols. Many of the non-commissioned officers and men did not want to serve in Australia: the North Gloucestershire Regiment (28th) sailed with its most senior non-commissioned officers on the verge of revolt because after thirty years' service they were being forced to go to the unknown southern continent. Many non-commissioned officers and men left military service and retired in Australia, a choice that entailed hardships of its own.

Ensign Abel Best of the 80th Regiment saw his first chain gang in January 1838. He observed the troops marched to isolated locations without billets, bedding or money for food and lodging on the way, sleeping on the ground, and carrying their rations which often rotted and were attacked by blowflies. Often it rained all night, and being without shelter or rations, and eaten alive by mosquitoes, their morale dropped to zero.[24] Under such conditions the soldiers often came to identify with the prisoners they were supposed to guard. One soldier sent to guard a group of recaptured prisoners at Portland, Victoria, in 1841 shouted through the bars of the lockup, "You buggers, why don't you break out? I won't prevent you my fine fellows".[25] In 1838 four men of the 80th Staffordshire Volunteers freed the prisoners they were guarding at Bathurst and provided them with arms to form one of the finest Australian bushranging gangs; a combined soldier–prisoner gang also operated at Cox's River.

The soldiers and the prisoners shared a common working class background and so far removed from the class structures of England it was not surprising that they often made common cause, despite ferocious military discipline which could impose up to 300 lashes for "mutinous conduct".[26]

Auxiliary and Paramilitary Forces

Up to twelve per cent of the Imperial regiments were seconded to serve as paramilitary mounted police, mobile forces capable of moving swiftly against individuals and groups. In addition, civilians were encouraged to enlist or were conscripted into local auxiliary forces. The first attempt to enlist civilians was made during the first decade of the invasion, when the Eora people of the Sydney region, led by Pemulwuy, put up a strong resistance. Settlers were conscripted by Governor Hunter to assist the military and it was made plain that they were not only expected to carry arms but were subject to military orders and discipline.

A formal attempt to enlist the local English settlers was made in 1800 when Hunter raised two groups of "loyalist" volunteers. One group of fifty in Sydney was commanded by a magistrate, William Balmain, and a second at Parramatta by Judge Advocate Atkins.[27] The Loyal Sydney and Parramatta Associations were to serve against Irish rebels as well as Eora war parties. They were issued with uniforms, rifles and ammunition but received no pay. The Sydney body was re-formed in 1801 as an artillery unit to man forts in Sydney. In 1804 they were called out to assist the New South Wales Corps in suppressing the Irish Rebellion and to take part in the Battle of Vinegar Hill. The defeat of the Eora and the Irish and the fading threat from Spain led Acting Governor William Paterson to propose in 1809 that the Loyal Associations be disbanded. They finally went out of existence on 9 June 1810, and only forty-four years later was any further effort made to enlist local auxiliaries.

In the meantime, however, the Veterans Company was formed from men of the New South Wales Corps who remained in Sydney after the Corps returned to England in 1810. Initially it formed a unit of Macquarie's Highland Regiment, then of successive Imperial regiments stationed in Australia until it was disbanded in 1823. It was as a lieutenant in the Veterans Company that William Lawson crossed the Blue Mountains in 1813, and his residence at Prospect Hill was called Veteran Hall.[28]

In 1854, the year of Eureka, the Imperial Government again authorised volunteer forces in the colonies. New South Wales led the way with the first Sydney Battalion of Rifle Volunteers, consisting of 330 men in six companies, a troop of yeomanry and a battery of artillery. At this time the six colonies together financed and armed a total of nearly 10,000 men, a formidable force to supplement the British army of occupation.

This was not the full extent of the militarisation of Australia, however. In 1824 the North Devon regimental commanders were instrumental in creating the paramilitary auxiliary known as the New South Wales Mounted Police. At the height of the war with the Wiradjuri people and in the year of the decisive Battle of Bathurst, Governor Sir Thomas Brisbane asked the Imperial authorities for permission to raise a troop of colonial cavalry as the infantry were too slow in action against the Wiradjuri war parties.[29] His request refused, he sought the alternative—mounted police drawn from various regiments. He received the necessary permission and the force came into being with a modest strength of two officers and thirteen troopers. Under the first commandant, Lieutenant Nathaniel Lowe, numbers peaked in 1839 at nine officers and 156 non-commissioned officers and men. Its headquarters were in Bathurst and until it was phased out in 1850 the mounted force was the spearhead of the war on the New South Wales frontiers.

The commandants were ruthless men who became a law unto

themselves.[30] Lowe was tried for killing warriors captured in battle, and Major J. W. Nunn was charged with massacring men, women and children in an ambush and was reported to enjoy "potting" blacks with his pistol. Both were tried but never convicted or even punished. Lieutenant Wilton of the North Devons commanded the force for its last twelve months, during which headquarters were at Parramatta. It had been responsible for destroying entire clans west of the Blue Mountains.

A second mounted force was raised in 1839 by Governor Sir Richard Bourke. Known as the Border Police, it was placed under the command of Commissioners of Crown Lands and was made up of soldier-prisoners released to serve on the frontiers. The Border Police remained in service for six years.

A third paramilitary group was formed, this one modelled on the Indian sepoy system, whereby the British Army raised auxiliary units of Indians under their command to fight fellow Indians.[31] Following a proposal by Captain Alexander Maconochie to Governor Bourke (in which recruits were to receive compensation for the expropriation of their land by invading whites) the Native Police Corps was established at Port Phillip on 24 February 1842. The first commander, Henry Pulteney Dana, a Western District squatter with a military background, sought the assistance of a local leader named Billibellary in recruiting men. Although suspicious of white intentions, Billibellary co-operated and the first twenty men were signed up. In the eleven years of its existence the force grew to be 100 strong with twenty-two white officers.

The men wore a dashing uniform–green jacket with possum-skin facings, green trousers with red stripes and a green cap with a red band. They carried a sword when mounted, a short carbine and a bayonet.[32] They were an impressive sight on parade but there it ended. During the decade that they killed at will, the Native Police found themselves cheated from their first day of active service. They received only basic rations as payment and were told to take what they needed from the land–in other words to steal from their own people.[33] Most of them were drawn from the Yarra and Western Port peoples and they were used in areas far from their own boundaries. The white officers were paid regularly, unlike the black non-commissioned officers. The whites also used unlimited numbers of black women as though they were whores, while the blacks had what they left.

It was nevertheless a formidable force, and in terms of riding and marksmanship proved a terrifying factor in the war. White officers encouraged and even ordered massacres. As hatred for them grew, the Native Police became more and more isolated; this only added to their effectiveness as they fought as a cavalry unit with solidarity. Every trooper killed in action was buried with full military honours, and Dana reserved the right to switch at his discretion from a police to a military role.

Queensland Native Mounted Police camp. JOHN OXLEY LIBRARY

As black resistance faded under the weight of constant military pressure the Native Police Corps was switched to gold escort duties and was much in demand on ceremonial occasions because of its drilled precision. Dana died of pneumonia on 24 November 1852 at the Melbourne Club,[34] and the following year the unit was disbanded, the troopers being dispersed as trackers to various police depots.

A northern division raised for service in southern Queensland in 1849 survived until 1909. It became infamous for its butchery of women and children and its ferocity in battle and was responsible for many of the 20,000 black casualties in the Hundred Years War.

Irregulars formed by the land barons or squatters and their stockmen were also part of the military forces engaged in the Hundred Years War. In Victoria black resistance peaked in 1838, when eighty-two settlers in the Port Phillip area, hungry for land, petitioned Governor George Gipps to step up military action.[35] They had in fact already formed up as irregulars and they told Gipps they would conduct the war if he did not. Within a month Gipps had established a series of military posts along a line crossing the Murray, the Ovens, Violet Creek, and the Goulburn. He used mounted police from Sydney and Melbourne to man the posts and authorised the police magistrate in Melbourne to send troops into action when requested. The mounted police were made up of trained soldiers with experience in action. They were ruthless. Typical of their operations was the massacre of forty black men, women and children on the Campaspe Plains. This was carried out by troops under Sergeant Leary in conjunction with a squatter, Captain Hutton, and his armed irregulars.[36]

The British regiments were the first line of power, the quasi-military auxiliaries the second and the "loyalist" associations the third. The colonial volunteers, which reached 10,000 in the first year they were formed as Imperial levees, were the fourth and a formidable force. For most of the 100 years of war the land barons in every part of the continent rode out with their hired hands to join the soldiers or their auxiliaries in battle. They constituted the fifth force in the military establishment that fought the war for the British Empire in Australia.

The Fortifications

The first defences raised on Australian soil were not English but French: La Pérouse, when he landed at Botany Bay in 1788, built a stockade guarded by two guns.[37] The redoubt built by the Marines as soon as they disembarked in Sydney Cove was supported within six months by a fortified position on Bennelong Point on the eastern side of the bay. Constructed by Lieutenant William Dawes, it was defended by eight cannon.

As the cold war with the Eora ended, Dawes was instructed to establish a battery on Dawes Point, on the western arm of the bay, and Sydney's third Fort, Fort Phillip, dominating it from high ground just behind. Fort Phillip boasted a garrison on twenty-four hour duty and cannon, as well as an observatory. It was the major fortification of the infant city. By December 1788 a redoubt had been built at Parramatta and fortifications were added in 1791.

For Phillip's successor, John Hunter, governor of New South Wales from 1795 to 1800, the twin enemies were the Eora and the Spanish. Following the rebellion in Ireland in 1798, he was also preoccupied by the threat of an attack by Irish prisoners in the colony. Four iron 12-pounder guns and two brass 6-pounders originally destined for the defence of Norfolk Island were retained in Sydney,[38] and "Loyalist Associations" of Englishmen were called out to help man the guns. Fort Phillip and Fort Bennelong were supplemented by batteries at Garden Island, Windmill Hill and Barrack Parade.

Although during his term of office the threats from the Eora, the Spanish and the Irish had largely passed, Governor Lachlan Macquarie strengthened the battery at Dawes Point and reconstructed Fort Phillip, adding a powder-magazine, which was the first construction undertaken by Francis Greenway, a prisoner on parole. Macquarie also commissioned Greenway to prepare an integrated plan for the defence of Sydney and to design a new fort, Fort Macquarie, to replace the one on Bennelong Point.

Fort Phillip occupied the site of what is now the Maritime Services Board, barely 15 metres from the southern end of Sydney Harbour Bridge. Sydney's major defence, it was built first as a hexagon with sides 100 feet (30.5 metres) long and later developed into a pentagon, long before a similar and larger structure, in the United States of America, claimed world attention.[39] The three key sides fronted the town, the Parramatta road (now George Street) and the harbour. The ramparts were faced with stone to a height of 10 feet (3 metres) and it was protected by a ditch 600 feet (183 metres) long, 18 feet (5.5 metres) wide and 6 feet (1.8 metres) deep; the moat was later deepened and widened. A bomb-proof magazine 14 feet (4.2 metres) square and 7 feet (2 metres) deep was built into the ramparts facing the harbour.

Fort Phillip developed into one of the most strongly defended positions of any power in the South Pacific region. Its planned armament was twenty guns: six 12-pounders, eight 6-pounders and six 18-pounders, part of which was brought from Norfolk Island. It remained a key fortification for many years. Its guns were fired from its upper levels for the last time in 1853 when the news arrived that the English hero of Waterloo, the Duke of Wellington, had died.

Macquarie also built another large barracks at what is now Wynyard Square, Sydney, which was completed in 1818, and extended the barracks at Parramatta by 1820. In Van Diemen's Land Anglesea Barracks was built in Hobart and Fort Mulgrave established on the southern point of Sullivan Cove.[40]

By the 1830s the British Army in Australia had been reinforced by a special unit of the Royal Engineers to attend to the network of forts. Prisoners were put to work creating new fortifications at Bradleys Head on the north side of the harbour and on the island of Pinchgut (now known as Fort Denison). During the 1840s further barracks were built or existing ones extended to accommodate the British regiments stationed in Australia. Victoria Barracks, at Darlinghurst, east of Sydney, was built and occupied by 1848 and Hobart's Angelsea Barracks were extended.

The resources of the occupation forces were stretched even further when garrisons had to be established in the new colony of South Australia, in Western Australia and on the northern coast of the continent. Military forays into what is now the Northern Territory were a succession of disasters; Fort Dundas, Raffles Bay, Port Essington and Escape Cliffs were forts set up only to be abandoned, either because of the hostility of the Australians or the isolation. The New South Wales garrison was reduced to almost a skeleton force in 1846, when Governor Charles Fitzroy was ordered to send 900 infantry to New Zealand to take part in the war against the Maori people.[41] By this time the battles against the Eora, Dharuk and Wiradjuri peoples of New South Wales had been won, the Irish crushed at Vinegar Hill and Spain driven out of most of the Pacific and South America. Within the year the Imperial authorities were seeking to tax the colonial populations to provide a stronger occupation force. In 1853, the year before the Battle of Eureka Stockade, the New South Wales legislative council, having been given control of tax revenues, decided to build two more forts—at South and Middle Heads in Sydney Harbour.

At the same time the Imperial forces in Australia had to recognise a new enemy of the English—the Russians. The Crimean War dominated the front pages of English and world newspapers until Eureka captured the headlines in 1855.

On the eve of Eureka the defences of Melbourne and Port Phillip were fortified and the Victorian colonial administration used tax money exacted from the diggers to maintain 700 British occupation troops in arms. Less than five months before the Battle of Eureka Stockade the new commander of the British Army of occupation in Australia, Sir Robert Nickle, arrived in Melbourne with a headquarters staff. Extensive military barracks were built on St Kilda Road and fortified points were established at Williamstown and Sandridge. Following the engagement at Ballarat in December 1854, the headquarters of the Imperial forces in Australia were moved from Sydney to Melbourne, while Sydney's defences were reinforced by a network of old and new forts including

View of Fort Dundas. NATIONAL LIBRARY OF AUSTRALIA

a strengthened Fort Macquarie. The defeat of the Eureka rebellion sounded alarm bells not only in London but among the "kings in grass castles" in Australia, who saw how close they had come to losing their power.

3. *THE HUNDRED YEARS WAR*

The period from the arrival in 1788 of the First Fleet to establish the first English settlement in Australia to the withdrawal of the last garrison of British soldiers in 1870 was marked by constant warfare. The heirs of the 2000 generations who had held the continent in trust for over 40,000 years fought and died in defence of their land for even longer, the last massacre of the first Australians being recorded in 1928. The century saw the Irish in rebellion, fired by visions of a republic in the Antipodes or of evacuation home; a brave Englishman in a bold bid to defy oppression; and what Mark Twain called the finest thing in Australian history, the Battle of Eureka Stockade. At the same time guerilla warfare raged in every part of the continent and at least a dozen pitched battles were fought between British regiments and their colonial auxiliaries and the embattled people of the continent.

Until the 1840s the original people of the Australian continent were in a majority, despite their losses in war and the ravages of foreign diseases. Their numerical superiority presented a threat to the invading forces in many locations, but while the invaders usually took the field with well armed units up to 200 strong, the defenders had to struggle to assemble and hold permanent fighting parties of that number.

The clans did not set out to make war. In fact in many cases they made a serious attempt to incorporate the newcomers into their society, categorising them as family members by making them part of their system of kinship. In this system people belong to one of two divisions or moieties—*dua* or *yirritja*, to use the words from north-eastern Arnhem Land. Marriage can only take place between people of opposite parts, for example, *dua* must marry *yirritja*, and *yirritja* must marry *dua*. The child at birth is assigned to the opposite half to its mother but the same half as the father, so that if the mother is *yirritja* then the children must be *dua*. The two moieties are then divided into four and then sometimes eight categories depending on the custom of the area. These categories, commonly known as skin groups, determine a person's relationship and behaviour to everyone else and dictate who the person may marry.

Once newcomers were put into a skin group they were part of the traditional culture, but in turn it was expected that they would then respect the Australian laws and fulfil their obligations to their new families. In the main, however, the invaders showed contempt for black law. In particular the taking as sexual partners, and in many cases the sexual abuse, of any women they fancied was incestuous according to traditional law.[1]

The seeds of war were sown when it became clear that traditional sanctions for wrongdoing could not be effectively carried out against the invading foreigners and that attempts to do so led to bloody reprisals. Once warfare began it was constant. A Queensland squatter named F. Newbolt told a large meeting of squatters in Rockhampton in 1865 that he and his men had been constantly at arms for five years.[2] Loaded guns hung in every room of every station homestead in Queensland and in the Northern Territory until the twentieth century.

Despite black resistance the British advance continued apace—in north and central Queensland in the 1860s the frontiers were extended by 2400 kilometres in just three years. As the *Townsville Times* of 5 January 1876 boasted, "the energy of the Anglo-Saxon race has been amply proved on many fields . . . ". Districts north of Rockhampton were once

> *a waste of howling wilderness, occupied by cannibal blacks amongst whom a white man durst not land for his life . . . let us cultivate the feeling of nationality first as Queenslanders (as North Queenslanders should circumstances demand it), and next as members of that great [British] colonising family upon whose domain the sun never ceases to shine . . .*[3]

The forces of Empire saw the black people as resisting their civilisation to the death and cited the Spartans and the Romans as examples of the necessity to enslave "brutish races" in the interests of the state and Empire.[4] The war was whipped up by newspapers such as the *Northern Miner*, which described the Australian people as "dogs and horses . . . irreclaimable brute[s] . . . the one argument a blackfellow understands is that delivered from a rifle or a six shooter".[5] In the summer of 1896 a writer described the pouring of 7000 bullets a minute into "an array of defenceless horror-stricken niggers".[6]

Defence forces had to evolve rapidly if they were to have any hope of stemming the takeover of their land. Their traditional social structure made it difficult to assemble the numbers of warriors needed to fight European-style wars. The basic units that took the initial brunt of the war were the bands comprising family groups. Sometimes larger groups became involved, as in the case of the Nyungar, the Eora, the Wiradjuri and the Kalkadoons where war leaders emerged and took command. Some individual nations were able to contain the invaders for up to ten years, but when it came to pitched battle firearms rapidly triumphed over spears.

At first the Australians greatly underestimated the power of firearms. Slowly and bloodily they learned by experience that the musket was more powerful than any weapon they had ever devised. In Victoria in the 1840s, for example, a group of warriors attacked a party of sixteen armed and mounted men using their shields to fend off the musket balls;[7] the mounted force wiped them out. The defenders also came to recognise the musket's limitations, however. Muskets often misfired and they took several minutes to reload: in the interval black defenders could come to grips with the enemy. As the century rolled on they had to contend with revolvers and repeating rifles. Daring open forays were now rarely possible and the massing of the peoples into armies became a policy of defeat. In the last battle of the war, at Battle Mountain in north Queensland, approximately 500 fighting men faced the last cavalry charge in Australian history on Australian soil; they were routed by superior fire power when they opted for two disastrous frontal attacks.

The success of the defenders lay in their knowledge of the terrain and the water and food supplies, their skill in medicine and their ability to strike and melt away again into the fastness of the bush. The greatest successes were achieved by small guerilla units operating at night in well planned attacks that were completed before dawn. A Tasmanian squatter described the whole art of war by the people of Tasmania as "concealed, silent and treacherous attack".[8] The careful gathering of intelligence, and the maintenance of constant observation of enemy movements was essential. Women and children acted as spies to report on the disposition of men and arms, and Black Australians forced to work on stations volunteered invaluable information. Through such networks they were able to accurately monitor many kinds of operations, including those of the Native Police, which became such a fearsome weapon against the defending peoples.

In defence of their land Black Australians also turned to economic warfare, marking for destruction the property of the invaders. Sheep were run into swamps or over cliffs or were speared, and cattle were stampeded or hamstrung. It was a custom of some clans to cut out the hearts from two animals and place them on poles stuck into the ground and facing one another[9]—a clear message that war had been declared. Bullock drays, a widely used form of transport, were easy targets. A group of drays struggling up a steep gradient would use several teams in combination to get the drays over the hill one by one; this would be the point at which a war party would strike. The importance of horses was quickly recognised and as many as possible were extirpated. Massive raids were made on

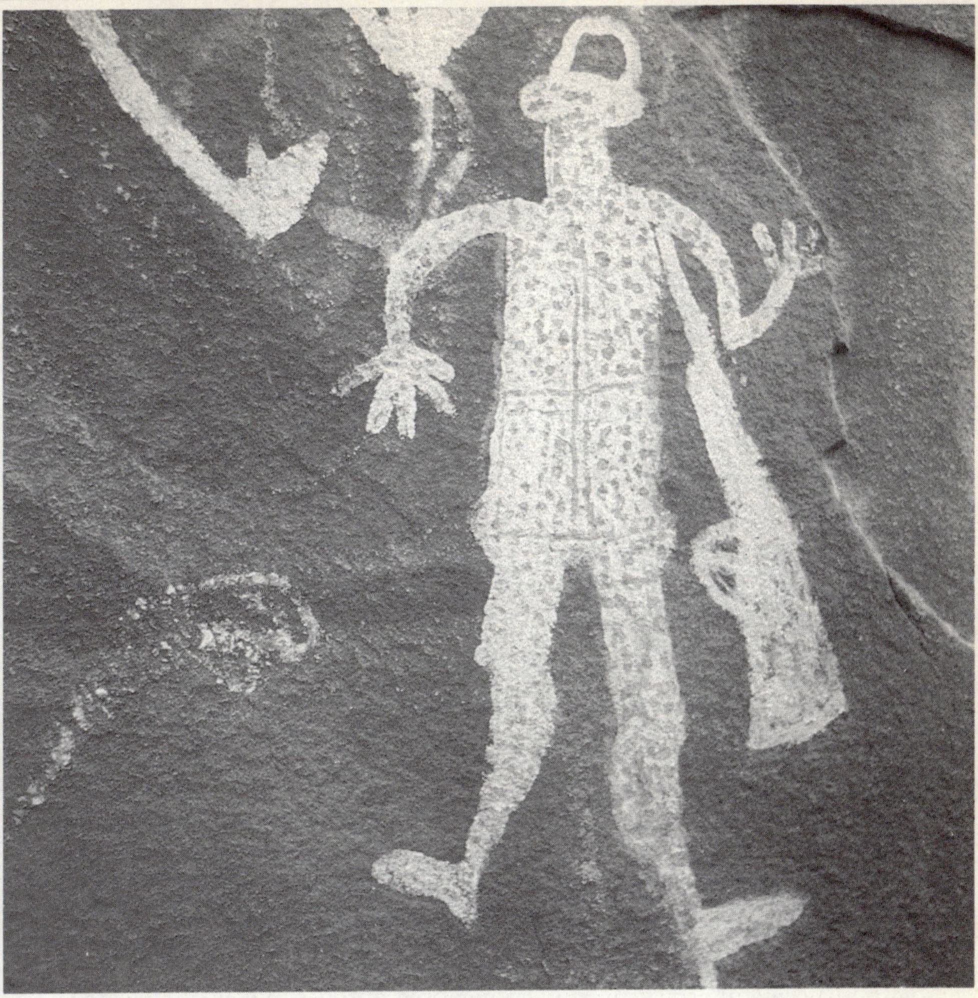

Black Australians could not hope to match the power of the invaders' firearms. Rock painting, Innesvale Station, Northern Territory.
PHOTOGRAPH BY ROBERT EDWARDS

miners' horses on the Palmer River in Queensland, where 200 were speared in ten years, while on the road to the Palmer from Cooktown 133 were killed during a six-year period in the 1870s.[10]

The economic war proved one of the most effective offensive methods at the defenders' disposal. One of their most ambitious plans was put into operation in 1843, when local clans combined to cut off all communication between the Darling Downs and the colonial capital of Brisbane.[11] They cut the main road from Ipswich to the Downs by blocking the highway with a barricade of timber and captured drays, while fighting men maintained vigil in the bush alongside the road. The British commander at what was then the settlement of Moreton Bay sent a regiment to break the blockade. They were in constant action along the road for three years, giving the defending forces at least temporary success in stemming the occupation of the Darling Downs.

The combined guerilla and economic wars were powerful weapons in the hands of the defenders in the open war, which New South Wales Judge Advocate David Collins considered had become general in 1795 when the New South Wales Corps clashed with the Dharuk people on the Hawkesbury.

New South Wales

The war of resistance was under way by 1790, when the Eora leader Pemulwuy made a successful attack on Governor Phillip's gamekeeper. In 1795 the neighbouring peoples, the Dharuk, suffered their first major defeat in battle near Richmond Hill on the Hawkesbury; they fought on for another twenty years, forcing the redcoats into what they called "Troublesome, Tedious Marches".[12] The Eora also continued the struggle with a successful attack on the Toongabbie outpost, but were defeated at Parramatta in 1797. Although guerilla resistance was maintained on the Sydney side of the Great Dividing Range for a number of years after, this battle broke the back of resistance in the Sydney region.

In 1804 the Irish rebelled against the English. They set out to capture Parramatta, march on Sydney, and proclaim an Irish Republic for those who wished to remain. They also planned to seize the warships in Sydney Cove to enable others to return to Ireland, and the English and Scots who had joined the rebels to return home. Their plans came to nought at the Battle of Vinegar Hill, near today's Rouse Hill.

The war moved over the Great Dividing Range with the crossing of the Blue Mountains in 1813. The stubborn resistance of the Wiradjuri people caused Governor Brisbane to declare martial law in the Bathurst district in 1824, and to send the 2nd Somersetshire Regiment to reinforce the local garrison. This regiment, backed by local paramilitary units, defeated the Wiradjuri led by Windradyne. After the battle he was forced to sue for peace, which was formally enjoined at a conference at Parramatta attended by Brisbane and Windradyne and his people.

Throughout the mid-1820s war also blazed along the Hunter River. There the newly formed British auxiliary, the Mounted Police, rapidly gained a reputation for brutality which would have been the envy of the SS in the Third Reich. A record of the "execution" of an Awabakal warrior from the Hunter region, known to his captors as "Jacky Jacky", tells how he was taken prisoner by Lieutenant Nathaniel Lowe, the first commander of the Native Police. Jacky Jacky was tied to a tree. One soldier fired and wounded him in the neck, a second fired and broke his jaw. The warrior turned his head with each shot until finally a third soldier fired at close range and blew his head to pieces.[13]

Other prisoners besides the Irish rebelled against the oppressive rule of the English administration. In 1828 women prisoners at the Female Factory in Parramatta broke out and marched on Government House at breakfast time. By the time the police and military arrived at the scene complete with guns and bayonets, the women had replenished themselves with loaves of bread and cold meats, and they returned to the factory jeering their oppressors as they went.[14] The following year a more prolonged rebellion took place at Bathurst, led by a young English prisoner named Ralph Entwistle.[15]

Born in Bolton in the North Country, Entwistle was convicted in 1827 of stealing some clothing and was sentenced to transportation for life. A bricklayer who could read and write, he was listed as Protestant and described as freckle-faced with sandy hair and 5 feet 8 inches (173 centimetres) tall. On arrival in Sydney he was sent to Bathurst and assigned as a servant to a local English settler called Liscombe, who was also clerk of the Bathurst Court. Entwistle soon became well liked and respected, and Liscombe recommended him for a ticket-of-leave, which would give him freedom of sorts and allow him to work for wages.

In November 1829 Entwistle and another prisoner were sent to take a bullock dray of wool to Sydney and bring back supplies, a journey of 225 kilometres over rough tracks that would take several weeks. On the first day out they camped on the banks of the Macquarie River near a ford in what is George Street in Bathurst today. It was a hot day and the men decided to strip off and have a swim. As they dived in Governor Ralph Darling with a military escort came into sight. He was to meet a large party of English landholders who had ridden out from Bathurst to greet him. The two prisoners promptly ducked under the water and out of sight.

They were seen by Lieutenant Thomas Evernden, Superintendent of Police. Evernden had been an officer in a regiment that had been garrisoned in the colony a few years earlier. He had retired from the army to become a police magistrate, and received a grant of 2600 acres (1052 hectares) of land about sixteen kilometres south of Bathurst. Evernden ordered troopers to seize the two men having an innocent swim, to drag them into Bathurst and give them fifty lashes each. To add to this Entwistle's ticket-of-leave was cancelled.

Such tactics were resorted to not only because the prestige of the military, and that of the English squattocracy, was at stake, but also because the land barons were outnumbered four to one by the prisoners. It was not, in fact, an unusual punishment. The records show that Evernden and his fellow magistrates dragged in prisoners on a daily basis and that floggings averaged more then 200 lashes a month. The reasons given for such treatment were often "insolence", "laziness", being sick and unable to work, and drunkenness. Every British "gentleman", because he was an officer or had an introduction from London, was given a handout of land, for example, 2000 acres (900 hectares), and up to forty prisoners, slaves who received nothing but food and shelter were assigned to work as stockmen, labourers and domestic servants.

Ralph Entwistle decided to rebel against these injustices. As soon as the floggings were over he gathered a few friends and fellow prisoners, stole arms and ammunition, and set out to make an example of Evernden. He was not on his property, but his overseer, who defied and abused the armed band, was shot dead. Entwistle was joined by a band of prisoners who had taken part in a similar rebellion in the Hunter Valley. Troops had driven them across the mountains to the Bathurst area and they were welcome recruits to Entwistle's little army, which rose in number to 124.

There were 1500 prisoners in chains in the Bathurst area, 600 of them Irish, and Governor Darling ordered the chains to be strengthened. The local squattocracy were called together and formed into a mounted volunteer unit, which first went into action against Entwistle and his men in a battle in which 300 shots were exchanged at Captain Cook Lookout in the Abercrombie Ranges. Entwistle, wearing a hat covered in green ribbons after the style of the Irish rebels, the Ribbonmen, drove off the volunteers and chased them into the darkness to find their way back to Bathurst. Entwistle's men suffered only a couple of minor casualties.

Major Donald Macpherson, commander of the Bathurst garrison, sent out a detachment of troops to attack Entwistle's force. Two soldiers and five horses were killed in the first charge, after which the rebels chased them back to Bathurst to join the defeated volunteers. Lieutenant Lachlan Macalister and his troops from Goulburn then tried their mettle against the rebels. They met in battle at Barona Plains and once again the rebels were victorious, killing and wounding troopers and horses, shooting Macalister in the thigh and sending them all scurrying back to Goulburn. By the time fresh troops of the 39th Regiment arrived from Sydney, under the dashing Captain Horatio Walpole, Entwistle's men had fought for weeks, defeating three strong forces. Wounds, weariness and illness were taking a toll and they were desperately short of food and ammunition. Walpole's force surrounded the rebels and defeated them after a short sharp battle. Ten survivors, including Entwistle, were taken prisoner.

A show trial, designed to strike terror into anyone who questioned the power of the Crown and its servants, followed in Bathurst. Chief Justice Francis Forbes, who presided at the trial, was one of the largest landholders in the colony; he was granted 2560 acres (1036 hectares) in 1835 and doubled his holdings, at Muswellbrook, the following year, in addition to other land at Emu Plains. The eight jurymen were officers and volunteers who had fought against Entwistle and had been defeated by him. The survivors of the revolt were condemned and hanged in public, opposite today's Royal Hotel in Bathurst. Half of them were Irish, the others English and Scots. Entwistle died with courage, as did his brave companions whose names are recorded here so that they may be remembered—William Graham, Patrick Gleeson, Michael Kearney, Thomas Dunn, John Shepherd, Robert Webster, John Kenny, James Driver and Dominic Daly.

The English invaders first began to probe the Liverpool Ranges north-west of Newcastle in the 1820s. By 1838 several dozen "kings in grass castles" had established themselves from the Gwydir River south to the ranges in what the administration in Sydney called the Liverpool Plains Pastoral District. This was an intrusion into the territory of one of the most powerful of all the nations of eastern Australia—the Kamilaroi. Late in 1837 the Kamilaroi, who had been pushed from their water supplies, robbed of their game and seen their women taken at the point of a gun, began gathering strength for an operation to rid the Gwydir of the intruders.

Colonel Kenneth Snodgrass, who was acting governor, ordered the Commandant of the Mounted Police, Major James Nunn, to take a strong detachment to counter the threat posed by what he estimated to be 1000 fighting men.[16] Nunn, Ensign George Cobban, three sergeants and nineteen troopers drawn from various regiments serving in the colony left Sydney before Christmas and headed north. By the new year they had reached the land of the Kamilaroi.

Arriving at Green Hatches Station on the Namoi, Nunn was told of a war party lower down the river. He marched his force overnight to surprise them in a dawn attack; he took fifteen prisoners, then released all but two, one of whom was shot trying to escape while the other was forced to act as a guide.

If this encounter was a disaster for the Kamilaroi the next, at Waterloo Creek, was worse: oral history has it that a massacre of Kamilaroi took place. In their third engagement, however, they fared better. Ensign

Cobban led a patrol along the Gwydir and found some Kamilaroi perched high on rocks; they taunted him and his patrol, shouting that they were not afraid of the soldiers.[17] The patrol beat a hasty retreat for fear of an ambush and left the Kamilaroi in possession of their strong point.

In the third week of January 1838 Nunn and his men, forty kilometres from today's Moree on the Gwydir River, engaged the Kamilaroi at a place now known as Slaughterhouse Creek. Coming across an encampment in which there was a large number of women and children, Nunn and his men charged. Kamilaroi warriors rallied to resist, spearing Corporal Hannan, who was at the head of the mounted party. The troopers then began intensive gunfire, which lasted for about an hour. After questioning some women, the troopers attempted to drive the survivors into a creek bed.[18] A detachment of troops repeatedly charged from either bank; the warriors dropped their weapons in a vain attempt to rescue the women and children who were in the direct line of fire from both sides. Hour after hour the firing continued until up to 120 lay dead, "shot like crows in the trees".[19] The force then withdrew to the south, shooting any black in sight. This was no battle but a massacre. Cobban later boasted to a member of the Legislative Council of how he had run his sabre through an unarmed black who was trying to escape up a tree.[20]

Other such incidents took place. Many Kamilaroi were shot and bayonetted after being surprised near a sacred bora ground at Terry Hie Hie near the head of Slaughterhouse Creek. The bora ground, which had been cared for for many generations, became the burial ground for those who revered it. The Myall Creek Massacre of 1838 took place when a group of armed auxiliaries, made up of squatters and their hired hands, murdered twenty-eight men, women and children, shooting them at point blank range or hacking them to death with swords.

By the end of the 1830s the war frontiers stretched from northern New South Wales to western Victoria and lay in the country of either the Kamilaroi or the Wiradjuri. The Wiradjuri defeat at Bathurst in 1824 and the massacres of the Kamilaroi along the Gwydir more than ten years later contributed to a development unique in the Hundred Years War. These two quite distinct and independent peoples came together in 1838 in an alliance which was born at a parliamentry style meeting. If the agreement they reached for a co-ordinated war strategy[21] could have been extended throughout the continent, the war could have taken a dramatic and different turn, leading to peace with honour rather than death and dispossession. The co-ordinated strategy was identified in 1839 by the then Crown Lands Commissioner, who noted the pattern of operations on both sides of the Murray and the Lachlan Rivers.

The Bathurst forces of the Wiradjuri had either been extirpated or subjugated, but this had not happened to the Narrungdera clan on the Murrumbidgee River around Narrandera. They had originally received the invaders with friendship and hospitality. Charles Sturt and his men spent two weeks within Wiradjuri boundaries in 1829–30 and received help and kindness. Even the landtakers who arrived in 1832 were received in friendship.[22] In 1838, however, Edward John Eyre, who was pioneering a stock route along the Murrumbidgee, reported from Ganmain Station that there had been punitive expeditions against Wiradjuri people, but that they had not yet declared war.[23] This was to come in January 1839, when the Narrungdera and other Wiradjuri people decided to strike back. Their first attack was on Brewarrena Station, which had strategic importance because of its rich water and food supplies.[24] The Wiradjuri killed one of the defending hired hands and burnt the outhouses, and followed up by destroying stock and driving out the intruders. The war had suddenly turned in their favour.

This declaration of war was made not only against a background of punitive expeditions against them, but also the decimation of the neighbouring group, the Ngunawal, whose territory was around Gundagai on their eastern boundary. Before the Ngunawal could ever organise on a war footing, firearms had beaten them time and time again. The Narrungdera people conferred with their brothers the Kamilaroi, still in action on the Gwydir, planning to organise themselves to combat the European invasion. They were capable of fielding 200 warriors for any given operation. Their four most famous leaders adopted the picturesque names given to them by the invaders: Brian Boru (named after the Irish high king and hero who saved Ireland from Danish invasion and occupation), Boney (an English nickname for the great Napoleon Bonaparte), Big Peter and Davey.

After the attack on Brewarrena Station the governor ordered a counterattack by a troop of Mounted Police and an armed auxiliary force of hired hands from the stations under the command of Commissioner Henry Cosby. It failed miserably. The force advanced ninety-six kilometres down the Murrumbidgee, spreading out 225 kilometres on both sides of the river, but failed to make contact with even one Wiradjuri.

While Cosby and his men searched for the seemingly invisible enemy, the Wiradjuri began an economic war on a scale not seen before in the continent. Ruthlessly and efficiently they set out to destroy the basis of the intruders' wealth and very survival. Commissioner Cosby, completely outmanoeuvred, could only list the losses during the year 1839: Brillinball, 200 cattle; Brewarrena, 22; Berembed, 250 missing and 250 speared; Ganmain, 140 missing, 38 speared; Tooyal, thirteen kilometres east of Ganmain, 40 speared. At Buckingbong, 40 cattle were killed and wounded, the station hands were driven off, the huts burnt and the land reoccupied.[25]

The invaders retreated, abandoning the lower Murrumbidgee. The Wiradjuri clans kept up the pressure of attack and the balance of terror was turned around—from cowering from punitive white expeditions they now struck fear into the hearts of their adversaries. The high point of the war was the Wiradjuri's reoccupation of ninety-six kilometres of riverfront, their traditional source of water and food supplies. Cattle losses of more than 1000 ended the white occupation of Berembed Station and the entire area west of Ganmain was reoccupied. The only exception was Yanco Station, where in a generous gesture unique at that time the Wiradjuri permitted the overseer and his wife to remain;[26] this couple had gained the respect and friendship of the Wiradjuri, which was reciprocated even at the height of the campaign. Not only were the whites expelled, but the overland track on the Murrumbidgee's north bank, the stock route to the new English outpost at Adelaide in South Australia pioneered by Eyre, was cut completely. After one of the most successful guerilla wars in the history of the continent, the governor was told that the Narrungdera people "had made themselves much dreaded . . . a perpetual state of war existed".[27]

Brian Boru had emerged as one of the main leaders. Standing head and shoulders above most of the Wiradjuri, he was credited with having immense strength and with developing and refining tactics that brought striking success in battle. The Wiradjuri's victory was all the more remarkable when it is realised that smallpox, brought by the invaders from the east, had earlier wiped out half the population.[28] For six years the Narrungdera people had run before the chill wind of occupation, but despite the terrible handicap of reduced numbers, the loss of their best land and the constant terror of raids and indiscriminate shootings they had turned and fought back. Their declaration of war, their recapture of the riverfront and the respect earned by Brian Boru combined to carve for them a place in the rollcall of heroes. Their victory would last only two years.

Governor Gipps, accepting Cosby's report of his defeat, simply recorded, "I do not find that anything can be done".[29] In 1841, however, the squatters set out to build their own army. Paying stockmen to fight was not new, but this counterattack was a planned strategy of extirpation. The opening attack by mounted irregulars trapped a party of seventy men, women and children on Murdering Island in the Murrumbidgee. In a surprise assault from both banks they killed them all except one young boy who hid in the reeds and lived to describe the massacre.[30] In the mid-1860s Wiradjuri survivors told T. A. Browne (a station owner better known as the novelist Rolf Boldrewood) that they were shot down "like possums".[31]

At Poisoned Waterholes Creek near Ganmain bags of flour were laced with arsenic and the water poisoned. A large party of more than 100 Wiradjuri arrived to camp, and within hours men, women and children were writhing in agony. Armed and mounted men then swept down on the camp from all sides, firing until the dead choked the creek. Australian writer Dame Mary Gilmore, who lived in the region as a child, described further massacres in the region.[32]

Brian Boru and the Wiradjuri survivors had to begin a long retreat, which took them away from the river as mile by mile the invaders recaptured the hard won ground. The bora ground at Darlington Point miraculously survived for another century and today the Wiradjuri have returned to Narrandera, Darlington Point, Griffith, Leeton and Hay. The white men who defeated them and carved out what became known as Wiradjuri Shire, called the citadel of their social power in Hay the Wiradjuri Club.

In the same period, war was continuing in the northern part of New South Wales, in the area the English were to name New England. There the Macleay, Hastings and Manning Rivers dominate a landscape of river valleys and mountains, waterfalls and forest known as the Falls Country. Here the Thungutti people retreated in the 1830s as the invaders pushed up the river valleys and down from the New England Tableland. They had hardly resisted as their lands were overrun, but when the weight of dispossession and oppression became too heavy to bear the Thungutti turned and fought. The white forces combined military skill with terror tactics, and twenty massacres along the lines of those suffered by the Wiradjuri were recorded. The Thungutti resisted, almost to the last man, for twenty-five years.[33]

They were still fighting a desperate rearguard action when a war of a different kind erupted at Lambing Flat, 320 kilometres north of Kiandra in southern New South Wales. Here, in 1861, redcoats of the East Suffolk Regiment (12th) and armed mounted auxiliaries went into action as race war broke out between Chinese and European diggers.

When colonial authorities in Victoria began to discriminate against Chinese in 1855, many moved across the border into New South Wales. The bid for a republic at Ballarat in Victoria the previous year alarmed the authorities, who subsequently found it convenient to use the Chinese as a scapegoat for their problems, including the recession which set in as the gold finds petered out. The European diggers were kept diverted from the real problems of the time by a constant barrage of propaganda against the orientals. The Chinese were driven from the field at Rocky River in New England in 1856, from the Buckland field in Victoria the following year, and moves to introduce restrictive legislation in Sydney provided many opportunities for racist outbursts against the 10,000 Chinese diggers in New South Wales.

OVERLEAF:
War drill in northern New South Wales, 1845. REX NAN KIVELL COLLECTION, NATIONAL LIBRARY OF AUSTRALIA

Late in 1860, on the newly proclaimed field at Lambing Flat, the European diggers set out to clean out the sly grog shops, brothels and gambling dens run by their own people. They marched through the town burning and destroying. A minority of racists went on to the Chinese camp where they continued the destruction, returning with pigtails cut or torn from their owners' heads hanging from their belts like Indian scalps.[34] Despite the persecution Chinese diggers persisted on the field, their numbers at Lambing Flat increasing to around 1500.

In January 1861 a Miners' Protective League, along the lines of the notorious San Francisco Vigilance Committee of 1851, had been formed in an attempt to exclude the Chinese from the field. With memories of the Ballarat Reform League (the precursor of the revolt at Eureka) still vivid, Governor Denison despatched a detachment of 130 men of the 12th Regiment with an artillery squad to the field. The League melted away before this show of force, but had revived by 30 June, when 3000 miners invaded all the Chinese camps in the area, burning and destroying them, and took over not just the town but the entire area.

They remained defiantly in control for two weeks, until a force of police troopers arrived from Sydney. Three diggers were arrested, the Riot Act was read, and ignored, and the troopers charged. Fighting continued for three hours before the rebels withdrew, with one dead and others wounded.[35] After this bloody clash on 14 July—more often remembered for Bastille Day than Lambing Flat—the police returned to Sydney. The diggers regrouped, setting up a Vigilance Committee to administer the area. There was constant drilling in preparation for the next battle.

The Chinese abandoned the area, taking refuge in Yass, while the governor and his administration kept in touch with events through the telegraph operating from Yass and Goulburn. The leader of the Miners' Protective League, J. Thorpy, called meetings to discuss the future. Thorpy's motivation was simple and venal. His syndicate had sold a claim to Chinese diggers who made a success of it, and wanted it back without paying for it. (Thorpy based his entire career on racism against Chinese people and continued the way he began: he was later elected to the New South Wales Legislative Assembly on a racist platform.) On 23 July a force comprising men of the 12th Regiment and sailors from HMS *Fawn* arrived in Yass from Sydney complete with artillery. They mounted an attack on Lambing Flat on 31 July. As they advanced the League leaders fled and the task force reoccupied the entire area without resistance. The 200 soldiers and sailors with their naval guns cowed 4000 armed diggers.

The Chinese diggers returned to the field, but racist agitators such as Baker, another future member of the New South Wales Legislative Assembly, attempted to cause more rioting. They failed but won in the parliament in November 1861 when the Chinese Immigration Act was passed. This repressive and discriminatory legislation was directed against

Chinese diggers, who made up sixty per cent of diggers on nearly every goldfield in New South Wales and nearly twenty per cent of the entire non-Aboriginal population. It was not until the Whitlam Government came to power in Australia in 1972 that racist state and federal legislation was wiped out, hopefully for all time.

Victoria

More than 100 engagements have been recorded in the war that began with the invasion of what is now Victoria in the 1830s. When Major Thomas Mitchell, then New South Wales surveyor general, set out from Sydney in 1836 to blaze the trail of British expansion southwards, he commanded his party of twenty-three men like a military unit rather than a peaceful group of explorers. On 24 May 1836, when they were on the northern bank of the Murray River near Euston (now in New South Wales), a party of 180 local people began to take an interest in the party. Mitchell decided to attack them a few days later, although there had not been any sign of hostility. Dividing his men into two groups he ambushed the unsuspecting people, who tried to escape by swimming the Murray River; they were shot in the water and survivors who reached the other side were picked off. The number of survivors is not known.[36]

Mitchell recorded his satisfaction at the massacre, named the site of the killings Mount Dispersion and completed his mission. His reward was an English knighthood and elevation to the lexicon of English heroes.

The pattern of invasion and destruction was set. By the 1840s the nations of Victoria had begun to build coalitions on the pattern of the Kamilaroi and Wiradjuri further to the north. This resulted in war parties of up to 600 men, particularly in the Goulburn Valley and Western District where resistence persisted. As the invaders moved out from seaports such as Melbourne, Geelong, Portland and Port Albert and from Sydney following Mitchell's route, the Western District and central and north-eastern Victoria were taken over. Gippsland saw its first invasion in mid-1840 and the north-west or Mallee about 1844.[37]

Melbourne itself came under attack. The Wurundjeri people, who met every year with neighbouring nations at Bulleen Ponds, planned a combined attack in 1835. The plan was abandoned, but was later revived when Billibellary became a leader of the Wurundjeri people. Billibellary studied the military disposition of the infant city, establishing that it was guarded by a force of soldiers under the command of Captain William Lonsdale, together with armed white settlers. Billibellary advised his people in council that the odds against them were too great for a full attack to succeed. Any hopes that survived were dashed in October 1840 when a military force directed by Lonsdale raided their main encampment on the Yarra and forced them to retreat.[38]

It was not Billibellary but a survivor of Tasmania'a Black War, named by his captors Jack Napoleon, who led a counterattack in 1839. Napoleon was one of sixteen Tasmanians who had been brought to Melbourne from Flinders Island to which they had been exiled following the disastrous end of their war. George Robinson, the Englishman who had persuaded the Tasmanians to surrender, had offered to bring the party to Port Phillip so that they could "civilise" their brothers still at war. Napoleon had been a war leader in Tasmania and resented the custody and lack of freedom which Robinson imposed. He was told to make contact with the Wurundjeri people with a message of peace, but instead told them of the Tasmanian massacres and the vain struggle of his people. He led five Tasmanians including three women (among whom was the outspoken Lalla Rooke, also known as Trucanini) to join the Port Phillip people in a glorious year of defiance.[39]

Using firearms captured in their first raids on outlying stations and covering up to fifty kilometres a day they staged a series of lightning raids. They wiped out some whalers at the Cape Paterson coaling station, west of Western Port, struck at Balnarring and swept down from the Dandenongs to the outskirts of today's inner Melbourne. Napoleon and his men were out to exact revenge for a generation of killings. It all ended on 20 November when Commissioner F. A. Powlett commanding nine mounted police, eight soldiers under Lieutenant Rawson, and twenty armed auxiliaries and black trackers, set out to confront them. Rawson's black assistants, bullied and bought off to oppose their own people, gave him an edge. Powlett's force was able to surprise Napoleon and his group while they were sleeping. Napoleon was taken back to Melbourne and hanged with Bob, his friend and comrade in arms. The three courageous women, who had handled firearms as well as their men, were sent back to Flinders Island as prisoners for the rest of their lives.[40]

As the invaders moved westward to Geelong and beyond, they encountered the Kurung and Wathaurung people, who had organised rapidly and by 1836 were in daily action. One of the most successful actions of the war in the area was the Wathaurung advance down the Leigh Valley from Mount Mercer with 200 warriors.[41] They attacked the Clyde Company Station and despite suffering dead and wounded locked up the invaders not only in that location but in forty-six stations in the Geelong area. They fought all the harder during the drought of 1838–39 in a desperate attempt to retain water and food supplies.

The Kirrae, Gunditjmara and Tjapwurong peoples in the Western District formed a coalition to take up the fight in those drought years. Their military actions in the Hamilton, Grampians and Glenelg River areas were made from a base they established in Stoney Rises, volcanic hill country stretching from Port Fairy north to Mount Rouse and Heywood and westward to Hamilton. This area was almost impenetrable on horseback, which reduced the whites' advantage. Rolf Boldrewood,

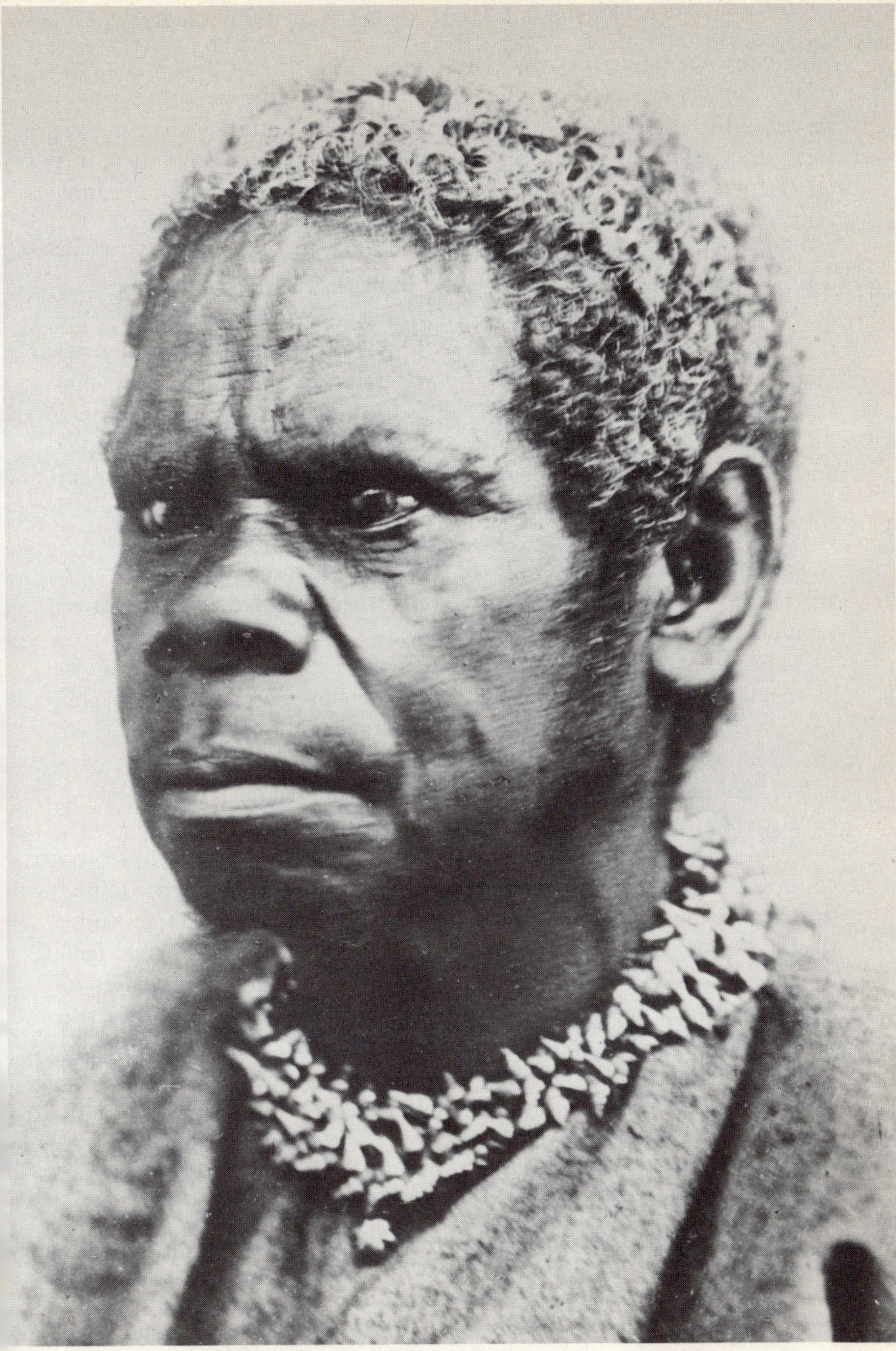

The most famous Tasmanian woman, Trucanini, 1866.
NATIONAL LIBRARY OF AUSTRALIA

who was then manager of Squattleseamere Station, recorded how every movement was watched and when the time was right the war parties would emerge from the fastness of the Stoney Rises and attack. Their targets were often economic—the crops and the stock—but sometimes there was an execution: Peter Codd, an accountant, was killed for raping and beating black women.[42]

Throughout central and north-eastern Victoria the Jaara, Ngurelban, Taungurong, Minjambutta, Pangerang and Kwatkwat peoples maintained a constant guerilla war aimed at driving back the landtakers, dispersing stock and cutting communications with Melbourne. One of their famous victories was at Broken River near Wangaratta. A combined force of 300 Pangerang attacked a strong party led by George Faithful, who was intent on taking land in the area. The war party killed seven of the armed hands and scattered the flocks while the survivors retreated. Faithful tried again on the Ovens River but again the Pangerang warriors drove him out.[43] A Pangerang war leader named Merriman led a guerilla group of twenty to strike at outstations; one attack was on Dr George Mackay's station where the only death was that of the hutkeeper, executed for his repeated rape and abuse of women.

The wet winters of 1843 and 1844 proved ideal for the prosecution of the war. On the upper Murray between present day Echuca and Corryong, the Jotijota, Pangerang and Kwatkwat peoples combined. Their strength was demonstrated on 7 August 1843 when they assembled a force of 600 fighting men and launched a series of attacks along the river, taking back great stretches of territory.[44]

Resistance in central Victoria, especially along the Goulburn, set the countryside ablaze. A Wurundjeri war leader called Winnaberrie joined forces with the Taungurong people in a role seen by his enemies to be that of supreme commander. He was successful in retaking a great deal of Taungurong land in a series of raids which forced the invaders to abandon their homesteads and retreat to Melbourne. During 1841 the whole area of the Goulburn and Lodden Rivers as far south as Plenty experienced daily raids: three war leaders named in the *Fort Phillip Herald* as Jackey Jackey, Tom and Alexander cleared the whites from Mount Alexander near Castlemaine;[45] and a war party of the Ngurelban people drove back both invaders and stock around Seymour. In another incident in January 1843 a combined force of 1000 gathered at the Broken River to join the Murray people in an attempt to reconquer the entire Goulburn Valley.

In 1841 Maraura warriors west of Mildura in the Rufus region cut the Adelaide to Sydney stock route. Four hundred warriors massed to deny passage to eleven whites and 5000 sheep near Lake Victoria; three of the intruders fell in the short, sharp engagement. Another attempted penetration of Maraura land from the south was completely defeated and the whites were driven back to Adelaide.[46]

Carefully planned opposition halted the occupation of the Wimmera, while the rugged Mount Arapiles was used as a base to attack in the Dimboola and Horsham areas. The Jaadwa people successfully attacked stations at Wonwondah and Longerenong. Mountainous Gippsland provided an ideal battleground for the Bratauolung people, who fought and survived longer than most and had Port Albert under siege.

The Bratauolung were one of the peoples who tried to secure firearms, realising that without them they could not match the firepower of the military and the colonial auxiliaries. The authorities, however, kept tight controls over the sale of weapons and it was this lack of firearms that caused the tide to turn. The beginning of the end came in August 1842 following a meeting in Melbourne to discuss the formation of a corps of Port Phillip volunteers. The colonial government responded by despatching armed border police and black troopers to the frontier. In 1845 the Native Police under William Dana, younger brother of the first commander, moved into Victoria like an avenger and in the Goulburn Valley combined with local auxiliaries raised from the stations to launch a series of attacks. The irregular auxiliaries, as in the Murrumbidgee area, began to exact a toll of terror which tipped the scales. George and William Faithful and Dr Mackay combined forces to attack the camps of the local people, firing from ambush and catching the people unaware.

The Border Police moved south with devastating effect. The new Adelaide settlement organised a military force, which Governor George Grey recognised as an official battalion, to advance along the Murray. The core of seventy heavily armed mounted men was augmented by scores of local auxiliaries and after a series of encounters the back of the war parties was broken. To keep the road from Sydney to Melbourne open Governor Gipps of New South Wales proposed a line of military posts.[47]

The combined forces in constant action with superior arms was taking a terrible toll of the defending nations, and by 1850 resistance to invasion had been broken in most areas of Victoria. The flames of war had died away almost completely, only to be rekindled by the rebellion at Ballarat, the bold strike for freedom and a republic in the Battle of Eureka Stockade in 1854.

Tasmania

The Black War in Tasmania reached its height in the 1830s and resulted in near genocide. The invasion of Tasmania, known as Van Diemen's Land until 1825, began peacefully enough about 1800 when sealers began arriving as seasonal visitors. They were incorporated into the Tasmanian kinship system, so there was a recognition of mutual obligations, but quickly gained a reputation for their brutality, particularly towards Tasmanian women.

The agricultural settlers who followed from 1807 to 1820 were mostly ex-prisoners from New South Wales. They used only small areas of land for which many paid "rent" to the Tasmanians in the form of potatoes, flax, tobacco, tea and dogs.[48] Again the Tasmanians sought to develop a system of ritual co-existence and to incorporate the newcomers into the kinship system by offering them wives. The whites were more interested in Tasmanian children as a source of labour and embarked on widespread kidnapping of both boys and girls from their families. By 1816 the Tasmanians were forced to defend themselves and launched a series of attacks designed to drive the foreigners into the sea. It was in the early days of the war that one of the most effective guerilla leaders came to the fore.

Musquito had been one of the war leaders in the Hawkesbury River and Broken Bay regions of New South Wales. He had been captured and imprisoned on Norfolk Island before being sent to Tasmania in 1813 and put to work as a stockman for one of the first English settlers, Edward Lord. The lieutenant-governor, Colonel William Sorell, sought Musquito's help to capture the bushranger, Michael Howe, promising him repatriation to Sydney; Howe was captured but Sorell broke his promise.[49] Musquito bided his time. When it became obvious that a takeover of the whole of the island was being planned by the English authorities, Musquito joined the Laremairremener people of Oyster Bay. He quickly welded them into a fighting force and began a guerilla war such as he had pursued with considerable success in his native land. Musquito seemed invincible and in 1824 Lieutenant-Governor George Arthur offered a reward for his capture. His several years of successful resistance came to an end when two bushrangers-cum-bounty hunters led by a renegade Tasmanian named Tegg tracked him down and shot him. They took the wounded Musquito and his fellow resistance fighter, Black Jack, back to Hobart. There, after recovering from their wounds, they were hanged.

By the late 1820s thousands of hectares of grazing land had been expropriated by the invaders, despite the fierce resistance, and Tasmanian women were being abducted by stock-keepers. This spurred the warriors on to greater efforts; they killed and wounded many more whites,[50] and also proved successful at disrupting the economy, destroying both stock and property. Arthur tried a tactic which was to work for the British in Malaya 150 years later and fail for the Americans in Vietnam—to remove people to strategic hamlets. The Tasmanians, however, refused to give up their land to go to Arthur's "retreat". Having failed to entice them, he ordered a military expedition designed to force them off the occupied lands.

On 15 April 1828 Arthur issued a proclamation dividing the island into settled and unsettled districts.[51] He placed troops along the frontiers at fortified points established at Launceston, at Waterloo Point at Oyster

Bay, at Bothwell on the Clyde River, at New Norfolk, at the Isis River and at Norfolk Plains. He placed giant posters along the frontiers, showing that his justice applied to black and white alike. Any Tasmanian wishing to cross the frontiers had to apply to Arthur for a pass.

The Tasmanians' response was swift—they ignored the frontiers and defied the troops, and launched an unprecedented series of attacks throughout what Arthur had called his "settled districts". In November 1828 Arthur declared martial law to justify shooting on sight any Tasmanian in those districts,[52] and in the winter of 1829 he sent nine punitive parties and troops to drive all Tasmanians out. He failed again. In the midst of growing panic amongst the white settlers Arthur wrote to his Imperial masters in London:

> *The species of warfare which we are carrying on with them is of the most distressing nature:—they suddenly appear, commit some acts of outrage, and, then, as suddenly vanish—if pursued, it seems impossible to surround and capture them, and, if the Parties fire, the possibility is that Women and children are the victims.*[53]

In the summer of 1829–30 there was some concern that the English might have to evacuate altogether. Arthur tried to stop the last detachment of the 2nd Somersetshire Regiment from departing for India, and appealed for reinforcements from the West Suffolk (63rd Regiment) in Western Australia but for the moment was unsuccessful. In the spring, however, when he decided on a full-scale offensive against the Big River and Oyster Bay people, reinforcements from the West Suffolk regiment did arrive. He ordered Major Douglas and the regiment to lead an action supported by the field police and every able-bodied Englishman in the colony.

They were to form a human chain across the settled districts from St Patricks Head on the east coast through Campbell Town in the midlands to Quamby Bluff in the Western Tiers. An extra flank at each end was designed to cover any escape points. For three weeks the Black Line, as this human chain was called, would move south and east across the settled districts until the forces were concentrated in an area bounded by Sorell at Pittwater, Richmond on the Coal River and Spring Bay on the east coast. Then the armed auxiliaries would be sent home and the troops would tighten the cordon until they reached East Bay Neck, the narrow isthmus of Forestier Peninsula, a month later.[54] The Tasmanians caught in this net would be driven south to the Tasman Peninsula, where Arthur planned a reserve.

OVERLEAF:
Survivors of Tasmania's Black War at Oyster Cove, c. 1860.
BEATTIE COLLECTION, NATIONAL LIBRARY OF AUSTRALIA

More than 2000 men were involved in the Black Line. There were 500 troops from three regiments, the 17th Leicester Regiment, the 59th and the 63rd West Suffolk Regiment, 700 prisoners and 800 English colonists. They carried 1000 stands of arms, 30,000 rounds of ammunition and 300 pairs of handcuffs.[55] For three weeks they advanced across the island, establishing fortified posts, getting lost in heavy rain and consuming huge quantities of government stores. They dislodged the Oyster Bay people, killing two and capturing two, but survivors slipped through the cordon to take refuge in the north-east. The people of the North Midlands and Ben Lomond also escaped to the north-east, where most of them were captured two weeks later. The Big River people were isolated in the mountains near the River Ouse, while the people of the North and the North Midlands as well as the North-east were contained north of Launceston ready for capture the following year.[56]

Arthur appointed George Augustus Robinson, a bricklayer who felt his mission was to influence the Tasmanians to surrender, to direct the last act of the tragic drama. Using a mixture of diplomacy and guile, Robinson spent three months in pursuit of the Big River and Oyster Bay peoples; they surrendered to him at the River Dee at the end of 1831. By 1832 the remnants of a once proud and relatively peaceful people surrendered. Fewer than fifty of the 200 Tasmanians who had inhabited the "settled districts" survived and at the time of the surrender there was not one man, woman or child who was not wounded in some way. Beyond the settled districts, in the west and north-west of the island, little more than 100 people were left to fight for their lands and their freedom. By cajolery or force, one by one, Robinson persuaded each of the remaining groups to surrender. By 1834 there were no Tasmanians left on the west coast.

British casualties in the war amounted to little more than 200 dead or wounded but a race had been almost wiped out. The Imperial Parliament in London established a commission of enquiry into the Black War and in the records held by the New South Wales Parliament the evidence pointed to the whites having pursued a policy of extirpation. Asked by a commissioner if that posed problems, one squatter giving evidence replied in the affirmative: to dispose of bodies it was necessary to drive the Tasmanians into the sea and shoot them there.

The remnants of the Tasmanian people were exiled to Flinders Island in Bass Strait. Among them was Trucanini, a heroic and tragic figure of the Tasmanian resistance. She was born about 1812 on Bruny Island in the D'Entrecasteaux Channel. By the time she was seventeen she had seen the English invade her country and murder, kidnap and abuse members of her family; she herself had been kidnapped and raped. People came to believe that she was "the last Tasmanian", and that when she died in 1876 her race died with her. Today, however, almost 3000

Tasmanians are still fighting, though these days peacefully, for their rights as Australia's first inhabitants.

South Australia

When the Imperial authorities in London decided in 1836 to promote an English settlement in what is today South Australia, they tried to avoid the bloodshed that had marred settlement attempts in both eastern and western Australia. The colonists were instructed to recognise the rights of the people to their land and to negotiate with them for it. This first attempt to secure land rights for the people of the continent was subverted from the moment of landing. The instructions from London were ignored and the usual orgy of land expropriation, backed by guns and bayonets, made South Australia no different from the rest of the continent.

By the late 1830s black resistance was beginning to stiffen. The leaders of that resistance, the Milmenrura people, who were called by the invaders the "Big Murray" group, had registered some success in discouraging the occupation of their lands. In 1840 a ship called the *Maria* was wrecked in the Coorong area and the ship's complement was attacked as they attempted to come ashore. Twenty-six were killed by the Milmenrura people, who regarded them as part of the continuing invasion.[57] The governor's response was to send an armed detachment to execute what he called "summary justice". The result was a campaign of terror. Fifteen men and fifty women and children were rounded up on one day, five women were captured and imprisoned on another occasion,[58] and young people harmlessly swimming were fired upon. The governor and his Executive Council decided to treat as a "foreign enemy" the Milmenrura people and any other nations if they resisted.[59] Two Milmenrura leaders, Moorcangua and Mongarawatta, were arrested and hanged. They were seen by their people as patriots and martyrs in the opposition to the invaders.

In 1841 armed auxiliaries took part in the war against people on the Murray. A combined force of 400 warriors, showing contempt for the firearms of their enemies, defeated them in one engagement, but in the long run the colonial forces bled them to death. Resistance continued throughout the 1840s wherever the invaders settled. In the remote parts, such as Port Lincoln, the fighting went on well into the 1850s. By 1856 the battle had been lost and the people dispossessed; for the rest of the century the survivors were steadily exterminated.

Northern Territory

The Spanish Crown had claimed all of the Australian continent but had never established a presence; the Dutch had explored parts of Australia and revisited many times, but over a period of 200 years had never made

Guerilla attack on a shepherd's hut, Port Lincoln, South Australia, 1864.
NATIONAL LIBRARY OF AUSTRALIA

any formal claims; and Captain James Cook claimed only half the continent for the British Crown, the other half being simply New Holland.

This was the position when Governor Thomas Brisbane, prodded by fears of French expansion, established a military outpost called Fort Dundas on Melville Island in 1824. The Tiwi immediately recognised the threat it posed to their peace and security and attacked the fort. By 1827 they had forced the garrison to stay within its walls. Soldiers moving outside the fort did so in battle array; those on guard duty were often picked off by marksmen with spears.[60] The Tiwi's military tactics were sophisticated, effectively putting the fort under siege. In 1829, after six years of hell, the garrison was withdrawn.

During the next forty years the English made three more futile attempts to establish a permanent settlement in the north—at Raffles Bay on Cobourg Peninsula (1827–29), at Victoria on Port Essington (1838–49) and at Escape Cliffs on Adam Bay (1864–67). The fourth, and at last successful, attempt to establish an English presence came in 1869, when a surveying team was sent to lay out the site of Darwin, then known as Palmerston. The people of the area attacked, killing one surveyor and wounding the other.

In 1870 the English began a more subtle probe, the construction of the Overland Telegraph Line connecting Adelaide to Darwin and then to the intercontinental telegraph. All along the line guerilla attacks were maintained on camps, hitting stores and parts of the line itself. The raids continued after the Overland Telegraph was completed but the landseekers were already on their way. Barrow Creek telegraph station some 280 kilometres north of Alice Springs was attacked in February 1874. Further north three determined raids were made on landseekers travelling through the East Alligator River region planning to take up pastoral country in Arnhem Land. South-east of Arnhem Land a combined force of the Anvella, Mbiah and Goodangi peoples produced a war leader of distinction, Mirrimicki, who led the resistance in the ranges at the headwaters of the McArthur and Limmen Bight Rivers.

In 1884 an attack was made on a copper mine at Daly River south of Darwin and three whites were speared. There were howls for instant reprisal. The *Northern Territory Times* on 4 October summed up the prevailing mood:

> *European settlers must be allowed to till the soil, and extract the wealth from the land which they have made their home, free from the murdering raids of these savages. Backward the natives must move before the tide of civilization, or, if they will not give place peaceably and show that their natures are as dangerous as the venomous serpent, even as every man will crush a snake under his heel, so must the hand of every man be raised against a tribe of*

When the invaders ignored repeated warnings, war parties attacked. A depiction of an attack on Ernest Giles' party at Ularring in the Great Victoria Desert, Western Australia, 1875. NATIONAL LIBRARY OF AUSTRALIA

inhuman monsters, whose cowardly and murderous nature renders them unfit to live . . .[61]

Inflamed by this rhetoric a paramilitary unit sanctioned by the government resident in the Daly River area killed 150 people including women and children. One of the party notched the figure "14" in the butt of his rifle to indicate his score. Another later described how he had shot an old man who was trying to escape by swimming a creek.

Such terror broke the resistance, but sporadic fighting continued into the 1930s. The Coniston Massacre, which occurred near Alice Springs in 1928, bears witness to the repetition of a tactic in which families were shot to death in the worst tradition of the Hundred Years War.

Queensland

The resistance of the Queensland people began in 1824 with the establishment of the first military post and prison at Moreton Bay. It was notorious for the cruelty of its commandant, Patrick Logan, a butcher of men who was put to death by Black Australians.

The Queensland clans maintained pressure on the invaders from the 1840s until the end of the century. War threatened the whole economy of the colony, which was part of New South Wales until 1859; stock losses mounted, stations were burnt, stores looted and lines of communication threatened. Small farms in coastal valleys and fertile tablelands were prime targets for raiding parties intent on taking corn, potatoes and bananas in forced exchange for the fish and game which the intruders had taken. Mines in north and north-west Queensland had to be guarded by armed men day and night. Guerilla forces dominated the road from Port Douglas to Croydon for a decade and mining camps on the Palmer were a special target in the 1870s.

A highlight of the Queensland war was the emergence of the charismatic guerilla leader, Dundalli.[62] In 1845 he brought the people of Moreton Bay and Wide Bay together in a grand alliance to stop the takeover of the countryside around Brisbane. He began his nine years of resistance with a raid on an isolated station near Brisbane, followed rapidly by an action that cut the main road from the infant capital. A military post was established at Helidon to combat Dundalli's forces. Men of the regiment stationed there carried out punitive expeditions for miles around, but despite the killings Dundalli remained at liberty and in command of a substantial guerilla force. His objective was to drive out the intruders and to replenish supplies with vegetables from the farms and sheep and cattle stations. Emulating his southern cousins, Dundalli successfully used economic warfare.

His brilliant career came to an untimely end at its height, when Make-i-light, the elder and lawmaker who had presided over the alliance of the three peoples and who guided Dundalli, was captured in 1854.

Dundalli went into Brisbane to free him in a one-man raid, but was captured and tried by a colonial court. A large war party of Ningy-Ningy warriors led by one of his faithful lieutenants, Billy Barlow, and an equally large force of his own warriors from Bribie Island attempted a rescue but failed. Dundalli was hanged publicly in front of what is now Brisbane's General Post Office, defiant, proud and fearless to the last. His death and Make-i-light's capture spelt an end to the alliance and the prosecution of the war.

Further to the north in the Maryborough area the Kabi Kabi people followed Dundalli's tactics, adopting a scorched earth policy in a desperate attempt to save their land. Their forces registered some striking successes in attacks on Frazer's Hornet Bank Station on the Dawson River in 1857 and in 1861 at Will's station, Cullin-la-Ringo. The combined white casualties were thirty-one and the two events struck renewed terror into British hearts. During the 1860s the Governor of Queensland asked the Imperial Government for troop reinforcements, it being acknowledged that the biggest threat to the colonial occupation was the bitter resistance of the original Australians.[63]

Resistance continued in the Dawson River area from 1857 to 1870, while further to the north the people vigorously defended their lands in the Mackay and Bowen districts. The fighting in the Cardwell district on the Palmer River and on the Atherton Tablelands continued into the 1880s.

A new invasion factor confronted Australians when gold was found in the Palmer River area in the early 1870s and thousands of Chinese diggers arrived. Before the goldfield was ten months old war parties had been formed and steps had to be taken to prevent the entire area being cut off by constant raids. The sheer number of invaders, both oriental and occidental, meant that black resistance had little hope.

The efforts of the mighty Kalkadoons in holding fast to their lands in the vicinity of Mount Isa and Cloncurry for ten years has been an inspiration to the generations that have survived. Their disastrous defeat at Battle Mountain in 1884 marked the close of the first 100 years of war, although fighting was to continue into the twentieth century.

Western Australia

Within eight years of the arrival of British warships in the Swan River in 1829 to take possession of the western part of the continent, the heroic resistance of the Nyungar people, whose eminent leaders included Yagan of the Swan River and Calyute of the Murray River, had been broken at the Battle of Pinjarra. Although this ended resistance in the Swan Valley and Murray River regions, their example fired other nations in the west to resist the invasion. Within two years the people of the Avon district had mounted their resistance. In 1850 the people of Champion Bay district

(Geraldton) reversed a generation of defeats and won a battle. The English forces on this occasion were led by Governor Fitzgerald, who was wounded while his forces retreated in the face of a steady attack.[64]

The occupation of Roebourne and the Cossack district was also marked by strong resistance. Armed whites captured some local people, for stealing, at Flying Foam Passage; a war party promptly descended on the camp, killed the guards and freed their black brothers. The success was not enjoyed for long: an armed detachment killed 150 people in a punitive raid.

By the 1860s the war spanned 2.6 million square kilometres. In the south a serious setback for black resistance occurred in the Esperance Bay area, where the people fought to prevent their lands being taken. In 1864 in the Lagrange district on the north-west coast a white force using six-chamber revolvers, "with six spare sets of chambers loaded ready for insertion, in addition to double barrelled guns or carbines" (which gave each man forty-four shots without reloading) ambushed and killed twenty warriors.[65]

South of Roebourne, through the Gascoyne and Murchison River districts, the people of the west fought for thirty years. This area of conflict was described by one Englishman writing home as paralleling the war in Ireland. The Australian "natives", he declared, had committed far greater atrocities on the British than even the Zulus had, and the British had "fearful respect" for them.[66]

In the Kimberley region the war lasted longer than anywhere else on the Australian continent, beginning in the 1880s and continuing until 1930. It was a heroic defence which utilised the rugged terrain and the experience gained over two generations of continual fighting. The sophistication of the guerilla tactics of the people of this region and the brilliant nature of their struggle is exemplified in the saga of the black patriot and hero, Pigeon, or Jundumurra, who became a resistance leader in the 1890s. The crowning glories of his career were the successful engagement at Windjina Gorge in 1894 and the following battle there in 1895.

Born in West Kimberley to the Bunuba people, Pigeon from his birth had heard tales of the white conquest, of abductions of children for forced labour by the pearlers, and of the devastating weapons the invaders used to enforce their will. The white frontier did not encroach on Bunuba country but two stations had been established nearby in the shadow of the Napier Ranges. From the mountains the Bunuba could observe the invaders and they would harvest their crops and take their stock when food supplies ran low. A few of them were enticed into the white workforce and Pigeon followed his mother and other members of his family onto William Lukin's Lennard River Station. He was still an uninitiated boy but he learned quickly. Lukin noticed him and gave him the nickname

Pigeon because he was swift-footed and small with a sunny personality.[67]

By the time he was fourteen Pigeon was the fastest shearer in the district and the best horseman; Lukin freely acknowledged that he was also the best stockman. He learned English and became popular with the Europeans. To him life was a grand adventure, not hard work, until he reached the age of fifteen, when the Bunuba elders decided that he should undergo initiation. Pigeon learned the secret songs and lore of the timeless history of his people, and the initiation and intense spiritual education had a profound effect on the boy. He chose to stay in the mountains with those Bunuba who had disdained to mingle with the invaders and in fact challenged their right to remain. This group, and a young man named Ellemarra, had a strong influence on him.

Ellemarra's courage, physical stature and hunting ability marked him out for respect by all. Ellemarra had been challenged by a white stockman on Lillimooloora Station when he was about to kill a sheep; the stockman had fired but Ellemarra had speared him. On another occasion, armed with spears and boomerangs, he had challenged a police patrol single handed. He was the first Bunuba to be arrested for stock killing, in 1886. Sentenced to three months hard labour he was sent to Roebourne prison. He escaped and walked 960 kilometres back to the Napier Ranges. Tall, strong and confident as ever, he was greeted with awe.

Pigeon was building a reputation among his people as a clever hunter, but as a result of his sojourn with the English was regarded as a little strange. He often preferred to be alone or to be in the company of young women, a practice frowned upon in a society with rigid sexual taboos.[68] Nevertheless, he continued to show leadership and attacked the white frontiers. In 1889 2000 sheep were killed on Lennard River and 4000 on Lillimooloora by war parties, led by Pigeon, spearheading the movement to retake their lands. The colonial authorities responded by reinforcing the troops in the area and setting up a military post near Windjina Gorge. It was there that a patrol of police troopers captured Pigeon and Ellemarra.

They were chained and marched to Derby, where Ellemarra went back to corrugated iron cells and chain gangs, while the still teenage Pigeon was put to work looking after police horses. He spent a year at Derby and after his release worked for a brief period on Lennard River Station. In his absence the troopers had waged a continuous war on the Bunuba, inflicting substantial casualties. On returning to the mountains his disregard for traditional law brought him into conflict with the elders and he fled to Joe Blyth's Brooking Springs Station, where he was indentured for two years.[69]

His boss was ruthless and Pigeon absconded, only to be captured and charged with escaping from bonded service. He was sentenced to serve as a police tracker some 110 kilometres north of Derby. Pigeon gave such good service in this strange territory that the authorities attempted to

Black prisoners of war.
FERGUSON COLLECTION, NATIONAL LIBRARY OF AUSTRALIA

use him against his own people. He was used in a raid on Bunuba land in which sixteen warriors were captured and marched to Lillimooloora homestead. Pigeon knew and was related to every one of them, and they told him that while he had been away, the English had invaded Bunuba land and a police trooper at Fitzroy Crossing had been killing his people indiscriminately.

Pigeon had served in Derby with the white man guarding the prisoners, Bill Richardson, and had once saved Richardson's life in action, but loyalty to his embattled people came first. He shot Richardson dead, released his compatriots, and assuming the role of war leader sent for other warriors to join him. He had the best qualifications for the job. He knew white tactics, he could handle firearms, and even the hero Ellemarra came forward to serve under him.[70]

Pigeon determined that if he was to win a military victory he must obtain firearms. In about November 1894 a wagon train of stock and weapons was ambushed successfully in Windjina Gorge, his first operation as leader. He captured a large armoury of weapons and ammunition, and quickly began to train his men in their use. He planned to ambush the patrol of police reinforcements and then lead his growing army down the Lennard River, clearing out the invaders.

The senior officer of the white forces, Sub-Inspector Drewry, mobilised all the troopers in the area and also commissioned fifteen hired hands. He sent six black stockmen from Queensland to pretend to join Pigeon, who knew something was amiss and did not trust them. Ellemarra wanted to kill them but Pigeon said his quarrel was with whites not blacks and sent them back. It was a terrible blunder, because they described his forces and location to the whites. At daybreak on 16 November 1895 the Battle of Windjina Gorge began. The white force of thirty divided into groups of ten and moved into the gorge from three directions in an ambush. Pigeon fought valiantly, despite three serious wounds, but the Bunuba were defeated and Ellemarra was among those wounded. With the help of the young women who had always been his supporters, Pigeon hid in a cave. For four months reinforcements poured into the area of the Napier, Oscar and Leopold Ranges. Attacked time and again, the Bunuba people and their neighbours could no longer resist.

Pigeon was not dead. It took him two years to fully recuperate, hiding in Tunnel Creek Cave about forty-eight kilometres south of Windjina, from which he emerged periodically to continue his fight. He was wounded again in an action to free Bunuba prisoners being marched in chains to jail, recovered, then raided Lillimooloora Station. Sub-Inspector Ord, who succeeded Drewry, was mocked by Pigeon as he stood on a mountain with his faithful band of thirty warriors, determined to fight on. Ord concluded that Pigeon would defy the whole British Army and enjoy it.[71] But sad losses were to come: in 1897 Ellemarra and another old comrade, Lillimarra, were captured and hanged in Derby. Pigeon's reply was yet another attack, this time on Oscar Range Station. The attack failed and he fled to his Tunnel Creek hideout. A black tracker named Micki caught up with Pigeon, now slowed by many wounds, and killed him near the hideout.

Resistance died with him. William Lukin saluted Pigeon as a man who could well have realised his dream of a combined league of nations sweeping the invaders to the sea. Pigeon never saw his beloved Bunuba country taken over, although this followed shortly after his death with the establishment of Leopold Downs Station.

The guerilla war was at an end. The new century saw a period of punitive expeditions, calculated operations of extermination. In 1922 there was a massacre at the Durack River; a similar massacre took place in 1926 in the East Kimberleys, at Gotegote-Merrie, Nowerre and Dala, in which more than twenty people were killed and burned by police. This marked the end of the killing era for Western Australia.

The Hundred Years War, which spilled over into the new century, saw the proud Australian people reduced in numbers from about a million to a remnant of perhaps 50,000. The press in England and Australia proclaimed that the race was dying. But the race refused to die and today's 200,000 Black Australians continue the fight—not with guns, but by challenging the conscience of the nation and the world.

4. THE TWIN BATTLES OF SYDNEY

Within two years of the first armed force landing in Sydney Cove and the proclamation that eastern Australia, including what is now New South Wales, had a new master, the original population around Sydney Harbour had been totally dispossessed of their lands and decimated by the invaders' guns and diseases. This was a period of phony peace, but it began to fall apart as early as the middle of 1788. There was no general outbreak of hostilities, but incidents multiplied until the real war began, the war between the Eora and Dharuk peoples and the English occupation forces that culminated in the Battle of the Hawkesbury in 1795 and the Battle of Parramatta almost two years later.

The territory of the Eora, who formed the front line of the resistance, stretched from Port Jackson to Botany Bay and inland to Parramatta. They had achieved within their boundaries an almost perfect balance between the land and its resources and the population. The stable food was fish (replaced inland by game such as kangaroos) supplemented with game, vegetables, berries and fruits. Their organisation was much the same as that of other Australians. Authority was dispersed and government was by negotiated consensus among senior women and men, the opposite of the hierarchical system that was represented by their invaders.

The Sydney people were good at languages, as are most of the original peoples, and picked up English more quickly and with greater facility than the English learned the Eora or Dharuk languages. They were fond of singing and in the early days of the invasion when relations were not so tense would learn English songs, and sing them with gusto, to the surprise of the English who after months could master only a few words of the people whose land they had come to take.

This pattern of life and customs was shared by the Eora's neighbours, the Dharuk, who lived along the Hawkesbury River to the north and north-west. They had a distinctive language but they and the Eora enjoyed friendly intercourse in peace and were firm allies in war.

Their weaponry was substantially the same. The principal weapon was the spear; there were three types, a simple pointed spear, a barbed spear and a jagged-edged war spear. The last was favoured by the Eora guerilla leader Pemulwuy, and was the type he used to kill the governor's gamekeeper, the action that heralded the beginning of the war. Woomeras were used to increase the range and accuracy of spears, and there was a range of war clubs, large and small. One had a flat head with a sharp point in the centre; the flat section was sometimes painted red with white stripes radiating from the centre. Hatchets, originally stone and then, as the invaders' technology was put to use, of metal, completed the armoury. Shields were of two types, one made from bark and not so effective in resisting spears, and the other of solid, fire-hardened wood.

The people were not particularly tall but were strongly built. Patterns of scarring adorned their arms and breasts and hair ornaments were made from animal teeth, lobster claws and small bones secured with gum. Many Eora men wore a bone or stick through a hole in the cartilage of the nose as adornment, and after initiation the right front tooth in the upper jaw was removed. On ceremonial occasions white clay and red ochre were used to paint appropriate traditional designs on the face and body. Eora men had bushy beards, but once they got used to the unusual custom of shaving those in Sydney Town often became clean shaven. The women were described by some lonely English officers as "sooty sirens" with physical charms that embarrassed or attracted the invaders depending on their disposition. They were diligent workers and they often had removed two joints of little fingers on the left hand, thought to be a sign of maturity and indentity. While the people did not feel the need for clothes in the hot summers, in the cooler months they wore elegant possum-skin cloaks.

Their dwellings were made from a piece of bark, bent in the middle and placed on end on the ground. On the coast the huts were larger, made of several sheets of bark put together in an oval with an entrance. These larger dwellings could hold six or eight people. A fire was always kept burning at the entrance to the hut. In some places families used as shelters the rock overhangs common in sandstone country.

The arrival of the First Fleet in Botany Bay was a signal for large parties of armed Eora to assemble along the shores; among them some would have remembered Cook's brief visit eighteen years before. But this was no lone ship. In the nine days between 18 and 26 January no fewer than thirteen ships entered the bay—eleven English ships under Captain Arthur Phillip and two French ships commanded by Captain de la Pérouse.[1]

A typical Eora warrior with weapons.
G. W. WILSON ALBUM, NATIONAL LIBRARY OF AUSTRALIA

Phillip was forty-eight years old when he was appointed captain general and governor-in-chief of New South Wales in 1786. Born in London, the son of a German-born language teacher, Jacob Phillip, and his English wife, Elizabeth Breach, Phillip joined the navy when he was fifteen. He served in the Seven Years War, was commissioned as a lieutenant in 1762 when he was twenty-four and was retired on half pay when the war ended the following year. He married but separated after six years and became a farmer in Hampshire in the south of England. In 1774 he was given permission to enlist in the Portuguese Navy where he was promoted to captain. After four years he returned to the English Navy to command first the *Ariadne*, then the warship *Europe*, on which one of the lieutenants was Philip Gidley King, also to be a colonial governor. Phillip was retired for a second time in 1784 and returned to his farm.

Phillip was recognised as a man of courage, able to inspire respect from the men he commanded. (The fact that the front tooth in his upper jaw was missing made him more acceptable to the Eora people, who often removed the same tooth as a sign of successful initiation into manhood—what was a disadvantage in English and Portuguese society became useful in the Antipodes.[2]) Historians, however, continue to speculate about why he was chosen.[3] His service in the Portuguese Navy against Spain in South America may have earmarked him as a man of special qualifications for the establishment of a distant base which could be used in offensive operations against remnants of the Spanish Empire in the Pacific.

If the Eora were to be both horrified and terrified by the arrival of Phillip's invasion force, on the other side of the world their fellow-English men and women in Portsmouth responded similarly when the prisoners were loaded onto the transports. "The shop-keepers, in terror, lowered their shutters; the householders barred their doors; the convicts overcrowded the transports; the women convicts lolled on the decks of the ships in dirt and half naked."[4] Rumours were rife and one, that the prisoners could be accompanied by their wives, brought a fresh invasion of hundreds of women clamouring to get aboard. Portsmouth breathed a sigh of relief when the fleet sailed: if they had known what was in store the Eora might have proclaimed a period of mourning.

Phillip concentrated on building a vision of the future—no slavery in a free land, pay for his troops, medicines for the sick, clothes for the naked women, execution for murder and sodomy only, give the people of the new land a high opinion of their guests.[5] He knew that the prisoners would have to provide the economic foundation for his settlement, and that the land on which it was to be built would have to be taken from the people there. His fellow officers were also pestering the English authorities; in one case to be given a servant to make life less uncomfortable. The marines petitioned for free grog as a necessity of life, while Lord Sydney, the Secretary of State for Home Affairs, told a

Catholic priest, Thomas Walsh, he could not go with the Irish prisoners because Catholic teaching would weaken English supremacy.[6]

There were in all eleven ships in the First Fleet. The warship *Sirius* was supported by a tender, *Supply*, six transports, *Alexander*, *Charlotte*, *Scarborough*, *Friendship*, *Prince of Wales* and *Lady Penrhyn*, and three storeships, *Borrowdale*, *Golden Grove* and *Fishburn*. The invasion force aboard comprised 19 officers, 24 non-commissioned officers, 8 drummers, 160 privates, 30 wives and 12 children. The prisoners, according to an official return three weeks before sailing, numbered 565 men, 153 women, 6 boys and 5 girls—729 in all.[7] The voyage from England, on which the fleet touched both the American and African continents, took eight months and one week.

The invaders did not know the language of the people they first encountered at Botany Bay, recognised nothing of their laws and regarded the entire country as their own. To them the Eora were simply a "great many Indians".[8] Phillip's instructions in relation to the people of Australia were conflicting. His first commission, issued on 12 October 1786, appointed him governor of the territory the English had named New South Wales and defined the boundaries as extending from Cape York to the southern extremity in the latitude of 43° 39'S and westward as far as the 135th parallel, and including all the islands adjacent in the Pacific Ocean. In effect he was given authority to take half a continent from the people who had lived there for 40,000 years without discussion, treaty or compensation.

On the other hand, in his second commission and instructions issued on 25 April 1787 he received orders to

> *endeavour by every possible means to open an intercourse with the natives, and to conciliate their affections, enjoining all our subjects to live in amity and kindness with them. And if any of our subjects shall wantonly destroy them, or give them any unnecessary interruption in the exercise of their several occupations, it is our will and pleasure that you do cause such offenders to be brought to punishment according to the degree of the offence. You will endeavour to procure an account of the numbers inhabiting the neighbourhood of the intended settlement, and report your opinion to one of our Secretaries of State in what manner our intercourse with these people may be turned to the advantage of this colony.*[9]

If Phillip had interpreted his instructions literally he would have had himself arrested for "wantonly" destroying and interrupting "the exercise of their several occupations". These instructions in fact left no doubt that, despite the mention of "kindness", to make the settlement possible the "natives" were to be driven from their land, which would then be fortified against them.

Phillip was also made Captain General with power to gaol or pardon, to "levy armed forces" which could be construed as the right to conscript, to erect forts and, of course, to grant land he had never seen and which had been expropriated by a single proclamation. Further, the commission stated that the prisoners were to be put to work and the fruits of their labour held by the Crown. The Church of England was established as the State Church and he was instructed to make sure that only the rites of that church were followed. Phillip's instructions in fact gave him the power of a supreme dictator.

The Phony Peace

The seeds of conflict were sown by the first actions of the invaders in Botany Bay—casting seine nets and taking a substantial supply of fish. The Eora indicated firmly that they were taking fish from their waters and that an offer of part of the catch was hardly adequate. Then the invaders began to cut down trees and shrubs to clear a path to fresh water, despite the strenuous objections of the Eora to the destruction of their main source of food and shelter. This invited another confrontation, but the English returned to their ships and no hostilities occurred.

The English were not impressed with Botany Bay. They described the soil as mere sand and there were no lush meadows such as Cook had described. After only one day Phillip led a small party north towards Broken Bay. Early in the afternoon of 21 January they sailed into Port Jackson, which Cook had named but not investigated. They found the "finest harbour" in the world,[10] a tribute which Phillip was well qualified to pay, being familiar with the great harbours of Rio de Janeiro and Montevideo. Phillip and his party explored the coves of the harbour and selected for settlement the one with the finest spring, later to be named the Tank Stream. He named the cove after Lord Sydney, whose name was an English derivative of the Greek name Dionysius.

The party returned to Botany Bay on the evening of 23 January with the exciting news of a better harbour and better land. Although considerable work had begun ashore for a settlement at Botany Bay, Phillip sailed posthaste out of the bay on 25 January to ensure possession of Sydney; the rest of the fleet followed the next day. The reason for his haste and some panic was the sighting off Botany Bay of La Pérouse and two ships of the French fleet. As the English pulled out and headed for Sydney the French sailed in. The Eora's hopes of losing their uninvited guests died. As good linguists they would have picked up the language and ethnic differences and must have pondered long and hard why two foreign forces had so suddenly descended on them.

As Phillip sailed up Sydney Harbour the Eora lined the cliffs and the coves, chanting "war-re, war-re". The invaders did not know whether it was a welcoming salute or a warning.[11] The first significant contact,

The First Fleet in Botany Bay, from the Illustrated Sydney News, *March 1871.*
NATIONAL LIBRARY OF AUSTRALIA

which occurred on Phillip's first visit, was described by Philip Gidley King. Phillip and a party of soldiers, preparing to put ashore in search of water, were confronted by an armed party brandishing spears, making it plain they were not welcome to land.[12] At the same time the Eora launched canoes and began inspecting the ships and the shore boats. Phillip showed some beads and ordered a sailor to fasten some to the stem of one of the canoes. He stood up in the long boat and indicated that he was searching for water. At once understanding a basic human need, the Eora indicated a source of water and invited the Englishmen ashore. They guided the visitors to a fine stream and Phillip approached them alone and unarmed and offered gifts of beads. No one would approach too closely, but they indicated the gifts could be left on the ground. One man was nominated to pick them up and the party retired, puzzled but not hostile, as the Englishmen went back on board their ship.

This first meeting was without incident mainly by accident. In advancing alone Phillip had unconsciously done the right thing, although he had not realised that Eora custom demanded that when someone in need sought water they should be given access. He failed other tests, however. By not naming himself,[13] by seeking the name of the man he approached and by pressing goods on strangers when they were not in a position to return the favour he had marked himself as foolish and ignorant.

These were minor incidents, however, compared with the great invasion of the afternoon of 26 January when officers and marines landed, hoisted the English flag and solemnly claimed eastern Australia for the distant King George III of Great Britain, Ireland and Hanover. The marines fired a *feu de joie*, everyone on shore cheered and the men in the ship *Supply* joined in. The Eora had withdrawn but they watched from afar as the number of invaders on shore grew to what was probably the greatest concentration of people ever seen at that cove. Hundreds of soldiers and sailors and great numbers of prisoners were soon set to work cutting down trees, clearing scrub, pitching tents and landing stores whilst another party of prisoners on the east side of the cove erected a portable canvas house, which had been brought from England for the governor.

The Eora must have realised with heavy hearts that this was to be no flying visit but a full scale invasion. After a few days observation of the strangers at Botany Bay and Sydney Harbour they would have noticed the differences between them. They disliked the red coats and the bayonets. They identified Phillip and his officers as people of authority, but the place of the prisoners, usually in chains, would have been bizarre and inexplicable. The Eora would have observed the orgy of 6 February, when nearly 700 prisoners got drunk, copulated and fought with each other, followed by attempts to escape, the first flogging and, soon after, the first hanging.[14] Within a few weeks of landing twelve prisoners had received a total of 1172 lashes. It was like a scene from hell.

All the while the invaders took, without compunction, anything that grew or moved, not recognising that every feature of the land was owned and cherished by the traditional owners, nor that they had ruined in a week the traditional balance between population and food supplies. Phillip, the most experienced of them all, tried hard during his four years in Australia to understand how the people survived in what he believed to be "sterile, foodless bush".[15] Another Englishman, William Bradley, took four months to discover that they ate other food than fish, and years later people like Burke and Wills remained just as ignorant.

During the first three weeks the invaders, except Phillip, were housed in tents. Land around the settlement was expropriated and doled out to civil and military officers to grow their own food, and a government farm was established. The trees, however, blunted the axes, the soil blunted the spades and picks, and the prisoners, who in most cases had never been exposed to heavy work let alone work in a hot climate, had to be lashed daily to perform even minimal tasks. The entire invasion force was balanced precariously on the edge of an unknown continent completely dependent on meat, peas, and butter brought from England and southern Africa. Problems were exacerbated by illness due to poor nutrition. The lack of green vegetables and fruits meant that scurvy took a heavy toll and the English officer Watkin Tench observed that "provisions were becoming scarcer than in a blockaded town".[16]

To the Eora people, who had withdrawn from the area and for the time being were able to live a disease-free, peaceful existence, the new lords of the land presented a sight both comic and threatening. They were comic because at first glance they seemed to be sexless, their clothes giving no indication of their gender and their hairless faces suggesting they were women. On one occasion a sailor was ordered to open his trousers and show them his sign of manhood to satisfy the people's enquiries. The Englishmen introduced to young women without clothes reacted in a variety of ways; King, for example, produced a handkerchief to cover up the charms exposed to the southern sunlight. On the same occasion King offered the Eora some wine, which they tasted and spat out. Despite such good-natured early encounters, for the most part the Eora made a point of avoiding contact. They found the soldiers threatening and kept away from them. If approached by other members of the invading force, they would simply move quietly away.

The invaders, conditioned by their background, often wrote the people off as "savages". To some they were the "Lowest in Rank among the Human Race . . . more like monkies than warriors . . . stupid . . . insensible . . . harmless". Other more honest observers admitted that the people were tractable when "no insult or injury was offered to them".[17] One wrote of "a Quiet, Inoffensive People" who were "total strangers to Personal Fear and have a Quick Sense of Injury".[18]

Yet the two years of phony peace could not and did not last without incident. During March 1788, for example, relations between the English and the Eora worsened. A party of English fishermen was ordered away from an important fishing ground and reluctantly retreated. In another confrontation two prisoners were speared, and later an Eora warrior confronted an English officer and threw a spear at him. The officer fired in retaliation but the warrior simply stood his ground and indicated that the Englishman should go.[19] Another cause of confrontation came when prisoners took and raped a number of Eora women.[20]

The Eora people had their possessions stolen, men and women had been injured, and they fought back. In May three prisoners who were seen to be interfering with the Eora environment were speared—one was badly wounded and two cutting rushes were killed.[21] Despite the fact that investigations by English officers into the cause of the clashes clearly fixed the blame for rape, killings, injuries and theft on the prisoners, Phillip himself led a search party to bring in the Eora warriors for punishment. They could not be found.[22]

By May permanent buildings were being erected. The Eora attempted to contain the spread of the invasion by driving off a party that wanted to land in another cove. They remained "aloof, out of reach, elusive, practising a standoffishness".[23] They either feared or despised the English too much to be anxious for a closer connection. The invaders who attempted to cultivate friendship by offering gifts were angry at being repulsed and threshed around for explanations. The antipathy of the people was so obvious that the thoughtful observer Watkin Tench wondered whether Captain Cook had perpetrated something terrible in 1770 that "prevented the intercourse which would otherwise have taken place".[24]

His observation was echoed by another young English officer, Lieutenant Newton Fowell, whose letters to his father, titled "The Sirius Letters", were first published in the *Sydney Morning Herald* in July 1987. Fowell spent eighteen months at Sydney Cove, then called Albion, in 1788–89. Describing Phillip's first attempt at landing at Botany Bay, he said the "natives" disputed the landing, brandishing their spears. Phillip directed the long boat some distance away and moved towards the Eora on land. He advanced alone to meet them carrying a gun, and the Eora would not approach until he had it laid down. Fowell said it was plain they had seen "Cook's people" carry out executions with guns. It does seem there was a bloody clash which Cook suppressed, perhaps with the doctrine of *terra nullius* in mind.

The gap between the two civilisations could not have been better illustrated than by Phillip's decision to try to give the Eora an understanding of English law. He instructed his troops to bring together as many people as possible to witness a flogging, lashing one of his own countrymen until his naked back was red pulp. The Eora showed disgust and terror at such ritual torture. It was obvious that the invasion force holed up in the hell's cauldron of Sydney Cove, while a fearful thing, was a fascination to the Eora. The ceremonial thundering of the cannon would have startled the people all along the coast, but despite the dangers and threats presented by the newcomers they began to drift towards the settlement.

An armed party from Sydney Town encountered a group of about 300 Eora between the town and Botany Bay, but was allowed to pass without hindrance. Reports came in of groups of warriors, 2000 were reported on one occasion, 400 on another. Panic grew.[25] Sydney Town took on more and more the appearance of a town under siege. Parties of fewer than six armed men were banned from going beyond the confines of the town, and at least one ship in harbour kept all its boats under guard in the cove. Incidents multiplied. Some English fish poachers had their catch confiscated; a prison party was chased several kilometres; several of the invaders were killed, others wounded; a marine disappeared.

Writing to Lord Sydney from his canvas house, however, Phillip still felt the colony he was establishing would be the most valuable England had ever acquired. He wrote his despatch following the celebration of the king's birthday on 4 June. Six 21-gun salutes to King George and his retinue of relatives had been fired during the day, and there was even a bonfire and a distribution of porter and spirits to all.[26] But it was hard to disguise the growing tension. Slow starvation faced both the invaders and the Eora. Food sources were being exhausted, trees and shrubs recklessly cut down. Acres of land had been cleared but were not yet producing. But still the Eora withheld from general hostilities.

On an expedition to Pittwater in September Phillip encountered a party of sixty local men, women and children. He gave them presents, as was his custom, and there was a generally friendly exchange, but he noted they seemed best pleased when he left.[27] On his way back to Sydney he watched a ceremonial encounter of about 200 warriors. Phillip noted that the harbour was being denuded of fish and commented that in one ordinary day only sixty-seven canoes and 133 fishermen and women were seen,[28] far fewer than the numbers originally encountered. He realised that his people were taking the food supplies of the Eora and even acknowledged it in his despatches to the Imperial Government. He also admitted that he had not got to know any of the people, although he hoped to induce a family to live within the town.[29]

Relations continued to degenerate. Much of the blame for the escalation of the killing was attributable to the prisoners, who were described in an English journal, *Blackwood's Magazine*, as being "the most murderous, monstrous, debased, burglarious, brutified, larcenous, felonious and pickpocketous set of scoundrels that ever trod the earth".[30] They banded together to abuse the Eora, ill-treating children, raping women, killing any man who protested,[31] and stealing their weapons and fishing and hunting gear. The male/female ratio among the prisoners was three to one, but one officer observed that the charms of the "sooty sirens" attracted the officers, soldiers and sailors as well. The troops also looted any unoccupied dwellings in their marching to and fro.[32]

Phillip warned London again in November 1788 that race relations were not improving: they "now avoid us more than they did when we first landed".[33] He imputed this to the outrages committed upon them by prisoners. As he was pursuing a policy of forcing the Eora away from Sydney, he was complaining that not one had been to the town for many months. Tired of the stalemate and in an astonishing turnaround, he decided to force the issue and devised a plan for kidnapping some Eora to teach the invaders the language and unveil the mysteries of their way of life.

The kidnapping policy was put in place and on the eve of the new year two men were singled out at Manly Cove. One escaped but the other, Arabanoo, was captured. Then about thirty years old, he was described by his captors as not tall but robust, with a face that suggested manliness, sensibility and thoughtfulness and with a soft musical voice.[34] His entry into Sydney Town in chains augured what was to come, but he conquered his captors with what they described as his cleanliness and decency, his courteousness to women, his gentleness and humanity, dignity and independence; he brooked no insult nor gave any. The English children loved him and flocked around, waiting on his words and gestures. Strong liquor repelled him and he turned from it with disgust. He also showed his horror of the floggings and the harsh discipline imposed by the military.[35]

Arabanoo was in Sydney when a new disaster struck the Eora. Smallpox, brought by the English, spread like wildfire, killing half of the Eora population in the Port Jackson area as well as countless others elsewhere. He helped his stricken countrymen and women, nursing them through the long weeks of the epidemic. Phillip was tremendously impressed and gave him his "freedom"—quaint concept that a man should be given the freedom of his own country. Arabanoo remained in Sydney and for a while was joined by two children, Nanbaree, a boy, and Abaroo, a girl, whose family had been wiped out in the epidemic. Sadly, after he had spent less than a year among the strangers, Arabanoo too died of smallpox.

Phillip's strategy, to build a bridge of understanding by kidnapping Eora people, simply did not work. Arabanoo spoke to none of his people outside the town boundaries. They in turn could only conclude that even if the English seemed friendly they were not to be trusted: the result could be kidnapping and chains. Yet Phillip persisted with his policy, which was in fact to propel the Eora into general warfare. Meeting the English for the first time they showed every sign of welcome and friendship, but once they became acquainted with the brutality of the invaders friendship changed to suspicion and then hostility. A Negro prisoner tried to establish a personal relationship but the Eora saw him as part of the evil empire of death and disease and repulsed him.

In November 1789 two more unsuspecting men were taken from their families by soldiers. One named Colby escaped after a week, while the other, Bennelong, remained in Sydney for five months.

Bennelong would have been able to see that behind the patrolled and guarded boundaries of Sydney Town all was not well with the English. They had destroyed much of his people's sources of food and shelter, but had failed to produce their own food from the areas cleared by convict gangs. Supplies of butter were completely exhausted, and the ration of all food except spirits was reduced to two-thirds. In the new year of 1790 English flour was exhausted and they began to use flour from southern Africa. The invaders were faced with starvation in four months.

Bennelong saw them send the *Sirius* to the Cape of Good Hope for supplies and as the weeks passed and March arrived even the rations of spirits were reduced. The officers were mostly pessimistic and spoke of abandoning Sydney; only Phillip remained convinced they would not have to starve or withdraw. But how shaky was their hold on the colony was brought home dramatically when news came in April of the wreck of the *Sirius* at Norfolk Island. All officers were summoned by Phillip to an emergency meeting. They were told the salt meat would be finished by 2 July, flour by 20 August and rice and peas by 1 October. Rations were reduced still further and the *Supply* was sent to the Dutch colony of Batavia for provisions.[36]

The Sunday religious services were now held in empty storehouses. The prisoners were dropping from hunger and their hours of work were reduced. One caught stealing food was given 300 lashes, a woman who ate too much too quickly died, an old man passed away as he queued up for his handout and when his stomach was opened it was found to be completely empty.[37] Phillip even put his private food reserves into the common pool. The prisoners, men and women, were half naked and the proud soldiers of the army of occupation were reduced to doing guard duty in their bare feet.

Phillip maintained his hope of building a dialogue with the Eora through Bennelong. Despite the desperate straits of the English the Eora did not make any general attack and for this Phillip was grateful. In fact, he wrote to Lord Sydney, he had always found them friendly, believing their hostility was born from being "ill used" and "robbed".[38] A concerted attack on Sydney Town in the grips of starvation with its barefoot soldiers would have had every chance of success, but in June 1790 the phony peace was holding despite a number of bloody incidents almost every week.

On the evening of 3 June 1790, when the invaders were at their lowest ebb, the flag was hoisted to announce the arrival of a ship in the harbour. It was the transport *Lady Juliana*, the first of the vessels of the Second Fleet. There were scenes of wild excitement. Despite the wind and rain women carried their children to see the sight of their deliverers, Tench ran to the harbourside and was joined by another officer from the tent next door. They were too overcome with emotion to speak and stood wringing each other's hands. Men and women alike cried and many took to the boats and rowed to the ship.[39]

The English had escaped disaster. The storeship *Justinian* reached Sydney on 20 June and the transport *Surprize* on 26 June, followed two days later by two more transports *Scarborough* and *Neptune*. Their numbers were considerably increased. A new batch of 218 prisoners on board *Surprize* was accompanied by officers, non-commissioned officers and privates of the newly formed New South Wales Corps. The later transports carried 188 male prisoners on one and 286 males and 76 females on the other,[40] a combined invasion of 768.

The Imperial authorities had made a decision to hold and expand what they had seized and the special army unit was an indication they were in no mood to abandon Sydney. Yet the forces were not as strong as they must have seemed to the Eora, and to Bennelong from the inside, as they watched them disembark in endless lines. In fact 267 men and women had died on the way from England and 488 arrived sick and unfit for work. More than half of the new work force was out of action before it even reached the continent. The hospital was extended by thirty tents, which were quickly filled with people suffering from scurvy, dysentery or infectious fever. The Eora watched with horror as naked, filthy, lousy wretches, many unable to stand or even crawl, were moved from the ships to the hospital. They had seen their environment polluted in many ways but the scale of the human pollution brought by the Second Fleet was a nightmare beyond imagination.

Bennelong had escaped from Sydney only the month before and rejoined his people, to whom he was able to describe the events of his five months in captivity. Phillip, out on patrol some months later, saw Bennelong and Colby, the other kidnap victim, but did not attempt to recapture them. In September, however, he encountered a large group of Eora warriors at Manly Cove. Catching sight of Bennelong among them, the governor went to approach him, but was speared by another man, Wileemarin, who thought he was to be another kidnap victim. It is believed he could have also seen Phillip as an enemy who had kidnapped or attempted to kidnap four people and who still held in Sydney Town a boy and a girl whose relatives wanted them to return.

Severely wounded in the shoulder Phillip ordered a military patrol to make contact with Bennelong, who had learned some English during his months in captivity and had developed a love of liquor, which he called "tumbledown", a word for grog that passed into the Eora language. (Bennelong also boasted a fund of stories about romancing the English women.) Bennelong convinced Phillip that his attacker had been punished by his own people.

At this point Bennelong began to fulfil Phillip's hopes of using him as an ambassador to bring more Eora into contact with the settlement. He and his friends began to move in and out of Sydney Town at will, often dressed as officers of the occupying military. It seemed they had surrendered their independence and were now mendicants of their conquerors, unlike their fellow countrymen, particularly those from the west of Sydney who had lost their lands and were demonstrating a new resentment and hostility.

The war was becoming more inevitable with every passing day. The invaders had gained greater power, they had imported food, the chain gangs were at work again from dawn to dusk, new buildings were planned, the new military force enabled the boundaries of the settlement to be extended and large tracts of land were cleared around Sydney and at Parramatta. In October the *Supply* returned from Batavia with more supplies and the Eora found themselves, instead of surrounding the fortified settlement and moving at will around its boundaries, being driven from more and more of their own land and confronted with more firepower than they had previously seen.

The Archduke Ferdinand of the Sydney war was a prisoner named John McIntire, who was employed to kill game for the governor—an occupation that put him in direct conflict with the Eora. He also had a reputation for attacking Eora people. On 10 December 1790 war was declared just as surely as it was at Sarajevo in 1914.

A sergeant of marines with three prisoners, including McIntire, had gone out on a shooting party. They camped overnight outside the town boundaries and were awakened by the approach of Eora warriors. As the party reached for their weapons a warrior named Pemulwuy leapt onto a fallen tree and targeted McIntire,[41] throwing a war spear that penetrated McIntire's body to a depth of nineteen centimetres. Mortally wounded, McIntire confessed to his companions the dreadful crimes he had committed against the Eora.[42] One of the prisoners broke off the spear and stayed with him while the other members of the party took off in pursuit of Pemulwuy, without success.

Despite the fact that McIntire was a guilty man, his execution seemed to drive Phillip into a new and terrible role. Almost overnight the peacemaker who tried, however misguidedly, to bring about intercourse between the English and the Eora, turned into a passable imitation of a Nazi such as Heydrich who ordered massacres when occupied peoples resisted Nazi rule. He ordered a devastating military reprisal; destroy all Eora weapons, bring in any two men as prisoners, put to death any ten more and finally cut off the heads of the dead. To this end he ordered hatchets and bags to be provided.[43] In a flurry of activity he also sent messages to Bennelong and Colby to bring in Pemulwuy, which they declined to do and in fact could not have done even if they wished.

Phillip told Tench, the marine officer appointed to command the reprisal party, to advance on any people he could find, and to show no signs of peace or amity. The killings were to be carried out and the two prisoners were to be hanged in the presence of as many of their fellow countrymen and women as possible. Tench suggested a modified program and Phillip then issued his final orders—if they could not capture six suspects for imprisonment, of whom two were to be executed, then any six were to be killed.

Tench assembled a party of fifty-two: Captain Hill of the New South Wales Corps, two subalterns, three sergeants, two corporals, one drummer, two surgeons and forty infantrymen.[44] On 14 December, with provisions for three days, they marched out of Sydney Town to the beat of the drum, bayonets shining. For three days they searched but the Eora had withdrawn and they were reduced to firing at shadows. The only Eora they met was Phillip's agent Colby, of Botany Bay; they filled him up with food and suggested he say nothing about the punitive expedition. A week later they tried again, but with no more success than the first time.

Phillip was to spend his last two years in the colony watching violence escalate. The new year began with an Eora raid on the outpost at Rose Hill, now Parramatta. A military force was despatched and attacked by guerillas and one Eora warrior was wounded in the encounter. Judge Advocate David Collins of the First Fleet wrote that the English must always be considered as enemies by the people they had dispossessed.[45] That Phillip had learned nothing from his encounters with the Eora was shown by his final bid to impress them with English justice. He had a prisoner who had stolen some fishing gear from them flogged, confirming in the minds of those he had rounded up to watch the torture that he was the chief of a nest of vipers.

The guerilla war gained momentum. During 1791 a farm dwelling at Prospect Hill was destroyed and there was constant tension on the borders of settlement. One well-known Eora warrior, Ballooderry, ventured into Sydney itself with a party of friends. The military attempting to capture him shot one of his companions, but he escaped. He was important enough for Collins to record his brief visit.[46] Paradoxically Phillip persisted with a policy of bringing within his boundaries as many Eora as possible, virtually putting them on the English payroll by giving them rations and tobacco. He thus created a situation that has existed ever since. The people of the occupied territories were encouraged to give up their independence, be disarmed, accept handouts and live as mendicants. All this earned them was the contempt of their gaolers and masters as well as of their fellow countrymen and women who carried on the fight for independence in the bush.

It may be that the Eora waited too long to begin their war of resistance. In July 1791 their enemies were again reinforced when the Third Fleet arrived bringing 1863 prisoners and more soldiers and arms and ammunition. In September a further fleet arrived which, if they had known it, brought hope of allies. From Ireland came the *Queen* crowded with 126 Irish prisoners of war, convicted by English drum head courts martial, and twenty-two women. These prisoners were so emaciated and feeble from lack of food and bad treatment that they could scarcely make the shore. Many did survive, however, to form part of a rebel force that would put fear into the English administration.

By February of 1792, when Major Francis Grose arrived in Sydney to take up his position as lieutenant governor, the fortress-town was firmly established and well based for further expansion. The Sydney boundaries were felt to be secure and to the west Parramatta became an armed base for strikes deeper into Eora country. A company of the New South Wales Corps comprising a captain, two lieutenants, an ensign, three sergeants, three corporals, two drummers and seventy infantrymen was sent to establish a permanent military presence at Parramatta,[47] and another outpost was established at Toongabbie.

The Eora watched but challenged neither this force nor the army of prisoners in chain gangs working to build access roads, cutting down trees and turning the ground from dawn to dusk. Working under overseers who held the power of life and death, they were housed in huts holding up to eighteen people and they had no beds or blankets, no bowls or plates.[48] The women prisoners were somewhat better off, although the most "fortunate" were those selected as mistresses, concubines or sometimes wives of the military and civilians. The civilians who had been given large tracts of Eora land lived like colonial princes: in mid-1791 the Macarthur family moved to Parramatta where Elizabeth, wife of the man credited with starting the wool industry in Australia, described boating parties, picnics and a sylvan existence.

Phillip's increasing ill health led to his resignation late in 1791. The following year, in December, he boarded the ship to return to England, taking with him Bennelong and another man, Yem-mer-ra-wan-nie, the first Australians to visit the seat of the Empire that was to wipe most of them out within half a century. Phillip saw further service with the British Navy, became an admiral, retired in 1805 and lived quietly on a pension in the English town of Bath. He married again, and lived until

1814; he was buried with full honours in the little town of Bathampton.

Bennelong spent two years in England being feted as a cannibal king by princes and paupers alike. Phillip called him "dooroow" or son while Bennelong addressed Phillip as "beanga" or father. He ate as elegantly as the Englishmen, bowed, toasted, paid the ladies compliments and loved wine. He grew to despise the customs of his own people but earned only the pity of the English. On his return from England in September 1795 his sister came with a young baby to welcome him home and he almost hid her from sight as he did not think she was appropriately attired. His wife Barangaroo returned to him but soon deserted him to return to her own people. Bennelong chased her and her new partner, breaking the latter's head and beating the faithless Barangaroo. He fought with English and Eora alike, but at the end of his life was cared for by his own people. He was about fifty when he died, in the bush, in January 1813.

The Guerilla War

On Phillip's departure Francis Grose became acting governor. Born in England in 1754, Grose became an army officer at the age of twenty, served in the American War of Independence, was seriously wounded and then retired for five years. He re-enlisted, was appointed to command the New South Wales Corps and arrived in Sydney on 14 February 1792. He proved to be no St Valentine's Day gift to the already hard-pressed Eora. He gave away 100 acres of land to all officers—John Macarthur not only received 100 acres but ten prisoners to work for him; the Reverend Richard Johnson was also given 100 acres as chaplain. Grose also gave land to non-commissioned officers, then to private soldiers, to civilians and finally to prisoners who had survived their sentences. How much land they received was determined by their station in life.[49] As word of this wholesale expropriation of Eora land reached England, more civilians embarked for the colony. Some received up to 120 acres as well as free seed and tools, prison labour and free food for two years.

By 1793 the phony peace had deteriorated and Grose was faced with an escalating guerilla war led by Phillip's old enemy Pemulwuy. Although Bennelong's name is commemorated by Bennelong Point, where his spirit was given the privilege of speaking the first words at the opening of the Sydney Opera House, Pemulwuy emerges as the most famous of all the Eora. The leader of the guerilla war from 1790 until he was killed in 1802, he displayed outstanding skills as a warrior and won the respect, if reluctantly, of the English.

Pemulwuy is believed to have been born in 1760. He was first described by the diligent Tench, who wrote that at the time the war began he was a young man with a speck or brown mark on his left eye.[50] At that time he was clean-shaven, an indication that he had been into Sydney Town and seen the invaders for himself. Bennelong, who in his role of informer

The guerilla leader Pemulwuy took part in this initiation ceremony in 1795, illustrated in David Collins' Account of the English Colony in New South Wales. NATIONAL LIBRARY OF AUSTRALIA

and governor's representative was supposed to help capture Pemulwuy, described him as "one eyed".[51] Tench was a more reliable witness. Pemulwuy had grown up among the Eora of Botany Bay but travelled over a wide area, from Sydney Cove itself, to other places in the harbour, to Castle Hill, Toongabbie and Parramatta. He may even have visited and fought with the Dharuk people on the Hawkesbury but of that there is no record.

Phillip attributed to Pemulwuy's group the killing or wounding of seventeen English soldiers and civilians. He had the same opportunity as Bennelong to join the payroll of the invaders, but having explored for himself life in their camp and seen the death and disease of the early days he returned to his people determined to lead the resistance to what was obviously going to be the total dispossession of the entire people.

Over a period of twelve years he witnessed the various phases of operations against the Eora which culminated in the terrorist tactics of Governors Paterson, Hunter and King. It is acknowledged that apart from his skill, intelligence, power and strength he possessed extraordinary vision and a sense of history.[52] He knew that if lost the first battle would be the last and it is probably this thought which stayed his hand even when the colony nearly faded away in misery and hunger. Pemulwuy was a legend in his own lifetime. His own people held him in such awe that a belief grew up that he could not be killed and would never be defeated.[53] His ability to avoid the lethal weapons of the English and to survive the most terrible wounds added to the legend, and even his enemies paid tribute to his courage, style and dash.

In the first year of Grose's regime the Eora guerilla forces commanded by Pemulwuy developed a pattern of operations, raiding settlements in turn and taking provisions. If there was resistance they would use force. The military sent out repeated expeditions against them, but as they gained confidence in their ability to match and sometimes outwit the English they became bolder. Just before Christmas a war party attacked a group of Englishmen returning to Parramatta after delivering stores to the Toongabbie outpost. The Eora war party collected the remaining loot and completely eluded the military which mounted an immediate search operation.[54]

In Sydney itself, by contrast, the Phillip doctrine of bring in, disarm and put on the payroll produced what seemed to be better relations. The English were even invited to watch ceremonies staged at what is now the end of George Street performed by the Eora people who once lived there.

Grose was transforming his military force, and many of the prisoners and civilians, into a mob of merchants, wholesalers and land speculators. Officers wearing their merchant hats thought nothing of selling rum to former prisoners who had shared in the land giveaway. Grose also offered an incentive to prisoners by allowing officers to pay them in rum for working outside "government hours". The prisoners were moving up in the world, and back to a traditional role, as the officers and military employed them as salesmen and shopkeepers. By August 1795 John Macarthur held 250 acres at Parramatta, of which 100 were under cultivation with wheat, corn and potatoes. His livestock included a horse, 2 mares, 2 cows, 130 goats, 100 hogs and poultry in abundance.[55] Game from Eora land graced his table to the extent of 300 pounds (136 kilograms) of meat a week. His mansion, situated in the middle of a vineyard and orchard, was close to the barracks so that the gentleman squatter could easily shift to his role as commander of the troops. Prisoners continued to work through the daylight hours in the fields, in the kitchen and at the table. Dairies provided milk, cream and butter. The atmosphere of a Little England had been created and locally born children were taught that Home was on the other side of the world.

As the English grew richer and stronger and better able to provide their own food and supplies, the Eora became more desperate and bitter, and more under threat. They were fighting a rearguard action. During 1794 the Eora maintained their resistance, now directing their attacks on the area between Parramatta and Prospect Hill. As they succeeded in striking and retreating without losses they extended their operations to Parramatta itself. Such was the situation in December when Grose, the pain from his old wounds becoming worse, returned to England leaving Captain William Paterson as administrator.

Paterson was an English soldier who had served in Cape Town in 1777 and led forays against the Hottentots. He later served in India, where he was commissioned as lieutenant. He was promoted to captain when he volunteered to serve in the New South Wales Corps. After arriving in Sydney in September 1791 he served on Norfolk Island for two years, and then at Sydney Cove. Thirty-nine years old when appointed administrator, Paterson was regarded as a soldier of competence but with a love of the bottle. He had shown an interest in botany and exploration as well as soldiering. In health, however, he was already an old man, often drunk and suffering so badly from gout that even a gentle breeze would send him back to the bottle to deaden the pain. He continued Grose's policy of giving land to all who asked for it among his officers, non-commissioned officers, former prisoners and civilians.[56] Pain and the bottle lent a ferocity to his orders to his troops to kill, to erect gallows throughout the bush and to hang people.

The expansion of the English into the Hawkesbury region north-west of Parramatta in 1794 was the beginning of the dispossession of the Eora's neighbours, the Dharuk. An estimated 2000 strong, they occupied the Cumberland Plain between Parramatta and the Blue Mountains.[57] The conflict was made worse by the fact that the yam beds on the banks of the Hawkesbury were basic to Dharuk diet. The yam beds were rapidly torn up and replaced with crops which the Dharuk were then forbidden to touch. A new landholder and his servant at the Hawkesbury were attacked. In October an armed posse captured a young Dharuk boy then tortured and killed him.[58] He was bound hand and foot, dragged several times through a fire and then thrown into the river where he was finished off with a bullet.

Relations between the Dharuk and the English were in sharp contrast to their initial contact. The first attempt at contact was made by Captain Watkin Tench and a party which pushed west in June 1789 from Prospect Hill towards the Nepean River. Tench found traces of their presence, but the Dharuk exercised the common tactic of pulling back to avoid the newcomers. In 1791 Phillip made the first actual contact when his party, which included Tench and two Eora men, Colby and Ballederry, as guides, moved into the area north-west of today's Parramatta. Even at that early stage, the Eora informed Phillip, most of the people in that part of the Hawkesbury had died from smallpox. The first Dharuk Phillip met was a man named Burowan. The party encountered him hunting and communication was established through the Eora interpreters. On 14 April 1791 Phillip's party reached a sandy bank of the Hawkesbury, north of what is now Richmond, where several Dharuk and their canoes were seen. An old man named Gomebeere explained they were collecting pebbles to make hatchet heads, and was soon joined by his son Yarramundi and his grandson Jimbah. The meeting was peaceful and Yarramundi demonstrated the Dharuk's prowess as *karadji* (doctors) by healing Colby's pain from an old spear wound.

In May Tench and William Dawes set out again for the Hawkesbury and were within three kilometres of Richmond Hill when they met Deedora, another friendly warrior. He lent them his canoe and with some friends who came down to watch the arrival of the strangers helped them to cross the river. Even a lost English soldier was rescued by the Dharuk and returned to his people.

There seemed to be mutual trust and goodwill, but it was not long before the first misunderstanding occurred. In July a number of former prisoners were given land at the foot of Prospect Hill. Shortly after they arrived they watched about 100 Dharuk warriors approaching in peace and curiosity and in panic began shooting.[59]

At the same time as the war was spreading along the Hawkesbury in 1795 Pemulwuy's leadership of the Eora shone more strongly than ever, giving courage and encouragement to his followers. Some of the English exacted petty revenge by seizing a young woman of Pemulwuy's family, raping and torturing her.[60] Pemulwuy was the number one enemy of the English at Sydney Cove, Botany Bay, Parramatta and Toongabbie and the Eora guerilla bands were now so well organised that he could penetrate at will to the harbour itself. In January of the fatal year of 1795 he attended the ceremony of *Yoo-long erah-ba-diang* (the tooth extraction ceremony) at Farm Cove to commemorate the graduation from initiation of some young warriors.[61]

On the western frontiers warfare was stepped up and in May Collins reported, "In their attacks they conducted themselves with much art; but where that failed they had recourse to force and on the least appearance of resistance made use of their spears or clubs".[62] It was obvious, however, that the Eora and Dharuk forces did not kill indiscriminately—and in many instances killed no one at all—in their raids for supplies and provisions. Their counterattacks were designed to drive the intruders and their animals out of their lands.

The English response to the increasing activity was to begin a campaign of terror with no pretence about justice being done. The owners of the lands the English had stolen were to be destroyed. In May 1795 Paterson gave orders for a killing party to be sent out from Parramatta to "destroy as many as they could meet with of the wood tribe (Be-dia-gal); and, in the hope of striking terror, to erect gibbets at different places, whereon the bodies of all they might kill were to be hung".[63] This squad of executioners carried out its orders, but it is not known how many were killed and hung on gallows from Parramatta to the Hawkesbury. They were able to take some prisoners for the first time—a crippled man, five women and several children. One of the women had been shot and her baby wounded.[64] Dharuk warriors counterattacked at Richmond Hill, killing an Englishman and a boy and wounding a woman. Another reprisal party of troops moved against the Dharuk but this time without success.

The landholders were horrified at this turn of events. They had not imagined that their occupation of other people's lands would involve them in a shooting war in which they as much as the troops were the enemy, Paterson, in a bid to stem the growing panic, distributed soldiers among the civilians.

In the same month Pemulwuy took the initiative again and struck right on the borders of Sydney Town near Brickfield Hill (at the end of today's George Street), wounding a prisoner before withdrawing.[65] Panic spread in the town and throughout the English Pale. There was talk of pulling back from the Hawkesbury and even from Parramatta. The scene was set for the first pitched battle between the armed forces of the English Crown and the people of the Sydney region.

The Battle of the Hawkesbury

The first of the two battles that decided the fate of Sydney Town took place in June 1795 along the banks of the Hawkesbury River in the vicinity of Richmond Hill. The Dharuk warriors, possibly augmented by some Eora fighting men, were traditionally equipped with spears, woomeras,

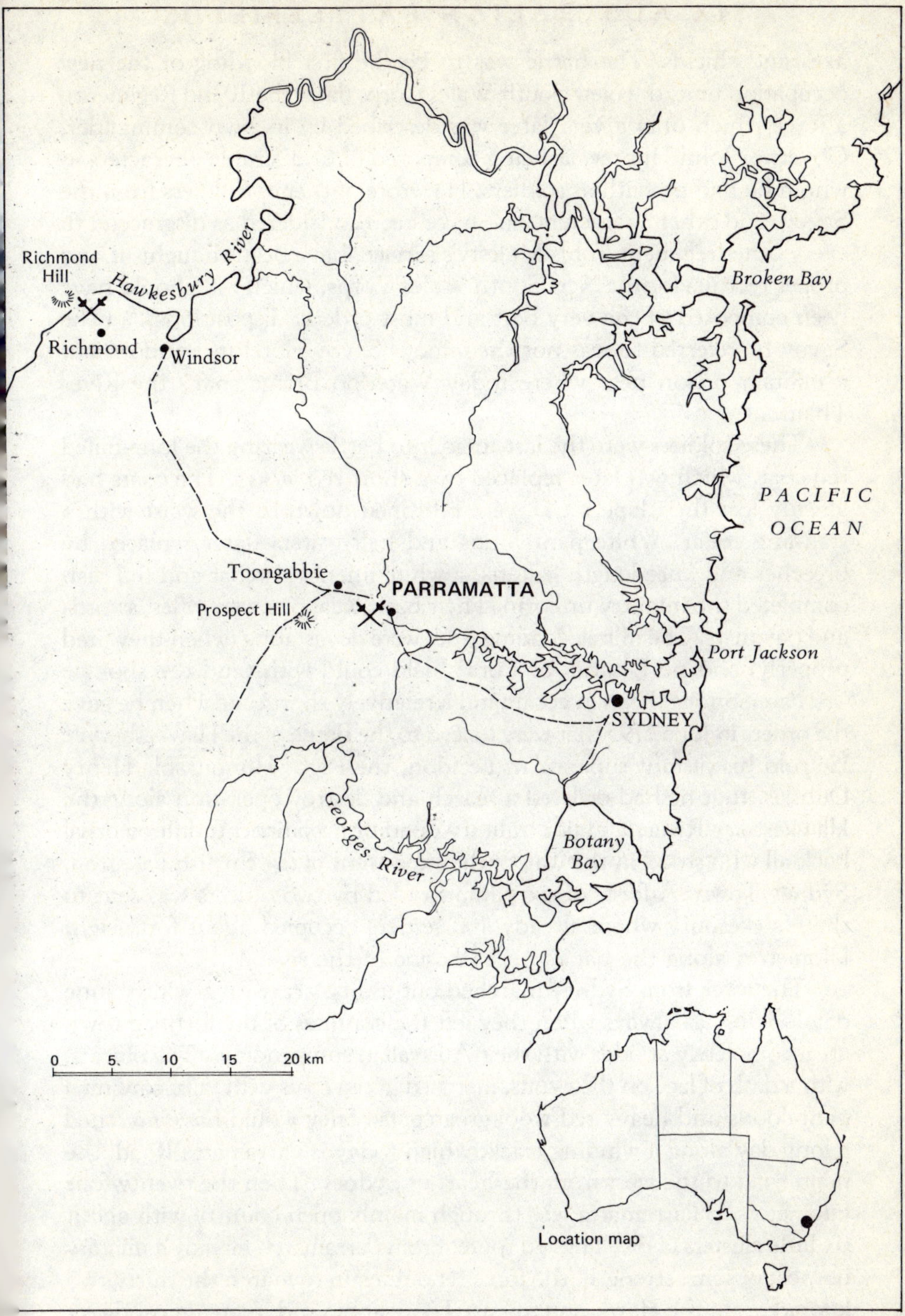
Richmond Hill
Hawkesbury River
Richmond
Windsor
Broken Bay
PACIFIC OCEAN
Toongabbie
PARRAMATTA
Prospect Hill
Port Jackson
SYDNEY
Georges River
Botany Bay
0
5
10
15
20 km
Location map

axes and shields. The battle was to be the first blooding of the new occupation unit, the New South Wales Corps (later the 102nd Regiment), a force which only a year later was described by its own commander, Governor John Hunter, as being composed of undesirable characters in whom he had no faith as soldiers. He wrote of them: "Soldiers from the Savoy, and other characters who have been considered as disgraceful to every other regiment in his Majesty's service, have been thought fit and proper recruits for the New South Wales Corps, which . . . should have been composed of the very best and most orderly dispositions".[66] (The Savoy he referred to was not the famous Savoy Hotel in London, but a military prison near where today Waterloo Bridge spans the River Thames.)

These soldiers were the last to go into battle wearing the long-tailed red coat, which was later replaced by a short red jacket. The coats had already lost their lapels and were buttoned down to the waist with a standing collar. White pantaloons and half gaiters (later replaced by breeches and knee length gaiters), a white linen waistcoat and red sash completed the infantry uniform. Their basic weapons were rifles, swords and bayonets. The muzzle-loading rifles were devastating (when they fired properly) and no Dharuk or Eora shield could withstand the shot.

Paterson had been in command a relatively short time when he gave the orders in June 1795 that were to lead to the Battle of the Hawkesbury.[67] He told his distant superior in London, the Right Honourable Henry Dundas, that he had ordered a search and destroy operation along the Hawkesbury River, a major military operation planned to kill or drive back all who stood in the way of the expansion of the English Pale from Sydney Town. A force of sixty infantry led by two officers was sent to the Hawkesbury where already 400 settlers occupied about forty-eight kilometres along the banks on each side of the river.[68]

The force from Sydney marched out in fine array on a wintry June day looking, as always when they left the confines of the fortified town area, completely at odds with their Australian surroundings. The officers, with a dash of lace on their cuffs, marched in red coats with tails, confining pantaloons and heavy red wool greatcoats. They would have marched a long day along a winding track, which today is Parramatta Road, the main road to the west from the heart of Sydney. Then the twenty-four kilometres to Parramatta was through mainly open country with about six little clusters of dwellings en route. From Parramatta, already a military outpost of some strength, the force set out again to march the thirty-two kilometres to the Hawkesbury, past Toongabbie and in an almost direct line to the river. Once at the river they camped on battle alert as the settlers had reported that there were Dharuk war parties in the area.

The next day the force deployed in the area but failed to make any contact. At the end of the comparatively short June day the English troops drew up in line of battle in an open area near Richmond Hill and moved on a Dharuk war party assembled in strength to resist their advance. Opening volleys cut down seven or eight warriors who were killed outright; more were probably wounded. Reloading and firing, reloading and firing, the infantrymen moved inexorably forward until the pride of the Dharuk withdrew into the bush. The troop commanders continued to advance until they tired and made hasty camp only to advance again with the dawn. When the Dharuk war party reassembled to overrun one of the farms and drive off the occupiers at night, the sweep continued with more killing. The commanding officer told Paterson "he was taking every measure he thought likely to deter them from appearing there again".[69] The clash ended with the virtual destruction of the Dharuk war party, and one warrior and four women taken prisoner.

Paterson reported the victory to his superiors in London and in doing so unintentionally wrote the epitaph of the Dharuk people. He said:

> *It gives me concern to have been forced to destroy any of these people, particularly as I have no doubt of their having been cruelly treated by some of the first settlers who went out there; however, had I not taken this step, every prospect of advantage which the colony may expect to derive from a settlement formed on the banks of so fine a river as the Hawkesbury would be at an end.*[70]

It was clear that he recognised that such effective resistence by the Dharuk posed a threat to the entire Hawkesbury settlement. The battle determined once and for all that the Dharuk would lose their land, that the survivors of the nation would be branded trespassers on the land they had owned for at least 40,000 years.

The Battle of the Hawkesbury was inevitable once the first English outpost was established. It was described by John Pilger as an "epic war" that was "not recorded in the imperial chronicle of Australia; growing up on one of its principal battlefields, I knew nothing about it".[71] That warfare continued even after the Dharuk defeat Governor Hunter blamed on the white people who had taken over Dharuk land: he exampled their barbarism by citing the killing of two Dharuk boys by a group of white men who beat them to death. It was kept alive by a deep hatred that grew up between the Dharuk and the English people stationed on the Hawkesbury. Again it was Hunter who pinpointed the reason, the killing, in his words, of a mother and child by a soldier in a shameful and wanton manner. Hunter's recognition of the cause of the conflict sadly was not shared by Governor King, who ordered a general attack on the Dharuk and the Eora in the western areas with the object of driving them either to the mountains in the west or to their death.

The Dharuk were to feel the full wrath of another governor a decade later. When they continued to try to limit the loss of their lands Macquarie ordered three punitive expeditions in 1816 and in one bloody sweep fourteen men, women and children were killed. The bodies of two men, Durelle and Kanabygal, were hung in trees after they had been shot to terrify their fellow countrymen.[72]

The battle epitaph of the Dharuk was written by David Denholm, who said, "The [Dharuk] resisted the Hawkesbury River settlers for twenty-two years and inflicted on the Hawkesbury settlers a casualty rate similar to that sustained by the Australian armed forces in World War II, about one in thirty-four".[73] Denholm goes on to explain that "the war on the Hawkesbury River was really a contest between Great Britain and a nation which, outnumbered and without guns, went down fighting to the last man, woman and child. In a land of cenotaphs, not one stands for those who fought and fell in their own country".[74]

Paterson, the battle won, the Pale extended and consolidated, left Australia still full of grog and gout but with the honours due to a victorious and successful commander. His reign had lasted less than a year when John Hunter arrived to take over as captain-general and governor-in-chief and prepare for the final battle against the Eora people and their leader, Pemulwuy.

The Battle of Parramatta

Hunter, who was born in Leith, Scotland, in 1737, had been a captain in the British Navy and had sailed into Botany Bay on the First Fleet with Phillip. As captain of the *Sirius* he went to South Africa for supplies late in 1788 and returned via South America. It was he who wrecked the *Sirius* in 1790 at Norfolk Island, where he was stranded for nearly a year. He returned to England in March 1791 by way of Batavia and was lucky to survive the voyage on which the captain, the mate and several sailors died. A tough man, he had previously served in the West Indies and survived severe injuries to his leg and right hand.

By 1794, at the age of fifty-seven, Hunter was facing retirement, but with the support of his patron, Admiral Lord Howe, was appointed governor of New South Wales. He arrived in Sydney on the *Reliance* on 7 September 1795. Also on board was Bennelong, returning from the Imperial capital full of condescension to those Eora who had been prevailed upon to stay within the confines of Sydney. For the benefit of his white audience he made speeches about bringing peace to his people and making them "love one another".[75]

Following the battle at the Hawkesbury all was quiet on the riverfront, but by the end of 1795 the Eora were escalating their guerilla war. Settlement after settlement was attacked and Hunter found himself sending his troops into action. Before he had been in command six weeks a military expedition had killed half a dozen Eora in one fight and four warriors had been taken prisoner. The Englishmen spoke of their opponents as being cruel, irrational and guided by their passions, yet they applied curious double standards to their own conduct: an English couple shot and killed the parents of a little girl who they then adopted. They taught her to despise her own people, but when the latter killed the girl the English couple turned on them and cursed them for the same crime.

Pemulwuy found that his enemies were not only the white Englishmen and other Europeans in the First Fleet. John Caesar, a black from Madagascar who had found his way as a seaman to England, was sentenced to transportation for seven years for a minor offence. He was one of several black prisoners on the First Fleet, which included a contingent of West Indians.

Black Caesar, as he was commonly known, was acknowledged to be the hardest working man in the colony but he had what Collins described as a gargantuan appetite and he stole to satisfy it. Another black prisoner known as Black Jemmey caught stealing with him was given 500 lashes, while Caesar's sentence of seven years was extended to life.[76] In May 1789 Black Caesar stole a musket and some ammunition and escaped, taking to the bush as the first Australian bushranger. Recaptured and put to work at Garden Island, he escaped again taking a musket, ammunition, a cooking pot and stores. This time he headed for Parramatta, then known as Rose Hill. He decided to throw in his lot with the Eora and in accordance with their traditions of hospitality they took him into their group.

The Eora had as little in common with Black Caesar as they had with the Englishmen, and it was inevitable, given his temper and brutal violence, that there should be a dispute. Caesar came off second best in his brush with the Eora warriors, but in a duel with Pemulwuy he almost accomplished what the English most desired, splitting Pemulwuy's skull with a blow that should have killed him. Caesar broke off the fight and made for the bush, but surrendered to the authorities at Rose Hill. After four years he escaped, was recaptured and flogged, and escaped yet again, going back to the Eora at Parramatta.

The association did not last long, but in January 1796, perhaps having watched and learned from Pemulwuy as a guerilla leader, Caesar gathered around him his own band of escaped prisoners. He defied the governor so successfully that a price of five gallons of rum was place on his head—rum had virtually replaced coin as currency. In February a man named Wimbow tracked Caesar to his hideout at what is now Concord; in a musket duel Black Caesar was fatally shot.[77]

Throughout 1796 Pemulwuy led the Eora in applying continuing pressure. Hunter, approaching his fifty-ninth birthday, was finding as unworkable as had Phillip his instructions to rob the people of their land while at the same time to make peace with them. In November, in growing desperation, Hunter virtually conscripted every man in the colony to defend the Pale against the Eora. If they failed to fight when called on by the soldiers they would be flogged or punished in some other way.[78] It was war with a vengeance.

The new year arrived and Pemulwuy remained at large and with a growing reputation. The Eora would have had many opportunities to celebrate. They could not know that their chance to push the invaders into the sea had died seven years before, but they had determined to limit the Pale to Sydney Cove. Their grand design for the reconquest of their western lands hinged on the destruction of the Toongabbie outpost, which would leave the 400 Hawkesbury settlers unprotected and open the way for an attack on Parramatta itself.

The military history of Parramatta had begun only ten months after the arrival of the First Fleet, when Phillip sailed up Parramatta River at the head of a detachment of marines to choose the spot for a new outpost. The first priority was given to marking out a redoubt and later ten prisoners in chains were brought to clear the area, which Phillip named Rose Hill in honour of an obscure public servant in the Imperial Treasury. He had second thoughts and three years later gave the settlement the Eora name, Parramatta. The township became a military centre for the duration of the black war.

The first recorded commandant at Parramatta was Lieutenant John Macarthur, who was appointed in 1793, only two years after he arrived in the colony with the New South Wales Corps. His original holding, which he called Elizabeth Farm, was on the eastern outskirts of Parramatta. Parramatta comprised the government store, the marine barracks and gardens and the first wharves on the south bank of Parramatta River. The Red Cow Inn no doubt did a thriving business a little way along what is Macquarie Street today, a primitive hospital had been erected, and there was a scattering of houses. Government House was on a hill just west of the settlement.

In March 1797 an Eora war party led by Pemulwuy executed the first stage of their plan. They attacked the network of settlements in the Toongabbie area,[79] capturing valuable supplies and ammunition. Armed and mounted landholders took to the field against them and a punitive party was despatched from Parramatta to fight the main force, which was reported to be 100 strong. Spears, clubs and axes challenged the guns of the enemy, and Pemulwuy abandoned some of the captured supplies to preserve the great advantage of his manoeuvrability. It was hit and run and hit again until the English forces gave up and retreated into fortified Parramatta.

For the moment the Eora were the victors, although the rout at Toongabbie was covered up. David Collins, for example, reported that the English had pursued Pemulwuy's forces towards Parramatta. The truth was revealed when he added that, "being fatigued" by the day's fighting and marching, they entered the town half an hour before Pemulwuy's arrival.[80]

It is a significant comment on the reduced morale of the English troops or on their increased respect for the battle prowess of Pemulwuy and his warriors that the English abandoned completely the tactics used at the Battle of the Hawkesbury. In that engagement they had opened fire in battle lines, charged with fixed bayonets and subsequently fired at will. In the Battle of Parramatta there was no such dashing charge. They simply held their line and their fire, awaiting the charge of Pemulwuy.[81]

The scene on that clear autumn day, only a stone's throw from the Parramatta River, symbolised the clash of civilisations. Drawn up in a disciplined line of battle were the redcoats with their superior firepower; facing them less than ninety metres away was a painted war party, exhilarated by their recent successes, waving weapons and shields and shouting the chants of battle. The terrain separating the two forces was gently undulating and virtually clear of any major obstacles. Once the Eora were within range of the guns there was nothing to protect them.

The battle began at a signal from Pemulwuy who, after a steady advance, threw the first spear. As the Eora began to charge the soldiers began firing. Pemulwuy, taller and more powerful than any other, was the main target as he led the charge. In the opening minutes he sustained seven wounds, including a massive head wound which struck him to the ground.[82] The first volley killed five Eora warriors,[83] but despite the apparent loss of their leader, the Eora pressed forward to the red line, using spears they had kept in reserve and wounding soldiers. Again and again the warriors charged, just how bravely they continued to fight is testified by one recorder of the events, Heaton, who put their losses, killed or wounded, at half the total war party.[84]

The Eora were eventually forced to retreat under the steady and sustained fire, leaving Pemulwuy for dead in a growing pool of blood from seven gaping wounds. The advancing troops found him among the bodies and with a rare show of admiration for a black leader took him to the hospital along what is now Macquarie Street, Parramatta.

The Eora were devastated. Their victory had turned into defeat, and they believed their great leader had been killed. The English, no doubt, were elated with their win and especially with the capture of the feared Pemulwuy. For days he lay unconscious or semi-conscious and his death was considered inevitable. Astonishingly he recovered. Biding his time for a few weeks he was able to break his chains and escape under cover of darkness with his leg iron still in place.[85] His escape took the edge off the English victory. To the Eora it must have seemed nothing more or less than a miracle, a sign that the great powers of the Dreamtime were with him despite the defeat and the heavy losses.

In the month that followed an uneasy peace descended on the

frontiers, and Hunter hoped his victory had ended all Eora resistance. When Pemulwuy encountered his protagonist, who was surveying with a small party between Duck Creek and Georges River for a possible site for settling retired members of the New South Wales Corps, there was no exchange of hostilities. Pemulwuy enquired whether the governor was angry and was told that Hunter was not but that he desired peace.[86]

Peace there was not to be. As Pemulwuy recovered his strength, the Eora renewed their harassment. In the past his war parties had attacked on the western outskirts of Sydney Town; now they moved north of the harbour. Lane Cove came under fire and houses were burned down and stock taken; a settlement at Kissing Point was attacked and the armed settler militia was called out to resist the raid. Hunter, beginning to feel the pressure building up again, issued a proclamation less than two months after the battle, warning that captured Eora warriors would be hanged in chains on a tree near the spot "as a terror to the others".[87] This order, similar to the tactics adopted by Nazi SS divisions in World War II in their struggle to contain resistance movements in France and Italy, he justified in his despatches to his new superior in London, the Duke of Portland.

At the same time Hunter began a new program of building forts. A detachment was sent to the Georges River to confront the Eora war parties there, while the Parramatta outposts, including the scene of the Eora victory at Toongabbie, were strengthened. He was also worried that some of his own people had deserted to join Pemulwuy. In his despatch to the Duke of Portland on 20 June 1797 he reported that some white people had joined large groups of Eora and had

> *taught them how to annoy and distress the settlers, who have many of them been murder'd by them, their houses burnt, and their stock destroyed. They have threatened to burn and destroy our crops upon the ground, and to kill our cattle wherever they can find them . . . I fear I shall be under the necessity of sending arm'd parties in all directions to scower the country. I have been out myself with a small party of officers, and I shall frequently do so, and prevent, as far as possible, the destruction of many of those people who are led entirely by the villains who have got amongst them. We are in much want of some small arms and some camp equipage, in order to take particular stations for preventing these mischiefs.*[88]

It is not clear whether Hunter was reporting to London that he and his officers were going out on search and kill expeditions of all the Eora people encountered or whether he was saying that he wanted to prevent it happening.

Despite Hunter's efforts, resistance continued into 1798 and Pemulwuy was at the head of every attack. He seemed somehow to have become invincible. The Eora, the Dharuk and other nations came to believe that he could not be killed by the firearms which defeated them so often. By the last year of the old century Pemulwuy was still trying to hold the line at Georges River where in May his people speared and killed an invader. There were many bloody reprisals. Armed settler auxiliaries captured two young Eora boys, tied them up with dog ropes, led them into a yard and shot them dead. In an apparent effort to contain the violence and terror Hunter had the five men responsible put on trial. They were found guilty and London was asked for a decision, but a reply never came and they continued to live on their properties as before.

Despite the bravery of the Eora and the steadfastness and skill of Pemulwuy and the way he had drawn even English prisoners to his cause, the English were building their strength and by the time Hunter left to return to England in September 1800 the population in the colony, settlers, prisoners and military, was nearly 5000. Eora women were always in danger, there being five men to every English woman in the colony, and Hunter continued to give land to all and sundry. His government charges brought criticism which implied he was pocketing the profits, and his inability to curtail the rum traffic and the trade monopoly of the military brought censure from the same Imperial authorities who ignored his submissions on convicted murderers. Hunter went home in disgrace, but the majority of the soldiers and settlers he had led for five years gave him an affectionate farewell and even some of the Eora people were there to see him off.

He had also failed to end Eora resistance and to kill or capture Pemulwuy, who remained at the top of the list of challenges confronting Hunter's successor, Philip Gidley King. Twenty-one years Hunter's junior, King was twenty-nine years old when he volunteered to sail with Phillip as second lieutenant in the *Sirius* in the First Fleet. He began to carve for himself a place in the roll of infamy almost as soon as he took up his responsibilities. He had already been in trouble—in 1779 he had been dismissed from his ship for ordering the crew, without the knowledge of the captain, to sign a power of attorney appointing him agent for any prize and plunder taken.

King came to the southern continent, however, to make a new start, to display a new high-mindedness. Phillip appointed him commander of the Norfolk Island settlement. He decided to abolish flogging, yet within six weeks he had a boy of fifteen given 100 lashes for a minor theft of rum. He spoke against sexual promiscuity and fathered two illegitimate children. He railed against drunkenness and began to drink heavily.[89] Through it all he kept up constant recitations of public piety, but in the twelve years from 1788 he turned from a fresh open-faced young officer who had only been guilty of a little racketeering to a "moody, maudlin, gout-ridden"[90] dictator.

By the time King commenced his reign in the colony in September 1800 he was a violent drunk, who would yell at people who annoyed him. He pushed an Irish woman named Bridget Kennedy down the street leading to his residence because she had asked him for a grog ration. In a drunken moment he once jumped into a basket of eggs and shrieked with laughter as the yellow mess soaked into his dress uniform.[91] Yet he began with kindness and amity towards the ancient nations, recommending forebearance and plain dealing as a means of ending hostilities: within five years all this had degenerated into pessimistic racism. His shining contribution, a rare example of dignity and nobility, could be his support for the legal rights of prisoners who had served their sentences.

Like Hunter, King had to contend with prices so high that it was cheaper for the Imperial Government to send supplies of salt meat from England than to buy from either public or private sources in the colony. One third of the population was fed from the public store, although they neither worked nor contributed in any way to the advancement of the settlement. But he found himself with a more urgent enemy than the entrenched racketeers who ran Sydney Town. The war on the close frontiers was continuing and Pemulwuy was by now a living legend to black and white alike. Using the power to conscript settlers to fight the Eora introduced by Hunter, King reinforced the impost on them to sustain the fighting. He was desperate to stop Eora attacks on the growing grain in view of the scarcity of food supplies. In 1801 he issued proclamations outlawing two Englishmen, William Knight and Thomas Thrush, who had joined Pemulwuy's forces and now set a reward on Pemulwuy's head.[92] The great guerilla leader was reduced by King's proclamation to the status of an outlaw. The rewards for his capture or assassination included twenty gallons of spirit, two suits of clothes for a free man, conditional emancipation if the captor was serving fourteen years or life or, if he had already been conditionally emancipated, free pardon and recommendation for a passage to England.[93]

In November 1801 King reinforced the detachment along the Georges River in an effort to protect the ripening wheat, and issued his first terror proclamation – the troops were orderd to fire on any people they saw and neither women nor children were exempt. "Every means is to be used to drive them off, either by shooting them or otherwise."[94] A second proclamation, the same in content, applied to the troops at Parramatta.

King's offer of rewards for Pemulwuy, dead or alive, was directed to his soldiers, prisoners and landseekers.[95] It also extended to any among the fighting Eora who would turn traitor, for if Pemulwuy could be "given up" then the Eora "should be re-admitted to our friendship".[96] Throughout 1801 all military efforts had been made to force those Eora around Parramatta, the Georges River and Prospect Hill away from these occupied areas. But on 30 October 1802 King reported to Lord Hobart that Pemulwuy had attacked more settlements, inflicted casualties and captured food and supplies. He was described as "an active" and "daring leader".[97] It was left to two unnamed and unheralded English settlers to stalk the leader, to catch him off guard and shoot him and a companion.[98] Pemulwuy's head was cut from his body, pickled, and sent to Sir Joseph Banks with King's assurance that the Eora were now more friendly than ever before.[99]

The assassination brought down a man who had defied five governors and captains-in-chief in battle, won the admiration of both black and white, and above all had contained for twelve years the cancer-like spread of the invasion into Eora lands.

Pemulwuy was dead and his head was on its way to London, but he left a son, Tedbury, who had fought at his side and who continued the war for another eight years. The main battles, however, were over. The Eora were decimated by war and disease, and Tedbury was never able to assemble guerilla forces equalling in strength those of his father. Like Pemulwuy, he attracted to his standard English prisoners who opted for the bush rather than the chain gang, but he began to seek and to use firearms in a way his father had not. Despite this, his operations were on a limited scale.

Tedbury was captured by an armed posse at Pennant Hills, nearly escaped and was later used, under threat of being shot, to track local bushrangers. Once out of military custody, he led attacks on settlements along the Georges River and on Parramatta Road at what is today Canterbury. He was shot dead in June 1810 by an English settler named E. Luttrill junior. It would seem to have been a private quarrel as a charge was laid against Luttrill, who subsequently went back to England.[100]

King was never able to extirpate completely Eora resistance, although the slaughter continued to such an extent that within twenty years of the invasion in 1788 an entire nation had been destroyed. Before his reign ended in 1804, however, King was to fight another battle, not against the Eora but against the Irish rebels who struck again for life and liberty after their defeat on the other side of the world in the Irish Rebellion of 1798.

5. THE BATTLE OF VINEGAR HILL

Among the dozen nationalities represented among the marines, sailors and prisoners on the First Fleet there was only a scattering of Irish men and women. It was the Second Fleet, which arrived in June 1790, that brought the first contingent of prisoners of war from Irish ports. Between 1791 and 1800 no fewer than 1140 men and 275 women were embarked from Irish ports as prisoners, a further 610 men and 91 women arrived between 1801 and 1802, and 546 followed in the next few years. By 1823 more than 8000 had been brought in chains to New South Wales,[1] comprising the largest single group after the English – the Scots, in contrast, numbered only 850 in the same period. Many of the Irish transported before the Battle of Vinegar Hill in 1804 could be described as prisoners of war captured after the Irish Rebellion of 1798. As political prisoners they formed a striking contrast to many of the other prisoners who had depended on crime for a living.

While the officially announced reason for the British settlement in New South Wales was to relieve the crowded state of English gaols there were other strategic reasons for establishing a military post in a continent that had already been penetrated by the Dutch, claimed by Spain, and made a target for possible annexation by the French. The race for possession of Australia led to much suppression of history, and there was no doubt that visions of a new province of the Empire dominated in the Imperial capital. In one of his letters, Joseph Banks, for example, looked to the day when Botany Bay would be peopled by "beings that would be an ornament to human nature", the product of prisoners and "the most beautifully formed women that the sun beholds" from the South Sea islands.[2]

The 37,000 prisoners, mostly men, sent to Sydney Town up to 1823 were used as a labour force. Most of them were English and in nearly every prison ship one third were from London, while a cosmopolitan dimension was added by Jews, blacks from Africa, Indians, West Indian blacks, a Ukrainian, Anglo-Indians, and French from Madagascar. Under English law transportation was the most severe punishment next to death. Sentences were for seven years, fourteen years or life, mostly for offences against property, although others ended up in chains bound for Botany Bay for more unusual crimes—"opening places of amusement or entertainment on Sunday evenings",[3] attempting to debate Holy Scripture if a Jesuit, or attempting to solemnise a marriage without an English licence.

Scottish law differed significantly from English law and punishments were milder. Sentences ranged over three, five or ten years and judges had discretion, in the case of youth, to take into account age, condition and temptation. While the English were hanging between ten and twelve men and women every day in the legal year, the Scots were despatching only six and they transported only three people to every 100 sent as captives from England. In 1793, in a flush of panic at the prospect of another rising of the Jacobites—the supporters of the Scottish Catholic Stuart kings, as opposed to the German Protestant kings occupying the English throne—Scottish judges sentenced to transportation five men who had committed the heinous crime of seeking to teach enlightenment in politics.

Most of the prisoners from England and Scotland were aged between twenty-four and twenty-nine years, but some barbarous judges even sent children of eleven in chains to the Great South Land. The female prisoners were even younger, generally aged between twenty-three and twenty-five, and included children sentenced for what today seem trifles—stealing a handkerchief in one case.[4]

If the English were characterised by their homosexuality—one English prisoner in eight to one in twenty engaged in homosexual practices, an activity punishable at the time by the lash—the Irish prisoners were characterised by their violence.[5] But Ireland was firmly occupied by British troops and English law was enforced in even more draconian fashion than in England—a man picked up on the street without a job or satisfactory explanation of why he was there could be charged with vagrancy and transported for seven years. After an abortive rising in 1796, men and women were arrested simply for opposing English rule; the mandatory sentence was transportation for life. The military repression enforced through alien courts and institutions meant in fact there was no rule of law except for those who held English title to land or property and acknowledged the sovereignty of England. Picked up from the street, the house or even the church, Irish prisoners were not even listed according to age or crime but simply described as "Irish" as if that was a crime in itself. Men from the northern counties of Ireland were brought

to Dublin, examined, given prison gear, sent to Cork and embarked from the port of Cobh direct for New South Wales.

The military dragnet after the 1798 rebellion netted rebels as diverse as three priests, James Dixon, James Harold and Peter O'Neill; three Protestant clergymen, Birch, Fulton and Simpson; an Irish landholder, General Joseph Holt; and a physician, Bryan O'Connor. Among other prisoners sent off by English courts was a former Lord Mayor of Cork, Henry Browne Hayes, who kidnapped a Quaker lady with a large fortune. He was sentenced to death, which was later commuted to transportation. During the voyage out in 1801 he quarrelled with the ship's surgeon and was jailed for six months on arrival.[6]

The arrival of increasing numbers of Irish in the colony after 1790 struck a note of alarm from the top level of society to the bottom. The military rulers were well aware that the new arrivals "despised their laws, defied their administration, and cursed all who collaborated with their

oppressors".[7] Even worse, they followed the Catholic religion, which enjoyed the same status in England at the time as did communism in McCarthy's America. The English prisoners also looked upon them with suspicion. None of them had been transported for political reasons and differences in language – a majority from the counties outside Dublin spoke Irish as a first language – values, religion and outlook fired fear of the unknown.

From their point of view the Irish reacted to life in chains on the underside of the world with wild hopes of liberation. An old Irish woman wandered around Sydney Cove like a soothsayer, assuring her suffering

ABOVE:
A chain gang in Sydney. Etching by E. Backhouse from A Narrative of a Visit to the Australian Colonies *by James Backhouse, published in London in 1843.*
NATIONAL LIBRARY OF AUSTRALIA

country men and women that their liberation by the French was at hand and that the English oppression would be ended forever.[8] There were rumours of an independent settlement to the south-west of Sydney free of English domination, and dreams that it was possible to walk from Sydney Cove to China.

Governor Hunter typified the fearful reaction to the Irish when he wrote of them as a "desperate set of villains"[9] who despised his courts, people with "fatuous religious beliefs", "superstitions" and the "worst of characters". He pleaded, vainly, for no more to be sent to New South Wales and kept them under constant observation. If a voice was raised against English rule, punishment was swift and ruthless. In April 1798 an Irish prisoner working in a chain gang at Toongabbie, driven to desperation by all-pervading misery, suddenly threw down his hoe and gave three cheers for liberty. He was seized by the military guards, taken before a magistrate, dragged back to the spot where the chain gang was working, tied to a post and given 100 lashes.

Hunter became paranoid about Irish plotting. If any group of Irish men and women met together they were immediately accused of being a "seditious assembly".[10] In 1800 a group of Irishmen who had been speaking in their mother tongue were brought to trial on this basis alone. In the hysterical climate of the time it was assumed by uncomprehending English eavesdroppers that they were using the language of sedition. This approach by Hunter's soldiers was adopted by many of the ignorant and arrogant who sought during the great migrant influx to Australia following World War II to ban the public use of all languages except English.

In September 1800 reports of a plan by a group of Irishmen at Parramatta to seize Sydney Town and sail home reached Hunter's ears. A commission of inquiry was set up, thus establishing in New South Wales a tradition for such commissions, sometimes designated "royal" and sometimes "judicial", with wide-ranging powers to raid, subpoena and set aside normal rules of evidence and conduct. It failed to shake the solidarity of the prisoners, who refused to become informers and resisted the assortment of blandishments, blackmail and torture that was used against them. The first called to give evidence was Father James Harold, although there was nothing to suggest he was associated with the plot. Despite the lack of firm evidence five other Irishmen were held to be the ringleaders and sentenced to 500 lashes. "James Harold called priest" was sentenced to witness the flogging of his compatriots and fellow religionists, and was banished to the hell hole of Norfolk Island for seven years.

The military condemned the Irish as "evasive" or "Jesuitical"[11] and continued the tortures. Samuel Marsden, an English cleric and hardline magistrate, ordered one Irishman named Galvin to be flogged until he revealed the wherabouts of the conspirators' pikes that Marsden was convinced existed. Galvin was flogged until the bones stood out of his back, stripped naked and flogged on his buttocks until they were a bloody pulp, then flogged on his back again. At the end of the bloody torture Marsden impassively assessed that Galvin would sooner die than become an informer. Other Irishmen were selected to receive 1000 lashes, some 500 lashes, some 200, or to be transported again to Norfolk Island.[12] Some were killed on the flogging triangles or died in agony afterwards; the survivors lived encased in a frame of scars.

Towards the end of this bloody interlude Philip Gidley King arrived to take over as governor from Hunter. King surrounded himself with a coterie of like-minded men: William Paterson, the commander of his troops, who favoured search-and-kill operations against both the Eora and Dharuk peoples; Richard Atkins, his judge advocate, who shared King's addiction to the bottle; and Marsden, his senior chaplain, who earned his nickname of the "flogging parson", concentrating on grabbing as much land as possible and squeezing as much work from the prisoners allocated to him as the lash could extract.

King put the Irish problem to one side as he contended with a revolt by one of his own officers, John Macarthur, who as commander of the Parramatta garrison used his own troops to seize spirits from the government store. Described by King as a racketeer with "art, cunning, impudence and a pair of basilisk eyes",[13] Macarthur avoided a court martial by resigning his commission. King also attacked the dolce vita of the colony where the military officers and a few civilian accomplices lived like feudal potentates, above and beyond the law which they determined and administered. Between them they had 356 men and women prisoners as personal servants whom the government fed and clothed, and they supported their lifestyle by operating a monopoly on importing goods and selling them at a mark up of up to 1000 per cent. The governor reduced the number of servants to ninety-four and put the rest to work on government land to produce food, and sought to break the military domination of the courts by having civilians sit on them.

The internecine struggles of the English, however, helped to provide opportunities for the Irish to organise following the age-old dictum that "England's difficulty is Ireland's opportunity".[14]

Governor Hunter had formed two local militias, which he called "loyal associations";[15] they paralleled the paramilitary "loyalist" organisations formed a century later in Belfast to resist Irish independence. Each comprised fifty armed men chosen for being loyal Protestant Englishmen possessing "property and good characters".[16] The Sydney militia was put under the command of William Balmain, a surgeon on the First Fleet, while Andrew Thompson, a former prisoner, was appointed commandant in Parramatta. King had hardly set foot on the continent when he issued a proclamation referring to "the constant state of alarm, and issued orders for handling" internal rebellion.[17] He was, however, nervous about the militias and had them stood down until 1802 when 200 Irish prisoners arrived on the *Atlas*.

Just as King used coercion, blackmail and money to bring about the assassination of the leader of the Eora people, he exploited the occasion of the enforced incorporation of Ireland in the United Kingdom by the Act of Union passed by the London Parliament into law in January 1801. When the news reached King in late May of that year, he ordered a major celebration, hoisting the new Union Jack and peddling the view that now Ireland was a part of the United Kingdom the old problems had been resolved.

Aware that the Irish and other Catholics now made up one quarter of the population,[18] King began to consider the idea of allowing them to practise their faith, but would not permit the three prisoner priests to teach the Catholic religion. His superior in London, Lord Hobart, was totally uncompromising that Catholicism, Jacobinism and the concepts of liberty, freedom and fraternity should never be seen in England and that a parliament of England should never yield to such "insolent demands".[19]

Nevertheless, King looked around for a willing agent who would be his ears and eyes. He found him in Father James Dixon who had been arrested and sentenced to death during the 1798 rebellion in Ireland for commanding a company of rebels in a town he had never been in. With support from his parishioners and members of the local Anglo-ascendancy, Dixon's sentence was commuted to transportation. He had arrived in Sydney in January 1800, accompanied by Father Peter O'Neill and Father James Harold. King discerned in Dixon a peace-loving man incapable of inciting anything very much; it says something about martial law in Ireland that the English authorities saw him as a rebel. In contrast to so many of his fellow countrymen, and to Father Harold, Dixon was given emancipist's freedom by King and paid a salary to carry out his ministry.

In granting permission for the Irish to worship in their own way King made every post a winner. His regulations began by reminding the Irish that "this extension of liberal toleration proceeded from the piety and benevolence of their most gracious sovereign, to whom, under Providence, they were indebted for the blessings they enjoyed".[20] He enjoined them to ensure that there were no seditious conversations at their places of worship, in their homes or elsewhere. Further, they were to show their gratitude and allegiance to King George III by informing on anyone who questioned his rule and the rightness of his system and servants. Dixon was to be held responsible for every action and word during the services, which were to be attended by the military as a double check that nothing was done or said against the King and English rule.

Father Dixon was permitted to perform his priestly duties at Sydney, Parramatta and the Hawkesbury (now Windsor) in rotation. Under these regulations masses were first said, officially and publicly, at Sydney on 15 May 1803, in Parramatta on 22 May and at the Hawkesbury on 29 May.[21]

By the end of 1803 King was well satisfied; his policies had brought about the assassination of the Eora leader Pemulwuy and the Eora forces had been soundly defeated in battle; he had set up a network of agents to watch the Irish and by bringing them together on a regular basis under the eyes of his police and using the offices of Father Dixon to suppress rebellion, he could turn once again to the problem of controlling his own military. On 1 March 1804, only three days before the rebellion and the Battle of Vinegar Hill, he wrote to Lord Hobart that Father Dixon's masses had had a most salutary effect on the Catholics—since the masses had been allowed there had been no cause for complaint among those who attended. But King's self-satisfaction was premature. His system of informers was not working, the 2500 lashes his predecessor had forced Father Harold to watch had not been forgotten, and his request for an Irish-speaking officer or servant who could report to him directly had been ignored by the British Government. Above all King could not know the strength of the bitterness, resentment and burning desire for freedom that had led to the great rebellion in Ireland, which culminated in the Battle of Vinegar Hill outside the town of Enniscorthy in the County of Wexford in June 1798.

The Irish Struggle for Independence

The Irish Rebellion of 1798 against English rule, which had such an important impact on Australian life and settlement, was but one chapter in more than eight centuries of struggle to regain independence.

Ireland had proudly withstood the might of Rome and survived the darkness that followed the latter's fall as the "island of saints and scholars". Led by Ard Ri or "High King" Brian Boru Ireland defeated the Danes and withstood the spread of feudalism; her kings were elected, and the great families and clans retained an independence all of their own. England, in contrast, became a Roman province, then fell to the Danes and was finally conquered by the Normans, who created a strong, centralised feudal state. Ireland, with divided loyalties and a tenuous national unity that depended on the strength of an elected monarch, was no match for her militarily more sophisticated neighbour.

The Anglo-Norman invasion of the thirteenth century was the beginning of the end of Gaelic Ireland, although Erin's call was heeded by Anglo-Norman families who became more Irish than the Gaels; many Anglo-Irish in later times were also to pledge themselves to their adopted country. But once the English occupation area around and including Dublin known as "The Pale" began to expand, the Irish suffered repeated defeats despite the help from time to time of their old allies Spain and

France. The massacres and devastation by the English leader, Oliver Cromwell, in 1649, followed by the defeat of Irish forces by a combined German, Dutch, Danish and English force under William of Orange in 1690, led to the wholesale dispossession of Irish families from their own land, which was then made available for resettlement by English and Scottish "planters".

The Statutes of Kilkenny enacted in the seventeenth century comprised one of the most savage provisions for repression ever enacted against a defeated people. The Irish language was banned, the religion was outlawed, and Irish men and women were prohibited from passing on land to their families or even owning a horse.

By the turn of the eighteenth century Dublin was the seventh largest city in the world but also among the most wretched, with disease and squalor worse than in Calcutta. Up to seventy people could be found sharing primitive houses so pathetic they often collapsed taking the inhabitants with them. While English political power was rising world wide, the Irish were struggling to stay alive in the famine of 1741. But although Irish pikes were rusting, the poets and "shanachie" (or storytellers) kept alive the language and the hopes and aspirations of the people for an Ireland that was free.

The American War of Independence dramatically encouraged Irish hopes, the more so since Ireland's old allies Spain and France supported the infant republic. The year after the English surrender to the Americans at Yorktown in 1781 delegates from a number of Ulster Volunteer Corps gathered at the parish church in Dungannon to pledge their support for independence. It was the beginning of the road that led to the Battle of Vinegar Hill. Debating societies with the proud name of United Irishmen became the basis for revolt. The national leader was Wolf Tone, son of a Protestant coachmaker, a young, slightly built barrister who was equally at home in Dublin and Belfast. In 1791 he formed the Belfast Society of United Irishmen and joined with the Dublin leader, Napper Tandy, to form a similar society in Dublin. It was a great "brotherhood of affection",[22] which brought together Catholics, Protestants and Presbyterians, artisans, businessman and peasants in a concerted bid for independence.

In 1796 Tone left Ireland for the United States, which he used as a stepping stone to reach France where the new republic was at war with England. Napoleon Bonaparte himself organised an army to help liberate Ireland, and Tone, in the heavy surcoat of a French adjutant-general, headed back to Ireland in December 1796 aboard the 80-gun flagship *Indomptable*, leading a French fleet carrying 14,000 men. Ireland lay at their feet, but the weather was with the English—a storm scattered the fleet and thwarted the invasion.

Despite increasingly draconian measures against the Irish the spirit of revolt could not be curbed and within two years the rebellion of 1798 began. It was violent, tragic and brief. In the space of a few weeks 30,000 people were killed. Peasants armed with pikes and pitchforks, supported by women and children, were cut down by sword and bayonet, shot or blown to pieces as they charged into the mouths of the English cannon.[23] It was an event that was burned into the folk memory of an entire people:

Who fears to speak of Ninety-eight?
Who blushes at the name?
When cowards mock the patriot's fate,
Who hangs his head in shame?

"THE MEMORY OF THE DEAD"[24]

The leader of the "Irish Directory" was the wild and handsome Lord Edward Fitzgerald, his hair cropped in the new style of the French Revolution. When he moved through Dublin with his beautiful French wife Pamela at his side he was hailed as the deliverer. Just before the rebellion was scheduled to begin, however, the Leinster Directory of United Irishmen was betrayed by a traitor to the cause, Thomas Reynolds, and a raid by British troops captured the entire leadership. Only Lord Edward escaped. When his hiding place was discovered on 19 May 1798, he fought like a tiger against eight soldiers but was mortally wounded and captured. As he lay dying in his cell in Dublin Castle rebel forces formed up to storm that citadel of English power, but a squadron of cavalry foiled the rescue attempt. Almost immediately a force of 800 British yeomanry unleased a reign of terror in the streets of Dublin, storming and wrecking the houses of anyone thought to be connected with the United Irishmen.

A few days later the rebellion began but the Dublin forces were leaderless and there was no national co-ordination. The men of Kildare led the way and then Wexford and Waterford rose together with the men of Ulster. English spies had estimated the Irish revolutionary army as 300,000 strong, but the fighting force that went into action in Wexford was no more than 20,000. Wexford, south of Dublin, became the proclaimed capital of the first Irish republic. The county was roused with the cry "Up the boys of Wexford" which was later to echo at Parramatta, Toongabbie and Castle Hill in distant New South Wales. The word "liberty" was painted on a thousand doors,[25] the words "Erin go bragh" or "Ireland forward" were carried before the republican army.[26] Hopes were high but Napoleon sailed for Egypt, not Ireland, soon after the rebellion began and the second French force failed to arrive until after the defeat of the Irish.

It was on 21 June 1798 that the fate of the rising was sealed at Vinegar Hill, the principal rebel camp just outside the town of Enniscorthy, 129 kilometres from Dublin. The English force of 10,000 soldiers with twenty pieces of artillery and 400 requisitioned coaches had taken four days to encircle the ill-equipped Irish army.[27] The artillery opened up a steady bombardment of new explosive howitzer shells. The Irishmen with their pikes were helpless. There was no cover on the hill and they were blown to pieces where they stood in bold defence. Then came the cavalry charge, and Vinegar Hill was drenched in red.

As the remnants of the Irish army escaped down the road to the town of Wexford itself, atrocities occurred which were to live in the memory of those transported to New South Wales. The Irish army had set up a field hospital in the centre of the town. The English troops captured the hospital and burned it to the ground; the bodies of the patients burned with it were still sizzling next day. Hundreds were cut down as they withdrew, their bodies used for sword play, or stripped of clothes and possessions. The Irish republic in Wexford had lasted three weeks: the rising in New South Wales would last even less.

The legacy of 1798 is "a story of incredible bravery and indescribable brutality. Yet, despite its failure, the United Irishmen movement profoundly influenced the thinking of later generations of Irishmen. The concept of a republic as the quintessential constitutional expression of Irish separatism originated with the United Irishmen".[28]

What of the heroes? Lord Edward Fitzgerald died in June 1798 of his wounds in the dank dungeons of Dublin Castle. Wolf Tone, accompanying another French expedition, was captured in September 1798 off Lough Swilly in north Ireland where a stronger English squadron defeated the French and took Tone back to Dublin. Although an Irishman and serving as a French officer, he was tried by an English court martial and condemned to death. Before he could be killed he cut his own throat in his death cell on 19 November. He took a week to die. His friends secured his body, which was buried in a grave still unknown.

No songs were sung more passionately to the heroes of '98 than to Father John Murphy whose name was heard in every sheebin or Irish drinking place throughout New Holland.

Come all your warriors, and renowned nobles,
Who once commanded brave warlike bands;
Lay down your plumes and your golden trophies
Give up your arms with a trembling hand,
Since Father Murphy, of the County Wexford,
Lately aroused from his sleepy dream,
To cut down cruel Saxon persecution,
And wash it away with a crimson stream.

"ODE TO FATHER MURPHY"[29]

Father John Murphy, of Boulavogue in Wexford, was forty-five at the time of the rising. The son of a local farmer, he had been eduated in an underground "hedge school" and was later sent to a seminary in Spain which gave Irish people automatic residence and citizenship. After his ordination he returned to Boulavogue to take care of several hundred parishioners.

Murphy had originally joined with thirteen other priests to give a testimonial of loyalty to the English authorities. Tragic events were to change him into a warrior priest. English soldiery and their local auxiliaries on their way to Wexford began to massacre prisoners rounded up at random, prompting Murphy to raise the county and fight. The soldiers responded by burning down his house at Tincurry, desecrating and destroying his little church at Boulavogue, and carrying his vestments on their bayonets. After the defeat of the Irish forces at Vinegar Hill, Murphy escaped in disguise to Taghman, where he was discovered and publicly hanged on 26 June 1798, only five days after the battle.

Napper Tandy retreated with French allies to France after a brief foray on Irish soil. He was later captured by British agents in Hamburg, brought back to Dublin and sentenced to death, but escaped hanging to die in France. Tandy's name was also commemorated in one of the ballads that would have been sung in New South Wales:

I met with Napper Tandy and he took me by the hand,
Saying, how is old Ireland? and how does she stand?
She's the most distressful country that ever yet was seen;
They are hanging men and women for the wearing of the green,
O wearing of the green, O wearing of the green,
My native land, I cannot stand, for the wearing of the green.

"THE WEARING OF THE GREEN"[30]

The only surviving leader was Joseph Holt, who was not a United Irishman but had joined the rebellion when his house was burned down by an English landlord. After the Irish commander-in-chief, Edward Roche, was defeated at Vinegar Hill, Holt assumed command and began to rally the remnants of the army. Despite the defeat and the pressure by the counter-attacking English Army, Holt, by sheer generalship, kept the rebellion alive in the whole of Wicklow and the borders of the counties of Kildare and Dublin. His successes, his bold strikes, brought recruits flocking to his standard and the English general Craig offered a reward of £300 to anyone who could capture him. Holt issued a counter proclamation offering twice the amount for the capture of Craig. After the collapse of the rebellion, Holt surrendered in November and was banished to Botany Bay. It was on him that the rebels of the Australian rebellion were to pin their hopes.

These were the names, the events and the songs that dominated the hearts and minds of the Irish who arrived in chains in the new English colony. For them nothing had changed. They were still in chains; they were still at the bottom of the scale, they were still distrusted, spied upon and, if they spoke out of turn, flogged like poor Galvin on the Toongabbie chain gang.

The links with the '98 rebellion were not all on one side. Francis Grose, first commander of the New South Wales Corps and acting governor of the colony in 1792–94, served in the Wexford command of the British Army during the rebellion. On his return to England he kept up a lively correspondence with friends in the colony whose main concern was that there might well be yet another Irish bid for freedom.[31]

Prelude to Rebellion

The Australian Battle of Vinegar Hill followed within three years of the decision in mid-1801 by Governor King to found a settlement at Castle Hill, eight kilometres from Parramatta, as part of his program to boost agricultural production from government land and so ease the payouts to private producers. By May 1803, 300 acres (123 hectares) had been cleared for food crops and by March the following year this had more than doubled. More and more prisoners were sent to Castle Hill, many of them Irish who had escaped summary execution in Ireland at the hands of courts martial and opted, like Joseph Holt, for transportation.[32] They were dispersed among private settlers under armed civilian overseers or were housed in barracks under military supervision.

The military maintained among them Irish-speaking informers who reported to the overseers, the latter being in a position to give favours, assign hard labour or easy work and make money available. Above all the overseers were always on the spot, by day guarding and observing the prisoners at work in the fields and on the roads, at night sleeping within earshot. The governor, apparently convinced that these measures would contain the "Irish problem", withdrew the Castle Hill garrison late in 1803 or early in 1804,[33] leaving only a small number of civilian officials to keep order.

Among the prisoners at Castle Hill were two young men from County Kerry, Phillip Cunningham, a skilled workman who was an overseer of stonemasons, and William Johnston. Transported for their part in the rebellion of 1798, both agreed they could not be worse off if they fought for freedom and died or were recaptured in the attempt. Secretly they began to plan a rebellion and to enrol others to their cause, particularly prisoners on the various farms and settlements between Parramatta and the Hawkesbury. Englishmen as well as Irishmen flocked to join them, embracing the slogan, "liberty or death". The provisional plan was for the rebellion to begin at Castle Hill, where a building would be fired as a signal to supporters on the surrounding farms to rise against their overseers and join the main force. They would attack and take Parramatta, regroup, then advance on Sydney. Once in control of the port, those

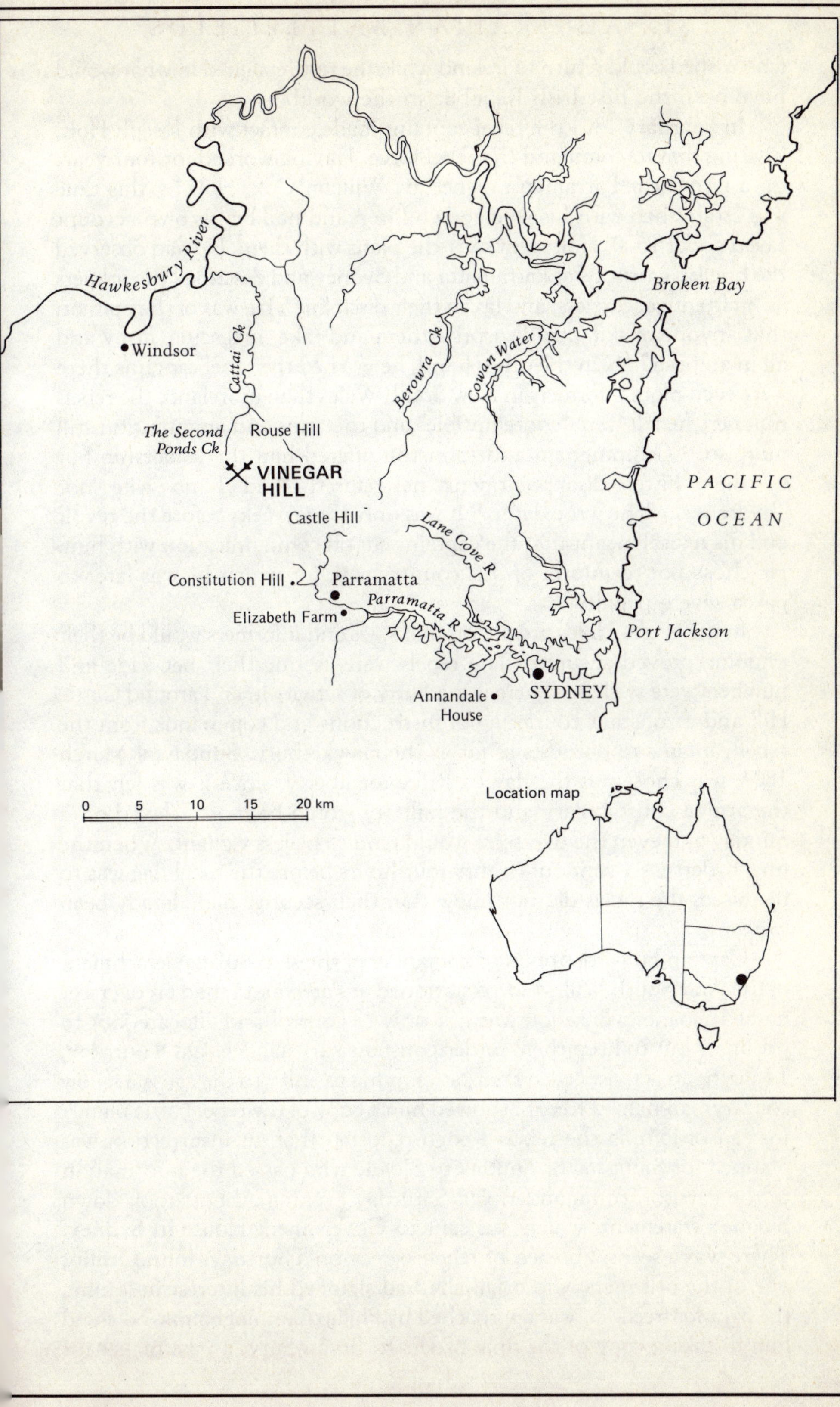

Hawkesbury River
Windsor
Cattai Ck
The Second Ponds Ck
Rouse Hill
VINEGAR HILL
Castle Hill
Constitution Hill
Parramatta
Elizabeth Farm
Parramatta R
Lane Cove R
Berowra Ck
Cowan Water
Broken Bay
PACIFIC OCEAN
Port Jackson
SYDNEY
Annandale House
0 5 10 15 20 km
Location map

who wished could return to Ireland while the rest remained in what would have been the first Irish Republic in the world.

In February 1804 the rebel captains made contact with Joseph Holt, inviting him to command the rebel force. Having worked for four years on a farm near Parramatta owned by William Cox, Holt by this time was established with his wife and children and had by his own account saved about £500. Holt went over the plans with them. He had observed the English garrisons at Parramatta and Sydney and described the soldiers as "inattentive, careless, and lax in their discipline". He was of the opinion that anyone of skill could surprise them and take "magazine, army and all in an hour".[34] On the other hand, he warned the rebel captains there were even more informers in New South Wales than in Ireland, the rebels numbers he felt were "contemptible" and the arms and ammunition still more so.[35] Cunningham and Johnston offered him the leadership but to their bitter disappointment he refused—"had I no wife nor children . . . ", he wrote later.[36] It was only three weeks before the revolt and his refusal meant that the captains cut off communication with him. He chose not to inform on his countrymen, for which he was later to pay a severe penalty.

In the event, Holt's prediction that spies and informers would be their undoing proved accurate. The rebels were casting their net wide and numbers were swelling. There was a flurry of activity in and around Castle Hill and a constant couriering of instructions and commands from the rebel captains to outposts as far as the Hawkesbury. Sunday, 4 March 1804, was chosen as the day to strike for liberty, since it was felt that the armed constabulary and the military would be more relaxed on a Sunday and even the overseers would tend to be less vigilant. When the final orders were sent out twenty-four hours before the rebel flag was to be raised, the rebels did not know that their security had already been broken.

Captain Edward Abbott, commander of the sixty-strong detachment of the New South Wales Corps stationed at Parramatta, had an overseer named Sloane, whose job was not only to control and allocate jobs to prisoners but to keep them under constant surveillance. On Thursday, 1 March, an activist called Poor, attempting to enlist to the cause a fellow countryman named Keogh, showed him a copy of the rebel battle plan.[37] Instead of joining the rebels Keogh reported that an insurrection was planned for Saturday or Sunday to Sloane who passed the information to the garrison commander. On Saturday evening Abbott took down Sloane's statement, which was sent to Government House in Sydney. There was a second breach of rebel secrecy on Thursday. John Griffin, one of the prisoners who originally had signified his interest in joining the fight for freedom, was approached by Phillip Cunningham, who asked him to take a copy of the final orders to Bryan Fury, a pike maker for the rebels. A prisoner named Lewis Bolger saw the orders and persuaded Griffin to destroy them. On Sunday, 4 March, Captain Abbott and Samuel Marsden at Parramatta took statements from Griffin and Bolger that the orders being circulated contained the date of the rising (4 March), the rallying points, and the password, which was St Peter, the founding Pope.[38] The information was conveyed immediately to the governor who on receiving this second report at midnight on Sunday noted on it, "Received by me at 12 o'clock at night . . . information that the insurrection had taken place at Castle Hill".[39]

Just how widely the rebel plans were known can be gathered from the later recollections of Joseph Holt. On Sunday, 4 March, returning home through Parramatta, he stopped to have a meal at the tavern there and met an acquaintance, an Englishman named Timothy Holster who was a chain gang leader. While having a leisurely drink after lunch Holt noticed men collecting in little groups and an unmistakeable air of tension. After some gentle probing Holster revealed that the government had obtained the plans for a rebellion and were even now moving to suppress it.[40] Although Holster knew Holt had been an Irish general, he perhaps also knew that he was not part of the rebellion, because he warned him not to stay out late that night. Holt went to Cox's farm and reported that rebellion was about to break out and they should fortify the homestead. The rebels made no move against Holt or the English family he was protecting, but they did go to Holt's own little property nearby, where they collected two weapons and a young English recruit named James Dobbs. Holt's two young sons were there but were neither molested nor threatened, despite the rebels' disappointment that the veteran of the Irish Battle of Vinegar Hill was not to join them.

Rebellion

Despite the fact that they knew a storm was about to break, those in authority at Parramatta had taken no special precautions. Elizabeth Macarthur and her family were dining peacefully at the Marsden's Parramatta mansion when the rebellion began as Cunningham and Johnston had planned at 8 o'clock on Sunday evening. One of the buildings in the government compound at Castle Hill was set on fire and the bell was rung.[41] As it tolled Phillip Cunningham marshalled the estimated 200 prisoners and directed the compound to be searched for arms. A man named Robert Duggan, who had been deemed a traitor and was known as " The Flagellator" because he had inflicted thousands of lashes on the backs of the incarcerated, was the first to be arrested by the rebels. As they approached his house he hid under the bed. He was dragged out, led to the triangle that had witnessed his excesses and flogged, although not, as had occurred when he was handling the cat-o'-nine-tails, to death.

Cunningham and William Johnston paraded the 200-strong force, gave them some elementary drill and laid out the battle plan. Under the grand strategy devised by Cunningham and Johnston, a "fifth column" in Parramatta was to set fire to Macarthur's Elizabeth Farm homestead to draw the garrison out of the centre of the town to the east. This would leave the town centre unprotected and prevent the rebel force from being trapped between the garrison and any reinforcements which might arrive from Sydney.[42] Another fire was to be lit in Parramatta to signal that the fifth column had risen, thus providing the signal for the main force to attack the town. Meanwhile raiding parties were to scour the outlying areas for arms and extra recruits before re-forming at Constitution Hill, between Government House and Toongabbie, where Phillip Cunningham would set up his headquarters. The second column under the command of Charles Hill was to storm the Parramatta gaol, capture its armoury and free its prisoners. After breakfast on Constitution Hill the columns were to re-form and march to present-day Windsor, then called Green Hills, to complete the call to arms. With the addition of the Hawkesbury men, the rebel captains estimated they would raise a total force of 1100 men.[43] The force would then return to Parramatta and assemble in front of Government House, where a tree of liberty was to be planted and all oppressed men would be invited to join them for the Battle of Sydney.

It must have been an intoxicating moment. The takeover of Castle Hill had gone like clockwork, and morale was high as the raiding parties set out. One group called at the nearby home of a French colonel, Verincourt de Clambe, possibly in a bid to enlist him; he was not there, but they satisfied themselves by seizing what arms they could find as well as a keg of spirits.[44] Others raided farms from the Field of Mars near present-day Ryde in the east to Prospect in the west, capturing in all 136 muskets, fourteen pistols and some bayonets and pitchforks.[45]

This was, however, the high point of the rebellion. One of the armed auxiliaries had escaped from Castle Hill when the revolt began and hurried to Parramatta to warn the garrison. Before 10 pm the drums had beaten "to arms" and Captain Abbott had hastened to secure the barracks and the gaol with the help of the loyalist militia. Some of the "principal families" of Parramatta and the surrounding district took shelter in the barracks, among them the Reverend William Pascoe Crook and his wife and daughter, and another parson named Hassall. Both these men of the cloth, being members of the militia, took up arms and went to their posts. Samuel Marsden and his wife, and Elizabeth Macarthur and her children fled the town by boat, floating down the Parramatta River to Sydney.[46]

The battle plans began to go seriously awry when Johnston and Cunningham's confederates in Parramatta failed to light the fires either at Elizabeth Farm or in the township itself. By the early hours of Monday, 5 March, Phillip Cunningham had assembled his column, as planned, on Constitution Hill and had ensured that each man had a weapon and a basic grasp of military manoeuvres. The column led by Charles Hill, although in a position for the planned attack on Parramatta gaol, waited in vain for the signal fire and realising the gaol was now heavily defended, made its way instead to Constitution Hill. The column led by Samuel Humes, amounting to more than seventy men, lost its way and became separated; Humes and some companions reached the rendezvous, but stragglers were captured between Seven Hills and Castle Hill Roads later that morning by an English platoon led by Lieutenant Davies.[47] The fourth column, commanded by William Johnston, had successfully carried out the first part of their mission but they too became hopelessly lost and only the iron determination of Johnston held the remnants together to reach Constitution Hill.

The rendezvous was now hours behind schedule, two of the rebel columns had been seriously depleted and as a result the tally of arms was below what had been estimated. The town of Parramatta, instead of being in rebel hands, was locked up by the English soldiery and their auxiliaries; wives and children were barricaded in their homes but the rebels in the town were in hiding, frozen in inaction. On Constitution Hill a camp was set up around the tent of the two captains and their two column commanders, Humes and Hill. The French colonel's spirits and a lot of other requisitioned grog was drunk, no doubt to toasts of "Liberty or death", "Liberty, equality and fraternity", "Up the republic" and "God save Ireland".

The dawn brought a conference and a decision by the captains led by Cunningham, who had assumed the overall command. The force of 250 rebels would march to the Hawkesbury and raise the rebellion there. Red-eyes, dry throats and little sleep not withstanding, the rebels set out in high spirits. They gathered strength along the march as new recruits and some of the stragglers from the third and fourth columns reported in, and by the time they reached a spot near Second Ponds Creek numbered about 400. From a nearby hill, which became known as Vinegar Hill, the captains were almost in sight of their objective, what is now the town of Windsor. Behind them, however, in Parramatta, the Union Jack of England was still flying.

The first news of the rebellion reached the British command in Sydney at about midnight. With some shock Governor King read Captain Abbott's express despatch outlining the rising and the taking over of Castle Hill. He scarcely had time to decide what action to take when forty-five minutes later Lieutenant Hobby brought the news that rebel columns were moving on Parramatta. King responded by calling the military in Sydney to arms and parading the Sydney English loyalist militia numbering thirty-seven under their captain, Thomas Rowley. He sent a message to Captain Woodriff of the warship *Calcutta* to come ashore with as many marines and armed sailors as he could muster.[48] Appointing Lieutenant Governor William Paterson commander-in-chief in Sydney, he set out on horseback for Parramatta. Before he had left the outskirts of Sydney, King was overtaken by his Provost Marshall Thomas Smyth, four troopers and several civilians. The party halted briefly at Annandale, the residence of Major George Johnston, who was to play the key role in the Battle of Vinegar Hill and later carved a niche in Australian history as a rebel himself. Major Johnston was roused from his bed by a trooper. Quickly dressing, he walked from his house to the Parramatta road where King and his party rode up at full gallop. King informed him of the rebellion and told him that there were about 600 in the rebel army. He would push on to Parramatta he said, and Major Johnston was to take command of a detachment of the New South Wales Corps, comprising a lieutenant, a quartermaster, two sergeants and fifty-two infantry, that was following behind on foot.

The troops reached Annandale at 1.30 am, about the same time as the rebels were establishing their headquarters on Constitution Hill. After ensuring they were all properly armed, Major Johnston formed an advance guard and marched the force down the Parramatta road, just filling it from one side to the other.

It was about 4 am when Governor King and his bodyguard swept into Parramatta with the news that Major Johnston and "one hundred men" were close behind; the governor perhaps inflated the number of troops to calm the considerable panic that gripped Parramatta. A Mr Joyce, an English settler from Seven Hills, had escaped the rebels and reported to the barracks for duty. Sent out to reconnoitre, he returned with the news that the rebels were massing close to the town. All through the long night the soldiers and the armed auxiliaries represented by the constables and the Parramatta Loyal Associated Company of twenty-eight men under John Savage had stood to arms, waiting for an attack that never came.[49]

It was about 5 am and dawn was breaking when Major Johnston and the reinforcements arrived. King met them at the barracks and told them that he had ordered a dram and a half of spirits and a loaf for each man. When they were refreshed they were to march to Government House for further orders. King himself rushed on to Government House and set to furiously scribbling orders for Johnston to carry out. He also issued a proclamation of martial law:

> *I do therefore proclaim the districts of Parramatta, Castle Hill, Toongabbee, Prospect, Seven and Baulkham Hills, Hawkesbury, and Nepean to be in a state of rebellion, and do establish martial law throughout those districts.*

I do therefore strictly charge and command all His Majesty's liege subjects to be assisting in apprehending and giving up to the nearest officer or magistrate every person they may stop who is unprovided with a pass, under pain of being tried by a Court-Martial.

And every person who is seen in a state of rebellious opposition to the peace and tranquility of this colony, and does not give himself or themselves up within twenty-four hours, will be tried by Court-Martial and suffer the sentence to be passed upon him or them.

And if they or any of them give up the ringleaders to justice it may be an effectual means of procuring them that amnesty which it is so much my wish to grant.[50]

Within a half hour the troops, despite their long march, were assembled in front of Government House. The governor handed Johnston his orders. Johnston tried in vain to read the orders. King, somewhat put out, replied that he had better read them to him. The equally tired Johnston responded that King might as well have given them to him in Greek.[51]

Johnston, King explained, was to take half the force to the Park Gate west of the town to confront the rebels; and if they had not advanced so far, he was to march to Toongabbie then "wheel to the right" and go to Castle Hill to await further orders. Major Johnston, King added, should open fire at anyone who attempted to run away, which Johnston said later was the only order he wanted to enable him to make up his mind whether to go into battle or not.[52]

Dividing his force in two, Johnston sent half under Lieutenant Davies along the road to Castle Hill and set out with the other for Toongabbie where he was told the rebel forces, about 400 strong, were on top of Constitution Hill, then known as Sugar Loaf Hill. He attacked the top of the hill only to find the rebels had gone. Casting around for information, he found several men who had fled before the rebel advance. They had picked up the news that the rebels were advancing towards the Hawkesbury. Despite the heat of the day and the obvious exhaustion of his redcoats Johnston pushed on in pursuit. When he reached the fence enclosing the government stock reserve he found he was only about 1.5 kilometres behind the rebels. Ahead of them, on Vinegar Hill, rebel scouts reported the redcoats' advance and the force formed up in battle lines, confident that the four columns under Hill, Humes, Cunningham and Johnston, the last facing his English namesake for the first time, would prevail.

The man they were opposed to, however, was an experienced soldier. Major George Johnston was born in the little town of Annandale in Scotland in 1764 and at a young age secured a commission in the marines, serving in the American War of Independence and in action at New York and Halifax. Transferred to the East Indies he was seriously wounded in 1786 and subsequently joined the marine detachment earmarked for the garrison at Botany Bay. It is claimed he was the first man ashore from the First Fleet, although an English prisoner, James Ruse, who later became known as the colony's "first farmer", also claimed the honour. Within a year Johnston was appointed commander of the marines and in 1792 Phillip gave him command of a company of the New South Wales Corps which took over garrison duties.

It was then that Johnston decided to remain in the new land. Following the custom of many English officers at the time, he had taken a mistress from among the prisoners during the four month voyage of the First Fleet. Esther Abrahams had been convicted at London's Old Bailey of stealing some black silk lace and was transported for seven years. A literate, skilled young woman with a dark beauty of her own, she remained at his side even when he was made aide-de-camp to Governor Hunter in 1796, much to the resentment of the English wives. Despite the fact she came from England herself there were persistent rumours linking her with the Irish rebels and their objectives, which King described as "seditious and republican". It is likely that many identified her, being a prisoner, as a sympathiser.

In 1793 Johnston secured 100 acres (40 hectares) of land on the road to Parramatta, which he called Annandale after his birthplace. The name continues in the suburb today. He was sent to England for court martial for paying his sergeants in spirits, was never tried and returned to Sydney, home and mistress in 1802, resumed duty with the corps and it was business as usual for the officer rum merchants.

At forty Johnston was older than his opponents, and had served continuously in the forces of the Empire for more than a quarter of a century. He had seen action against the Americans and the French, and now he was to be tested against the Irish.

The Battle of Vinegar Hill

The sun was high in the sky as Johnston's force approached Vinegar Hill. Major Johnston, in his account of the battle, confessed to using a flag of truce, his own white handkerchief, to try to bring about a parley while he organised his forces and perhaps gained time for Governor King to join him.[53] Trooper Handlesack was sent to tell the rebel leaders of the forces advancing on them and order them to surrender. He came back unharmed with the flints taken out of his pistol and a message that there would be no surrender. Still playing for time Major Johnston sent another emissary. He had brought with him, whether by force or not is not known, Father James Dixon, the Catholic priest who had been put on the

The Battle of Vinegar Hill, a watercolour by an unknown artist.
REX NAN KIVELL COLLECTION, NATIONAL LIBRARY OF AUSTRALIA

governor's payroll by King. The rebels quickly sent him back with the same message, no surrender.[54]

It was at this point that Major Johnston, still parleying under the white flag of truce, decided on his ultimate trick, one which paralleled a rebellion against the English crown some 500 years before. As the rebels stood firm in line of battle on Vinegar Hill, Johnston's detachment formed up less than a kilometre away. Both sides were waiting for orders to attack.

It was just such a moment that turned the tide of English history when in 1381 the downtrodden peasants revolted against the government which ruled in the name of the boy king, Richard II. The English workers were in the straitjacket of a law called the "Statute of Labourers", which established a maximum limit on wages; poll taxes were imposed and the peasant worker also had to pay to his lord a range of other taxes—when he married off a daughter, for example, or sold a pig, or when somebody died.

In June 1381 a spontaneous revolt broke out. Wat Tyler of the English county of Kent, a charismatic leader of great eloquence and organising ability, brought the rebel forces together, maintained strict discipline and swept away all opposition to arrive at the very gates of London. The Great Company (Magna Societas), as the English rebels were described, was seen by later historians as a parallel to the United Irishmen. The powerful priest Father John Ball, also of Kent, had been setting alight the countryside for twenty years with his calls for justice for the oppressed. Now he preached a sermon which incited the crowd and coined the famous lines

Whan Adam dalf and Eve span,
Who was than a gentilman?[55]

which no doubt ran through the minds of some of the young Englishmen who joined the Irish rebels in 1804.

After the rebels entered the city, attacking the gaols and penetrating Lambeth Palace and the Tower of London, young King Richard rode out to parley with them. He promised them everything they asked for and more, and then, during the final parley with the King, the Mayor, William Walworth, struck Tyler with a sword and a minor squire ran a sword twice through his body. Tyler rode away shouting "Treason".[56] His supporters got him to hospital, but Walworth had him dragged back to the square where he had been struck and beheaded on the spot.[57]

The two men who killed Tyler received knighthoods from Richard II, and Tyler's head ended up on a spike on the walls of London.

It was not so much different at Vinegar Hill. Major Johnston, showing raw courage, now rode himself within pistol range, calling to the leaders to parley with him. They indicated that he could ride up to them and the flag of truce would be respected. The major challenged the rebel captains to come to him—"you have very little spirit if you don't come and speak to me".[58] Trusting the truce, Phillip Cunningham and William Johnston came forward. The major, playing the game out with consummate skill, spoke reasonably to them, pleaded with the captains to avoid bloodshed, said he only wanted a peaceful resolution of the problems, and promised to bring up Father Dixon again for a further discussion.

Having returned to his own lines, Major Johnston brought a detachment of ten men closer to the rebels and rode out again, this time accompanied by Father Dixon and Quartermaster Laycock. He noted that the rebels held their line of battle, stretching from the top of the hill down to Second Ponds Creek. Once again the captains came forward and Major Johnston and Dixon took it in turns to plead for surrender to prevent bloodshed. Phillip Cunningham's final reply was to cry "death or liberty",[59] whereupon, taking the captains by complete surprise Major Johnston pulled out a pistol he had stuck in his sash, put it to Cunningham's head and ordered him back to the English lines or have his soul blown to hell. The quartermaster, in an obviously prearranged plan, did the same to William Johnston.[60]

Cunningham had shown his adversary every courtesy. He arrived, took off his hat and hand on sword had entered into discussion. He was totally unprepared for the Englishman's duplicity when suddenly the gun was held at his head while Laycock prodded him with his sword. William Johnston was seized and held by the detachment of redcoats that Major Johnston had moved up as part of his plan to dishonour the flag of truce. The eyewitness to the deception and its sordid end was John Byrne, one of the insurgents who was also an associate of Joseph Holt, to whom he reported after the battle was over and who recorded the incident after he had returned to Ireland.

Having taken his captives back to the detachment, Johnston immediately ordered an attack on the rebel lines, which with the sudden and unexpected capture of their commanders were in confusion. The redcoats began to advance, pouring out their deadly fire while the rebels were still trying to come to grips with the fact they were leaderless and without orders. The rebels recovered sufficiently to return the fire but after firing a second volley the redcoats closed with bayonets. The rebels rallied for a second volley in reply, but were already under bayonet attack before it had been completed and the line broke.

It was the beginning of the end. The retreat quickly became a rout, the discharged muskets and pikes proving useless. More than twenty rebels were killed and wounded in the opening fire and the bayonet charge, and the English troops went on to take twenty-six prisoners.[61]

Although they had marched more than seventy kilometres since leaving Sydney, the victory gave Johnston's men renewed energy and they pushed on in pursuit of the rebels to Windsor. Here the ugliest act of revenge was perpetrated. Phillip Cunningham, certainly wounded and, according to some accounts, dead, was hanged the same evening from the staircase of the Government Stores as a warning to others.[62] Skirmishing continued all day as rebels fought a hopeless rearguard action. Rumours of reprisals ran rife through the colony; of how Johnston and his troops shot every third man among the captured rebels; how he strung up young men like dogs. The mists of time obscure many incidents on the battlefield itself, and estimates of the rebels killed range as high as sixty.

Three days later, on 8 March, a court martial was convened at Parramatta presided over by Captain Edward Abbott with all the pomp of the victorious Empire. The rebel captain William Johnston, captured on the field of battle by a trick, was there, together with Samuel Humes, Charles Hill and seven others. All were found guilty and sentenced to death, Johnston and Humes to be hanged in chains. Hill, Humes and John Place were hanged the same evening at Parramatta, Johnston, John Neale and George Harrington followed them to a tortured death at Castle Hill the next day, and John Brannon and Timothy Hogan were hanged in Sydney on 10 March. John Burke and Bryan McCormick were pardoned by King for reasons never recorded.[63] Seven other rebels were sentenced to receive between them 2600 lashes. Two more, Dennis Ryan and Bryan Riley, apparently sick or wounded, were sentenced to receive as "many lashes as they can bear" without killing them;[64] as a result of this act of mercy they received 164 lashes and 100 lashes respectively.

This was not by any means the end of the reprisals. Another group of thirty Irishmen were held in chain gangs, "incommunicado", until they were sent to a new penal settlement at Coal River (later Newcastle) where their beaten and starved bodies became the shield for the military expedition which was to take yet another parcel of land from the original people of the continent.[65] They were sentenced not only to silence but to work without rest except to eat and on the Sabbath.

The English establishment determined to take no chances that such an event would happen again. Persecution of the Irish continued relentlessly. Joseph Holt was arrested even though he had spent the entire time holed up with an Englishman and his family. Just as a precaution—there was no trial, no proof of guilt—he was sent to Norfolk Island.[66] Miraculously he survived, eventually returning to Ireland where he died and was buried in peace and honour. His offence was being Irish and refusing ever to deny his origins. It was said by an Irish historian that there are two categories of Irish—those who may come from Ireland and those who are indeed Irish men and women; Holt remained an Irishman. In his memoirs he was critical of the rebel captains for falling for the English trap. He wrote, perhaps harshly, of the young Phillip Cunningham: "But what else could have been expected from the conduct of a general who

Rebel prisoners were hanged publicly within days of the battle. Frontispiece from Life and Death of John Carpenter, *published in London in 1805.*
REX NAN KIVELL COLLECTION, NATIONAL LIBRARY OF AUSTRALIA

would condescend to take off his hat to the captain of an opposing force? If I had been in Cunningham's place I would have taken Captain Johnston's head instead of my own hat".[67]

This was the spirit of General Holt who had kept the whole of County Wicklow and the borders of the counties of Kildare and Dublin in a state of insurrection. Tribute was paid to his boldness and his army of 1500 men which had forced most of the English forces in Wicklow to flee before him. Had he been the general commanding at Vinegar Hill, cut off Major Johnston's head, surprised his small force and scattered them to the winds, perhaps the rebels would have captured Parramatta and marched on to Sydney to proclaim the first Irish Republic.

The final act of retribution and one long-lasting result of the Battle of Vinegar Hill was the view taken by the Imperial authorities of Catholics of all backgrounds. Martial law was lifted within seven days but after only twelve months of religious freedom King and his successors suppressed the practice of the Catholic faith in the colony for ten long years. In defiance of either evidence or commonsense, King held Father Dixon responsible for failing to prevent the rebellion. For "very improper conduct, and to prevent the seditious meetings that took place in consequence of the indulgence and protection he received",[68] King cut off his salary. Having been appointed prefect apostolic of New Holland by Rome, Dixon remained in New South Wales for another four years.[69] While it can be imagined how his work was made almost impossible by his own role in the betrayal of the Irish captains, he continued to officiate at marriages, baptisms and funerals. He survived, however, by permission of the English, who felt he had served them well, and on the cold charity of his own. He returned to Ireland in 1808. Father Harold, the singer of Irish songs, returned from Norfolk Island in the same year; he later went to the United States and eventually returned to Ireland where he died.

The night of persecution which descended on the Irish and on Catholics generally was fostered by people such as Samuel Marsden, who proclaimed, "It is more than probable that if the Catholic Religion was once allowed to be celebrated by Authority, that the colony would be lost to the British Empire in less than one year".[70] Carried away with anti-Irish spleen and his own religious bigotry, Marsden said of the Irish prisoners that they were "wild, ignorant and savage . . . men that have been familiar with Robberies, Murders every Horrid Crime since their infancy . . . destitute of every Principle of Religion and Morality".[71] The Mass was simply an assembly to plan assassination, arson and destruction and encourage the "natural ferocity" of Irish Catholics. His solution was simple—complete suppression of the faith and the seizure of all Irish children to be forceably indoctrinated with loyalty to the British Empire.

Until 1818 Catholics in the infant colony were abandoned by all. Not one voice was raised for them from Rome to Dublin to London.

Catholic prisoners were compelled to attend English church services; if they refused they were sentenced to twenty-five lashes, if they refused a second time they were given fifty lashes, and if they persisted they were sent to Norfolk Island. It is little wonder that the Catholic Church in Australia held one hymn above all others:

O Faith of our fathers, living still
In spite of dungeons, fire, and sword:
Oh, how our hearts beat high with joy
Whene'er we hear that glorious word!
O Faith of our fathers! Holy Faith!
We will be true to thee till death.

Our fathers, chained in prisons dark,
Were still in heart and conscience free:
How sweet would be their children's fate,
If they, like them, could die for thee!
O Faith of our fathers! Holy Faith!
We will be true to thee till death.

O Faith of our fathers, we will love
Both friend and foe in all our strife,
And preach thee too, as love knows how,
By kindly words and virtuous life:
O Faith of our fathers! Holy Faith!
We will be true to thee till death.[72]

No doubt remembering the French support for the Irish in 1798, King lost no time in expelling François de Riveau (spelled variously Duriault or Girault), one of two Frenchmen brought out by the government in 1800 to grow grapes for wine making. The other, Antoine Landrien, had already applied to return to England and was supposed to sail on the *Calcutta*, whose departure had been delayed by the rebellion. De Riveau left under armed guard when the *Calcutta* finally departed on 16 March; he was never charged but was believed to have aided and abetted the rebellion. This was small revenge against a tiny French presence in the colony but revenge nonetheless.[73]

Having dispersed the Irish and suppressed the practice of their faith, and banished the French, King turned his attention to the last of the five men who had been tried in Scotland in 1793 and 1794 for such crimes as advocating democracy, only two of whom were actually Scottish born. By the time King arrived in New South Wales two had died in Sydney. Thomas Muir, who was sarcastically described by King as one of the "Scottish martyres", had escaped in 1796 and died in France three years later. Palmer had completed his sentence and went to Guam where he died in 1802. This left Maurice Margarot, who had been transported from Scotland for advocating constitutional reform. King had him "dispersed" to the outer bounds of settlement.[74]

The final act of repression was an attempt to wipe the Battle of Vinegar Hill from the memory of all Australians. In colonial history books it was ignored, or recorded only as a footnote about "revolting Irish convicts". Even the name Vinegar Hill failed to survive on the post office which was opened there in 1857: it was changed to Rouse Hill. But the folk memory is persistent. Just fifty years after the Battle of Vinegar Hill during another strike for freedom at Eureka the password was "Vinegar Hill", and today the site of the battle is part of our national heritage.

The young Irish captains died in their prime, their names all but forgotten until more than a century later. Major George Johnston, in contrast, went on to rich rewards. In 1804 he was given 2000 acres (808 hectares) of land in the Cabramatta district and then in 1817 another 1500 acres (607 hectares) in the Illawarra. He kept Esther by his side despite suggestions of her support for the rebels. It was even rumoured that the Irish captains had come forward so readily to parley with Johnston under the white flag of truce because they had a message from Esther that he would take his troops and join them in a bold bid to establish an independent colony of free men and women.

It was a mere dream, or a vain hope, but paradoxically Major Johnston, backed by John Macarthur, started his own rebellion only four years later on Australia Day 1808. He seized the apparatus of government, put Governor Bligh under arrest and attempted to deport him, suspended Judge Advocate Atkins and all other civilian officials and proclaimed himself lieutenant governor. This military junta lasted a half a year and was much to the advantage of Macarthur, who virtually ran the colony, maintaining the rum business as usual and continuing to distribute huge tracts of land among the band of officers whose power Bligh had unsuccessfully challenged.

Johnston survived the reimposition of London's rule, married his mistress and founded a successful and eminent family. Esther built her own fortune, by 1828 having amassed holdings of 2460 acres (995 hectares) in her own name. One of her sons became an officer in the English navy, and a grandson was auditor-general of New South Wales.

History turned the full circle on 4 March 1983 when the first official commemoration of the Battle of Vinegar Hill was held, 179 years after the event. The ceremony was attended by Bert Weston, a great grandson of George and Esther Johnston, and another of their descendants, John Higman, who were welcomed by the then Mayor of Blacktown, Kevin Kelly, whose family survived the defeat and the dungeons to become part of modern Australia.

The battles for liberty at Vinegar Hill and Eureka were lost but the war was won in the long run. Irish Australians today comprise more than a quarter of the population and are represented at every level of society. The Federal Cabinet has more Irish men and women than any government outside Ireland itself. The independent Republic of Ireland maintains an embassy in Canberra; Australia reciprocates with an embassy in Dublin. The Irish language is heard on radio in most of Australia's capital cities and Irish national day is observed across the continent.

The young captains and the men who died with them at Vinegar Hill can rest in peace. We have the liberty they fought for.

6. THE BATTLE OF BATHURST

The decisive battles of Parramatta and the Hawkesbury and their bloody aftermath broke the back of the resistance of the Eora and Dharuk peoples within twenty years of the invasion. The conquest was all but complete, the land occupied and the people dead, driven south and west, or reduced to tragic dependence on their conquerors' handouts. The combination of the English invaders' firepower and the diseases they carried with them like an arsenal of secret weapons proved irresistible, but the English appetite for land was insatiable and the march to the west continued. The shields of the Eora and Dharuk peoples may have been hurled aside but the invaders soon found themselves confronted by a third proud and powerful nation, the Wiradjuri, one of the great nations of eastern Australia. Although they had been alerted by the disasters that had befallen their neighbours, once again the social and political organisation of the Australians proved inadequate for the waging of continued, sustained and total war.

Breaking Out of the Pale

The struggle for the lands west of the Great Dividing Range, which culminated in the Battle of Bathurst in 1824, began according to the accounts of the time in 1804 with the crossing of the great natural barrier, the Blue Mountains, by an escaped prisoner whose reward was a lashing and transportation to Norfolk Island.[1] The official credit, however, goes to Gregory Blaxland, William Charles Wentworth and William Lawson, who crossed the mountains in 1813 and penetrated to within several kilometres east of the crest of the Divide to a spot now known as Mount Blaxland. The people of the area withdrew before them, making sure there was no contact with what they rightly assumed was an advance party of the invading force already entrenched in the Sydney area. The

Englishmen were aware they were under observation. In his journal Blaxland recorded that at Cox River they stumbled upon a camp with fires still burning and the flowers of the native honeysuckle, a source of food, still scattered everywhere; he observed that the flowers shaped like a bottlebrush were full of honey.[2] It was perhaps significant that he found also shavings and pieces of sharp stones which had been used for sharpening spears littered around the site.

Although Blaxland, Wentworth and Lawson had not crossed the Divide, they had conquered the major obstacle to westward expansion—the sheer cliffs and deep gorges of the Blue Mountains—and news of their success must have pleased Governor Lachlan Macquarie.

Often hailed as the most outstanding of all English governors, Macquarie was in fact a Highland Scot born on the island of Ulva in the Scottish Hebrides. Accompanied by his second wife, Elizabeth Campbell, and the Royal Highlanders (73rd Regiment), he had been sent to clean up a colony in total disarray. After years of corrupt and inept administration by the New South Wales Corps, which culminated in the Rum Rebellion and their arrest of Governor Bligh, periodic shortages of basic foodstuffs were common, public prostitution was a way of life, the few public buildings were in ruins, roads and bridges were impassable, rum was the basic currency and barter the usual mode of trade, and speculation in land was rife. Typical of life in Sydney Town is the story of two drunken army officers who noticed a woman they fancied in Pitt Street. They propositioned her in plain, Anglo-Saxon terms and she ran into the house of a couple she knew. When they banged on the door, the owner opened up and told them, "Oh, oh, if it's fucking you want, I can give you enough if you do not be off". The officers beat him to death and as they left one said, "If he is dead let him die, and be damned".[3] They were subsequently fined one shilling and sentenced to six months in gaol.

Macquarie's fighting Highlanders were to replace the New South Wales Corps, and at Rio de Janeiro he heard that the leaders of the rebellion, Johnston and Macarthur, had left for London. On the last day of 1809 Macquarie stepped ashore in Sydney to the roar of the guns from the warships and the Dawes Point batteries, and who but Lieutenant-Colonels William Paterson and Joseph Foveaux were there to receive him.[4] After a grand parade of all the forces—the battle-hardened Highlanders as well as the somewhat seedy New South Wales Corps—more firing of muskets and roar of cannon, Macquarie made a speech that left no one in doubt about his resolve to govern rightly and strongly. Significantly, he called for an end to the hostilities with the people of the continent and asked for "kindness and attention" to replace molestation.[5] Needless to say the rebellion was over.

This formidable protagonist was to prove, perhaps with Captain James

Life in Sydney Town in the early decades of the nineteenth century was not as idyllic as this view from The Rocks by convict artist John Eyre might suggest.
HANDCOLOURED AQUATINT 1806, NATIONAL LIBRARY OF AUSTRALIA

Stirling in Western Australia, the most effective officer ever to serve in Australia. He reorganised the administration, laid the foundations of organised commerce and finance and imported Spanish dollars for Australia's first coinage. During his term of office more than 200 public buildings were erected in Sydney, Hobart, Newcastle, and the towns of Liverpool and Windsor which began to develop after the defeat of the Eora and Dharuk peoples. He also made the decision to invade the lands of the Wiradjuri people. The Imperial authorities were still footing a large bill for the occupation and maintenance of their toehold on the continent with little prospect of cash returns. Macquarie faced the task of demonstrating that a continuation of operations was worthwhile, the alternative being the abandonment of the colony.

Almost from the beginning of his rule Macquarie looked to break out of the coastal areas to the west. To the prisoners groaning under the terrible tyranny of the time, the land beyond the Blue Mountains held out dreams of a new life of freedom. The new owners of the Eora and Dharuk lands also had dreams. But greedy for quick returns they had cleared vast areas of virgin bush, overstocked and overworked the land and now faced the eternal Australian problem of drought. In 1812 the shortage of stock feed was made worse by plagues of caterpillars,[6] which for some years defended their native heath even more effectively than the people. In that year a House of Commons committee established to look at the colony observed: "The settlement of New South Wales is bounded on the north, west and south by a ridge of hills known by the name of the Blue Mountains beyond which no one has yet to penetrate the country . . . beyond these, it is stated, the colony will not be capable of extension."[7] Macquarie continued the policy of handing out land (he gave away 228,000 acres (92,268 hectares) in less than ten years), but the graziers wanted still more. Blaxland, Wentworth and Lawson were all graziers, motivated in their push to the west by the search for new pastures. The trio's successful venture thus came at an appropriate time and was rewarded in the fashion of the day by land grants. William Lawson, who had come to Sydney with the New South Wales Corps in 1800 had been commandant at Newcastle in 1808, was the surveyor of the party and received 1000 acres (400 hectares) west of the Divide as a reward. Wentworth and Blaxland received similar grants, although the latter, whom Macquarie found a pushy member of the ruling clique, did not think it was sufficient.[8]

Within six months of their crossing Macquarie ordered a further expedition led by Assistant Surveyor George William Evans to complete the conquest of the Great Dividing Range. For five or six days Evans and his party climbed and stumbled until they reached the summit five kilometres from Mount Blaxland. Looking across the wide almost treeless plains, Evans recorded that they could see forty miles (sixty-four kilometres) towards the western horizon. They pushed on, descending the western slopes until they reached and crossed the Fish River and camped near Bindi Hill. They had crossed into the lands of the Wiradjuri. Fascinated by the open country they followed the course of the Fish River until it joined the Campbell; the confluence Evans named Macquarie in honour of the governor. On 1 December 1813 Evans became the first Englishman to see what would become the site of Bathurst.

For mile after mile the intruders had been watched by the Wiradjuri, as Evans was well aware: "I think they are watching us," he was to write in his journal.[9] Time and again they encountered fresh tracks and still-warm camp fires but the Wiradjuri withdrew, avoiding any contact. In three weeks in Wiradjuri country Evans and his party did not see a Wiradjuri let alone meet any. He reached a point on the Macquarie River near Killongbutta and continued downstream, passing the junction of Winburndale Rivulet, until he reached a point eleven kilometres south of the present town of Hill End and nearly 160 kilometres west of Mount Blaxland.[10]

There the party rested and three days later, on 21 December 1813, on their way back, the first historic meeting took place. Evans had been reconnoitring away from the river and on his return saw smoke on the north side of the river. At sunset the Englishmen were quietly fishing when two Wiradjuri women and four children appeared. Stumbling on the armed men was a frightening experience. The women screamed, the children cried, but Evans sought to reassure them. He gave them presents of fish, some fishhooks, twine and a tomahawk. The women indicated their thanks but two of the children ran away. The women tried to communicate with the strangers and the gesticulating on both sides led to some good humoured laughter before the Wiradjuri continued on their way to camp, which was indicated by the smoke Evans had noticed.[11] The peaceful encounter took place in the vicinity of Mountain Pleasant, about eight kilometres down the Macquarie River from the present city of Bathurst. Evans reported the meeting in full and told Macquarie he estimated the entire area was heavily populated[12]—camp fires had blazed all around them, although the Wiradjuri held to their policy of strategic withdrawal.

The fortunes of Evans, who hailed from Warwick in England, had fluctuated since his arrival in the colony in 1802. He had supported Bligh in the Rum Rebellion; was at one stage charged with fraud; but in his mid-thirties was appointed deputy surveyor of Van Diemen's Land by Macquarie. As a reward for his successful reconnaissance of Wiradjuri land he was handsomely rewarded with both cash and 1000 acres of land in Van Diemen's Land.

Once Macquarie had received Evans' detailed reports he began to plan, carefully and methodically, the invasion of the west. As 1814 dawned

Governor Lachlan Macquarie. NATIONAL LIBRARY OF AUSTRALIA

he was reporting to London that "all vegetation is again at a Stand. The Ponds and Streams again Exhausted, and the Cattle once more Sickening and dying from Actual Want of Food and Water".[13] The drought and the relentless attacks by patriotic Australian caterpillars on the invaders' crops were wreaking havoc, lending urgency to the graziers' pleas to move their stock west. But Macquarie had no intention of allowing his lines of advance to be extended in an unplanned and uncontrolled way, and guided by his military experience in Egypt, India and Sri Lanka he determined to build a new highway aimed right at the heart of the Wiradjuri country, which he proposed to call "West-more-Land". The road was started in July 1814 and followed closely the Blaxland and Evans route. Prisoners who volunteered to work on it were offered free pardons if the road was completed on time, and the project was placed in the charge of William Cox, who had joined the New South Wales Corps in 1797 as a lieutenant and in 1799 sailed to Sydney. (His name is also associated with the Battle of Vinegar Hill as the Irish prisoner General Joseph Holt was his overseer.)

Macquarie was delighted when Cox reported in January 1815 that the road had been finished, and in record time. He named both the Blue Mountains pass down Mount York and the river just below it after Cox, to whom he gave 2000 acres (800 hectares) of land across the river from Bathurst. Lawson and Cox thus vie for the honour of being the first Englishmen to be allocated Wiradjuri land. In his report on the new lands to his distant superior, Lord Bathurst, the governor also recommended that Cox should receive a payment of £300 for his labours, and that he be made commandant of the proposed settlement at Bathurst.

In April 1815 Macquarie decided on a personal foray across the mountains. On 25 April he set out like a conqueror, accompanied by his wife and a retinue of more than fifty people including Cox, Evans, Surveyor General John Oxley, his ADC Captain H. C. Antill and the naturalist and artist John Lewin. Ever the cautious soldier, Macquarie had no intention of pushing into possibly hostile country without an advance guard, and sent a detachment of military and prisoners ahead of the main party to form a base near the junction of Vale Creek and the Macquarie River at the lower end of what today is William Street, Bathurst.[14] The silent watchers of the Wiradjuri let them pass without let or hindrance and when the base was established and it appeared the party was determined to stay for a while the second recorded contact was made. Perhaps it was the friendliness of the good Evans that influenced three Wiradjuri men and four marvelling young boys to appear as if from nowhere in their long possum-skin cloaks.

They stayed to watch the arrival of Macquarie on 4 May with carriage and horses and all the pomp and ceremony of a potentate on the move through conquered lands. The Englishmen, soldiers and prisoners alike, had attempted conversation with the Wiradjuri and friendship was established by frantic and sometimes amusing gesticulation on both sides. Macquarie was to write in his journal that the Wiradjuri cloaks were neatly sewn and carved in a unique manner, and that the people were friendly and clean.[15] Captain Antill made similar comments, and described how a military barber cut the beards of the warriors to demonstrate the use of scissors. They were interested in everything, laughed a great deal at the visitors and their antics, and impressed everyone with their friendliness, good humour and mild manners.[16]

Macquarie later wrote in his journal: "At this beautiful spot I have established my Headquarters for the present, intending hereafter to erect a town and township here for the convenience and accommodation of such settlers as may be indulged with grants of land in this new discovered country".[17] Three days later, on Sunday, 7 May, he officially inaugurated the town of Bathurst, which he named after Henry, Earl Bathurst, who had the responsibilities for the colonies of the British Crown. Richard Lewis, one of Evans' earlier companions, was appointed superintendent of the "Government settlement at Bathurst" with a garrison of six soldiers and six prisoners who were given orders to clear and establish crops on several hectares of land.[18]

The Wiradjuri watched the goings on, oblivious to the fact that the three cheers, the unfurling flag and the cries of "God save the Queen" meant they had been dispossessed and that the invasion and inevitable war with these seemingly friendly if overdressed popinjays would soon be upon them.

Macquarie's sally into the lands of the Wiradjuri was marked by friendly relations. In his journeying around the area he met an old, infirm Wiradjuri woman with her grandson. She was terrified by the apparition of horses and soldiers. Macquarie gravely presented her with some biscuits, which she put in her bag and hurried away to join her grandson.[19] The next day he came upon a bora or ceremonial ground (which, although it is more than a century since the last ceremonies in the area were performed, still survives today).

On 10 May Macquarie recorded that the English camp was visited by a delegation of Wiradjuri warriors. It is believed to be the first meeting between the great Wiradjuri leader Windradyne and the leader of the English colony. Macquarie was impressed. He described the three warriors as "handsome good looking young men",[20] and they must have looked regal in their long ornamented cloaks, holding their spears like long sceptres as they came forward. Macquarie, ever sensitive and observing, noted the leader as the "best looking and stoutest" and very properly made him a ceremonial presentation of tomahawks and yellow cloth.[21] Windradyne solemnly accepted the gifts as from one leader to another and in return made a present to Macquarie of one of the possum-skin cloaks which the governor had obviously admired from his first contact with the Wiradjuri. The friendly intercourse continued. The same afternoon the Wiradjuri delegation returned with eleven more warriors and again there was an exchange of gifts, Macquarie giving them black leather caps and tomahawks.[22] Lewin made sketches of much that occurred and painted a portrait believed to be of Windradyne who he called "A native chief of Bathurst".[23]

On 11 May Macquarie and his party began the long trek back to Sydney. As an obvious sign of respect and friendship Windradyne and his party came to take their farewells, which Macquarie noted with appreciation. The return was triumphant: he had pushed across the mountain barrier, founded a new town and established friendly relations with a powerful people, which none of his predecessors had ever been able to do.

Before leaving, he sent a small party under George Evans to explore south-west of Bathurst. On 13 May Evans set out along Queen Charlotte's Vale Creek and by 25 May had reached the Lachlan River, which he named for the governor, several kilometres downstream from the site of the present town of Cowra. He followed the Lachlan until 31 May, when he was near what is now Nanami, before turning back. That word of the amicable meetings at Bathurst had spread among the Wiradjuri became apparent on this trip. The Australians abandoned their strategy of retreat and often waved to Evans' party, but undoubtedly for many there was an element of fear. Two or three times a day the Englishmen saw Wiradjuri, but they kept their distance. On 31 May a woman who had obviously wandered away from the family found herself confronted by these apparitions. Evans gave her presents, including a tomahawk, and after relieved thanks the woman ran back to her folk.[24] Shortly after, they took a warrior by surprise. The startled Wiradjuri, spear and boomerang in hand, climbed the tallest tree in sight and ignored every inducement to come down. Evans gave up and stuck a tomahawk in the tree as a present.[25]

On his return to Sydney Governor Macquarie made it clear that no land would be granted west of the mountains until approval was received from the Imperial authorities. To prevent unauthorised occupation he stationed a military detachment on the new road and issued a general order that no person, civil or military, was to attempt the crossing without making written application to the governor. Individuals he described as "gentlemen, or other respectable free persons" could be issued with permits to at least inspect the new frontiers.[26]

He did, however, allow stock to be taken over the mountains to escape the drought. As early as July 1815 William Lawson moved 100 head of cattle to his promised grant—the first in the area—south of the Fish River. In 1818 Macquarie decided to allow ten men each to take up fifty acres (twenty hectares) of farmland and a two acre (almost one hectare) town allotment on the north bank opposite Kelso. In that year, too, William Cox received his promised appointment as commandant at Bathurst. By 1820 Cox had 5000 sheep on his Bathurst property and had built a complex of farm buildings. His son William acquired 700 acres (283 hectares) in the district in 1823, when Cox secured a further grant of 1000 acres.

In 1819 Lawson replaced Cox as commandant of Bathurst and was appointed commander of all English troops west of the Blue Mountains. He used Bathurst as a base to open up the Mudgee district in 1820–21, establishing a track from Bathurst north to what would become Mudgee on the Cudgegong River and through to the Goulburn River. He amassed properties in the Mudgee district, which extended to the Talbragar River. In 1824, the year of the Battle of Bathurst, he resigned his post at Bathurst and retired to Prospect.

Despite Macquarie's restrictions, white settlement continued steadily, although land south of the Macquarie River was closed to private settlement. By the time Macquarie made his second visit to Bathurst in 1821 the white population numbered 287 of whom 210 were prisoners. In 1823 Assistant Surveyor J. McBrian surveyed grants on the north side of the Macquarie and on the Fish River and Winburndale Rivulet before handing over to Robert Hoddle.

Up to this time there was no general outbreak of hostilities between the invaders and the Wiradjuri, but tension grew as white numbers increased and the sheep and cattle herds expanded dramatically.

Macquarie had already given some thought to the position of Black Australians in the colony. He told Bathurst in London that while the people of the continent were "rude and uncivilized" they had qualities which "if properly cultivated and encouraged might render them . . .progressively useful to the country either as agricultural labourers or a lower class of mechanics". They needed "the fostering hand of time, gentle means, and conciliatory manner".[27] In 1814 he established a training institution for black boys and girls at Parramatta and a farm on the shores of Port Jackson to teach agriculture.[28] But he failed miserably in his efforts to Europeanise them and at Parramatta most of the children were taken away by their parents. The war against the Eora and the Dharuk was only ten years behind and the people had not forgotten their defeat, the loss of their land, and their treatment by white predators without women: there were still sparks of resistance among the survivors that flared occasionally.

In 1816 Macquarie reacted with harshness which contrasted strangely with his friendly stance at Bathurst the year before.[29] On 10 April he sent three detachments to the Hawkesbury, Grose and Nepean Rivers with the express purpose of driving the remaining Eora and Dharuk people away from "British settlements" into "remote parts of the country". A score or more warriors were killed and far from expressing regret that innocent women and children had also died, Macquarie hoped that this would "strike terror" amongst the defenders of their land. On 4 May, while the operation was still in action, the governor issued a proclamation addressed to the Eora and Dharuk—"the Ab-origines or Black Natives of this country".[30]

The proclamation began by offering testimony to the strength of the resistance which despite two major defeats was causing "great Terror, Loss and Distress" to the English settlers. For this reason, it then declared, from 4 June 1816 (the birthday of the by then mad King George III) any Black Australian, whether singly or in a group, was prohibited from approaching within one mile of any town, village or farm occupied or owned by any "British subject" if they were carrying spears, clubs or waddies. If they did they could be shot.[31] If a group of more than six people, even though unarmed, ventured near a farm they could be shot. Ceremonial assemblies, even for religious purposes and whether on occupied or unoccupied land, were banned.

The proclamation thus gave landowners and their yellow-clad prisoner servants the right to treat as an enemy both armed and unarmed Black Australians and to kill them at will.

To those who were prepared to abide by these restrictions and to acknowledge the authority of the British Crown Macquarie offered a "passport", signed by the governor, that would protect them from English bullets. He also offered a grant of some of their own land, food for six months, tools and seeds, and clothes and a blanket from government stores to any who agreed to settle down on that "farm".

The 1816 proclamation also inaugurated an annual feast and conference—a levee in the tradition of the British Empire in India—which Macquarie hoped would encourage the Australians to consult about their concerns.[32] To be held in the market place at Parramatta on 28 December each year (unless this was a Sunday), the conference also provided Macquarie with an opportunity to reward those who had given good service. Among the first so recognised were Nurragingy (alias Creek Jemmy) and his friend Colby to whom Macquarie promised a grant of thirty acres (twelve hectares). Land adjacent to Bell Creek beside the present Richmond Road was granted in 1819; their families held it until about 1920 when the State in the form of the Aboriginal Protection Board assumed control of it.

The conferences were continued by Macquarie's successor Thomas Brisbane but were discarded by Governor Bourke in 1835 when it was not considered worthwhile assembling the survivors of nearly fifty years of white occupation.

It was a major stain on Macquarie's rule that he sanctioned the killing of unarmed people and banned them from coming together for any purpose. The essence of the 1816 proclamation was used for a century as an excuse to kill on impulse. Seemingly so out of character, its harshness may have been influenced by a bout of ill health brought on by syphillis which he had contracted while on service in Egypt.

Macquarie was able to hold the peace beyond the mountains until he returned to England in 1822, and his own people in fact gave him more concern than the Wiradjuri. The coterie of military bandits and their civilian accomplices who had enriched themselves from land and the rum trade monopoly were jealous of their newly won status. Macquarie, however, seemed to despise them and outraged them by extending a hand in friendship and reconciliation to prisoners who had served their time. He and his wife frequently dined with these emancipists and he appointed them to posts of authority and significance. The flogging parson, Samuel Marsden, led attacks on Macquarie,[33] both in Sydney and in the Imperial capital, pouring out calumnies as prolific as his hellfire sermons, which threatened in the name of God all who disagreed with him or questioned his very questionable gains.

Ilnesses and the wear and tear of more than forty years of active service led Macquarie to seek permission to resign and early in 1822 he sailed from Sydney. He retired to his rain soaked cottage on his estate in Mull, but died in London only two years after his return. History vindicates his place in Australian history and Australia treasures his tomb in Mull (it is administered by the National Trust), while he, his wife and son have more places named after them than any family in the history of the continent.

Macquarie's successor, Governor Brisbane, who was to declare war on the Wiradjuri people, was an imposing man in his late forties, 182 centimetres tall. A Scotsman from Ayreshire with the given names of Thomas Makdougall, he joined the British Army at the age of sixteen and after a career of soldiering in Europe, the West Indies and India went on to become a lieutenant general. He fought against Napoleon in Spain, against the invasion forces of the United States in Canada and was part of the occupation forces in France after the defeat of Napoleon. Both the Duke of Wellington, one of the heroes of the Battle of Waterloo, and Joseph Banks recommended Brisbane for the position of governor of New South Wales. By the time of his arrival in Sydney in November 1821 his main interests were science and astronomy.

Brisbane was accompanied by his wife and infant daughter, his sister-in-law, his wife's personal physician, a German astronomer, a Scots astronomical instrument-maker, a Scots governess, several Irish maids and a French chef—the English butler, however, had been abandoned

Governor Thomas Brisbane. NATIONAL LIBRARY OF AUSTRALIA

in Rio de Janeiro for drunkenness.[34] He arrived with more luggage than anyone in the colony had seen before. It included a fine piano for his wife, a harp for her sister, several boxes of astronomical equipment and an extensive wine cellar purchased at Madeira on the voyage from England.[35]

Brisbane was far too wrapped up in a vice-regal lifestyle and his astronomical interests to become very much involved in administration. The colony was virtually run by two men, John Oxley, who was the surveyor general, and Major Frederick Goulburn, the colonial secretary, who held a brief for the land barons bent on adding to their holdings.[36] Both were opposed to the Macquarie policy of welcoming into the fold the prisoners who had served their time.

Brisbane's main contribution to the problems of the day was to cut back the expense of the colony to the Imperial government. He saw a colony with a good climate and unlimited supplies of land and cheap labour in which the government was supporting the people when the people should, and, he believed, could, be supporting the government. Briefed by Macquarie's enemies, he cast his eye around Sydney and disapproved of the large number of prisoners employed on government works.[37] Work on roads and bridges was stopped and the prisoners were put into chain gangs which were hired out to landholders for tasks such as land clearing. From the 3s 6d per week received for the prisoners at work, Brisbane decided to pay cash to the convict overseers who previously had received increased rations and convict servants.[38] For each prisoner maintained free of expense to the administration a landholder would receive 100 acres.

Brisbane found the landholders had an "insatiable greed" for more land but because he failed to govern diligently the two men who exercised power in his name, Oxley and Goulburn, allowed the unplanned and unregulated occupation of thousands of hectares of Wiradjuri land along the Fish and Macquarie Rivers.[39] From 1822 to 1824 the invasion went ahead, without Brisbane approving or knowing; Frederick Goulburn, in fact, used to alter Brisbane's orders, issue other orders in Brisbane's name on his own authority and when necessary put words into Brisbane's mouth.[40] Bathurst itself was developed as a military and supply base. The friendship with the Wiradjuri established by Macquarie and Evans faced incredible strains as the redcoats arrived with yellow-clad prisoners, directed by the land barons to take over at musket point the best land and permanent water supplies and to occupy the Wiradjuri camp sites which were usually close to water, well drained and with ready access to food resources.

The invasion happened so quickly and from so many points along the Wiradjuri's open frontier that each week saw fresh incursions. The Wiradjuri noted with alarm the deadly nature of the firearms of the invaders—game of all kinds was shot, not just for food but for sport, and what the guns failed to kill the hunting dogs the English brought with them did. The invasion by the soldiers and chain gangs was bad enough, but the great herds of cattle and sheep that came with them destroyed the Wiradjuri's vegetable foods and fouled their water supplies. Taken off guard the people found themselves being dispossessed almost overnight. Colonel Godfrey Charles Mundy, an Englishman who visited the Bathurst district some thirty years after the arrival of the first settlers, observed that the land had been taken over "neither by inheritance, by purchase nor by conquest but by a sort of gradual eviction".[41]

> *As our flocks and herds and population increase, and corresponding increase of space is required, the natural owners of the soil are thrust back without treaty, bargain or apology. A tract of rich verdant pasture is heard of through a surveyor, or through some adventurous settler or stockman, riding in search of fresh "runs", and in an incredibly short time it is overrun with livestock.*[42]

Mundy pointed with amazement to the speed and totality of the invasion: "stations are built, the natives and the game upon which they feed are driven back—the latter chased and killed by the Englishmen's greyhounds, the graves of their fathers trodden underfoot by strangers . . . "[43]

The invaders took the peaceful confusion of the Wiradjuri, faced with the superior firepower of the military, for weakness. Armed also with the view that as conquerors they had a right to do as they pleased, and having already taken land and food at will, they now turned to the Wiradjuri women. Husbands and parents saw wives and daughters taken by force and raped, repeatedly abused publicly and collectively. By 1822, when the Wiradjuri gathered their strength to strike back, there was already on their soil the blood of individuals who had died in defence of their families.

One of the early landholders in the district was George Suttor, who received a grazing licence from Brisbane in 1822 and later a grant on Winburndale Rivulet that became the Suttor family home, Brucedale. One of his sons, William Henry Suttor, a member of the New South Wales Legislative Council, defended both those who set out to expand without violence and plunder, and the reaction of the Wiradjuri.[44] "So it came to pass", he wrote,

> *that the blacks were not allowed to wander at pleasure, hunting kangaroo and emu and chopping out the sleepy o'possum everywhere as had been their custom. And as without such hunting . . . the hunger was providing rather a bar to the peaceable settlement of the country and no doubt ill-feeling was thereby created between the two races.*[45]

Suttor saw the tragedy of the Wiradjuri being forced from their own land and driven into the barren hills and mountains to starve. He recognised that among the English settlers there were some with a desire to make peace not war, but that the soldiers and the prisoners—the dreaded wearers of the coats of red, blue and yellow—raped and looted and regarded the Wiradjuri as "a sort of dangerous wild animal whose speedy extermination was the best possible thing that could happen".[46]

The Wiradjuri

The lands of the Wiradjuri people covered an area larger than England, extending from the western foothills of the Blue Mountains and today's city of Lithgow just over 500 kilometres west to the Hay district, north beyond Dubbo and south to the Murray River and Albury. The Wiradjuri occupied almost the entire length of the Murrumbidgee and Lachlan Rivers and 100 kilometres along the Upper Murray. How populous they were can be gathered from the number of people that participated in ceremonies at one of their main bora grounds at Darlington Point near Griffith on the Murrumbidgee River. Local knowledge has it that about 5000 people came from a wide area of the state to take part, although the demographer L. R. Smith has estimated the population as being about 3000.[47]

Like the other Australian nations the Wiradjuri were divided into clans, each belonging to a defined territory. Family groups travelled over their land, which contained their water and food supplies and the sacred sites essential to the religious and ceremonial life of the people. Those clans centred on Wellington, Mudgee–Rylstone and Bathurst had territories estimated to be about fifty kilometres in radius.[48] The family units usually comprised the elder, his wives, and his sons and their wives and families. Descent was through the female line and the system of marriage, with its precise limitations on who was permitted to marry whom, was much the same as that of their northern neighbours, the Kamilaroi.[49]

The Wiradjuri shared a common language, although even young boys entering manhood and girls approaching womanhood were able multilinguists. The entire socio-political structure was based on decentralised power-sharing from the family, the clan and the nation itself.

Disputes which took place from time to time—mostly concerning arguments about people marrying outside the permitted limits of kinship or about game or other food supplies—were settled in a ritual way in which actual conflict was limited both in participation and the time permitted for it. Two opposing formations of warriors, "their bodies and shields glistening with fresh colour" and symbols would "leap and twist with speed and great dexterity as the battle was played out".[50] It was rare for anyone to be actually killed as the intention of the opposing groups was ritual wounding. As late as 1870 the Murrumbidgee clans took part in a ritual

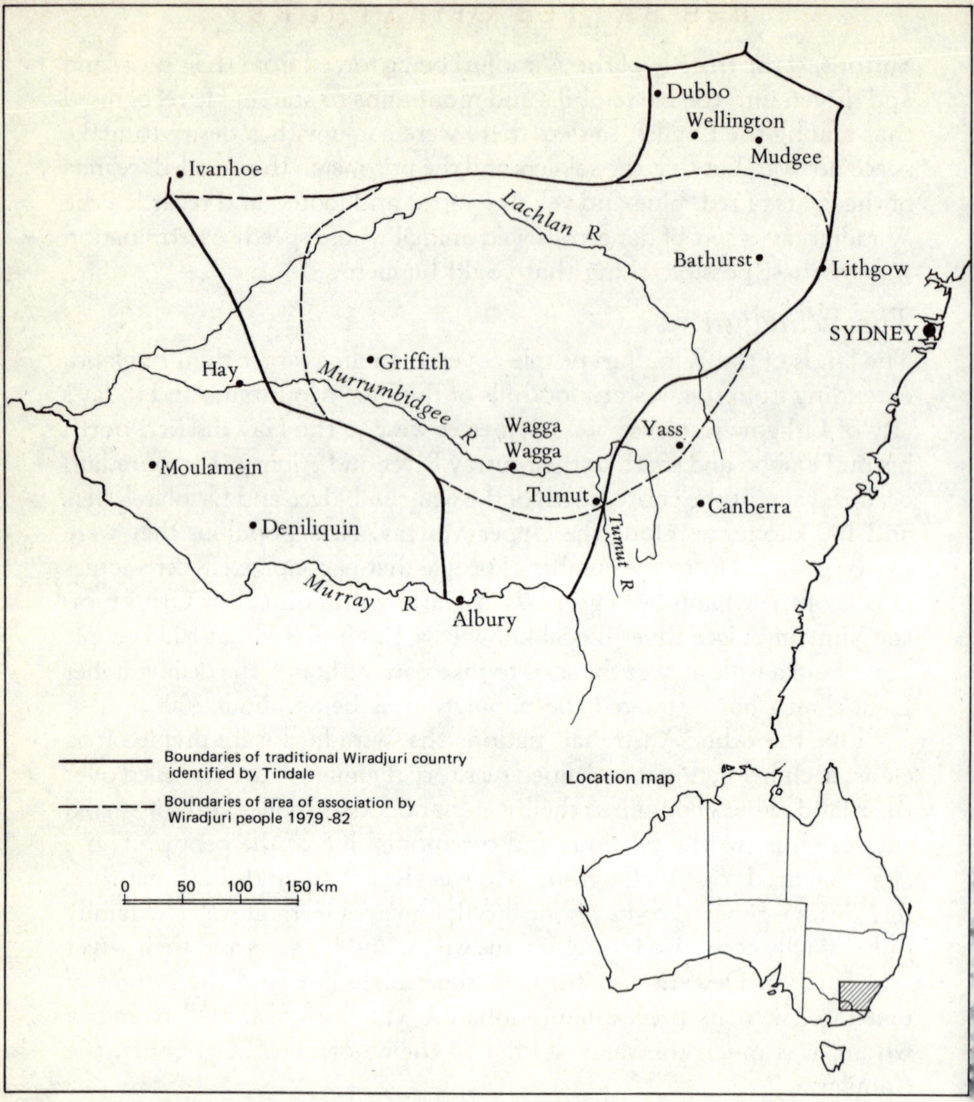

AFTER P. J. READ, A HISTORY OF THE WIRADJURI PEOPLE OF NEW SOUTH WALES 1883–1969. PhD THESIS, AUSTRALIAN NATIONAL UNIVERSITY, CANBERRA, 1983

joust against the Tumut people, their southern neighbours at Wagga Wagga; more than 1000 people are believed to have been involved.[51] Apart from these ritualised inter-group battles, only those who broke the law and particularly those who carried out revenge killings by stealth would have been forced to face violent punishment.

The Wiradjuri were a handsome people, who looked even more impressive in their great possum-skin cloaks decorated with striking geometric designs characteristic of the art styles of the people. The skins were sewn together with kangaroo and emu sinew, and from eighteen to eighty pelts could be used in the production of one cloak. It is unfortunate that only three cloaks seem to have survived today,[52] one of them in a museum in West Berlin.

The art of this part of Australia has been described as possessing an aesthetic excellence: "The style of line and mysterious intent of these designs, sculptured from the living wood of standing trees or finely carved with often chiaroscuro effect to transform the surface of men's weapons, are the distinctive features of the artistic system".[53] It has been favourably compared with the more famous carvings and art traditions of the New Zealand Maoris, the Sepik River people in Papua New Guinea and the Trobriand Islanders of Melanesia.[54]

Scattered the length and breadth of Wiradjuri country were the bora grounds, where 500 people commonly gathered for ceremonies; at some national gatherings thousands might attend. The word *bora* comes from the Kamilaroi *bor*, which signifies a belt of manhood, and many ceremonies at the bora grounds were associated with the initiation of young men.[55] When a gathering or *gaboora* was planned a message stick or *merri merri* was sent out to people as far as 600 kilometres away. The *merri merri* was a round stick thirty-eight centimetres in length with notches and markings at each end.[56] Old rivalries would be put aside and clan disputes suspended when the trek began to the ceremonial grounds.

The bora ground at Darlington Point comprised two circles, one thirty metres in diameter and the other fifteen metres, linked by a path 1.5 metres wide running east–west for 180 metres. Both the path itself and the giant circles were created by scraping away the earth and building raised circular embankments more than thirty centimetres high. The path was scraped away and the earth used to build an embankment on either side.

In the smaller, most important circle, the *goonaba*, were a number of stakes 1.5 metres high and about 4.5 metres apart decorated with strips of bark. Along the path were various devices and images, the largest being a representation of Baiame, the Father of All, and near him his wife, Gooberangalnaha, human outlines made with loose soil. Other figures including the emu, snakes, kangaroos and other animals as well as representations of the great serpent were drawn at intervals along the pathway.[57] Imitations of the nests of the scrub turkey, bower bird, kangaroo rat and other fauna were built in suitable places. Along each side of the path and around the circles trees were carved with images of wombats, possums, goannas, fish, the moon and lightning. Around the circles other trees were uprooted and stood with their roots to the sky. Platforms made from roots were placed on top and decorated with paint, grass, feathers and anything that added to the colour and decoration. The rims of both circles were marked with raised embankments. No stone was used at the Darlington Point bora ground, but in the Bathurst region Macquarie observed permanent monumental stone cairns.

The circle with the earth moulded figures, the Ground of Baiame, was the most sacred part of the bora ground. No women or uninitiated young men were permitted near it. It was in this circle that the ceremonial removal of a tooth proclaimed to all that a young man had passed his tests in education, practice and study and was admitted to manhood. The Grounds of Baiame were the cathedrals of the Wiradjuri, but were neither recognised nor acknowledged by their conquerors. The religious ceremonies were times of great trading, feasting, singing and dancing. The people painted their bodies for the occasion with ochre and pipe clay, and added a wide variety of ornaments fashioned from hair, bones, teeth, leaves or feathers.[58]

Carved trees, or dendroglyths, a feature of the cultures of this part of Australia, were also associated with burial customs. The designs carved into the bark were repeated on weapons and cloaks or were painted on bodies; they were the coats of arms of the people. Often the graves of significant warriors, hunters or healers were marked by these elaborately carved trees. It is possible that the designs may have commemorated events in the life of the dead man—great battles or other feats.[59] The burial trees formed a permanent record of events in the history of the people. Young men going through initiation were told of the events recorded in these monuments, so that as they approached the high altars of their people, the grounds of the transcendental being, they would appreciate the links between the living, the dead, and the spirit ancestors the All Father had sent as his personal emissaries.

This was hardly a people that could be marshalled into a cohesive force to meet the onslaught of firearms. To them, total and continuing war was an almost incomprehensible idea. Their war organisation could not hope to match the invaders, and their weaponry was no better than that of their brother nations which had already been subdued. The Wiradjuri had two types of shield. One of them was solid and narrow and was designed to parry the forceful blows of clubs, usually in individual combat. The other was broad and thin with a convex outer face and a concave under surface, with a handle carved from solid wood.[60] It was used in general combat, particularly to deflect spears. The surfaces of both types of shield were either incised or painted with elaborate designs, the "coats of arms" or their equivalent of the owner. Standard battle equipment included large boomerangs, tomahawks and stone hatchets, clubs covered with elaborate designs or simply rubbed with ochre and oil to enhance their colour and sheen, woomeras, and a range of spears similar to those used by the Eora and Dharuk. Some Wiradjuri warriors also became proficient in the use of captured firearms.

By 1820 the Wiradjuri were facing a more powerful English presence than there had ever been in Australia. Nearly 24,000 people lived and worked within the expanding Pale, which was Sydney, Botany Bay, the Hawkesbury, Coal River (Newcastle) and the Illawarra. A new factor they had to face was that the white population was becoming indigenous: nearly 700 men and more than 800 women had been born in the English settlements.[61] The Wiradjuri were not to know it but the odds were being increasingly stacked against them.

Prelude to the Battle

The fighting west of the Blue Mountains broke out on an organised scale early in 1822 when, after long terrible months of watching the encroachment of the landseekers with surprise and astonishment, Windradyne emerged as one of the leaders of his people. War leaders were not part of the Wiradjuri tradition, but the Eora had already shown the way in following Pemulwuy and the Wiradjuri were to follow that example.

The signal for the beginning of the war was the action in 1822 by the commandant at Bathurst, who determined to exert his authority and show the iron fist to the Wiradjuri. Rightly determining that Windradyne, who had already met Macquarie as an equal leader, was a key figure, he had him seized after a raid on a property near Bathurst.[62] It took six men to secure him. Almost all his ribs were broken by repeated attacks with the butts of muskets, one of which was actually broken on his body. For four long weeks he was held in chains in a cell attached to the barracks, until, at the commandant's pleasure, he was released with the arrogant message to his people to keep their place.

The gauntlet had been thrown down and it was quickly picked up. The beginning of the war was recorded by Judge Barron Field in his account of his 1822 excursion across the Blue Mountains.[63]

The first attack was at Cudgegong River on one of the stations owned by George Cox, one of the roadbuilder's sons. A war party drove the armed stockmen away, released cattle from the yards and scattered them and killed as many sheep as possible. The counterattack was swift. George Cox armed six men at Bathurst and returned to the station, while his brother, William junior, went to Penrith to seek military help. A few months later on another property William Lawson reported that one of

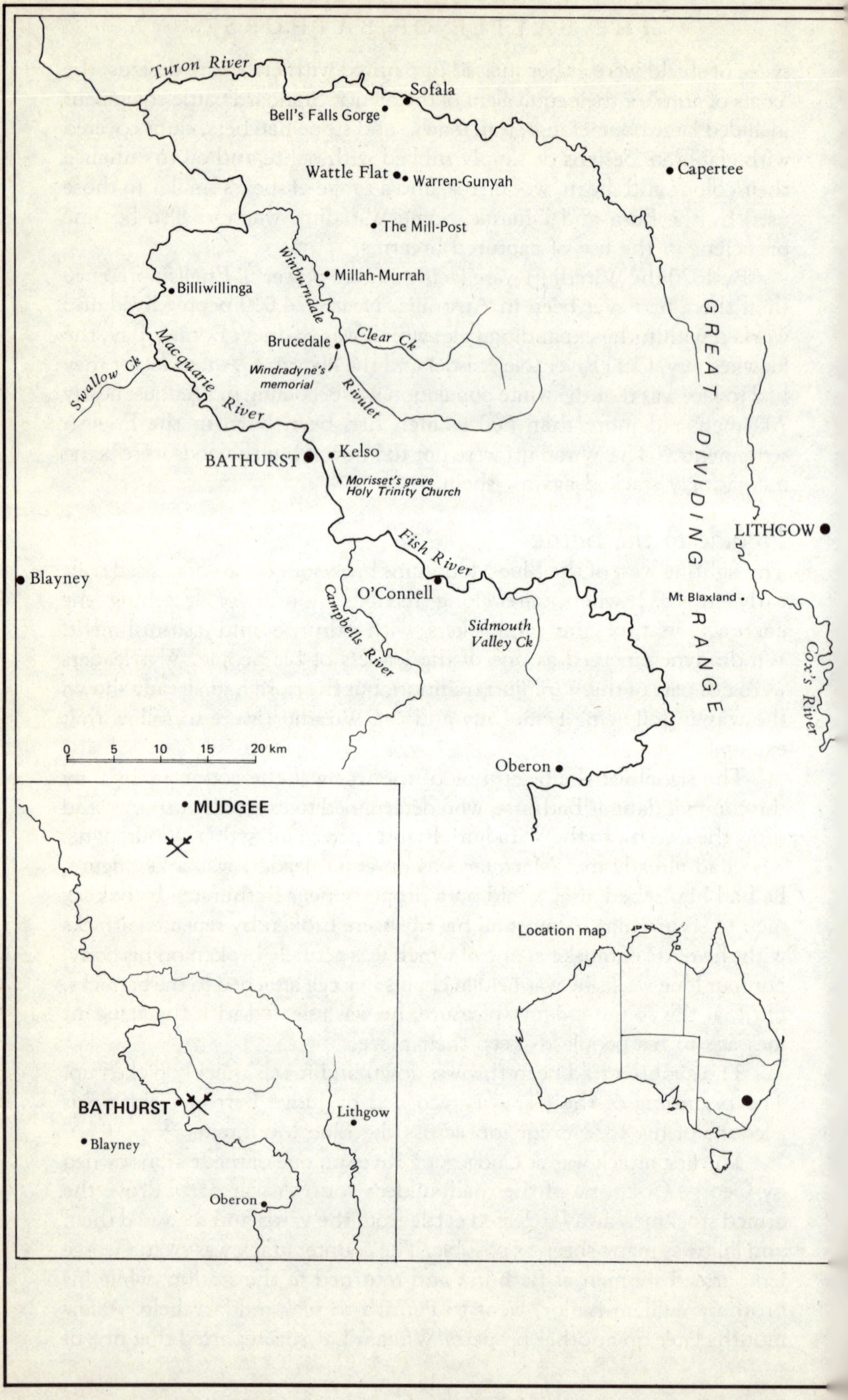

Turon River
Sofala
Bell's Falls Gorge
Wattle Flat
Warren-Gunyah
Capertee
The Mill-Post
Winburndale
Millah-Murrah
Billiwillinga
GREAT DIVIDING RANGE
Clear Ck
Brucedale
Windradyne's memorial
Macquarie River
Swallow Ck
Rivulet
Kelso
BATHURST
Morisset's grave
Holy Trinity Church
LITHGOW
Fish River
Blayney
O'Connell
Mt Blaxland
Campbells River
Sidmouth Valley Ck
Cox's River
0 5 10 15 20 km
Oberon
MUDGEE
BATHURST
Lithgow
Blayney
Oberon
Location map

the prisoners in his employ had been killed by a Wiradjuri war party. Lawson conceded that there was justice, or at least provocation, on the side of the people who were beginning to fight back.[64] Swallow Creek was the next target and the results of the operation were described by Barron Field. Within sixteen kilometres of Bathurst he found deserted huts and houses following the successful raid which had forced the English to withdraw in face of the strong war parties.[65]

The attacks continued in 1823 as the Wiradjuri maintained their pressure, determined to force a general withdrawal from their soil. In September the Wiradjuri attacked William Lee's station, about sixteen kilometres north-east of Bathurst, and killed one of his men. In October and November station after station—Wylde's, Palmer's, and Samuel Marsden's, who had seized even more land in his relentless greed—fell to the war parties. They would raid, kill or drive off the guards, scatter the herds and spear the cattle, until the invaders were intimidated and forced to retreat. The government station at Swallow Creek was closed and the surviving cattle brought into Bathurst.[66] The invaders sought military assistance and Lawson agreed that more soldiers were required. But the Wiradjuri held the initiative for the whole of 1823.

It does little credit to the English invaders that they now resorted to what the world today calls chemical warfare. Long before the poison gas of World War I the Wiradjuri were to experience its horrors. The treatment of scab in sheep involved the use of arsenic, which was now used in the preparation of damper or wheaten cakes left for the war parties and to poison water supplies used not only by the warriors but by their families.[67] The result was agonising death and twisted corpses across the countryside.

Even friendly gestures by the invaders often ended in bloody disaster. On the river flats opposite Bathurst a war party led by Windradyne passed by a modest market garden which they had no intention of touching. The farmer was known not to be an aggressor and at this stage most Wiradjuri raids targeted known predators and places where Wiradjuri had been killed, robbed or raped. In what was to be a fatal act of friendship the farmer offered the warriors some potatoes, which they gratefully accepted, expressed appreciation and went on their way. The next day the party returned and in his absence helped themselves to some more potatoes, obviously feeling that they had been offered a share of the produce of the paddock in the same way in which they themselves shared food supplies. They were not to know there was no such thing as common ownership in the colony of New South Wales.

The alarmed farmer assembled an armed party, not seeking hostilities but merely to protect his crops. Sadly communications broke down and the Englishmen opened fire, killing and wounding a number of the Wiradjuri.[68] Windradyne was forced to withdraw, bitter at what he considered an unprovoked attack on people who had shown peace to the farmer concerned. It was to him yet another example of the brutality and duplicity of the invaders who had come first in peace and friendship, but had then returned to rob and plunder and remained to poison and kill. Yet even in his anger he was noble enough not to seek revenge for its own sake.

One of the invaders who had earned the respect of the Wiradjuri people was William Henry Suttor of Brucedale who had been among the first wave over the mountains in 1822. Unlike most of his fellow countrymen Suttor established friendly relations with the people and learned to speak their language fluently. In 1824 he invited a Wiradjuri man named Penneegrah to help him find his way around the rough country between Bathurst and Mudgee. Suttor and Penneegrah were visiting an outlying hut when they encountered a war party led by Windradyne. Recognising him, Suttor addressed him as one leader to another. They spoke together in friendship and, despite his burning anger, Windradyne took a polite farewell and left them in peace.[69] Although the war was pursued with a vengeance, Brucedale was spared.

Windradyne's raiding parties continued to attack outlying stations, burning down the buildings, killing the garrisons (for they were all armed) and destroying as many sheep and cattle as the spears could dispose of. Bathurst became something of a refugee centre for both men and stock. The attacks were directed first at those who had been indentified for crimes against the people.

In one of the most celebrated raids Windradyne led the warriors against the stations of Millah-Murrah and Warren-Gunyah near Wattle Flat in May 1824. Millah-Murrah Station settlement had been built with supreme disdain by Samuel Terry on the site of a bora ground.[70] Three armed station hands were killed in the attack on Millah-Murrah. The war party occupied the complex for three days and destroyed everything that had been built on the most sacred site of the people. They captured one musket, two bayonets and considerable quantities of ammunition. At Warren-Gunyah three men, blazing away at the warriors, were forced to retreat to a hut. The raiding party set fire to it and two of the men were burnt to death. The other Englishman fought to the death with five spears in his body and others piercing both his hands.[71]

Windradyne had a brief period in which to take stock of the situation. His offensive was succeeding, and he and his warriors had firearms and were becoming proficient in their use. He was determined to maintain the pressure on the retreating enemy. But early in June the troops at Penrith and Bathurst were reinforced from Sydney: their counterattack is surely one of the most inglorious episodes in English history.

Troops of the 2nd Somersetshire Regiment (the 40th) moved out from Bathurst to confront Windradyne and his warriors. They found instead three women, who were killed on the spot, their bodies being left to rot in the sun. In another violent incident three women and a young boy were shot by a party of soldiers and settlers despite their cries for mercy, and their bodies thrown into a nearby waterhole. Two of the women were actually young girls and even the Sydney authorities felt this was murder without reason. The *Sydney Gazette* of 10 June 1824 actually condemned the killings and five of the six men, said to be servants, were eventually sent to Sydney to stand trial for the murder of only the older woman.[72] They were found not guilty.

By late May other Wiradjuri were carrying the war to areas south and south-west of Bathurst. At O'Connell Plains south of the Fish River a raiding party of fifty warriors attacked huts at Brisbane Valley. The Arkell Station near Rockley was attacked and almost 500 sheep driven off, four armed men on the Lawson Station on the Campbell River were killed in a raid and two more were killed near Kings Plains. The deployment of the extra soldiers from Sydney and armed parties began to take a toll of Windradyne's men. In more than a dozen successful raids from late May until mid-June perhaps twenty Englishmen had been killed, but the *Sydney Gazette* of 22 July estimated Wiradjuri casualties in the same period at sixty to seventy dead,[73] while the Wesleyan Mission put the figure at 100, including large numbers of women and children.[74]

In Sydney absentee landholders like Samuel Terry were pressing for a major military response, a crushing blow. But the bloodletting by the military and their armed auxiliaries was beginning to cause a backlash. On 19 August an anonymous letter writer to the *Gazette* protested against "indiscriminate slaughter", "massacre" and "unpardonable murder". The writer, who signed himself "Amicitia", attacked the view that the slaughter of some would impress the others with a "due sense of superiority". Commenting on the views of the advocates of slaughter, he wrote that the blacks "never doubted that the body of whites is greatly superior to the whole body of blacks. If they had ever thought that our collective strength was inferior to theirs, they would long ago have made some attempt to drive us altogether from their shores . . . "[75] Two letters published on 5 August reflected opposing views. One called for rule by terror, regretting that the armed "mounty" killings had not been immediately followed up by military action by the troops.

> *The government of the United States have experienced this evil to a greater degree, even up to the present day, and after exhausting their ingenuity both in measures of vengeance and mildness (and of late years they have not been accused of unnecessary acts of the former) have declared that it is impossible to give security to their backwoods settlements, but by terror . . .* [76]

The other writer pleaded for the restoration and preservation of peace

English settlers under attack, an illustration from Australasian Sketches, *May 1874.* NATIONAL LIBRARY OF AUSTRALIA

by reaching agreement with the people on whose lands the English were trespassing.[77]

By July 1824 the trespassing was of great proportions. Beyond the Blue Mountains 41,000 acres (16,600) hectares of land had been seized, and 83,000 sheep, 15,000 horned cattle and 300 horses introduced.[78] Reports on the fighting poured over the mountains, not only to the governor but to the *Sydney Gazette*, which chronicled the death of English men and English livestock with equal indignation. In the end it was the land barons who got their way for what was described by the *Gazette* as "an exterminating war".[79]

In June Governor Brisbane had written to Earl Bathurst, Secretary for the Colonies, in London, that as a "consequence of the native attacks and the retaliatory forays by settlers",

> *I consider it most indispensably requisite to obtain Your Lordship's sanction to raise a Troop of Colonial Cavalry . . . not only with the view of keeping the Aborigines in check . . . but also for the general Police of the Country, which I consider will derive most essential benefit from it . . .* [80]

Brisbane was attempting to seek legal status for the mounted and armed auxiliaries which were in action almost daily with the military. Barely two months later, on 14 August 1824, the governor proclaimed martial law in the country "West of Mount York". Although he may not have favoured rule by gun and bayonet, the effect of his proclamation was to deliver absolute power into the hands of the commandant at beleaguered Bathurst, James Thomas Morisset.

Then forty-three years old, Morisset was born in England, joined the army at seventeen and saw action against the French army in Spain. He arrived in Sydney with his regiment, the 48th, in August 1817 and the following year was appointed commandant at Newcastle. He succeeded Lawson at Bathurst in November 1823 at the height of the Wiradjuri offensive, and immediately put his military knowledge to work.

Welcoming the proclamation of martial law, Major Morisset declared, "Mutual Bloodshed may be stopped by the Use of Arms against the Natives beyond the ordinary Rule of Law in Time of Peace; and, for this End, Resort to summary Justice has become necessary".[81] To reinforce the proclamation, and Morisset's view that a state of war now legally existed, a further detachment of the 2nd Somersetshire Regiment was sent to Bathurst, bringing the total number of soldiers stationed there to seventy-five.

The 2nd Somersetshires must have made an impressive sight as they marched into the little military post crowded with refugee men and stock. The officers were splendid in jackets of red with blue facings and gold lace and a white edging to the collar, cuffs and lapels. The trousers, cut

Cossack fashion, wide at the knees and tapering to the ankles, were light bluish grey with a crimson sash.

After Waterloo and the return of peace, English Army uniforms became more elaborate and even more impractical and costly. The shiny shako worn by the New South Wales Corps had been replaced by what was called the Prussian model. Made of felt, it was about twenty-one centimetres in height with a broad top nearly twenty-three centimetres in diameter and a polished leather peak. These splendid high hats had bands of yellow or white lace—gold or silver for officers—around the base and top, with worsted plumes about fifteen centimetres high fitted into a metal socket behind a black leather cockade with the regimental button on the upper band.[82] Officers' hats had a hackle feather thirty centimetres high.[83] On the front of the shako was a brass crown bearing the regimental number.

Coats were worn by all ranks, those of the infantrymen having a skirt at the back. Officers' coats had swallow-tail skirts, padded shoulders and chests, lace hooks on seven centimetre high Prussian collars, and epaulets embellished with lace, embroidery, beading and bullion fringes. The troops arriving at Bathurst were permitted to wear overalls instead of pantaloons and knee boots. Officers carried swords with gilt half-basket hilts with a royal cypher between the outer bars in black leather scabbards with gilt mounts. The sudden turn of the English Army in peace to fancy dress also affected the Scottish regiments with higher feather bonnets, ornate dirks, cairngorm shoulder brooches (once only worn by women and girls) and silver bells on the sporrans.[84]

Morisset's strategy was to use these gaily dressed soldiers, augmented as before by armed mounted auxuliaries, to strike out in a number of directions on search-and-kill operations. The columns would then converge towards a preplanned position. No warnings were given, no prisoners taken, and women and children were killed as readily as warriors. Any sightings of Wiradjuri brought immediate fire, which continued until the party was extirpated. Those who broke and ran were driven into the guns of the approaching columns.

The policy of massacre was brutally carried out. One of the worst episodes took place in the Capertee district north-east of Bathurst,[85] where a camp, a refugee centre, had been established principally for women and children. A party of soldiers opened negotiations with the camp. The women and children and the few men present were invited to leave the camp and take food which had been placed within musket range of nearby station buildings. As the people came forward to take the food soldiers treacherously concealed in the buildings opened fire. They did not cease until the entire group was dead. Of perhaps thirty people none escaped, not even babes in arms.

On the Turon River north of Wattle Flat troops drove a party of women and children with a few accompanying warriors into Bell's Falls Gorge. Trapped, they were systematically shot.[86] The same tactic was used in a gorge near the headwaters of Clear Creek, and in the two killings local estimates put Wiradjuri casualties in the hundreds. Morisset's firepower and tactics were taking a grim toll, forcing Windradyne onto the defensive for the first time in nearly two years. Yet Windradyne's standing with his people and with his enemies stood higher than ever. His strength and stamina had become legendary and it was recognised that his leadership was the key to the prosecution of the war.

Only eleven days after the proclamation of martial law a further proclamation was issued by Colonial Secretary Goulburn announcing that

> *FIVE HUNDRED ACRES OF LAND will be given to any Individual, who will apprehend, or give over to any of the Civil Authorities, SATURDAY, a Black Native and who is supposed to have been a principal actor in the late murders committed on the White People, at Bathurst.*[87]

For some reason no one has recorded Windradyne was named Saturday by his enemies and his bold bid to free his country of intruders was reduced by Goulburn to "murders". No one, black or white, was either willing or able to do the deed and events were to march on to the fatal spring days when the Battle of Bathurst decided once and for all the fate of the Wiradjuri republic of this region.

The Battle of Bathurst

The Battle of Bathurst was not one short, sharp engagement but two days of intensive fighting followed by a two-month campaign of extermination by the men of the Somersetshire Regiment and their mounted auxiliaries.

It began about 10 September 1824 when a Wiradjuri war party set out to clear stock and people from an area on the Cudgegong River, about 130 kilometres north of Bathurst, occupied by George Cox. They had collected a mob of cattle and begun to drive them away when three of Cox's hands, including his overseer, Chamberlane, who were on their way to the Mudgee district to collect the same cattle, picked up their tracks and began to follow.[88]

About eighty kilometres north north-west of Bathurst the trio encountered the Wiradjuri party at least thirty strong. The mounted men rapidly beat a retreat, but the Wiradjuri, showing tremendous stamina in challenging the pace of the horses in the rough terrain, came close enough to throw their spears and boomerangs. One of the leaders threw a boomerang which hit the overseer's horse. Chamberlane wheeled around and shot the warrior dead, retreated, reloaded and shot a second warrior, and repeated the manoeuvre a third time killing a third warrior, the closest to the fleeing Englishmen.

The station hands made good their escape and under cover of night they dismounted and hid in the bush, not even daring to light a fire. At daylight they set out again to try and locate the war party. About thirty-two kilometres from Bathurst, just as they had decided to turn back, they stumbled across a Wiradjuri camp with several fires and an immense stockpile of weapons. But it was deserted: the entire group had suspended operations to bury the three dead warriors with all the traditional honours.

The three men immediately set about gathering up the weapons and burning them. They had disposed of the greater part of the cache of arms when the Wiradjuri returned.[89] A party of forty warriors moved away from the women and children and attacked the intruders. They quickly expended the few spears, boomerangs, clubs and tomahawks that had not been destroyed in the fire. Chamberlane and his party, realising they were being pursued by defenceless men, dismounted, tied their horses together and took up positions under cover. As soon as the Wiradjuri came within range they began firing. When half had been killed or wounded they fixed bayonets and charged.[90] Bare hands had been no match for firearms and were no match for bayonets.

The Wiradjuri retreated, leaving sixteen dead and taking their wounded with them. Not only had the strongest war party to take the field in some time been decimated, but a large quantity of weapons had been destroyed. An even greater disaster was that one of the Wiradjuri leaders, named Blucher by his adversaries, had been the first to fall to the English guns.[91] It was a great tribute by the Englishmen to name a black warrior after the great Prussian general who shared with the English Duke of Wellington the honour of defeating Napoleon at the Battle of Waterloo.

The three Englishmen, who had demonstrated both courage and fighting expertise, rode back to the Cudgegong Station to report their victory. Scarcely pausing for food and rest, Chamberlane rode at full gallop to Bathurst to report to George Cox that he had lost 122 head of cattle to the Wiradjuri, who had also successfully raided Lawson's property in the same area. Cox immediately took Chamberlane to Major Morisset, who then assembled the largest force yet seen in action in the area.

The seventy-five infantrymen of the Somersetshire regiment, augmented by 100 local mounted auxiliaries, were divided into four flying columns. One column headed by Morisset advanced north, Magistrate Walker was given command of the left division and moved west and the other two, commanded by Magistrate George Rankin and Lawson, moved east.[92]

On about 18 September 1824 the columns moved out of Bathurst in the culmination of the "exterminating war".[93] In a great sweep they covered an area up to 160 kilometres around Bathurst, east as far as Mount York, north to Capertee and the Cudgegong River, and, later, to the south. For about ten days they sought out and killed and systematically destroyed everything Wiradjuri—people, camp sites, weapons, implements, cloaks, utensils. Individuals were hunted like dogs, groups surrounded and shot. Entire clans were rounded up, driven into gorges and cut down. Relentless fire killed the families of warriors trying desperately to regroup in the deep valleys of the Capertee country. W. H. Suttor commented of the daily massacres that the English Army seemed to have decided to rid the land of Wiradjuri, the "pests of the period", now fighting so doggedly for hearth and home.[94]

One of the first sweeps yielded only a young unarmed woman and a child: being the enemy it is probable that they were shot. The excuse that gave the semblance of legality to the killing of women of all ages, from hobbling grandmothers to nubile girls and young mothers, was that they were armed—with their digging sticks.[95] Nowhere is it recorded how toddlers barely out of their mothers' arms could have been construed as members of a war party.

The warriors failed to rally with either arms or numbers, even in the fastness of Capertee. Daily they received reports of the wholesale slaughter of their families. The land was in lament, the morale of the warriors in shreds as the guns of Morisset and his men took their deadly toll. On 28 September the troops returned to Bathurst, where Morisset held a victory dinner at the barracks. The following day they set out again, and for two more long months the killing continued. No skill in organisation of war could enable Windradyne to strike back. Defeat was stark and complete, yet the reward of 500 acres to assassin or traitor failed to tempt any of his people. In those weeks of horror there is not one recorded attempt to betray him: in life and death the Wiradjuri were loyal. But fight on they could not. As black September died into history October saw the first surrenders. Five warriors came into Bathurst in mid-October, an advance guard to see if it was possible to surrender without being shot.[96] When they were neither killed nor imprisoned, the remnants of two clans, numbering only sixty people, followed them in.[97] They were given blankets and food,[98] and placed in guarded camps, where they were told they would remain until their leader surrendered.

In the first week of November Brisbane informed his superiors that the Wiradjuri were "hourly coming in to tender their submission and sue for peace and protection".[99] There was no talk of a treaty, however: the vanquished could only be grateful they were not killed outright. Morrisset waited until 20 November before presenting his report to the governor, and on 11 December 1824 Brisbane lifted martial law, formally ending four months of hostilities.[100] Morisset was not entirely satisfied: he wanted his great adversary Windradyne dead or alive.

In the long, drawn-out pain of the Battle of Bathurst, in which retreat and rout turned into massacre, it is estimated that one third of the entire population of the Bathurst area, perhaps more than 1000 men, women and children, perished. By 1900 there may not have been more than twenty or thirty Wiradjuri living in the district.[101]

Aftermath

On the last day of 1824 Brisbane informed Earl Bathurst that he was "most happy to have it in my power to report to Your Lordship that Saturday, their great and most warlike chieftain, has been with me to receive his pardon and that he, with most of his tribe, attended . . ."[102]

Windradyne had continued to move through the Bathurst district with an elite guerilla unit of four to eight men. Morisset, unable to kill or capture him, was finally persuaded by Brisbane to offer peace with honour, the only accolade won by the Wiradjuri in the war of extermination. The man who had orchestrated the war from the safety of Sydney wanted to meet this warrior who had defied his soldiers for so long, the man who had become a legend in his own lifetime. Messages were sent back and forth across the mountains and it was arranged that Windradyne and his people would meet Brisbane in the market place at Parramatta at noon on Tuesday, 28 December 1824.[103]

After a seventeen-day march across the mountains, Windradyne led some 260 Wiradjuri men, women and children into the market place at the appointed time. They were watched by the governor and his staff, his officers in red and blue with lace and shining buttons and waving cockades, Attorney General Saxe Bannister (who had been the legal instrument of the declaration of martial law), important merchants and visiting English gentlemen, and reporters from the *Sydney Gazette*, all agog to see the great war leader.

Clad in their long cloaks, Windradyne and his followers were joined by other Wiradjuri clans until some 400 were present. They sat in a circle, waiting quietly, grouped around the clan leaders who were each given a chair in recognition of their rank. The central position was given to Windradyne.

The scribes from the *Gazette* were impressed not so much by Windradyne's height (he was more than 182 centimetres tall) as by his muscular physique and "his noble appearance and piercing eye". Despite his dreaded reputation, they wrote, his countenance was "calculated to impress".[104] They could not find enough superlatives to describe "the most manly black" they had ever seen.

Looking at the soldiers formed up with their firearms, his hard-eyed foes whose bayonets had so recently dripped with the blood of his kin, Windradyne appeared nervous. Watched by his wife, Brisbane and his staff did what they could to reassure him. The governor formally proclaimed the lifting of martial law and announced that the war was over and that peace would now reign. Windradyne was presented with

J. W. Lewin's sketch of "A native chief of Bathurst", made in 1815, is believed to be a portrait of Windradyne, the war leader of the Wiradjuri.
PHOTOGRAPH BY MARJI HILL

a straw hat decorated with a label bearing the word "peace" and a little branch representing the olive.

About 2 o'clock in the afternoon, after the proclamations and the presentation to Windradyne, the peace feast began. Brisbane had spared no expense to make it worthy of the occasion. There were forty loaves, twenty-two "monstrous" dishes of inviting roast beef, thirteen massive plum cakes, a huge cask of soup, several tubs of potatoes and a whole hogshead of "three-watered grog".[105]

Before leaving, the governor made a point of paying the first and last courtesies to Windradyne. He spoke to each clan leader, reassuring them of his intention to promote peace. He actually made the rounds twice to make sure his message was understood. As he took his final leave, the Wiradjuri rose spontaneously and cheered. Brisbane's own troops, who had also dined well, echoed them with a single cheer. Attorney General Bannister made his own rounds of the assembled Wiradjuri. Knowing, as did the governor, that the war had turned into massacre and that there were ugly stains on the hands of the troops and auxiliaries, he was noted to be saddened by the "awful consequences" of the war.[106] It was strange indeed, to find peace celebrated by a feast at which the victors were overcome by the bravery of their opponents and saddened by a victory that had been won at such a terrible cost in human life and forfeited honour.

After two hours of feasting the Wiradjuri women packed the leftover food in their baskets. As the clans began to leave the market place, the *Gazette*'s reporters noted that the prostitutes of Sydney began their traditional revelry. Windradyne and his people camped on the Parramatta Domain for several days before returning over the mountains to Bathurst.

Never again would Windradyne lead his depleted ranks against the invaders. He continued to give leadership, trying to hold his people together, to bind up their wounds and try to come to terms with the occupation of their lands. In December 1825 he was again invited to Parramatta, this time to meet Brisbane's successor Ralph Darling. The governor and the great and powerful of the colony eagerly awaited his arrival, but were disappointed. Windradyne sent an ambassador with his apologies: he was busy arranging a ceremony with a neighbouring clan and was unable to come, but would try to meet the governor at a later date.[107] His absence was the lead story in the *Australian*.

The *Sydney Gazette* continued to cover Windradyne's exploits. In May 1826 it reported that he had established his headquarters at Capertee, a location which had served well during the war. Another report described an altercation with some neighbouring people whose leader, in abuse of Windradyne's hospitality, challenged him to combat. Bested by Windradyne he fled the field of combat and hid in the house of a clergyman named Hassett (possibly Thomas Hassall), who offered to turn on a feast of roast bullock if they would end their differences.[108] Ever friendly in peace, Windradyne agreed and with laughter and camaraderie joined the feast with the English peacemaker and his Australian protagonist.

Wherever he went he was saluted with affection. In August 1826 an anonymous Englishman who signed himself "Colo", writing from Brucedale, described him as a "very fine figure . . . [with] limbs [that] are of a beautiful symmetry . . . a mind not unconscious of his mental superiority . . . a good model for the figure of Apollo".[109] "Colo" also wrote of his songs of praise for the brave and generous, of ridicule for the cowardly and mean, of a song depicting an English settler who was cruel and morose, and of many laments for the dead warriors and the women and children. In their songs and stories Windradyne and his people even found room to forgive Bannister, the attorney general, who made such an effort to make up for his part in the war. "Colo" spent long hours at the camp fires of Windradyne, his Australian "Apollo", and spoke of the Wiradjuri relaxing in the summer sun, the men around Windradyne in one group singing their songs, the women in another laughing at the pantomime of husbands and fathers.

By this time Windradyne's camp boasted the food supplies of the invaders—bread and milk, tobacco and sugar—but if offered spirits of any kind Windradyne would decline with thanks, tapping his head in disapproval and to indicate the bad effects it could have.[110]

Windradyne may have made his peace with the English, but he still had disagreements with some of his neighbours. When a group from the south, possibly the Gandangara people, came to visit him, a dispute broke out and Windradyne was wounded in the knee. He was taken to Bathurst Hospital where Dr George Busby dressed his wound and handed him over to the care of women prisoners rostered to serve as nurses.[111] Finding the confinement of the hospital too much to bear, he tore off his bandages and headed to Brucedale where there was a Wiradjuri burial ground. His wound became gangrenous and he died on 21 March 1829, five years after the Battle of Bathurst. The date of his death has also been recorded as 1835, but all agree on the manner of his burial. Surrounded by his family and people he was given a Wiradjuri ceremonial burial, wrapped in his possum mantle and with his weapons bearing his insignia beside him.

The grave was marked with a large mound of timber and earth flanked by two wild apple trees. One hundred and twenty years later the Suttor family erected a memorial over the grave in a generous tribute to a fallen foe, an honour in stark contrast to other leaders who fell in battle throughout Australia and wait to be honoured yet.

His old adversary Brisbane came in for lively criticism of his administration from his London chiefs. In May 1825 he was sacked by Earl Bathurst with one short sentence: "I am commanded by the King to signify to you that His Majesty is pleased to relieve you from the exercise of the Government of New South Wales."[112] He returned home seven months later and devoted the rest of his life to his scientific interests. He died on 27 January 1860 in the room in which he had been born.

James Morisset went to England in the same year as Brisbane, but returned in 1827, becoming superintendent of police and then commandant at Norfolk Island until 1834, when he retired. He bought a property at Winburndale Rivulet near Bathurst in the heart of the land of the people he had conquered. He died on 17 August 1852 and the town of Morisset near today's Newcastle was named after him.

Victor he may have been but today his foe Windradyne commands more admiration and affection from not only the Wiradjuri but the descendants of the English who came and conquered so long ago.

7. THE BATTLE OF PINJARRA

Fought on the banks of the Murray River, eighty-six kilometres south of Perth, Western Australia, on 28 Octotber 1834, the Battle of Pinjarra was the culmination of five years of successful black resistance to the British invasion and settlement of the Swan River Colony.

The Invasion of the West

Although the Portuguese were nominally part owners of the continent according to the Pope's division of the world in the 1494 Treaty of Tordesillas, the race to invade the western half of Australia involved the Dutch, the English and the French. The Dutch were both the first and the more persistent.

The Dutch supplanted Spain and Portugal in what today are Indonesia and Malaysia. The ships of the Dutch East India Company—the instrument by which the Netherlands created a great empire based on trade and commerce—were the first to report on the west coast of Australia to which they were carried often by accident because of inaccurate navigation aids and the ocean currents.

The first recorded sighting of the west coast was made by Dirk Hartog in the *Eendracht*. He left a pewter plate nailed to a tree on the island that now bears his name, recording his visit in 1616. The *Zeewulf* came unexpectedly to the coast two years later, followed in 1619 by two ships under Frederik de Houtman, who was nearly wrecked west of today's Geraldton on a dangerous reef he named Abrolhos, and in 1622 by the *Leeuwin*, which sighted and named the south-west tip of the continent.

The Dutch also recorded the first Englishmen to reach Australia—the crew of the *Tryal* wrecked in 1622. In June 1629 the *Batavia* with some 200 men, women and children aboard was wrecked off Houtman Abrolhos. Attempts to establish friendly relations with the people of the mainland failed and after mutiny and many deaths the survivors were eventually rescued by the gallant Captain Pelsart, who sailed 2000 kilometres to Indonesia in an open boat to bring help. The crew and passengers on the *Gulden Draak (Gilt Dragon)*, wrecked in 1656, were less fortunate: of nearly seventy survivors only seven reached Batavia.

The great Abel Tasman, on his second voyage in 1644, charted the north-west coast from Darwin to Dampier, but avoided contact with the people. In 1658 Captain Peerebroom in the *Elburgh* recorded observations of the Nyungar people of south-west Australia near Cape Leeuwin, but it was another forty years before a Dutch fleet gave the Swan River the name it bears today.

The voyage of Willem de Vlamingh in 1696–97 was the final large-scale effort by the Dutch East India Company to find new worlds. It also marked the last attempt by the Dutch to penetrate the mysteries of the last continent. The fifty-six-year-old commander, a veteran of Indian and Arctic Ocean navigation, anchored off Rottnest Island in December 1696 with three ships, *Nyptang*, *Geelvink* and *Wesel*. His instructions included searching for lost ships of earlier years and when camp fires of the Nyungar people were seen on the mainland it was obvious that a landing was necessary in the interests of this part of their mission as well as to explore the area.

The decision to land was made by de Vlamingh and the ship's council on 4 January 1697 and eighty-six soldiers and sailors and African guides landed on Cottesloe Beach, where a monument marks the location today.[1] They decided to explore inland along a river but the Nyungar people strategically withdrew before them. The Dutch pushed further inland and came across some Nyungar dwellings. They were deserted. In a rare display of sensitivity by invaders of the time, the Dutch sought to avoid alarming the people by making a slow, deliberate approach, but the Nyungar took the opportunity provided to evacuate.

For two weeks the cat and mouse game continued. The Dutch would light friendly fires hoping for contact; the Nyungar would extinguish theirs and retreat again. The Dutch shot a few cockatoos and swans, and fell seriously ill after eating the attractive-looking nuts of the Zamia palm. They could not know the Nyungar treated these nuts to neutralise the poison they contained. For two long, hot weeks Vlamingh and his men explored the countryside but faced by lack of contact and inadequate supplies of fresh water they returned to the outpost at Cottesloe to board their ships again. For several more weeks they persevered, sailing north along the coast in the summer heat looking for friends and survivors. They found neither and late in February 1697, near what is now Dampier, Vlamingh fired a five-cannon salute and said farewell to the southland forever.[2]

The Dutch East India Company flourished for another 100 years and other Dutch ships invaded western waters and some were wrecked, including the *Zuydorp* near Geraldton in 1712 and the *Zeewyk* on Houtman Abrolhos in 1727. From its peak in the seventeenth century, when it boasted nearly 200 ships and an army of 10,000 soldiers, the company declined as the British and French empires began to rise, and the Dutch simply abandoned the west.

The forerunner of the invasion force that was to change the face of the west was an English pirate, William Dampier, who with a group of English buccaneers in a stolen ship, the *Cygnet*, landed in King Sound near what is now Derby in 1688. His contact with the people was limited, with not a word exchanged, but peaceful. Their reward was to be described as the "miserablest People in the world".[3]

This opinion did not prevent Dampier selling the idea in England that the west might be the place for a new colony. A ship, the *Roebuck*, was fitted out, and Dampier arrived back in the west in 1699. He landed near Port Hedland and took prisoner a number of the local people and attempted to make use of them as slave labour. Ordered to carry barrels of water to the ship, they simply stood like statues, took off the cast-off rags they had been given and laid them down.[4] In another incident further south Dampier captured a young man and tried to force him to lead the party to fresh water. An English sailor was speared, the first shot in the war against the invaders in Western Australia was fired and the first Black Australian lay dead. Dampier and his men retreated, the first invasion attempt a failure.

In the late eighteenth century, when the English colony at Port Jackson on the other side of the continent was struggling to survive and the French were beginning their probing of the continent, the English stepped up exploration. In September 1791 Captain George Vancouver in the *Discovery* discovered and named King George Sound, but the Nyungar repeated the tactics of withdrawal and evacuation they had employed so successfully against the Dutch and he failed to make any contact. He felt that the land was a place of famine and distress.

Captain Matthew Flinders commanding the *Investigator*, who followed in December 1801, had more success. For the first time friendly overtures were made between a group of sailors and a group of Nyungar. The local people made a visit to the English camp where gifts were exchanged. The strangers were not permitted to visit the Nyungar settlement nor to even see women and children, but the men made daily visits to watch the activities of the sailors as they made ready to go to sea again. The contact ended as happily as it had begun. Flinders arranged for the marines to stage a farewell drill parade and as the drums sounded, and the muskets and bayonets gleamed in the sun, the Nyungar appeared delighted by the spectacle. Flinders and his men sailed away in peace.

The inspiration of Napoleon Bonaparte carried the French to the

A Nyungar spearman, an illustration from George Grey's Journal of Two Expeditions of Discovery, *published in London in 1841.*
NATIONAL LIBRARY OF AUSTRALIA

furthest corners of the world, probing and taking where resistance was weak; the declining Spanish Empire conceded Tahiti and other islands in the Pacific and in the west, Captain Nicolas Baudin commanding *Le Géographe* and *La Naturaliste* arrived in Western Australia in 1801. In February 1803 Baudin and his men also established contact with the Nyungar people at King George Sound; they were friendly but, as Flinders had noted, kept women and children away from the strangers.[5] Baudin's respect for the people of the west is illustrated by the fact that when he came across two graves surrounded by spears embedded with their points uppermost, he paid tribute to the dead warriors by leaving two French medals on the graves. After this voyage, the west was *Terre Napoléon* to the French. Perhaps if the French Empire had triumphed in Europe the Nyungar people would have faced a different invasion from that which eventually overwhelmed them.

Tragically, the peace of the south-west was shattered by gangs of sealers from Bass Strait, who began to raid Nyungar dwellings to kidnap women and female children,[6] who were raped or used as slaves before being killed. The sealers also brought with them infectious diseases to which the Nyungar had no resistance, and cultural corruption.

Phillip Parker King followed up the visits of Vancouver and Flinders to King George Sound in January 1818, but the Nyungar withdrew and he failed to make any contact. He returned in December 1821, however, to a warm welcome and offers of hospitality. During the week's stay one side laid down muskets and the other spears, and vigorous trading resulted in the crew of the *Bathurst* securing 100 spears, 300 woomeras and 150 knives at the rate of half a biscuit per item.[7] King left in peace once again and returned a third time almost a year later. The Nyungar helped him to take on fresh water and there was another round of trading at mutually satisfactory exchange rates.

Four years later, in October 1826, Captain Dumont D'Urville commanding *L'Astrolabe* landed at King George Sound to establish a scientific observatory. Once again the Nyungar were friendly. They helped the French with their linguistic studies, and during the long evenings entertained them with traditional songs and dances while the French responded with songs of home.

The age old rivalry between England and France flared as soon as the French flag was seen in Australian waters. The London government and its colonial administration were immediately suspicious that France might claim and colonise that half of the continent not covered by Cook's proclamation of 1770. Anxiety to forestall any French invasion led to the hurried establishment of garrisons in northern and southern Australia in the 1820s and lent impetus to Darling's approval late in the decade for a survey of the Swan River area in the west. In March 1826 Governor Darling received instructions from London to have surveys made of Shark

Bay and King George Sound, and early in November Major Edmund Lockyer left Sydney with some twenty soldiers and twenty prisoners to establish a garrison at the latter.

Lockyer was able to maintain the amicable relations established by the earlier French and English explorers, despite the fact that the Nyungar's initial warm welcome was followed by some misunderstandings that could have led to an outbreak of warfare. Lockyer set in train policies that kept the peace for ten years. This garrison appropriated little land from the people, did not force them into slavery or steal from them. They also made friends by helping to curb the excesses of the sealers. Only weeks after their arrival Lockyer reported that a party of sealers had killed a Nyungar man, marooned four others, and had taken four women for whom they had gambled. One of them, an Englishman named Samuel Bailey, also had a seven-year-old girl for his use and abuse. With information from another party of sealers, a cosmopolitan group which included North American blacks, Englishmen, a New Zealander and a Sydney black named Pidgeon, Lockyer was able to rescue the women and return them to their people. The little girl was apparently from Sydney and the Nyungar indicated that it was Pidgeon's responsibility to care for her.[8]

This small settlement was a rare example of the two peoples coming together in peace and amity and enjoying mutual respect. The peace was shattered for 100 years when dispossession began and the people were made trespassers on their own land, foreigners in their own country. The Nyungar could not know that the ceremonial firing of muskets and cannons and the hoisting of their flag by the English at King George Sound would have the same results in the west as similar ceremonies had had in the east. They saw only a group of people who restricted themselves to a small portion of land, had shown respect and friendship and would probably leave, as had their earlier visitors, in due course.

The day of reckoning for the Nyungar arrived in 1829, when the British Government decided to establish the colony of Western Australia and appointed Captain James Stirling as lieutenant governor.

Stirling, who was born in the town of Drumpellier in Lanarkshire, Scotland, in 1791, had joined the British Navy in 1803. Within six years he was promoted to lieutenant, in four years more he was a commander and he was appointed captain in 1818. He fought with his uncle, Admiral Charles Stirling, at the Battle of Cape Finisterre against the French in 1805, was in operations against Spain along the Rio de la Plata in 1807, in the West Indies again in 1811 and had his own command, the sloop *Brazen*, in 1812. He also took part in the naval war in the Atlantic until the defeat of Napoleon in 1815 and he remained with his ship in the West Indies until 1818 when he was put on half pay and left on shore for seven years.

Governor James Stirling. NATIONAL LIBRARY OF AUSTRALIA

During that time Stirling enjoyed a well-earned holiday and met and married Ellen Mangles, with whom he had five sons and six daughters. Stirling disliked inaction, however, and events in Australia gave him his chance.

A settlement had been established in 1824 on Melville Island on the extreme north coast of Australia, but it had struck difficulties and the British authorities decided to move it to another site. Lord Bathurst decided that HMS *Success*, one of the first ships of war appointed to the East India Station, should be directed to north Australia to find a new settlement site and in April 1826 Stirling found himself in command en route to Sydney. When he arrived at the end of November, however, the onset of the cyclone season prevented him from going north. In view of the reports of French ships in southern and western Australian waters, Stirling persuaded the governor of New South Wales, Ralph Darling, to allow him instead to search for a settlement site on the west coast.

In March 1827 he arrived at the Swan River and proceeded to explore upstream where he made his first contact with the people. A group of about thirty Nyungar men decided to open a friendly dialogue with the strangers and in a bout of vigorous trading exchanged artefacts, the English contributing clothing and three swans, and the Nyungar spears and woomeras. After a stay of nearly two weeks Stirling took his ship south and his second major meeting with the people of the west took place near today's Busselton, where a Nyungar leader made a gesture of peace by leaving his spears behind him and stripping himself of his handsome kangaroo-skin cloak to show that he concealed no weapons. The story of these early meetings was set out by Stirling in a detailed report to Governor Darling.[9] Darling was so impressed with Stirling's work he gave him 2560 acres of land in New South Wales in the vicinity of Bathurst. (It was the practice to give land to naval captains, who usually handed it over to an agent to lease as they saw fit on behalf of the absentee landowner.)

In May 1827 Stirling went to north Australia to fulfil his original mission. He selected a site on the mainland at Raffles Bay, which he claimed for the British Crown, and directed the establishment of Fort Wellington. The fort was built in the form of a hexagonal stockade of solid timber, with eighteen pound carronades mounted at four of the angles and in the centre a six metre high tower. Barracks for the troops and prisoners were built outside the stockade. The fort was manned by a commandant, a surgeon, a storekeeper, thirty soldiers of the Dorsetshire (39th) Regiment, fourteen marines and sailors, twenty-two prisoners, a Malay interpreter and his own two women, and five children. This was Stirling's first attempt at establishing a settlement, valuable experience for his future in Western Australia.

His task in north Australia completed Stirling joined his East India

Station squadron. Illness, however, forced him to return to England. Anxious to push his Swan River project he made representations to the Colonial Office. His wife Ellen, twenty years old at the time, had generously offered her family fortune to help out the Stirling family, while James sought to build his fortunes by offering himself to the British Government as the commander of any settlement on the Swan River. At the same time Thomas Peel's syndicate approached the Colonial Office with a scheme for settling the Swan River. The scheme was accepted in a modified form, and this together with Stirling's enthusiasm led to orders being given to annex the region. In 1829 Stirling was sent back to form the settlement with the rank and authority of lieutenant governor.

Not only was he given authority to seize all the land belonging to the people of the west without discussion, treaty or agreement of any kind, but he received a personal present of 100,000 acres. Stirling was equipped with instructions from the Imperial Colonial Secretary, Sir George Murray, who wrote from Downing Street, London, on 30 December 1828, to tell him that in the absence of any civil, legislative, judicial or financial institutions he should act on his own initiative with "firmness and discretion".[10] He was instructed to establish a town, and ensure that a "due proportion" of the expropriated land be reserved for the Crown and the clergy of the Church of England. Settlers were invited to "locate themselves" on any land he felt fit to suggest; if they argued between themselves he was to have their claims settled by a Court of Arbitration.

Captain Charles Fremantle was sent from the Cape of Good Hope in another English warship, HMS *Challenger*, to forestall any last-minute French invasion of the area named by the Dutch more than a century before. He anchored in the mouth of the Swan River on 25 April 1829. His instructions were to be "constantly on the alert to prevent surprise from the natives and especially to be very guarded with respect to the women". He was also to take possession of the entire west coast, of which fact the Nyungar, as with Lockyer, were unaware. But he did not appropriate their land or exploit them and in fact established good relations characterised by trading. Even Fremantle traded his captain's hat for a string of possum furs.[11]

The *Parmelia*, the first ship carrying settlers from England, arrived on 2 June, 1829; it promptly stuck on a sand bank and Fremantle and his men came to their rescue. On 18 June Stirling proclaimed English rule, by which all the people of the west became "British subjects of King George IV". It was not thought worthwhile to consult them, although they were from that moment subject to British laws and regulations. Stirling is reported to have expressed concern for their welfare and conceded that they should be able to keep some of their land for their own use.

From August to December 1829 no fewer than eighteen immigrant ships arrived at the Swan River, launching the great migrant rush of 1830. Settlers quickly spread over the land, taking the most fertile areas and the river lands, which they cleared of timber to establish homesteads and sheep and cattle runs. The land was either granted in proportion to the capital and labour supplied by each settler or purchased for nominal sums. The British were for the most part unaware that all the land, every billabong, creek, river, hill or valley, was the property of people whose religious belief was that the ancestral beings of the Dreamtime had given the land to them to be cared for in perpetuity, and that the land belonged to the people and the people to the land in this life and the next.

The security of the port and the colony rested on the muskets of the officers and men of the West Suffolk (63rd) Regiment and the arms of the crew and marines of the warship. In addition almost all the settlers had access to muskets and swords. Within five years the English bridgehead was nearly 2000 strong; an overwhelmingly male population of soldiers, sailors and landowners armed with the most modern weapons confronted the spears and woomeras of the Nyungar. If there was any strategic weakness in the English position it was that the landseekers had spread out over a wide area away from Perth itself.

Many of the settlers were victims of conditions in the United Kingdom, of poverty and industrial and social discontent, and arrived steerage; others travelled with servants, taking first class passages to the new colony where land could be had for the asking. The majority came from England but all parts of the United Kingdom were represented. Once on their blocks they faced a struggle to survive in a completely alien environment. To put up a house, to grow some food, just to survive in the early days totally occupied them. But consciously they set out to duplicate their homeland, ripping out local trees and shrubs and substituting roses and oaks, scattering the region with English names such as Guildford, Bayswater and Huntingdale.

Their early contact with the Australians was limited, as they kept to themselves in the vicinity of their homesteads. Many friendly meetings took place, however, and it is doubtful if the Nyungar realised that these people, unlike their earlier visitors, were there to stay. Misunderstandings there were but overall peace reigned in that first year.

The Nyungar

What kind of country had these invaders come to from their restless homeland in the grip of the industrial revolution, and who were the people in whose country they were settling? The Nyungar's territory covers the southwest of what is now Western Australia from the Geraldton district north of Perth, south along the coast to Cape Leeuwin, east to Esperance and back to Geraldton. The region enjoys a good climate and is well watered by rivers, pools, springs and swamps. The Nyungar had occupied this south-west triangle for thousands of years. Current scientific evidence places their occupation at around 40,000 years; tools found at Upper Swan Bridge have been dated 38,000 BP and other similar finds in the Swan Valley at 29,000 years BP.

At the time the British arrived the Nyungar formed a fairly distinct socio-cultural bloc and could rightly be called a nation. They were not necessarily a closely integrated social group, and interaction beyond the level of family groups was very limited. It was not until 1940 that ethnographer Norman Tindale identified the Nyungar as comprising thirteen linguistic groups; naming the various groups with any certainty was difficult since the traditional society had collapsed and the lawmen had died before a complete study could be made. These linguistic groups represented peoples who spoke dialects of the common south-west Nyungar language.

One of the principle distinguishing features which set the Nyungar apart from other Australian nations was the absence of subincision and circumcision in the ritual associated with initiation. In place of these rites the youths' nasal septums were pierced and their bodies were patterned with ritual scarring.[12] In other ways their culture was similar to that of the rest of the population of this continent.

The Nyungar lived in family groups, coming together at regular intervals to enact the religious ceremonies essential for their existence and the maintenance of religious life. They had a body of law similar to that found in other parts of Australia and elders were responsible for interpreting and enforcing it. Meetings were held to discuss law matters. Unlike Western cultures with their hierarchical forms of leadership, social control was built into the structure of society, eliminating the need for strong centralised leadership. Reports of powerful chiefs or kings were based on post-conquest developments or the imaginations of some early observers.[13]

The Swan River settlement was established on Nyungar land called *Mooro*, while the site of Perth itself was known as *Boorloo*. The elder and lawman who acted as spokesman for the people of that area was Yellagonga. His *kaleep* or main camp was on the sloping hill Byerbup, which gave him a commanding view of the town and the river flats. He was dispossessed by the soldiers of the 63rd Regiment who pitched their tents on the spot which is today the site of the Anglican Bishop of Perth's house in Spring Street.[14] The Nyungar were at first able to maintain their lifestyle and often traded fish and game for bread and flour. They wandered in and out of the town of Perth, where twenty-eight were named in the census of 1837. When Yellagonga died in 1843 the *Perth Gazette* printed his obituary under the bold headline, "Death of the King of Perth".[15]

That this curious peace was maintained was due both to the leadership of Yellagonga and to the Nyungar belief that the strangers were *djanga* or spirits returned from the dead. English men and women often found themselves being greeted as returned fathers or mothers, brothers or sisters. So the Nyungar tolerated the intruders while the intruders, for their part, felt they were showing toleration because Stirling had proclaimed the Nyungar British subjects. The seeds of war were sown in the different cultural concepts of land and its management.

At the end of the first year of the invasion the Nyungar began to fire the land, an annual practice to encourage growth, hunt out game and increase soil fertility. Firestick farming, however, was a threat to the homesteads of the settlers and to their crops and livestock. The English took the traditional game of the Nyungar such as kangaroos as they pleased, yet viewed their livestock as private property, representing indeed their capital investment. The Nyungar, as they saw their livestock being taken, simply reciprocated by taking the cattle and sheep, just as they used introduced crops as substitutes when food plants and trees were cleared to make room for agriculture and grazing. Before long they were branded as thieves and rogues.

Typical of the clashes that resulted was an incident in the first year of the invasion, when a party of Nyungar, finding their food game gone, turned to some chickens. The Englishman defended his chickens, the military were called and fired on the Nyungar to drive them away. They did not shoot to kill, but the damage was done. The Nyungar had found a new rule: "We take what you have but you can't take what we have".

By 1831 such incidents had multiplied, but the Nyungar developed new strengths under leaders such as Yagan in the Swan River area, Weeip, the leader of the Upper Swan groups, and Calyute, whose territory south of Fremantle extended from the west coast to the ranges and hills inland of Pinjarra.

Calyute had emerged as a leader following a traditional upbringing. By the time he entered into manhood he had learned the history of his people, their faith, their relationship with the land, and the skills of living—how to hunt, how to recognise the plants which could provide food and water and those which were part of the people's pharmacopeia. A tall, very strong young man, Calyute would have cut an imposing figure with his sweeping kangaroo-skin cloak casually fastened around his shoulders, clutching his spears and woomeras as he moved through the bush. Because of his height and build he stood out among his people and his bravery was demonstrated many times during the years of guerilla warfare. He remained uncircumcised in accordance with custom, but had a nasal septum and ritual scarring on his body, and wore a beard. Not yet thirty years old, he had achieved the status of elder and lawmaker. He had a number of wives and several of his children fought alongside

All over Australia families were dispossessed, denied access both to their traditional foods and to the invaders' livestock and crops.
NATIONAL LIBRARY OF AUSTRALIA

him, including a son, Unia, who was to die in the Battle of Pinjarra. The fighting force he led ranged from youths to greybeards. Many of them carried scars from wounds sustained in guerilla actions, and all would have lost relatives killed by white diseases.

Calyute achieved a unity among the Murray River people but he allowed himself to be outmanoeuvred by Stirling in relation to his allies in the Swan River and the Upper Swan. He failed to hold together a grand alliance with the two other leaders, Yagan and Weeip, and thereby allowed himself and his people to be isolated in the struggle against the intruders. While some of his people, and he himself, had handled firearms Calyute did not use them against the enemy, preferring to rely on traditional weapons. This failure to utilise the new technology made it impossible to withstand frontal attacks against the guns of the enemy. He also failed to develop support techniques to sustain a high level of guerilla activity.

Calyute and his people made some concessions to new technology—using glass chips instead of stone flakes on spears and substituting metal axes for stone. The weaponry with which they faced the militia and the British Army comprised spearthrowers or woomeras, which had a hook or wood or a kangaroo tooth lashed to one end with animal sinew, spears, axes, shields, boomerangs and throwing sticks. The point of the distinctive fighting spear was edged with razor-sharp quartz or glass flakes embedded in hardened tree gum, similar to the teeth of a rude saw. As it penetrated an opponent's flesh the quartz edges severed the blood vessels; when it was withdrawn or was dragged out by its own weight, pieces of quartz would break off and remain inside the victim.[16] Based on a good knowledge of human anatomy, it was designed to inflict maximum damage. It was propelled by a woomera, which increased its range, speed and accuracy. Shields were used for protection in action, but were designed to deflect spears not bullets.

Military Action Begins

The response to the growing resistance by the Nyungar was widespread demand for military action. It was led by Thomas Peel, whose family hailed from Peelford, near Blackburn in the county of Lancashire in middle England. Thomas was a cousin of Sir Robert Peel, 2nd Baronet, who founded the London Police Force, became Chief Secretary for Ireland and went on to become Prime Minister of England for two terms.

Hailed as one of the founders of the colony of Western Australia, Peel was a big, strong, healthy boy who did reasonably well at school but did not get on well with people when he came to make his own way in the world: the shadow of Cousin Robert was ever present. Thomas's father decided he should go into the family's cotton manufacturing business. Thomas baulked, and his father put him instead into an

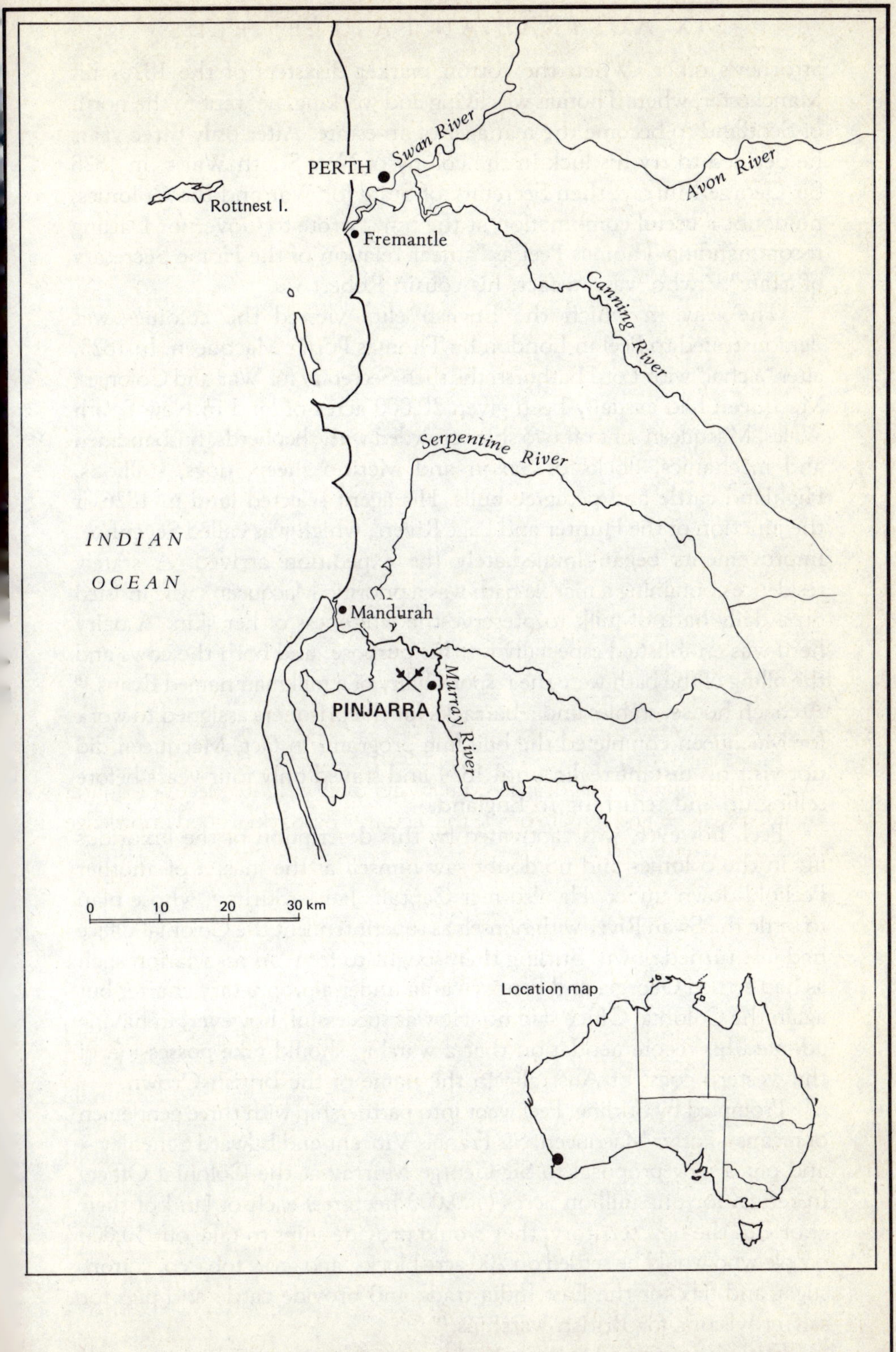

Swan River
PERTH
Avon River
Rottnest I.
Fremantle
Canning River
Serpentine River
INDIAN
OCEAN
Mandurah
Murray River
PINJARRA
0
10
20
30 km
Location map

attorney's office. When the cotton market disasters of the 1820s hit Manchester, where Thomas was living and working, he went to the north of Scotland to become the manager of an estate. After only three years he decided to try his luck in the colony of New South Wales. In 1828 Sir George Murray, then Secretary of State for War and the Colonies, no doubt a useful combination at the time, wrote to Governor Darling recommending Thomas Peel as "a near relation of the Home Secretary of State",[17] who was, in fact, his cousin Robert.

The way in which the English elite viewed the colonies was demonstrated to Peel in London by Thomas Potter Macqueen. In 1823, after "a chat" with Lord Bathurst, the then Secretary for War and Colonies, Macqueen had casually been given 20,000 acres of land in New South Wales. Macqueen sent off two ships crowded with shepherds, husbandmen and mechanics, flocks of Saxon and Merino sheep, dogs, stallions, Highland cattle and pedigree bulls. His agent selected land in 1826 at the junction of the Hunter and Page Rivers, which was called Segenhoe. Improvements began immediately the expedition arrived. A stately residence containing a marble bath was a priority: Macqueen's wife insisted on a daily bath of milk to preserve the whiteness of her skin. A dairy herd was established especially for this purpose, and both the cows and the filling of the bath were the responsibility of a milkman named Evans.[18] A coach house, stables and a barracks for the prisoners assigned to work for Macqueen completed the building program. In fact, Macqueen did not visit his distant realm until 1834 and stayed only four years before selling up and returning to England.

Peel, however, was captivated by this description of the luxurious life in the colonies and no doubt saw himself as the master of another Peelfold down under. He also met Captain James Stirling, whose plan to settle the Swan River with himself as superintendent the Colonial Office had just turned down. Stirling then sought to form an association such as had settled Georgia and Pennsylvania under a proprietary charter but again the Colonial Office said no. He was successful, however, in having adopted his recommendation that a warship should take possession of the western coast of Australia in the name of the British Crown.

Prompted by Stirling, Peel went into partnership with three gentlemen of means—Potter Macqueen, Sir Francis Vincent and Edward Schenley—and put a new proposal to Sir George Murray at the Colonial Office. In return for one million acres (400,000 hectares) each of land of their choice in the new territory, they would provide ships to take out 10,000 people who would be settled on 200-acre blocks, and grow tobacco, cotton, sugar and flax for the East India trade and provide cattle and pigs for salt provisions for British warships.[19]

Stirling continued to press for his own appointment as governor of the colony, and for first choice of 100,000 acres (40,000 hectares).

Eventually the Colonial Office acceded to his demand and also accepted the partnership's proposals in modified form but offered in return only one million acres in total. The three London gentlemen, apparently slighted by such a paltry offer, withdrew their financial backing. Dining alone in despair at the Windham Club, Peel found an unlikely saviour. Solomon Levey, a former convict turned Sydney merchant, put in enough capital to save the scheme, although both he and Peel thought it prudent not to reveal this fact to the Colonial Office.

The association's first ship, the *Gilmore*, which sailed from London with 179 emigrants in 1829, was delayed by a mutiny before it got as far as Plymouth, and during the voyage Peel was credited with fighting a duel with the commander, Captain Geary. When the vessel reached Fremantle on 15 December Peel found that the 250,000 acres he had selected on the Swan and Canning Rivers had already been taken. Stirling sent him instead to the coast near Fremantle where a new town to be called either Georgetown for the present English King George IV, or Clarence for his heir apparent, was planned. Unsatisfied, Peel and some of his settlers moved south to the fertile lands of the Murray River near the present town of Mandurah.

Once established there, he built a home which he called Mandurah House from where, in August 1831, he led the campaign for more military action against the Nyungar. Writing strongly to the colonial secretary, he urged that a military post be established on the Murray; Peel was anticipating extending his land holdings and was threatened by the increasing Nyungar opposition. The demands must have found official support since by the end of 1831 Captain T. Ellis, who had been given the somewhat condescending title of Superintendent of Native Tribes, was stationed with troops at Mandurah; there were also small garrisons at Perth, Upper Swan and Kelmscott, at Clarence, and on the south coast at Augusta and Albany.

Despite this deployment, Nyungar resistance gathered momentum during 1832–33. Isolated farms became targets for guerilla attacks and many settlers became worried about venturing away from their homesteads. As the tension grew citizen forces were recruited to assist the military and a warning system of signal shots and bugle calls was developed to alert the community and signal a stand to arms.[20] Much of the activity was on the Swan and Canning Rivers. On 14 June 1832 a group of Nyungar speared a bullock belonging to one of the settlers; it was another instance of the Nyungar finding their traditional food having been replaced by cattle. The reaction was a raid by ten armed Englishmen on a camp of fifty men, women and children. There were deaths on both sides before the camp surrendered. The surviving Nyungar men, women and children were herded together, their kangaroo-skin cloaks were removed, their bags, knives, woomeras, axes and spears taken, before being driven off with a warning not to touch the sacred cows again.

Fear of a massed attack on Perth grew. Food depots were established outside Perth and Fremantle in an effort to prevent the Nyungar from moving around the settlements. Troops were placed at the present Causeway to provide early warning should large numbers of warriors attempt to cross the Swan by way of the swamp flats. Troops were also strategically located to harass raiding parties retreating from the town.[21] Captain Ellis was given the task of recruiting a mounted force of armed troopers to maintain communication with scattered homesteads. He and his assistant superintendent, Charles Norcott, were instructed to observe the Nyungar people and learn their habits, to estimate their strength, and to identify their leaders and their pattern of movement. It was an intelligence operation of high priority.

Some voices were raised against the treatment of the Nyungar. One outspoken settler, Robert Menli Lyon, condemned the aggressions against them and declared in an impassioned speech: "You have seized upon a land that is not yours. Beware, and do not as a people, add to this guilt of dipping your hands in the blood of those whom you have spoiled of their country".[22]

Lyon established a dialogue with Yagan, the resistance leader of the Swan River region, and wrote a series of articles on his talks with him, which were published in the *Perth Gazette* in March 1833. Further, he offered in a letter to the acting lieutenant governor, Captain Irwin, to accompany Ellis and his assistant to the Murray River to attempt peaceful negotiations. He believed that the only obstacle in "civilizing of the native tribes [would be] found in the backwardness of the Local Government".[23] Before his offer could be taken up, more clashes took place and Captain Ellis was seeking to engage Yagan. Each incident inflamed passions, regardless of where the guilt lay. The killing of the Velvick brothers near Fremantle in April turned them into pioneer martyrs although they were an unpleasant duo who had been convicted and punished by their own people for mercilessly beating Nyungar men and women. They had murdered Domjum, the brother of Yagan, who in turn killed them both. Subsequently, Yagan's father, Midgigooroo, was captured and shot on evidence given against him by a twelve-year-old boy.

Yagan himself was shot dead by two young shepherds, James and William Keats, in July 1833. His body was skinned, and his head hacked off, wedged in a hollow tree-stump and smoked. Several months later the hair was combed, possum fur string tied around the forehead, and red and black cockatoo feathers added. Ensign Robert Dale acquired the trophy and took it to England, where it was displayed as the head of a "Swan River Chieftain".

The voices of restraint were more often than not drowned out. Meetings such as that held at Guildford in 1832 were warned that the colony would have to be abandoned and the military and settlers withdrawn if peace with the Nyungar could not be achieved. There was a call for a special negotiator to be appointed, but those seeking conciliation were accused by others of lack of concern because, being wealthy, they were able to tide themselves over any troubled period. The hawks simply rejected peace and brought out their guns.

By the beginning of 1834 the fate of the colony hung in the balance. Numbers within the Pale remained at almost 2000, but the introduced herds of sheep and cattle had been reduced by poison weed, poor husbandry and the constant attacks by Nyungar guerilla bands. Military and administrative changes had also weakened the colony. Stirling had left for England with his wife on the *Sulphur* in August 1832 to try and enlist the Imperial Government's aid to resolve the problems of the colonists. Three military commandants, Captains Irwin, Daniell and Beete, acted successively as lieutenant governors during his absence. In May 1834 the experienced 63rd Regiment was replaced by troops of the Royal North British Fusiliers, 21st Regiment, commanded by Captain Daniell. This regiment had been moved from Tasmania but was only a garrison force and below the strength the settlers wanted to face the increasing resistance of the Nyungar.

As the frontier war hotted up even the Peel family felt the sting. In March 1834 Thomas Peel's sixteen-year-old reputed son Fred came up from the pastures at the back of Mandurah House to see about dinner. He was reaching for some kangaroo meat hanging from a branch near the kitchen door when a dozen Nyungar men rushed out of the soldiers' quarters and surrounded him. One of the guerillas put a spear to Fred's chest, but at that moment Captain Byrne of the garrison appeared. His soldiers, caught off guard, were frantically priming their muskets, but when Byrne simply told the Nyungar to withdraw, they did. Thomas Peel arrived in a hurry to shout the troops ale from his stock and launch a tirade against the colonial administration for not having more troops in the field.[24] Byrne had reluctantly to confess that he was unable to prevent such guerilla operations.

It was becoming obvious that the Nyungar could not be written off as kindly childlike folk who would submit to losing their patrimony in exchange for a pat on the head and a hand-out of bread and flour. They had learned new skills of co-operation, and with a fearless and skilled leadership were waging a guerilla war which contained the invaders within their Pale and regularly challenged them on its frontiers.

While Yagan will always be remembered for his role in rallying the Swan River people, and Weeip equally well remembered in the Upper Swan, it was the Murray River leader, Calyute, and his people who were seen as the most effective resistance fighters in the south-west of Western Australia. They were described in letters and despatches to England as "the fiercest and most warlike in the colony".[25] Yet neither the Murray people nor the other Nyungar regarded all the invaders as enemies. Many settlers established friendly relations with the Nyungar, who often made the homesteader, his wife, children, servants, shepherds and labourers members of the family group. The English, however, often failed to understand that if they then did wrong, they were equally guilty and eligible for spearing.

Exacerbating the tension was the terror among Nyungar communities when they discovered that men, women and children were being mysteriously struck down, that inexplicable death was coming to live permanently in what had been happy and contented if frugal communities. As in eastern Australia, infectious diseases to which they had no resistance, such as cholera and whooping cough, had arrived with the English settlers. They rationalised that the deaths must be due to the new arrivals—and they were right—but saw them as a deliberate evil that called for payback action and spearings. As entire families were wiped out by the mysterious deaths a new and savage urgency came to the drive against the strangers.

The Nyungar were increasingly being denied access to their own food sources and water supplies, refusals which were backed by the guns of the militia and the muskets of the troops. The now Governor Sir James Stirling returned from the Imperial capital in August 1834 convinced that to survive the colony must both increase its population and control the Nyungar. He introduced military initiatives designed to prevent them assembling in effective fighting forces. A series of military outposts, the nuclei of future towns, would be established between Perth and Albany and connected by roads. Military escorts would be guaranteed for coaches and mail carriers and the English Pale extended by opening up inland areas for farming to increase the English population, outnumber the Nyungar and build an enduring strength.[26] So confident was Stirling of the success of these plans that he chose large areas of land in the Williams, Harvey and Albany districts as part of his already large personal entitlement.

The main obstacle to the plans was the Murray River people whose traditional lands straddled the road he planned to drive south. In selecting Pinjarra, on the Murray River about nineteen kilometres east of Mandurah, as a site for a township and military post on the proposed road, Stirling was throwing down the gauntlet: he knew that Pinjarra was the capital, the meeting place for all the Murray River people. But he made his plans carefully, not wanting to risk general warfare along the frontiers, which could result in his defeat and the annihilation of the settlers. He did not underestimate the fighting prowess of the Nyungar and paid tribute to their skills in guerilla war in his despatches to the British Colonial Office in 1834. Writing after his victory in the Battle of Pinjarra, he conceded that "there was danger, that their success in this species of warfare, might tempt other tribes to pursue the same course, and eventually combine together for the extermination of the whites".[27]

Putting his new strategy into effect Stirling used the classic tactic of divide and rule. He sought to negotiate a truce with Weeip to prevent a joint attack on Perth by his forces from the north-east and Calyute's forces from the south.[28] It was a tribute to Stirling's negotiating skills that he was able, in August 1834, to conclude a peace with Weeip, who proclaimed he would personally enforce it and spear any of his people who violated the agreement.

As the right hand spoke of peace to Weeip the left threatened death to Calyute and his people. The *Perth Gazette*, on 6 September 1834, reported the governor's thundering:

> *In case of any future misconduct, the punishment would be different to what it had hitherto been, that a great number of men would be mounted on horses whose business it would be to ride through the Country punishing with severity, any of the blacks who molest the white people, and offering protection to the blacks so long as they behaved well. But if the black men committed any violence or robbery, [Stirling] would not leave one man [alive] on this side of the Hills.*[29]

By mid-October Stirling had established the Mounted Police Corps, most of whom had previous military experience, to protect settlers, safeguard mail carriers and, as an afterthought, to "maintain a friendly relationship with the Aborigines".[30] They were issued with green uniforms and weapons with 300 rounds of ball cartridges. Their training and drill was under the supervision of Captain Ellis and Charles Norcott. The Nyungar, meanwhile, were confronting their own difficulties in building unity out of a political structure specifically designed to prevent aggregations of power and authority. They were also struggling to evolve the defensive techniques necessary to maintain a successful and prolonged guerilla war against European technology. Their strength lay in speed of attack and quick effective withdrawal.

A major incident, which was one of a series leading to the battle itself, took place on 24 April when Shenton's Mill on the Swan River near Perth was attacked by a guerilla group of Murray River people, led by Calyute, who were carrying the struggle away from their own land and towards the heart of enemy territory. A war party of about thirty had reconnoitred the mill a few days earlier. George Shenton, the mill owner, had asked them where they came from and they told him. They returned to raid the mill, holding Shenton prisoner, while they carried off 980 pounds (about 450 kilograms) of flour. They then freed Shenton who alerted the military. The raid was not only a significant act of defiance against the English but also a raid into the territory of the Swan River people who it was felt had not pulled their weight in the struggle since the loss of their leader, Yagan.

The Swan River Nyungar, annoyed, named the Murray River men and Captain Ellis and a detachment of the 21st Regiment set out in pursuit. At Mandurah Calyute and two lieutenants—his son Monang and Yedong, who was seventeen years of age—were surrounded by soldiers and forced into the barracks. Monang escaped and ran into the bush under a hail of shots. He was wounded three times but reached a nearby swamp and disappeared into the reeds.[31] Calyute and young Yedong did not give up without a fight. Yedong tried to climb through a window but was stunned by a rifle ball that grazed his head above the ear. Calyute struggled against impossible odds and was taken prisoner only after he had been bayoneted.

His wounds notwithstanding, Calyute was immediately taken in a cart to Fremantle together with Yedong and two other captives, and then by boat nineteen kilometres up the river to Perth. Here an emergency meeting of the Executive Council was called, an indication of his importance. It was decided he should be publicly flogged, then held hostage against any reprisal by the Murray people. He was given sixty lashes with a knotted rope that same day and the *Perth Gazette* of 3 May reported that he hardly made a sound as his back was ripped apart. Despite his strength, the effects of his wound and the lashes combined to send him falling to the ground when he was cut down from the flogging post.[32]

Calyute's stature among his own people, the respect and affection in which he was held, was demonstrated when he was dragged off to Fremantle Prison. Throughout six weeks of imprisonment his friends and supporters never left him, hiding by day in the bush outside Fremantle and when darkness fell creeping right up to the walls of the gaol, which still stands, as forbidding now as then. They would call soft cooees and wait for the answering call from Calyute to assure themselves he was still alive. In mid-June Calyute was released after being taken outside the gaol walls and given another sixty lashes.[33] Bloody but unbowed he joined his waiting lieutenants and set out for the south to resume his leadership and continue the struggle.

The Murray River people now embarked on a campaign against Thomas Peel, whose claim on 100,000 hectares of their land had been confirmed that year. In July, deciding to set a trap for Peel, they set loose some valuable mares on his property hoping he would go out to search for them and so could easily be taken prisoner. Monang volunteered to take Peel to his missing horses, but shrewdly he declined, sending instead a man named Edward Barron, who had come down from Perth to buy one of the horses, and Private Hugh Nesbitt of the 21st Regiment.[34] Monang led them five kilometres from Mandurah House to the shores of Lake Goegrup, cooeeing along the way to let the other Nyungar know where he was. By the lakeside they attacked. Barron, with three spears in his body, galloped back to Mandurah, dismounting just as the Peel family were sitting down to the evening meal by tallow candlelight. They bandaged up his wounds, while Peel called for medical help from Fremantle and military assistance from Perth. The following day a military detachment found Nesbitt's body by following the mournful howling of his little terrier which had not left his side.[35] He was found to have sustained thirty wounds and had obviously fought bravely to the last.

Although Nesbitt was a soldier and was killed in the line of duty the military and the hawks among the settlers called for war, describing the Nyungar as "callous", "treacherous", "deceitful" and beyond the understanding of "civilized man".[36] Captain Ellis and his men swept through the Murray lands seeking an engagement, but the Nyungar had withdrawn. The entire area was panic-stricken; every man walked from his house to the fields carrying guns, the military were constantly patrolling and rumours ran riot. The *Perth Gazette* solemnly reported:

> *It is, we believe, generally allowed that the natives when desirous of avoiding us in the bush have a peculiar method of rendering themselves* invisible, *although at a short distance. That they are aware of this power was evinced a few days ago by an acknowledgement of Weeip that he had seen Mr Bland pass along the road from York and with a significant gesture he gave that gentleman to understand that he was aware he could not have seen him.*[37]

The alarm was such that the settlers would believe anything. Strange tales grew out of apprehension of the unseen enemy who seemed to be winning a war that was accelerating daily. The silence of the bush and the oppressive loneliness fed the fantasies. A settler in the Murray area wrote to the *Gazette* describing how the Murray people had told him of a creature, a huge amphibious animal whose head stood as high as the ridge of his house, which could "scream like a pig but five times as loud" while also producing "a blubbering sound which shook the ground".[38] Sights beyond comprehension were reported: a "great greyish column . . . whirling rapidly down one of the wide reaches of the river and a boat in its path vanished forever". On another peaceful "sunny afternoon, people had watched a huge silvery flash dazzle the sky, appear and disappear again and again over a far bank" of the stream. That one was a waterspout and the other the sun's reflection of the white underwings of a wheeling cloud of small snipe did not prevent the unexpected producing feelings of awe.[39]

Time was running out for the colony and Stirling knew it. Calyute, and the Murray River Nyungar, continued to defy him despite flogging, imprisonment and every attempt to cow him into submission by demonstrations of military strength and power. Yet the weapons at his disposal formed a striking contrast to the spears of the Nyungar. The Royal North British Fusiliers were equipped with muskets that could hit a man at a range of ninety metres. These weapons had barrels more than a metre in length, weighed more than four kilograms, and were fitted with bayonets forty-three centimetres long; they fired ball cartridges.

The private soldier was a colourful sight in a red coat with collar and cuffs of regimental facing colour and white turnbacks. The coats had white worsted epaulets and were decorated with loops of white lace on the front, collar, cuffs and pocket flaps of the coat tails. Dark trousers in winter and white trousers in summer completed the ensemble. Equipment consisted of a black pack and a grey blanket worn on the back and a black ammunition pouch worn from a belt suspended over the left shoulder. All the straps were white. Officers were even more exotically arrayed, although Stirling kept to the more workmanlike naval rig. The longer the British regiments remained in Australia the more exotic touches of lace and ribbon were lost, but the heavy, colourful and ornate uniforms were more an asset to Calyute's fighting men than to Stirling.

The Battle of Pinjarra

The continual guerilla warfare waged by the Murray River Nyungar was a major obstacle to Stirling's plans for the expansion of the colony. He was left with no alternative but to try and break their resistance. On a cloudy spring weekend in 1834 the opposing forces began to take up positions for a battle initiated by Stirling, the first time the English took the offensive in a major military action in Western Australia.

On Saturday, 25 October, Stirling left Perth on horseback with Surveyor General John S. Roe. At Preston Point ferry, three kilometres from Fremantle, they rendezvoused with two non-commissioned officers who had brought a boat load of supplies from Perth. The supplies were loaded onto spare horses and the party, now four, skirted Fremantle and moved as secretly as possible to next rendezvous at Hamilton Hill. Here they were joined by Captain Ellis and five mounted troopers, and later by Captain R. G. Meares and his son Seymour.[40] Now twelve strong, the party rode on to Mandurah to the Peel homestead. The final link up of the English force took place on Monday morning, 27 October, when eight privates and a corporal of the Royal North British Fusiliers arrived. The intelligence unit established earlier in the year by Stirling had done its job well. The entire force had been brought together in three well-planned movements. It was a strategy of surprise and it worked like clockwork.

The entire force commanded by the governor now numbered twenty-five, having been joined by Ellis's assistant Norcott, Surveyor George

Smythe and none other than Calyute's old enemy Thomas Peel himself, who brought along an armed servant for good measure. Well armed and equipped with ample ammunition and supplies for a campaign of several weeks, they rode out from Mandurah that same morning, the red coats of the soldiers making a splash of colour as they moved rapidly south-east towards the Serpentine River. They reached the Serpentine where at that time it joined with the delta of the Murray River to form a single estuary, shallow enough to enable them to ford the combined streams. An examination of the sandy banks disclosed fresh tracks made by Calyute's people. The signs, which were easily read, showed the spears dragged alongside the heavy tread of the men, the smaller tracks of the women and the erratic footprints of children playing in the bushes as they moved with the main party. The tracks clearly indicated that the Nyungar were only one hour away and heading south-east in the direction of Pinjarra.[41] Stirling's force had moved so rapidly that the normally watchful Nyungar had been caught off guard. A council of war called by Stirling determined by late afternoon to halt the advance and make camp at Jim-Jam, about 2½ hours ride from Pinjarra and close enough to the Nyungar to make an early morning strike.

Probably for the first time the tables were turned on the Nyungar. It had always been the Nyungar who had watched their enemy blunder through the bush in their red coats, picking them off at will, hit and run in classical guerilla style, keeping military posts constantly under observation, and harassing the garrisons to such an extent that only a short time before the British Fusiliers had retreated to Perth. Yet now a heavily armed force had been assembled in three distinct operations at the Peel homestead, which to Calyute was the source of the greatest threat to his people and which he had raided many times, and brought undetected to within only a few hours of the heart of the Murray River people's homeland. The distance from Mandurah to Pinjarra is only nineteen kilometres, but with swamp and thick bush slowing the pace, a steady ride would take a mounted party about four hours. Stirling had led his force to Jim-Jam without encountering an enemy scout.

Tuesday, 28 October, dawned to stormy skies and drizzling rain. The soldiers and their auxiliaries rose two hours before dawn. The horses were saddled, the weapons were readied and preparations for the attack were completed by firelight. They even ate a hot breakfast. It was 5.30 am when the force moved out of Jim-Jam, with the drizzle continuing and the fog lying close to the ground. It was as if the elements themselves had been organised by Stirling to facilitate his strategy of surprise.

The force followed the bend in the Murray River for a short distance and then struck out across country directly to Pinjarra. Their progress was slowed as they travelled across the plain made swampy by winter rains. Less than one kilometre from the present town of Pinjarra they crossed the river at a ford where the water was about seventy-five centimetres deep and running at about two kilometres an hour to the north. The ford today is a pretty place where children swing out over the river on ropes tied to the overhanging trees. On that morning there were no children, no people, and even more extraordinary no watchful Nyungar scouts. They continued upstream for 1.5 kilometres until they heard voices from the Nyungar encampment. Stirling ordered his men to turn their horses towards the river.[42]

Stirling sent Peel to scout ahead, to try and establish whether Calyute and his principal lieutenants were there, the fighting leadership of the people who were his objective. The force was deployed out of sight as Peel went forward. In a tactic that was tried with tragic success at the Battle of Vinegar Hill thirty years before, Peel was to attempt to entice the leaders away from the main party; he lacked, however, the flag of truce and the services of a priest that had been employed to trick the leaders of the Irish rebels to come forward in good faith to parley, only to be shot and captured.

Peel returned to report that about seventy Nyungar were at the camp with its beehive-shaped huts on high flat ground on the eastern side of the river and were making so much noise they could not hear his call for parley.[43]

Stirling then sent Ellis, Norcott and three of the troopers across the river, which at this point was thirty metres wide with red loam banks six metres high—an ideal location for an ambush. Stirling remained in place with the main force, while Roe was put in charge of the baggage and four fusiliers who were strategically placed to cut off any retreat by the ford.

The rain began to fall heavily, deadening the sounds of the troops' movements to such an extent that they were able to take up strategic positions and strike with complete surprise. Captain Ellis and his troopers were not sighted until they advanced on the village. The men rushed for their spears and woomeras while the women and children withdrew towards the river. Ellis gave the order to charge and within minutes was in the middle of the village. The Nyungar turned to face the charge. Norcott, armed with a double-barrelled shotgun, recognised an old enemy. "There's that old rascal Noonar," he yelled. Undaunted, Noonar replied, "Yes, Noonar me," and threw his spear.[44] Norcott shot and wounded him.

In the first charge, five Nyungar warriors were killed, valiantly fighting mounted troopers whose superior weapons made a mockery of bravery. The Nyungar retreated towards the river only to find themselves caught in deadly crossfire. They attempted to rally their forces on the river bank but the charging horses on one side and Stirling's marksmen on the other cut them down as they stood vainly looking for targets for their spears and often hurling them in desperation up the steep, flood-scoured bank.

The fusiliers could fire down on the struggling mass below with impunity. The only alternative for the trapped spearmen was to seek some kind of cover. They hid behind logs and branches or in holes in the banks or dived under water, coming up for air from time to time or keeping only their faces out of the water.[45]

The troops noted with amazement that despite their desperate situation no Nyungar called for surrender. They held on to their spears, came out of cover to hurl them or trod water, trying to reply to the fusillades from the banks. They never ceased to try to take the offensive, but every attempt to throw their spears exposed them to Stirling's marksmen. Some attempted to break out of the trap in a concerted charge only to be cut down by a hail of bullets. It was not long before more than half of the fighting men of the Nyungar had been killed. Captain Ellis was wounded by a spear and fell from his horse, and Corporal Heffron was wounded in the arm, but no other casualties were sustained by the British troops.[46]

The fusiliers dismounted and formed a thin red line at the top of the steep river bank firing at will into the spearmen trying desperately to find a foothold on the slippery clay, to hide from the fire and at the same time hurl their spears at the line of soldiers. With incredible bravery they persisted, and a few found their target, one narrowly missing Stirling himself, a veteran of more than a decade of war across the world, commander of a warship at twenty-one and still only forty-three years old. His death could have turned the tide. It would not have won the battle for the Nyungar but it would have given heart for further resistance and perhaps won to Calyute's standard the warriors of the Swan and Upper Swan.

As the battle raged eight women and a group of children were taken prisoner and held under guard. They saw their men cut down as they struggled to take the offensive and then, when the fight was hopelessly lost, watched the survivors attempt to flee on foot or escape downriver in the water. The soldiers under Stirling's command ceased fire and mounted to pursue the survivors. John Roe, who stayed at the ford, heard the cries of the survivors as they were caught and shot. The soldiers and troopers remaining on the battlefield set about killing the wounded. None survived. One and a half hours after the first shot was fired the bugle sounded to signal the end of the Battle of Pinjarra.

The casualties sustained by the Nyungar were subsequently minimised by the victors: Stirling reported only fifteen dead, Roe mentioned fifteen

---

OVERLEAF:
Although not of Pinjarra, this scene from the Illustrated Sydney News *of 1872 is very similar to the battle site on the Murray River.*
NATIONAL LIBRARY OF AUSTRALIA

to twenty, while Captain Daniell, who was ordered to survey the battleground after the engagement, found several mass graves. Other estimates are as high as fifty, and it would seem that more than half the Nyungar at Pinjarra that day were wiped out.[47] The victors acknowledged killing only one woman and fewer than a dozen children.

Calyute escaped death both in battle and during the aftermath, but his youngest son, Unia, was killed and two of his wives were wounded. Yornup had his right leg shot away and was also shot twice in the left thigh. Mindup was shot twice, once in the left arm and once in the thigh. Gummel, one of Calyute's trusted lieutenants who had been with him on the raid on Shenton's Mill, was among the dead.[48] After the bugle sounded the end of the engagement, the three English units formed up together on the east bank of the river ready for further action, but Calyute and the remnants of his fighting men, many of them bleeding and torn from bullet wounds, unable to rally again, escaped into the bush. The few captives were released with instructions to tell the story of Stirling's victory and spread the message that the army would return "to destroy every man, woman and child", to use the words of G. F. Moore, who kept a diary of the events.[49]

By 10.05 am Stirling had reassembled his men and they reached Mandurah late that afternoon. The wounded Captain Ellis died after lying in a coma for two weeks. In contrast to his foes, who fought so bravely and well, he was buried with full English military honours. The bodies of the Nyungar dead lay where they had fallen. It was left to the defeated people to return, silent and unseen, to bury them in mass graves, the sites of which were kept secret by Nyungar people in the area for more than a century. Over the years repeated floods have altered the terrain but even today the Nyungar know where the fallen were buried.

Captain F. C. Irwin, who was lieutenant governor in Stirling's absence, said in a book he wrote the following year that the battle was needed to demonstrate to the Nyungar "their inferiority in power to the whites".[50] Yet the settlers felt the victory was not enough. They believed Calyute would raise another force and seek to unite all the Nyungar clans for a grand onslaught on Perth and the English Pale. It was a fantasy. In fact, the people of the Swan, Canning and York, instead of seeing the battle was the death knell of their independence, felt the defeat of the famed Murray River spearmen might actually advantage them by making available their possessions.

Thomas Peel continued to agitate for a final solution, a ruthless extermination of the entire people, the young and the old, men, women and children.[51] Neither he nor anyone else realised that Stirling had dealt a death blow to the hope of the Nyungar people of the Murray to free their lands of the intruders. The reality was revealed five months after the battle when an emissary of the Murray people sought peace with the victorious governor. After what was reported as careful thought, Stirling agreed to send a formal reply and chose Miago, of the Swan River people, to invite them to meet him in Perth.

The peace conference was held in March 1835 with Munday and Miago acting as interpreters. The Murray leaders pledged their support for the present and future decisions of the governor, followed by a similar pledge from the Swan River men.[52] It was, in fact, as unconditional a surrender as that of Germany and Japan after World War II. There were no concessions, no recognition of land rights and no guarantee that the Nyungar would ever be consulted again. They never were until the latter half of the twentieth century. At a ceremony to celebrate the peace Stirling displayed his power and charity by distributing fifty loaves of bread before going back to Government House to reflect on his triumph. The Mooro group of the Swan people adjourned to a creek called Doodinup, now in Spring Street, Perth, while the gallant Murray people went to a waterhole at Dyeedyallalup near today's ABC studios.[53]

Calyute, the proud warrior, the fearless leader, the loved and respected lawman and elder, survived, living out his life to die an old man, unheralded and unsung by the conquerors and remembered only in the laments of his people.

That Stirling fully recognised the quality of his foes is shown in a despatch to London written on 12 June 1836: "If they had the inclination and the power to combine their efforts, it would be useless to attempt to maintain our conquest with our present numbers".[54] A year later Stirling resigned as governor and early in 1839 returned to England to re-enter active service. He commanded battleships in the Mediterranean in 1840–44 and in 1847–50. He climbed further up the ladder of success to become a Lord of the Admiralty for a short period in 1852 and his final active service was as Commander-in-Chief in the East Indies and China in 1854–56. Like his opponent he lived to be an old man, dying on 22 April 1865 at Guildford—not the place he named in Western Australia but in the English county of Surrey. Unlike his vanquished foe he was honoured in death and his grave became a shrine for his family, friends and admirers. The defeated Calyute lies in an unknown unmarked grave within the boundaries of the lands held and conserved and cherished for 40,000 years, only to be lost in the Battle of Pinjarra.

8. *The Battle of Eureka Stockade*

The Republic of Victoria was proclaimed in Melbourne on 1 January 1855. The provisional president was Peter Lalor and the vice president Raffaello Carboni. The English governor of Victoria, Charles Hotham, retreated to Sydney to prepare a report to London in conjunction with the New South Wales governor, Charles Fitzroy.

Had it not been for the tactical ability of an English officer whose achievements have been ignored for nearly 130 years, this would have been the result of perhaps the best known rebellion in Australia's history, which broke out in Victoria in 1854.

The Invasion of Victoria

The area that now comprises the state of Victoria was the homeland of thirty-eight Australian nations, which varied greatly in size depending on the richness of their land. One of the things that distinguished the people of Victoria from those of the rest of the continent was that some groups established permanent villages where they lived in U-shaped or semi-circular houses with low stone walls and low ceilings of rushes and sheets of bark surrounded by a timber frame. A number of stone houses have been found in south-western Victoria around Lake Condah and Condah Swamp; in one paddock alone there were 146. In these villages the people stayed put because the lakes were teeming with food resources, including eels which were smoked on hearths made of basalt rocks. This image contradicts the stereotype of traditional Australians as being lean, hungry nomads, constantly on the move in search of food and water.[1]

The decentralised power structure of the Victorian nations was similar to that in the rest of the continent, leaving the people open to invasion and occupation. Despite the fact that the great Portuguese navigators, Cristovão de Mendonça, may have sailed along the coast as far as present day Warrnambool in 1522,[2] for most of the people of south-east Australia the pale strangers from overseas remained only a rumour, a fairy tale for late night storytelling around the camp fire, right up to 1800. The English navigators Bass and Flinders, who were based at the new colony in Sydney Cove, briefly explored the coast in the region of Port Phillip in 1797. At that time the Victorian coast was also occasionally penetrated by the notorious sealers and whalers, by escaped prisoners and sometimes by shipwrecked innocents. In 1801 an English ship commanded by Lieutenant James Grant, who had set out from Sydney on a probing expedition of the Bass Strait area, anchored for a few weeks in Western Port Bay, where he established crops and a dwelling on Churchill Island. The following year two ships would have been sighted in Port Phillip, one commanded by Lieutenant Murray who discovered the bay, the other by Matthew Flinders who charted it. Earlier in the year Flinders had bumped into the French navigator Nicolas Baudin in the waters around the Victorian and South Australian coast.

On the recommendation of Governor King in Sydney the British Government sent Captain David Collins to establish a prison settlement at Port Phillip. Late in 1803 Collins set up a small military station just inside the heads at what is now Sorrento. It was at this point that the first hostilities probably occurred with the Bunurong people, whose land encompassed the Port Phillip area. This may have been one of the reasons for Collins abandoning the post only a few months later and removing the entire complement to the Derwent River in Van Diemen's Land, where a military post had been established in September 1803. Apart from occasional incursions Victoria remained largely free of occupation for the next thirty years. Assuming the hostility of the Bunurong was responsible, this was a significant triumph never to be achieved for so long a period in any other part of the continent.

One of the interesting sidelights of the Collins military post was the escape of one of the prisoners, William Buckley, who made his way to the western side of the bay. He settled with the Kurung people and lived with them for thirty years, not rejoining his own people until he was fifty-five years old.

The first incursion from the land occurred in 1824 at the height of the war against the Wiradjuri people in New South Wales. A group of pale skinned men appeared riding on the backs of weird animals and carrying with them portable shelters in a dray pulled by other animals never seen before. The party crossed the Murray River watched closely by the Pangerang people into whose land they trespassed. They reported to their neighbours that the invaders had brought with them a strange sickness that left people either dead or pockmarked. The leaders of this party are recorded as W. H. Hovell and Hamilton Hume. The people who watched them come and go believed the sickness was caused by the

Mindi, the destroying spirit who could bring misfortune.[3] News of the incursion spread rapidly across the countryside as the invaders moved south to Corio Bay, where the coastal nations woke one morning to find a dread sickness had suddenly struck them also. Rumours spread that the heavens were likely to fall and prevent the sun moving across the sky, and that all the people of the land would be killed.[4] The presentiment was only too accurate, but for the time being the sun and the moon continued their journeying across the heavens and the cycle of life continued as it had done for more than 40,000 years.

In the mid-1830s the British started to occupy their lands. The forerunners were Edward Henty and Henry Camfield, two English free settlers who arrived at Portland Bay with four prisoners and a mob of sheep on 19 November 1834. In 1835 the Port Phillip settlement came into being with the arrival of two separate parties under John Batman and John Pascoe Fawkner, heralding an invasion that saw the British roll over the land like a juggernaut. Within three years more than 1000 invaders had reached the Port Phillip District; by 1841 there were over 20,000[5] and by 1851, when the colony of Victoria was proclaimed, 77,000[6] people from Europe and Asia were occupying the Australians' land.

In the short space of fifteen years the resistence of the Australians had been completely broken and the population reduced by nine-tenths.[7] Their complete subjugation was inevitable but one event consigned them even more rapidly to the back pages of history—the discovery in 1849 of a sixteen ounce gold nugget at Daisy Hill. This was the signal for a new and overwhelming invasion: by 1861 Victoria had a population of 540,000 Europeans and Asians,[8] ten times that of the thirty-eight nations they had dispossessed.

Initially, the invasion of Victoria came not directly from the English colonial capital of Sydney but from Van Diemen's Land. The Derwent River military post, which Collins had moved to the present site of Hobart after abandoning the first Port Phillip settlement in 1804, had become a prison on a scale even larger than Sydney. Van Diemen's Land also attracted wealthy settlers and by 1835 demand for good grazing land had outstripped supply. Landseekers such as the Henty brothers were quickly followed by others from Tasmania eager to establish themselves on the mainland.

Early in 1835 John Batman formed an association comprising fifteen members to set up a colony of their own in the Port Phillip area and engage in stock breeding. In May that year, in a way which did him credit, Batman sought out the owners of the land in the Port Phillip area—the Bunurong, Wurundjeri, Kurung and Wathaurung nations—and with much sincerity negotiated a treaty to allow the members of his association to settle on their land by mutual agreement rather than conquest. This famous treaty ceded to John Batman and his heirs 100,000 acres (40,000 hectares) on the southern shore of Geelong harbour, and, by a second deed, 500,000 acres (200,000 hectares) around the present city of Melbourne stretching as far south as Geelong.[9] Neither Batman nor his associates were aware that the eternal laws of the people could not permit or even envisage the sale of land, that the terms of the treaty could have been neither understood nor accepted by the four nations.

Batman returned to Van Diemen's Land and tried to have the treaty approved by his own administration. Meanwhile a fellow Vandiemonian, John Pascoe Fawkner, sent an expedition to Port Phillip. When Batman returned he found to his annoyance that Fawkner's party had settled themselves on the banks of the River Yarra opposite the site he had selected for a village. Both parties appealed to the governor of New South Wales, Sir Richard Bourke, who moved rapidly to protect the British Crown's title to the land by right of conquest. Bourke declared that any treaty with Black Australians was illegal, but, realising he had no hope of preventing settlement in the area, decreed that the land would be sold by auction. Batman was consoled with a valuable land grant at Geelong, and no more was heard of making treaties with the people of the land. They were to be dispossessed in the name of the English king on the basis of *terra nullius*, that the continent was a land without people.

The growth of Batman's village on the Yarra was dramatic and the invasion of south-eastern Australia swift. Within five years Melbourne had 4000 people, thirty hotels, three newspapers and hundreds of tradesmen. The Western District had been penetrated and the traditional lands had been overrun by more than 300,000 sheep.

Hard on the heels of the invaders from Van Diemen's Land came people and herds from the north. A drought in the Monaro district in New South Wales after 1841 sent people and livestock flooding across the Murray River into northern Victoria. Despite sustained resistance the invaders were overwhelming. The pastoralists were reinforced by shiploads of immigrants sent to Melbourne to serve those who had seized the lands of the thirty-eight nations. By the late 1840s the only parts of Victoria not taken from the original people were the arid areas in the north-west of the Mallee district and the mountains and heavily forested parts of Gippsland and the Otway Ranges. The British Crown reserved all land for itself unless it specifically granted title to an individual or a company. Thousands of people who poured into Victoria had no legal title at all under English law, and of course none under the law of the Australian nations.

The presence of the British Crown was established by Governor Bourke, who sent Captain William Lonsdale, as military commander and magistrate, with soldiers and colonial police to set up a military post on the Yarra in 1836. Bourke visited the village himself the following year and ordered a town to be laid out and named Melbourne in honour of his London superior who administered the far flung colonies. In 1839 Charles Joseph La Trobe was despatched from England as superintendent of the settlement of Port Phillip. La Trobe, who was born in London in 1801, was the son of a minister of a German refugee church (the Moravian Church) in Manchester. He became a tutor and a writer, and was thirty-eight years old when he arrived in Melbourne. He reported directly to the governor of New South Wales—at first Sir George Gipps and from 1846 Sir Charles Augustus Fitzroy—and presided over an increasingly diverse mixture of people who seemed to develop a spirit of independence all their own. When transportation to New South Wales was suspended in 1840, for example, an attempt to divert prisoners to Port Phillip was met by its inhabitants with resolute opposition.

From the outset there was impatience with Imperial rule. Although Port Phillip was ruled from Sydney, it soon developed its own lands office, a branch of the Supreme Court, and its own customs and police officers. The taxes and revenue, however, went to Sydney, and when the Yarra village was only five years old a petition was made to sever administrative links with Sydney. When the first partially elected Legislative Council was established in New South Wales in 1842–43, the Port Phillip District and Melbourne were given only six of the twenty-four elective seats. This added fuel to the fires of separatism, and it was difficult to find anyone prepared to travel so far to attend sittings. The electors of Melbourne made a complete farce of the system in 1848 by voting in as their representative in Sydney the English minister, Earl Grey, then Secretary of State for Colonies.

In 1850 the English Parliament succumbed to colonial pressure and passed an Act described as being "for the better Government of Her Majesty's Australian Colonies".[10] This set up a new colony to be named after the English Queen Victoria, who had succeeded her uncle, William IV, in 1837. The northern boundary ran north-west from Cape Howe to "the nearest source" of the Murray River, which it then followed downstream to the border of South Australia. The folk history of the Riverina people, the south-west province of New South Wales, is that the original boundary was to be the Murrumbidgee River, but that either a clerk in the Colonial Office in London got his rivers mixed up or the wily Port Phillip push did not want Riverina because it was drought-stricken at the time and dotted with dead people and stock.

Melbourne celebrated for two weeks non-stop when the news came from London. A new Legislative Council was to consist of thirty members of whom twenty were to be elected. However, as Melbourne itself was to elect only three and since franchise was restricted by property qualifications, power remained firmly in the hands of those who held the land—the pastoralists. In addition, the remaining ten members were nominated by the governor, who also appointed an Executive Council of up to four with whom he was to exercise his authority.

The colony of Victoria was proclaimed on 1 July 1851 with La Trobe as lieutenant governor. It was the discovery of gold, however, that dictated the course of history in this part of the continent.

Gold

Dreams of gold had long dominated the Australian scene. The first find, only six months after the arrival of the First Fleet, was reported by a prisoner named Daley, who produced a clump of earth complete with gold particles to prove it. There was a rush to the site nominated by this overnight hero near Sydney, but no more was found. He eventually confessed to melting down some gold and salting the patch of earth in the hope of a pardon and return home for his "discovery". Lashed mercilessly and made to wear a canvas coat marked with the letter "R" for rogue, he was hanged within a few months as a thief.[11] Hell hath no fury like those disappointed in sight of boundless wealth.

A year before the Battle of Bathurst in 1824, Assistant Surveyor James McBrian found particles of gold near the Fish River, some twenty-four kilometres east of Bathurst. Nothing more was recorded for sixteen years until in 1839 Paul Edmund de Strzelecki, the Polish explorer, geologist and mineralogist, confirmed the evidence of gold near Hartley in the Bathurst district. Strzelecki was anxious to pursue his finds, but Governor George Gipps opposed the initiative, perhaps frightened of a great rush of people that could sweep him and his rule into oblivion. An English clergyman and geologist named W. B. Clarke found gold in 1841 at Cox River in Wiradjuri country, and on the Wollondilly. As a clergyman he saw gold as something to be feared in a land in which he considered his fellow countrymen and women either dishonest or immoral or both.[12] In effect he sat on the information for several years.

Many shepherds had discovered gold but tried to keep the information to themselves. A man named McGregor, nicknamed "the gold-finder", was believed to have mined gold to the value of £200 sterling.[13] Such secrecy was essential as far as the gold seekers were concerned, because under English law all gold and silver belong to the Crown.[14]

During the 1840s Sir Roderick Murchison, an Englishman who had lived and worked in Australia for ten years, was telling the Royal Geographic Society in London that there was a strong resemblance between the Blue Mountains chain in Australia and the Ural Mountains in Russia. This similarity, he told his London audience, had led him to search for gold in Australia, and particularly in the Blue Mountains. Murchison had looked in the wrong place, but in 1849 he found a sixteen ounce nugget at Daisy Hill in Victoria. That same year there was a major gold discovery in California, which was to link Australia and California closely for a decade.

While Australia had been seized by the British Crown, California had been taken by the Spanish, and both colonial powers adopted a similar attitude to the conquered peoples resulting in the dispossession of the vanquished. As early as 1820 there were rumours of gold finds in the vicinity of San Luis Obispo in southern California. In 1842 a *ranchero* named Francisco Lopez discovered gold at Placerita Creek not far from the present city of Los Angeles,[15] but it was not until an Anglo-American named James Marshall discovered alluvial gold uncovered by a water flow at Sutter's Mill that California became world famous.

Gold fever gripped Sydney when the news of Marshall's find broke. In January 1849 six ships crowded with gold seekers and their supplies sailed for San Francisco.[16] Sydney merchants suddenly became aware of a huge new market for food, clothing and other supplies at a time when prices for flour and grain were low in Sydney and high in San Francisco. Tasmanian ports also geared themselves to ship grain and lumber, but Melbourne was not ready to join the trade rush and the authorities warned people not to be lured to California by "feverish dreams". It was six months after the first ships sailed from Sydney that a ship left Melbourne, on 23 June 1849, for California.

By the end of the year more than 800 people from Australia had landed in California and the numbers increased in the following year.[17] The London authorities saw the invasion of California (which was not ceded to the United States until 1850) by British subjects as a way of extending their influence, the Sydney authorities viewed the loss of manpower with sour disfavour, but the Californians were downright worried.

The "Sydney ducks", as they were known, banded together in San Francisco, Sacramento and other centres. In San Francisco, where they grouped together in "Sydney Town",[18] later to become the Barbary Coast, their wild ways stimulated a rash of anti-foreign feeling and demands for restrictions on immigration. A Bill was introduced for the "Better Regulation of the Mines and the Government of Foreign Miners".[19] A tax on foreign diggers was also proposed, but the main thrust of legislation was to close the doors against the multitudes from what were described as the "worst populations" of the Mexican and South American states and New South Wales. The Californian legislature had its committee on finance investigate the invasion and concern was expressed that boatloads of convicts from Botany Bay, Mexico and Chile were carrying away a great deal of gold. Another Bill, passed in April 1850, made it a felony to bring convicts into California,[20] which in fact prohibited the great majority of the "Sydney ducks" from landing.

"Sydney Town" continued to flourish, however, and finally in 1851 San Francisco's first vigilante groups were formed. Two "Sydney ducks" were arrested in February of that year for robbery and beating a San

Francisco merchant. Seized by a lynch mob, they narrowly escaped being hanged by the intervention of the authorities. Almost four months later San Francisco suffered the fifth and most damaging of a series of fires for which it was widely rumoured the "Sydney ducks" were responsible. A mob rampaged through "Sydney Town" and found loot from burned homes. Soon after John Jenkins, an English thief who had come to San Francisco from Sydney, was hanged. The Committee of Vigilance boarded ships from Sydney searching for "convicts"—those discovered were held in custody and put on the next vessel back—and the entire coastline around San Francisco was watched for "Sidney men".[21]

Once news of these activities reached Sydney there was widespread resentment and a decline in numbers heading for California, but while the rushes lasted up to 8000 people poured north across the Pacific. The flow was not always in one direction, however, as many returned disillusioned from the Californian fields. One of these was Edward Hammond Hargraves, who had been a sailor, a station overseer, a shipping agent and a publican before he left Australia for California in July 1849.[22] He returned, empty-handed, at the beginning of 1851 and set out to win the reward being offered by the New South Wales Government for the first find of payable gold. As he said himself, he simply compared the gold-bearing geological formation he had seen in California with similar formations in Australia and decided they too must carry gold. Early in February he found a few specks in Lewis Ponds Creek in the Bathurst district, but nothing more. Four men who he had taught to pan, however, made a real find. Hargraves reported it to the authorities in Sydney and, sure of the reward, leaked the news to the press. By May the rush to Ophir had begun.

The gold discovery in California had taken place only nineteen days after California was ceded by Mexico to the United States. Spanish-Mexican mining laws were soon superseded by a licensing system for foreign miners such as the Sydney men in an attempt to control conditions on the goldfields. In Australia it was obviously impossible to stop the rush, so the English authorities followed California's example. They could do little else. As men of every rank and profession converged in their hundreds on Turon Gully, Lewis Ponds and other places, Governor Charles Fitzroy sent a detachment of troops and armed police to set up a military post on the goldfields, and from 1 June 1851 no digging could take place without a licence, which cost thirty shillings a month. The applicant had to show he had been discharged as a prisoner or that his employer would let him go.

The discovery of gold in Victoria followed quickly—at Smythesdale in 1849, at Clunes the following year and in the Pyrenees Range by the German mineralogist Dr G. H. Bruhn. Like Hargraves, former mail coach driver James Esmond had tried his luck in California, and in fact had returned home in the same ship. He was working as a station hand in the Pyrenees area when he met Bruhn, who told him of a good prospect near Clunes. Fired by Bruhn, Esmond went off with a companion and struck it rich at Deep Creek, a small stream running into Loddon River. Soon there was a band of diggers panning the alluvial gold. A strike near the Yarra River only a few kilometres from Melbourne was overshadowed by new finds at Buninyong, Golden Point and Specimen Gully, all leading to the historic Ballarat rush of August 1851.

Ballarat was followed almost as quickly by Mount Alexander and the great golden trove of Bendigo and within a few months more than 80,000 diggers were on the fields.[23] This was to be Australia's greatest decade in people building. In the first year of the gold rush 77,000 immigrants landed in Victoria—more than the entire Commonwealth of Australia gained in a single year in the 1980s. They came from more than thirty different countries, spoke as many languages and practised many different religions.

In California an immigrant had to prove that he was not and had never been a jailbird, particularly if he came from South America or New South Wales, and as a foreigner he had to pay a tax to the authorities; no American citizens were taxed. In Victoria a tax in the form of a mining licence was applied to everyone, before he even began to dig for gold.[24] The individual who was unsuccessful and spent his little fortune on trying was still in debt to the government. The Victorian authorities went even further by limiting the size of a claim to 144 square feet (thirteen square metres);[25] Californian claims could be as large as 2880 square feet (over 250 square metres). Australian diggers were doled out parcels of land so small that their chances of success were limited from the start.

Victoria also followed their trans-Pacific cousins by passing an "Influx of criminals prevention Act",[26] which was not designed to keep out "Sydney ducks" but people coming from Van Diemen's Land. Any Vandiemonian arriving in Victoria had to prove that he was not a prisoner of less than three years freedom otherwise he or she was refused permission to land. A heavy fine was the penalty for any captain who brought a prisoner or former prisoner to a Victorian port.

Not only immigrants flocked to the goldfields but the people whom the Victorian authorities relied upon to run their administration. A report submitted to Lieutenant Governor La Trobe illustrated that Melbourne was bleeding to death. The postmaster general said his operations were grinding to a halt; the surveyor general reported in the same way; the deputy registrar said his entire staff was leaving for the goldfields; the superintendent of police increased pay for all, but fifty out of fifty-five constables resigned to search for gold and only his clerk and senior constable remained; the Crown Solicitor said he was embarrassed and the Denominational School Board feared a loss of teachers. To maintain law and order on the goldfields La Trobe was forced to rely on his black mounted police force, which he sent to patrol the diggings and inspect mining licences. The black police were known as "Joes" as their official police authorities were signed "Charles Joseph La Trobe".

Ballarat, built on Wathaurung land close to the border of Kurung territory, was the scene of one of the most dramatic of all the great rushes. In a confined space of a few hundred metres thousands were at work, the sides of the creek so thickly lined with miners that it was impossible to cross without asking someone to step aside. As mining progressed the work became more difficult. Shafts up to forty-five metres deep had to be sunk and they often filled with water which seeped through the porous soils. Pumps run by steam engines were used to keep them dry.[27] To operate mines like this miners formed companies of ten to twenty, working in shifts to pump out the water. When the going was tough, companies often did not have even enough money to buy bread with their shaft only half finished.

Huge quantities of gold, including nuggets, were found in both deep and shallow diggings, but many claims gave no return at all. It was a gigantic sweat shop. The claims were so small that violent arguments broke out over only a few centimetres of dirt. A claim had to be worked at least a few hours every day and if not worked for twenty-four hours it could be taken over by someone else.[28] If a miner sweating blood over a sterile claim tried to switch to another, his neighbours could jump either his old one or the new one because he was not permitted two. In the event of disputes the Goldfields Commissioner, assisted by four assessors from among the miners, was supposed to adjudicate, but in the rivalry and tension of the time most disputes were resolved by the pick or the gun, or the threat of them.

Men from all parts of the world and of all religions, some educated and some not, artisans, literary men, priests, pastors, soldiers, a host of ex-prisoners from the English gaols of the Australian colonies and even Black Australians were caught up in the rape of the soil. A Polish digger, Seweryn Korzelinski, recalled:

> *A colonel pulls up the earth for a sailor; a lawyer wields not a pen but a spade; a priest lends a match to a Negro's pipe; a doctor rests on the same heap of earth with a Chinaman; a man of letters carries a bag of earth; many a baron or count has a drink with a Hindu, and all of them hirsute, dusty and muddy, so that their own mothers would not be able to recognise them.*[29]

They shared the common designation "digger" despite colour of skin, accent and background. Technical English was the lingua franca—everyone understood "bucket", "aye aye" and "pull up"—and during breaks from the exhausting work below ground they stretched out in the fresh

air to share experiences with their neighbours.

Korzelinski remembered how "a happy-go-lucky German tailor, a brawny English smith, a slightly-built French cook, a Polish Jew, an American or Dutch sailor, . . . a Swiss hatmaker, an impoverished Spanish hidalgo, . . . a black Negro head, a brown Indian face or the olive countenance with slanting eyes of a 'child of the sun' " would gather to yarn.[30] Nearby a group might include a Swedish sailor away from his whaling ship, a Norwegian reindeer herdsman, a gaucho from La Plata,

a Creole from Malabar or Mozambique.

Within months of the beginning of the rush Ballarat could boast a street of traders and stores, public houses, butchers and bakers, a canvas chapel and bands of Czech musicians who travelled the fields playing

ABOVE:
A view of the site of the Eureka Stockade at Ballarat, 1854.
NATIONAL LIBRARY OF AUSTRALIA

love songs on their traditional harps. Tents were occupied by one or two miners or sometimes by whole families. Packing cases were used as pantries to protect bread and rice from mice; coffee, tea and sugar were kept in the same place but meat was hung high in a tree or at the top of the tent pole so the dogs could not reach it.[31] A candle in a bottle served for light at night.

As darkness fell the diggers began their nightly shooting spree, firing the old cartridge and reloading to make certain that the piece would not fail if needed. These salvos, which also served as a warning to marauders, often continued late into the night and sometimes a sleeping digger was accidently shot by a neighbour with poor aim.[32] As night drew on the firing died away, to be replaced by the sound of diggers returning from a night's drinking. At dawn, everyone had to queue for water—in some places, such as Mount Malaga, the charge was 2s 6d a bucket.

Sunday was the only holiday apart from Christmas and Easter but the English diggers celebrated Queen Victoria's birthday and in 1852 went into mourning for the passing of the Duke of Wellington, the English commander at Waterloo. The North Americans were not so impressed with Wellington and his deeds and there was often pin pricking between the two. Overall, however, camaraderie prevailed, and the flags of a score of countries flew proudly above the tents.

Immigration to Australia in 1852 was seven times higher than in the previous year. Before the rushes ended Victoria alone attracted more than 5000 North Americans, 6000 Germans, up to 40,000 from Asia (mainly Chinese) and thousands of Irish, English, Scots and Welsh.[33]

It was the people they quaintly termed "Celestials" who caused the Anglo-establishment, ever mindful of their superiority in numbers, most concern. New South Wales imposed a double miners' tax on people described as "aliens", who included not only Chinese but all "non-British subjects". Victoria went further by imposing in addition a £10 poll tax on Chinese on arrival and limiting their migration to one person for each ten tonnes of a ship's burden.[34]

Soon the most isolated and most visible group in the community, the Chinese were often discriminated against by those who themselves were discriminated against by officialdom. The dictum of divide and rule was promoted vigorously by the Anglo-establishment. Squeezed into a minority they looked in panic at the numbers ranged against them and pondered how best to keep the power they had seized. After the English, the Chinese were the most numerous. The official strategy was to isolate them, to make them the scapegoat for the savage taxes, the repression and the lack of sound economic management. The rulers succeeded in creating this division and when the rebellion came the Chinese took no part in it.

By mid-century too, the prisoner content of the workforce had dropped to one per cent, and half of the entire population was locally born, the "currency" lads and lasses. This boisterous new generation of locally born whites had developed a challenging egalitarianism, which represented a growing threat to the dictatorial rule of English governors who imposed local edicts with the co-operation of a handful of English land barons. Frequently rewarded with English titles and English medals, they could be sure of a warm welcome from officials in the Imperial capital when they went "Home". As events unfolded during the 1850s, the English establishment became more and more isolated and alienated from the majority of the population, the locally born whites and the diggers from the rest of the world.

Another ingredient in the giant demographic crucible that was Victoria, and indeed Australia, in the 1850s was the Americans. As the Californian fields began to peter out their eyes turned south to the newest world. American imagination was captured by the Antipodes for the first time. James Gordon Bennett, owner of the *New York Herald*, wrote of Australia's future: a "great country . . . a real Ophir, from the hills and valleys of which gold is rolled out, not by penny weights, as in North Carolina, not by ounces and pounds, as in California, but by the ton . . . This is the golden age, and Australia is the real El Dorado".[35]

A year before Eureka the *Boston Post* was predicting:

> *Soon republican institutions will be there . . . monopoly, under the impious plea of divine right, will not be allowed to filch bread from the mouths of those who earn it—as is done in England now; as the development of republican principles is sure, [there] will arise a new government, another America, that will rejoice and profit together with its elder brother Jonathan, in free trade and free institutions.*[36]

This was the America which had risen in rebellion and won its fight for independence to establish the first republic in the New World.

Only one American in nine was actually in Ballarat, where it is estimated there were about 600. They were immediately identifiable by their colourful rig and bandana, and an air of alertness and confidence. Despite their colourful clothes they were as a group sober and industrious, and brought with them both expertise and a spirit of co-operation which made their mining operations more sophisticated than most. Above all they were organised, energetic and proud of their young republic.[37] They tended to keep their own counsel on the goldfields, and the Fourth of July was their only celebration,[38] but they did not hesitate to speak up for republicanism, which they equated with freedom and prosperity. Their words found an echo not only among the Irish, Germans and Italians but also among English working class and the Australian-born whites who were beginning to feel the stirrings of nationhood.

The Seeds of Rebellion

In August 1851 Lieutenant Governor La Trobe, following New South Wales' lead, announced that a monthly licence tax of thirty shillings would be imposed on those on the goldfields. Goldfields Commissioner Doveton, accompanied by a contingent of troops and armed police, was despatched to Ballarat where on 20 September he announced that fifteen shillings was immediately payable for what remained of the month, with thirty shillings due on 1 October and monthly thereafter.[39]

The announcement brought a swift reaction, and not just from those who, struggling to find money to buy tools and supplies at rocketing prices, could not pay or found it a hardship. The diggers had believed that no licence tax would be payable until October and were outraged by the postage-stamp size of the claims they were to be permitted. (A measure of the savagery of the tax is the fact that shepherds in 1850 received a wage of eighteen to twenty pounds a year, plus rations; licence fees of thirty shillings a month amounted to an annual tax of eighteen pounds.)[40]

After a protest meeting of shocked and angry diggers, a delegation went to Doveton seeking postponement of the tax until October and an enlargement of the allowable claim size. "I am not here to make the law," Doveton told them, "but to administer it and if you don't pay the licence I'll damned soon make you pay it."[41] Despite this bravado, the solidarity of the diggers and their well-armed numbers persuaded him to abandon any idea of collecting licence fees until October.

In December La Trobe proclaimed that licence fees would be doubled to three pounds a month in the new year and would apply not just to miners but to anyone "concerned" with the search for gold. This was the equivalent of a year's wages for rural workers which by 1853 rose to between twenty-six and forty pounds a year in the face of labour shortages. La Trobe came under attack in the Melbourne *Argus* where he was accused of appointing "foppish whippersnappers" to positions of power and his minions described as "mushroom puppets of a rotten government".[42] The commissioner on the goldfields was accused of corruption and it was alleged that diggers paying for licences in gold received much less than the going rate.

Protest meetings attracted thousands of concerned people, not only in country centres such as Bendigo, Ballarat and Castlemaine but also in Melbourne where a meeting in Flagstaff Gardens resolved that the diggers, who by then made up half the population of the colony, had a right to be consulted on the tax. At one meeting a speaker reminded La Trobe that "it was such taxation that lost Great Britain America".[43] Captain Harrison, who had been a popular and prominent figure in the Anti-Transportation League, addressed 12,000 people at Castlemaine. Pledges of "self defence" were made, and the demand for guns, pistols

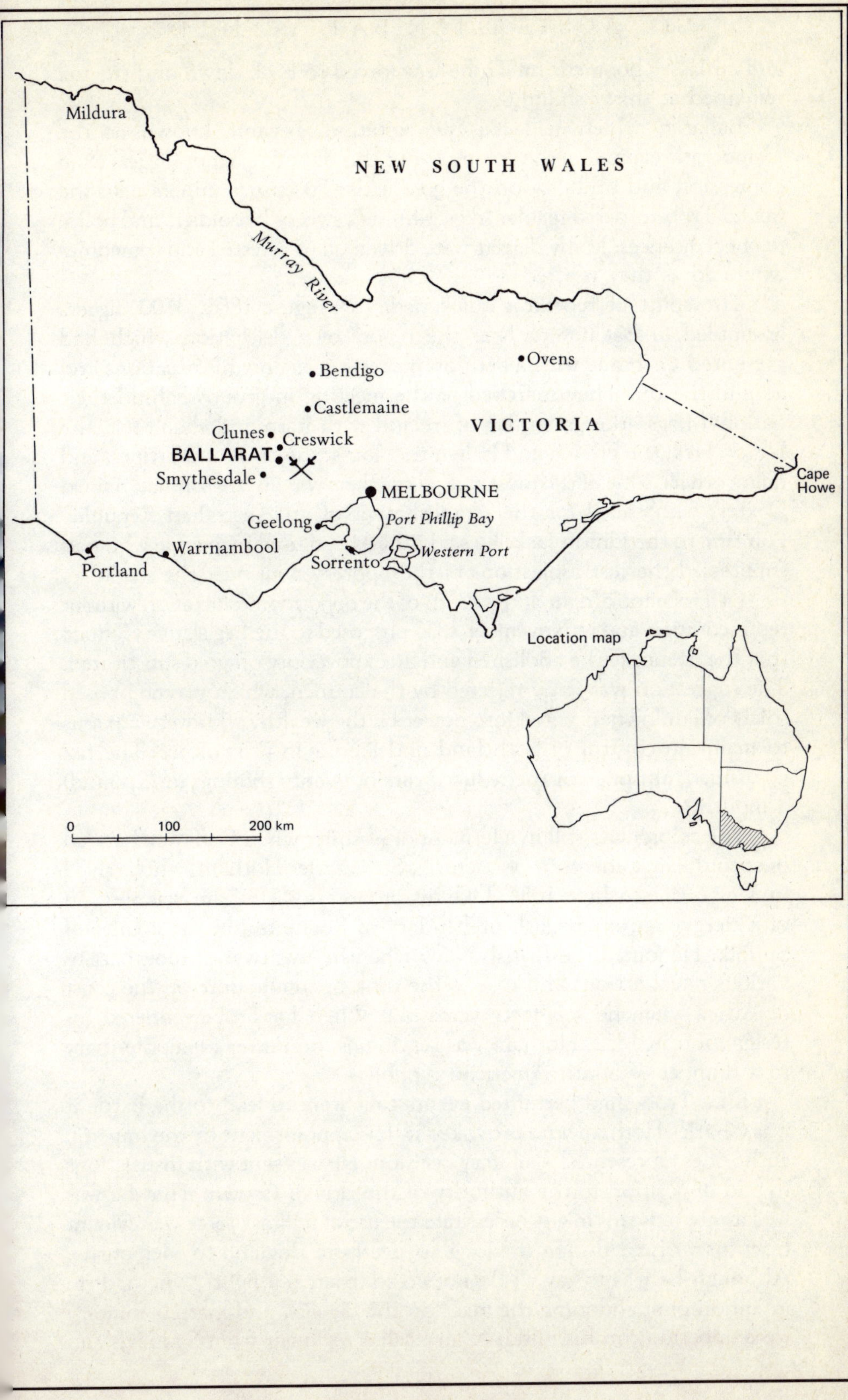
NEW SOUTH WALES
Mildura
Murray River
Ovens
Bendigo
Castlemaine
VICTORIA
Clunes
Creswick
BALLARAT
Smythesdale
MELBOURNE
Cape Howe
Geelong
Port Phillip Bay
Warrnambool
Portland
Sorrento
Western Port
Location map
0
100
200 km

and cutlasses boomed. La Trobe was forced to back down and the tax remained at thirty shillings.

Ballarat, which had led the agitation, became known as the "democratic capital" of the colony.[44] But this did not exempt diggers from oppression and brutality on the goldfields. To ensure miners paid the tax La Trobe ordered regular "digger hunts", sweeps by soldiers and police to check licences. Many diggers were driven off or arrested and sometimes wounded as they resisted.

The spirit of rebellion quickened. In August 1853, 3000 diggers assembled in Ballarat to hear the report of a delegation which had presented La Trobe with a petition protesting against his exactions and administration. They marched to the meeting in groups behind their national flags—the green flag of Ireland with harp and shamrock, the Union Jack, the French and Italian tricolours, the Stars and Stripes, and many others. One of the most radical speakers was an Englishman named Dexter, who called for the establishment of an Australian Republic. Pointing to the Union Jack, he said it had been used by people who had suppressed the just aspirations of the oppressed all over the world.

La Trobe took fright at the depth of the opposition to taxation without representation and in November 1853 proposed to the Legislative Council that the licence fee be abolished and an export duty on gold substituted. The suggestion was flatly rejected by the council, which was composed solely of landowners voted into power by the wealthy who were anxious to maintain control of both land and labour in the colony. The tax continued, although at the reduced rate of twenty shillings (one pound) a month.[45]

The colony was still in a ferment of hostility when La Trobe handed over to the first governor of Victoria, Sir Charles Hotham, who arrived in Melbourne in June 1854. Like his predecessor Hotham was the son of a clergyman, an English prebendary of Rochester, in the county of Suffolk. He joined the British Navy when he was twelve, took part in various naval actions and rose to the rank of commodore on the coast of Africa when he was forty years old. When La Trobe tendered his resignation in 1852, Hotham was serving as a minister plenipotentiary to a number of South American republics.

If La Trobe had permitted events that were to lead to the battle it was Charles Hotham who provoked it. His appointment by the Imperial authorities represented a military decision. He was sent with instructions to end opposition to the authority of the British Crown. That he was well aware that this might necessitate the use of military force was evident from his writings during the long voyage from England to Melbourne. Although he was to say, "I do not go to (coerce) a fight",[46] he had no intention of abandoning the taxes on the diggers, and matters military were uppermost in his mind: "Can I call a regiment from Sydney, Van

Diemens's Land or New Zealand?"[47] When he took charge of the administration, he gave orders rather than listened to advice, effectively ignored the Legislative Council except when it agreed with him and ran the colony like a military dictator.

Briefed by the same closed group of advisers who had led La Trobe along the path of confrontation, Hotham decided in August 1854 to visit the "democratic capital" and show the flag. The diggers were misled into thinking he was bringing them a change in policy, and even cheered him when he described them as "true hearted" and "loyal",[48] although most must have wondered who they were expected to be loyal to. They rapidly became disillusioned: Hotham failed to mention goldfields reform in his first speech to the Legislative Council. In addition, in an attempt to overcome a shortfall in colonial revenue, he ordered in September that the monthly raids by the military and police to inspect licences be increased to twice a week.

Colonial Secretary Foster, Chief Commissioner Rede at Ballarat, Goldfields Chief Commissioner Wright and Chief Commissioner of Police MacMahon all warned Hotham that the confrontation was growing daily more bitter.[49] While the colonial administration spent all its time, energy and bullets in enforcing an unjust tax they ignored the simple needs such as roads, and even the prevention of crime. During October 1854, for example, Raffaello Carboni, later a leader of the rebellion, reported a man murdered and thrown into a mine shaft, a boy left to drown in a creek, horses stolen daily, the nightly hold-up of stores and tent dwellings, and a public murder only a dozen metres from Ballarat's notorious Eureka Hotel where robbery of drunks was routine.[50] Despite the breakdown of law and order the police and magistracy did nothing and evidence mounted of massive corruption in the police force.

Compounding the terror of crime let loose was a dramatic change in the mining scene as surface and alluvial gold was exhausted. Miners now spent months digging deep shafts and worked underground in appalling conditions. They had to find capital to purchase special equipment and machinery and to tide them over the months when there were no returns at all.[51] Many faced starvation for the first time. The military raids simply added to their misery and to the insult they felt at being taxed without representation or consultation, and at not being accorded even basic justice.

Melbourne was no alternative as far as employment was concerned, since the city, and colony, had been in the grip of a financial crisis since 1853, when the squatters and merchants who dominated the Legislative Council combined to avoid taxes and duties themselves and sought to shift the burden to the diggers. There is no doubt that the diggers saw the English governor and his squattocracy as deliberately exploiting them. The daily oppression stung them into a realisation of their political powerlessness: they had no vote and no say at any level of government yet were subject to an arbitrary tax. Again and again at protest meetings and in the passionate discussions that raged wherever diggers gathered, the parallel was drawn with the Boston Tea Party and the American revolution with its catch cry of "No taxation without representation". Throughout October newspapers such as the outspoken *Geelong Advertiser* were warning that disaffection was rapidly increasing,[52] and Hotham was called upon to recognise that the spirit of rebellion was abroad.

La Trobe, aware of the potential military power of the diggers, had proposed that licence holders be given a vote but in London the Colonial Office told Hotham bluntly that there should be no yielding to what they saw as the diggers' intimidation.[53] This same Imperial office that had lashed the American colonists into revolt was making the same mistake again, and went on to record that a fight to maintain English ascendancy in the Australian colonies was expected.

The chain of events that led to the explosion of rebellion in Ballarat began with the murder of a digger at the Eureka Hotel, which had become notorious for its fleecing of diggers and the standover tactics used to extract money from them. On 6 October 1854 a Scotsman named James Scobie sought a drink at the hotel. He was told it was closed, which probably meant he did not have enough money. He protested and there was a brawl in which he was killed by a blow from a shovel, which witnesses testified was struck by the hotel owner, J. F. Bentley, a ticket-of-leave man from Tasmania. When a coronial inquest failed to indict him, widespread protests forced a charge and a trial. Again Bentley, his wife and a hired hand were found not guilty by a police magistrate named Dewes, who was known to be in debt to the publican and regarded as being on his payroll.[54]

Incensed at what was seen as another instance of government corruption, more than 5000 diggers gathered on 17 October to show their dissatisfaction. A committee was set up to seek the reopening of proceedings against Bentley and to offer a reward for information leading to the identification and conviction of Scobie's murderer. After the meeting a group of miners moved off to the Eureka Hotel. Passions ran high, the hotel was burnt down and Bentley and his family and hired hands escaped only with the help of the police.

Hotham immediately despatched 450 police and soldiers (from the 2nd Somersetshires, 40th Regiment, the regiment that had distinguished itself in the indiscriminate slaughter of the Battle of Bathurst) to reinforce the Ballarat military, and gave instructions to find the ringleaders of the destruction of the Eureka Hotel. Although he also ordered the re-arrest and retrial of Bentley, the seeds of rebellion had been sown by the merciless military raids, the naked oppression by the authorities, the hounding of the diggers, and the corruption of police and judiciary which had allowed crime to become a lifestyle and a threat to every hard-working family, not only in Ballarat but throughout the goldfields of Victoria.

At every stage the English governor and his local henchmen strove to divide and rule: they had succeeded in making the Chinese scapegoats, alienating them from the rest of the population, and now tried to divide the remainder. Gubernatorial despatches claimed the disaffection was all due to the "foreigners", to "foreign anarchists and armed ruffians". "Nursed in intrigue . . . members of secret societies in Europe [were] conspiring with the worst class of the Irish on the goldfields, and no vile art was wanting among the desperadoes whom Italy, Germany and France had yielded to the Australian mines".[55] The lie to this colonial propaganda was given by events themselves, when in late October 1854 the Ballarat Reform League began to take shape. Organised by two Englishmen, a Welshman and a Scot, who combined their efforts to oppose oppression and injustice, the league rapidly became the driving force in the politicisation of the diggers.

When Hotham had three English diggers, Andrew McIntyre, Thomas Fletcher and Henry Westerby, arrested and charged with leading the riot and burning Bentley's hotel, a protest meeting was called at the Gravel Pits, one of the most heavily worked areas at Ballarat, on 23 October. The meeting condemned the "almost daily violation of personal liberty . . . and . . . the manner in which the laws are enforced at Ballarat",[56] and offered full support for the three diggers. The Diggers' Rights Society came into being and resolved to confront the English authorities whenever they acted unjustly.

Colonial Secretary Foster, primed by Hotham, told the Legislative Council in Melbourne that the laws would be upheld "no matter what the result".[57] London had foreseen that a battle might be necessary, and its servants in Melbourne had endorsed that policy. The Ballarat correspondent of the *Age* wrote, "Excitement here is by no means decreasing".[58] Hard-line Hotham decided on a political show trial of the three diggers, but thought it prudent to conduct it in Melbourne rather than in Ballarat. When another mass meeting of protest was held at Ballarat on 1 November it was obvious that despite the show of force by the military and the armed police, authority was slipping away from the English governor.

The meeting received complaints about corruption and about the torture by police of a crippled Armenian, Joannes Gregorius, servant to the local Catholic priest, Father Smyth, but it was dominated by John Humffray, George Black and a Scot named Holyoake, who guided the diggers onto the broader path of political reform. The *Geelong Advertiser*, recognising this trend, reported on 8 November: "It is evident that the agitation is about to assume a new shape. The consideration of the [tax] matter *per se* has passed away, and in the future, every constitutional exertion is to be used to ensure the obtaining of withheld political rights".[59]

Another meeting of miners and other citizens was held at Bakery Hill on Saturday, 11 November, and it was on this historic day, so closely bound up with events in Australian history, from the execution of Ned Kelly and the armistice of World War I to the dismissal of the Whitlam Government by another autocratic governor more than a century later, that the Ballarat Reform League was officially inaugurated. A dozen bands played and there was a great display of national flags—the Stars and Stripes, the Italian and French tricolours, the German eagle, the green flag of Ireland, the Welsh dragon, St Andrew's cross of Scotland were all there. Thousands of diggers listened to speech after speech not only outlining the oppression, the atrocities and the corruption but calling for political rights and reform. The League, which was described by the *Ballarat Times* as "the germ of Australian independence",[60] drew up a political manifesto calling for "the right of the people to full Parliamentary representation. Manhood Suffrage. No Property Qualification for Parliament. Payment of Members. Abolition of Diggers' and Storekeepers' Licences."[61]

A century later Australian parliaments display the English Magna Carta and Australian Federation Act but not one displays to today's Australians the manifesto that was the foundation of our democracy. In backwaters such as Tasmania the demands of this first democratic manifesto have still not been heeded: limited franchise prevails in the most primitive Upper House in the world.

Humffray was elected secretary and the meeting condemned the government for its oppression of the diggers and demanded the removal of an English sergeant-major of the Somersetshires who they said had perjured himself to convict the three diggers of the Eureka Hotel riot.

By 23 November Bentley's retrial had been concluded and he had at last been convicted of manslaughter. The corrupt magistrate Dewes was dismissed, as were a number of police. But McIntyre, Fletcher and Westerby had been sentenced to terms of imprisonment, despite the fact that it was acknowledged at least 1000 people had personally been involved in burning down the hotel. The jury considered it would "never have had that painful duty to perform if those Government officials at Ballarat had done their duty properly".[62] The irrepressible *Geelong Advertiser* bluntly said, "we can ensure justice only by the complete abolition of the present system of misrule".[63]

A delegation of Humffray, Black and Tom Kennedy, a Scot, from the Reform League met Hotham on 27 November and demanded a pardon for the three diggers. Hotham, incensed by the word "demand", threw them out. Kennedy, in a parting shot, said, "let the men go or there'll be war".[64] The *Argus* agreed, warning the next day in an editorial headed

"Government by Artillery" that "Canada could not get a British statesman to listen to her grievances till she broke out in rebellion".[65] And indeed signs of rebellion were everywhere, as United States Consul Tarleton saw for himself when he visited Ballarat on 28 November.

Tarleton invited local colonial officials, including Goldfields Commissioner Rede and Police Magistrate Hackett, to a reception. During the dinner the air was electric; officials were constantly scurrying away on secret missions and sporadic gunfire was heard. The evening culminated in a dramatic incident when the chairman of the dinner, a local Englishman named Otway, began the official toasts by proposing "The Queen". He was met by a hostile silence. If no British subject would respond, he said, he would drink alone. *Geelong Advertiser* correspondent Samuel Irwin jumped up and said, "While I and my fellow Colonists claim to be, and are thoroughly loyal to our sovereign lady the Queen, we do not, and will not respect her men servants, her maid servants, her oxen, or her asses".[66] When Irwin pointed to the empty chairs of Rede and Hackett, who had rushed away when the gunfire intensified, the room broke into tumultuous applause.

It was not until after the dinner that the reason for the gunfire became apparent. Yet another detachment of troops had arrived from Melbourne and when the news reached Ballarat the first digger militia was quickly formed to intercept them. The troops, who were bringing up cannon, were commanded by Captain H. C. Wise, who was to play a key role in the battle to come. Halted by diggers demanding to know if the wagons contained cannon, he replied he would not give any information to rebels. The diggers rushed the convoy, overturning one wagon and capturing another; they shot several English soldiers and one of the escort drivers, and killed the regimental drummer boy.

The troops retreated rapidly to the military camp commanded by Rede, who then sent out a detachment to pursue the rebels. The captured weapons had been dispersed and when the troops attempted to enter the diggings they were met with a hail of missiles and gunfire. The troopers drew their swords and cut their way back to the security of the camp in which they were rapidly becoming besieged.

The same evening a group of Reform League leaders met to discuss the new direction of the movement—from the constitutional reform of the League to the proclamation of independence and the formation of a new directorate to carry forward the now inevitably armed struggle. The gathering was presided over by Peter Lalor, a young Irishman who had emerged as a leader.

Lalor was born in 1827 in Raheen in the Irish county of Leix, where the house in which he was born still stands and now bears a plaque presented by the Australian Government acknowledging his contribution to Australian liberty and democracy. By profession a civil engineer and a graduate of Trinity College, Dublin, Lalor was one of the few diggers who had no financial worries. His family was comfortably off, he himself had a sought after profession and had in any case come to Australia with what the Irish would call a "rough sufficiency". He was not therefore motivated by his own poverty or hardship but rather by the calls for justice. Although he had never taken part in any political agitation either in Ireland or in Australia, he was heir to one of the finest revolutionary traditions of the nineteenth century. His brother, James Fintan Lalor, uncompromising in his stand for Irish independence, penned the immortal words on behalf of his oppressed country: "Who strikes the first blow for Ireland? Who draws the first blood for Ireland? Who wins a wreath that will be green forever?"[67]

Peter Lalor was more in the mould of his father, Patt, who fought for freedom in the English Parliament as another of his sons, Richard, would also do. He had the world, or at least the British colony of Victoria, at his feet in 1854. He had more money than most, a degree and a skill, and was engaged to be married (to a woman named Alicia Dunne). The licence fee did not affect him personally—he could pay and indeed had paid. It was the events at Eureka that made a rebel of him, that brought him to assert "if a democrat means opposition to a tyrannical press, a tyrannical people, or a tyrannical government, then I have been, I am still and will ever remain, a democrat,"[68] in an age when to be a democrat was similar to being a communist in the USA during the McCarthy era.

This meeting of leaders at which Lalor first came to prominence agreed that the movement should have a flag, a symbol, and so the first Australian flag was born. The design was suggested by Captain Charles Ross of Toronto, who was the first to die defending it. Only seventeen years earlier demands for the same rights of democratic representation had seen both upper and lower Canada in tumult. Events at Toronto followed almost the same pattern as at Eureka; Canada's Peter Lalor was William Lyn Mackenzie, whose forces were routed by those of the British Crown. Arthur Lower in his book *Colony to a Nation* observed, "As in the American Revolution the number of active spirits was small, the number of sympathisers large and the number of people who tried to avoid a decision larger still".[69] The Australian rebels at Eureka had greater proportional support than the groups that launched either the successful American rebellion in 1771 or the disastrous Canadian rebellion in 1837. Both would have influenced Ross and there is evidence that Canadian events shaped his thinking in Australia, even to the design of the flag of stars.

While the council of war continued, two English migrant women toiled through the night to produce the flag, of which Carboni wrote there was "no flag in old Europe half so beautiful as the 'Southern Cross' . . . the flag is silk, blue ground, with a large silver cross, similar to the one in our southern firmanent; no device of arms, but all exceedingly chaste and natural".[70]

The next day 15,000 diggers assembled on Bakery Hill to hear the report of the delegation to Hotham. In Ballarat and other towns notices had gone up proclaiming "Down with Despotism! Who so base as to be a Slave!" and "Down with Licence fees!"[71] During the morning a team of men had been hard at work erecting a stage and a flagstaff twenty-four metres tall, beneath which Captain Ross stood, sword in hand, surrounded by his rifle division. The *Ballarat Times* waxed almost as lyrical about the flag as Carboni himself. At 11 am "the Southern Cross was hoisted, and its maiden appearance was a fascinating object to behold. There is no flag in Europe, or in the civilized world, half so beautiful and Bakery Hill, as being the first place where the Australian ensign was first hoisted will be recorded in the deathless and indelible pages of history".[72]

It was two in the afternoon when Timothy Hayes called on Black to give his report. As he rose to speak he was greeted with cheers as one of the founders of the Reform League, but his description of Hotham's curt rejection of the miners' petition set a new mood. Black, Kennedy and Humffray had tried the peaceful way, but speaker after speaker pointed to the only results—more digger hunts, more troops, more threats.

Peter Lalor, implementing the strategy put together at the critical council of war the night before, proposed that a new Central Committee be elected and that each of the forty members or delegates should have the right to elect one delegate to the committee. The digger militia had already been formed and had seen action against English troops the previous evening; the flag of independence had been hoisted; now Lalor was proposing the establishment of a provisional government.

The next to speak was Raffaello Carboni, who used his skills in Italian, French, German, Greek and English to translate the proposals to diggers whose English was not as good as his own. Supporting Lalor's call for a provisional government he cried, "I hate the oppressor, let him wear a red, blue, white or black coat".[73] Carboni called on all diggers, irrespective of religion or nationality, to salute the Southern Cross flag as the refuge of all oppressed people from all countries on earth. Later Hotham was to write of the historic moment, "The Australian flag of independence was solemnly consecrated and vows proffered for its defence".[74]

As the first act of independence Frederick Vern, a Hanoverian who had had some military experience, called for a decision to abolish all licences—existing licences should be burned and no more paid for. The resolution was carried when Chairman Hayes asked if any member should be dragged to the lock-up for not having a licence, would a thousand men volunteer to liberate him. The response was roared:

"Yes! Yes!"

"Will two thousand of you come forward?"

"Yes! Yes! Yes!"

"Will four thousand of you volunteer to march up to the Camp, and open the lock-up to liberate the man?"

"Yes! Yes!", in a deafening crescendo.

"Are you ready to die?" he shouted, stretching forth his clenched right fist.[75]

The cheers of the assembled thousands gave him the answer.

The decision was followed by volleys of rifle and pistol shots, and fires were lit and licences thrown on them. When the final resolutions had been processed the assembly was adjourned, and as if to demonstrate how the British Crown had failed to keep order and safeguard the innocent, the diggers dispersed so quietly and in such good order that the *Ballarat Times* was constrained to comment, "Nothing could exceed the order and regularity with which the assemblage, some 15,000 in number, retired".[76]

The Challenge

The reaction of the authorities was swift. Hotham issued orders to "stand firm" and reminded Commissioner Rede that he could call on military, police and civil power. Hotham's view was that the military had been insulted and challenged; he intended to take up that challenge.

The next morning, 30 November, Rede ordered his forces onto the diggings to check for licences, an action which Humffray described as "a base piece of gold and silver lace revenge"; a later writer, H. G. Turner, called it the "last kick of the tyranny".[77] As soon as the police reached the field and gave orders for the now non-existent licences to be produced, the digger militia came forward to resist. In accordance with English tradition Rede read the Riot Act, which gave the Crown the right to suspend any right of protest and order the dispersal of any assembly. As he finished reading, the signal was given for the troops to advance. The cavalry on both flanks and in the centre charged and the troops advanced in battle order. The diggers retreated in all directions. Rede seized eight of them, despite resistance, and charged them with not having licences.

Hotham had a ready instrument in Rede, who on the eve of the Battle of Eureka Stockade wrote, "I am convinced that the future welfare of this colony depends on the crushing of this movement in such a manner as it may act as a warning . . . we may be able to crush the democratic agitation at one blow".[78] Supporting this view was Captain Charles Pasley, acting aide-de-camp to Captain Thomas, the commanding officer, who after the digger hunt called for strong measures to put down sedition by force. Hotham, Rede and his military commanders matched words with deeds.

The digger leadership acted quickly in the face of what amounted to a declaration of war. The constitutional reform group of the Reform League vacated the leadership and a military directory comprising Peter Lalor, Raffaello Carboni, Frederick Vern and Captain Ross took charge. A further general assembly on Bakery Hill was called at 3 o'clock the same afternoon. The Southern Cross was solemnly hoisted and Peter Lalor's voice once again boomed over the crowd as he called them to arms. Holding a rifle with his left hand he mounted a stump and called on the diggers to fall into divisions behind their captains to prepare for war. His call was answered by a cry of unanimous acclamation and an army of 500 immediately formed up. Lalor then said:

> *It is my duty now to swear you in, and to take with you the oath to be faithful to the Southern Cross. Hear me with attention, the man who, after this solemn oath, does not stand by our standard is a coward in heart. I order all persons who do not intend to take the oath to leave the meeting at once. Let all divisions under arms fall in in their order round the flag staff.*[79]

Kneeling down, Lalor received the salute of the captains of each division and then, with his right hand pointing to the Southern Cross flying in all its glory in the afternoon breeze, proclaimed, "We swear by the Southern Cross to stand truly by each other and fight to defend our rights and liberties".[80] The diggers stretched their hands out to the flag and answered in unison, "Amen".

The first acknowledgement of the military directory's authority came later on 30 November when Father Smyth, whose servant had earlier been arrested and tortured by corrupt police, came with an English digger, George Black, one of the founders of the Reform League, to propose a deputation to the military camp to demand the release of the eight diggers seized that morning, and to demand that the troops take no further action in the area. Carboni was appointed to accompany them.

The delegation was met by Commissioner Rede, Sub-Inspector Taylor and Police Magistrate Hackett. Black spoke bluntly to his fellow Englishmen in the service of the Crown: "To say the least, it was very imprudent of you, Mr Rede, to challenge the diggers at the point of the bayonet. Englishmen will not put up with your shooting down any of our mates, because he has not got a licence".[81] Rede, incensed at being challenged, roared back that he was the authority and declared, "The whole affair is a strong democratic agitation by an armed mob!".[82] Black stuck to his point about justice and freedom for the imprisoned diggers, but Rede dismissed him as a "cat-paw" of more designing people.

Early on Friday, 1 December, the army of the Australian revolution began to assemble. The 500 or so men who had taken the pledge on Bakery Hill swelled to 800, and numbered 1000 by the time they marched to Eureka. Here they buckled down to work under Frederick Vern's direction,

Taking the rebel oath of allegiance on Bakery Hill, 30 November 1854, from Illustrated Australian News, *August 1888.*
NATIONAL LIBRARY OF AUSTRALIA

establishing a headquarters and drilling ground of about forty hectares of mining claims and rebel huts, which was hastily enclosed with mining slabs, logs and any other material available. Parties of men began drilling, others were sent to scour the countryside for arms and ammunition; a German blacksmith was making pikes to "fix red-toads and blue pissants especially".[83] News of the rebellion was spreading rapidly and in the afternoon 300 to 400 diggers arrived from Creswick. The colony was aflame and all eyes were turned to the democratic capital of Ballarat.

Peter Lalor called a meeting of the directory leadership and the captains of the divisions, which formalised the revolutionary administration. In a room in Diamond's Store the twelve men sat around a plain wooden table, a black bottle and a tumbler in front of each man. Present were Lalor, Carboni, an Italian patriot who had fought with Garibaldi to liberate Italy, and Vern; Edward Thonen, of Prussia, who was described as a man of deep thought and prompt action; Timothy Hayes, who had presided at the great assemblies on Bakery Hill with more than a dash of Irish humour and was able to quote the great Irish poets saluting the rebels of a generation before; Patrick Curtain, an Irishman and captain of the pikemen's division, one of the first military units to form after Captain Ross's rifle brigade; and John Manning, another Irishman who had emerged at the outset as a supporter of armed struggle. Captains Ross and Nealson, George Black and his brother Alfred, and Captain Nelson completed the council of twelve.

It was Manning who proposed and Carboni who seconded the motion formally inaugurating the Council for the Defence and that Lalor be elected provisional president. He was elected unanimously. That he was president of the council of war was clear but there is no doubt to many he was also taking on the mantle of president of the republic-to-be.

John Manning took the initiative again to propose Carboni as commander-in-chief, pointing to his active service with Italian patriots against Imperial rule from Vienna. Carboni declined on the grounds that he did not have the physical vigour to be a successful commander who he felt would be better coming from one of the majority groups on the goldfields. Frederick Vern then put himself forward, referring to his experience as a soldier and promising a German rifle brigade 500 strong. Lalor was closely questioning him about the likelihood of such a brigade materialising when Carboni intervened to nominate Lalor himself as having the confidence of the people.

The nomination was immediately seconded by Edward Thonen, who also had military experience, and enthusiastically endorsed. It was at this point that Lalor gave his famous pledge:

> *I make no pretensions to military knowledge. I have not the presumption to assume the chief command, no more than any other*

> *man who means well in the cause of the diggers . . . if you appoint me as your commander-in-chief, I shall not shrink; I mean to do my duty as a man. I tell you, gentlemen, if once I pledge my hand to the diggers I will neither defile it with treachery, nor render it contemptible with cowardice.*[84]

Lalor was elected by eleven votes to one. As Lalor's deputy, Carboni moved around the stockade, spreading word of Lalor's election. The authority of the president and commander-in-chief and his revolutionary council was respected throughout Ballarat and the news of its formation rapidly reached neighbouring towns and settlements. A modest military success by Captain Ross and his division brought heart to the rebels. The Crown forces decided to attempt to move out of their camp and set up a post on the Eureka field itself. Ross and his men attacked, driving them back to their camp and capturing arms and ammunition and a splendid horse on which Ross rode back to headquarters in triumph.[85]

By Friday evening word of the rebels' activities had reached Hotham in Melbourne. The remaining companies of the Somersetshires and the East Suffolks and two field pieces were ordered to leave for Ballarat, together with two howitzers and seamen and officers from two English warships, HMS *Electra* and HMS *Fantome*, then lying in Port Phillip Bay. Major General Sir Robert Nickle, commander-in-chief of English forces in the colony, himself assumed overall command.

Activity at the stockade continued until late and the Council for the Defence was in almost constant session. Reports flooded in from near and far, among them information that reinforcements were on their way from Melbourne. Captains Ross and Nealson rode out with their divisions to try to intercept and ambush them before they reached Ballarat. Although they stayed out until the next day, they were unsuccessful.

They were still absent at 8 am on Saturday, 2 December, when Father Smyth came to the stockade to request Lalor's permission to address the diggers. He told them that the British strength in the military camp was 700 or 800, well armed and well equipped.[86] He appealed for more negotiations and for everyone to attend Mass on Sunday morning. His services to the diggers had been widely appreciated and he was heard with respect, but he could not break the mood of solidarity.

During the afternoon 200 men of the Independent Californian Rangers' Revolver Brigade commanded by James Magill, a former lieutenant in the US Infantry, swung into the stockade. Their arrival was a shot in the arm to the rebels and Lalor came out to greet them; they were an impressive sight with a military air and Colt revolvers and Mexican knives on their hips. Magill's military knowledge speedily won respect and he was invited to become second-in-command to Lalor as commander-in-chief and thereby an ex officio member of the Council for the Defence. Another American contingent, the First Rifles led by Nelson was considered one of the best and included veterans of wars against Mexico.[87]

Among the Americans who had already enlisted in the rebel army were two blacks, James Campbell, who came from Kingston, Jamaica, and John Joseph, from New York and Boston, who had come to Ballarat to run a refreshment tent, and Davis Calwell from Pennsylvania, who shared a hut at Eureka with his brother, Dan, before Dan went to New Zealand to try his luck. When the fighting was over Calwell was to obtain twenty-eight hectares on the Western Moorabool River. He lived to see his grandson, Arthur Augustus Calwell, become a minister in the Australian government and the architect of the twentieth century's greatest planned migration scheme.

The stockade was alive with rumours of a pending British attack and the Council discussed whether they should pre-empt it by launching an attack on the British military camp first. It was felt, however, that Rede and his troops were satisfactorily bottled up in the camp and had in fact abdicated control of Ballarat to the revolutionary Council, and persistent reports indicated the greater danger was posed by the men and arms due from Melbourne. It was decided that the headquarters should be more adequately guarded, to be undertaken by the Californians, and security was tightened throughout the stockade. The Council instituted a password, and in accordance with the Irish contingent's view of the struggle "Vinegar Hill" was chosen to commemorate the Battle of Vinegar Hill outside Sydney only fifty years before.[88]

Each member of the Council had a special responsibility—security, for example, was given to Thonen, who kept under observation the comings and goings in the stockade. Carboni was everywhere; spreading the news of the Council's decisions, spying in the vicinity of the military camp, collecting intelligence of troop movements from Melbourne. On one occasion when he returned to headquarters he forgot the password and found his way barred by the Californian guards. Fortunately Vern arrived and reminded him. Out and about again, Carboni investigated complaints from storekeepers that diggers claiming to act in the name of the Council had been requisitioning stores.

The preoccupation of Lalor and the Council with the reinforcements on their way from Melbourne was a tactical error that led to disaster. The rebel forces were potentially formidable, quite capable of challenging the British, but their dispersal in the ambush attempt left inadequate numbers to defend the headquarters of the revolution. After Ross's success against Thomas's men on 1 December, the strength and experience of the force in the military camp was left out of the Council's calculations. The infiltration of the stockade by Thomas's spies, while not overlooked (one named Peters was spotted by Carboni), was not dealt with effectively.

Just how serious was this moment in the history of the British hold on Australia can be gathered from the fact that Melbourne was in crisis. In despatching the reinforcements Hotham had gambled on one decisive battle, virtually denuding the capital of troops. He called out the home militia. The civilians, mostly bourgeois traders, professional men, junior clerks and the like, were given uniforms and arms and ammunition and turned out under Army officers to patrol the armoury and the government offices.

Hotham knew only too well that loyal Englishmen were very much in a minority at that point. Many of his fellow countrymen had joined the rebels; the Irish, Germans, Italians, French, and the overwhelming majority of Americans, who were in Melbourne, as well as Greeks, Welshmen and others were opposed to what they saw as British tyranny. If the battle was lost at Ballarat British power would be lost in Melbourne, for there was no way that the patriotic militia could withstand even a mild reaction in Melbourne itself, let alone an onslaught by veterans of wars in Mexico, Ireland and Europe. In a despatch to his Imperial superior, Colonial Secretary George Grey, the governor confessed that Melbourne was virtually under siege and there is reason to believe that a contingency plan was devised, providing for the evacuation of himself and his officials by the warships in Port Phillip in the event of a defeat, while members of the squatter-dominated Legislative Council would retreat to the security of their rural castles.

It is clear that the Imperial authorities made the decisions that provoked the rebellion. The repeated reports of opposition to their colonial rulers led them not only to anticipate a battle but to see it as inevitable and indeed as a desirable way of suppressing dissent once and for all. Hotham was the ideal man for the job.

The Battle

By the morning of Sunday, 3 December 1854, Rede had handed over command of the armed forces and responsibility for the battle plan to Captain John Wellsley Thomas of the 2nd Somersetshires, selected because of his experience in India. In December 1843 Thomas had been awarded the Maharajpoor Star for his part in the suppression of the Maratha people at Gwalior in central India. The medal adorned his tunic when, at 2.30 am, he assembled his forces for a surprise attack on the stockade.

From the troops and police at his disposal, Thomas marshalled 100 mounted men and 176 on foot.[89] They moved silently out of the camp and by 4 o'clock, before the sun had risen, had covered the 2.4 kilometres to the stockade. They had taken up positions within 275 metres of the rebel stronghold before their advance was discovered by a sentry.

It was a moment of disaster, for the forces at the stockade were seriously depleted. Lalor's second-in-command, James Magill, with the bulk of the Californian Rangers' Revolver Brigade, Captain Nelson and the American First Rifles Brigade and Captain Nealson with a strong detachment had been sent out to search for and intercept the reinforcements on their way from Melbourne. Most of the 400-strong Creswick contingent had dispersed to search for and commandeer arms and ammunition, while at the stockade men under the command of Captain Ross and others had been stood down to go to their homes. Some had gone off to collect their families to attend Mass with Father Smyth, others for a night of revelry. Carboni, dog tired, had said good night in German to Thonen, who was on night duty, and had gone to sleep in his tent outside the stockade area. Just before he left he had reported to Lalor, who after forty-eight hours without sleep had gone to bed protected by his Californian guards and was dead to the world. Of the 2000 armed rebels who could have crushed any English force in the colony fewer than 200 remained in the stockade on Saturday night.

While Carboni and his aids had been busy spying on the British camp, Thomas, with military thoroughness, had set out to establish the strength of the rebel forces. He was certainly well aware that only a skeleton of the rebel army remained on duty in the stockade, and that Lalor, preoccupied by the possibility of an attack from the Melbourne road by Hotham's reinforcements, which were not expected to arrive until Monday, 4 December at the earliest, had failed to anticipate that the discounted forces in the military camp would have the temerity to move out.

Captain Thomas deployed seventy mounted police on his right flank and thirty mounted infantry of the Somersetshires on his left; the main attacking force was made up of forty of the Somersetshire and East Suffolk men together with twenty-four police on foot. The remainder of the force—some 200 men—was held in reserve on Stockyard Hill where they held a commanding view of the stockade.

The rebel sentries sounded the alarm. Thomas gave the order "Forward and steady men. Don't fire until you hear the sound of the bugle".[90] The cavalry rode into position and the infantry advanced to within 135 metres before drawing fire from the rebel army. Within minutes the combat was hand to hand. An American commander was shot in the thigh but hopping on one leg kept up a rapid fire at the redcoats; Captain Ross was shot down defending the flag he helped to create;

OVERLEAF:
A plan of the attack on Eureka Stockade, published in 1870 in W. B. Withers' The History of Ballarat.
REX NAN KIVELL COLLECTION, NATIONAL LIBRARY OF AUSTRALIA

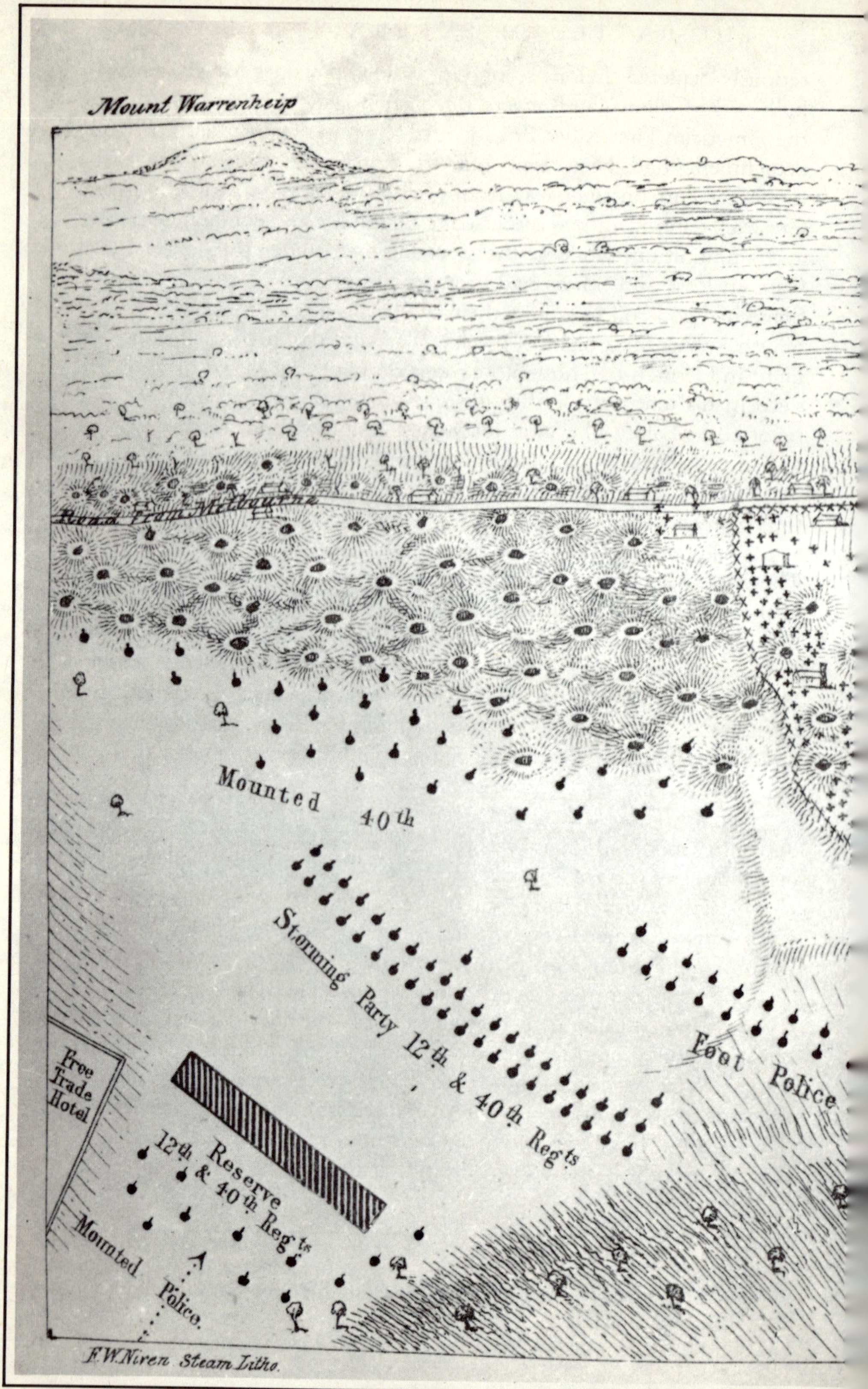
Mount Warrenheip
Road from Melbourne
Mounted 40th
Storming Party 12th & 40th Regts
Foot Police
Free Trade Hotel
Reserve 12th & 40th Regts
Mounted Police.
F.W.Niven Steam Litho.

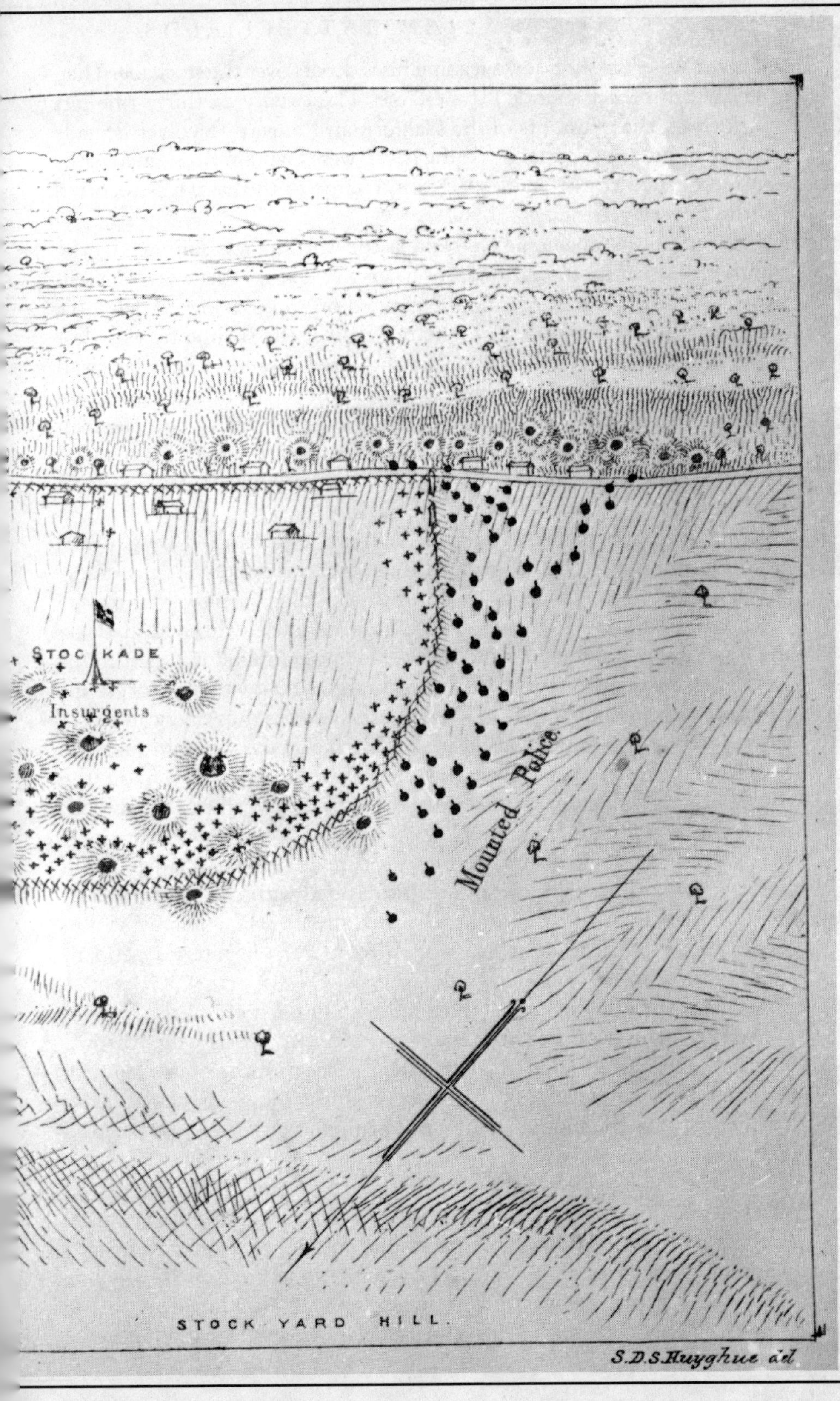
STOCKADE
Insurgents
Mounted Police
STOCK YARD HILL
S.D.S.Huyghue del

Captain Wise was shot down leading his redcoats over the stockade. Then the English bugler sounded the charge. The twenty or thirty rifle pits manned by the remnants of the Californian Rangers' Revolver Brigade took the brunt of the attack. To the north were Captain Ross's men while Thonen defended the south. Vern, in charge to the east, was reported as the first to retreat.

Peter Lalor had emerged as soon as the warning was sounded by the sentries and had taken immediate and effective charge. As he saw Captain Ross shot and Vern retreating, he jumped on top of a logged defensive position to rally his forces; silhouetted against the skyline he was shot by an English sniper and fell with a shattered shoulder. Ross lay dead with a gaping wound to the groin but with his men Thonen battled on until he was shot in the head. He died almost instantly. The pikemen on the bulwarks of the stockade, many of them brave Cornishmen, stood their ground against the English cavalry and were cut down by sword and bayonet.

An Irishman named Tomas O'Neil, his legs mangled by gunshot wounds and sword cuts, continued to defend the capital of democracy, swinging his pike around his head until the infantry blew him to bits with repeated fire. The German blacksmith, Hafele, who had made so many of the pikes, fought by O'Neil's side until his skull was cleft to his shoulders with a sabre—he was still fighting as his twitching corpse hit the ground. Among those who fought to the last was the American black, John Joseph, who miraculously survived as the troops went through the stockade bayoneting the wounded and venting their speen on the Southern Cross flag, which, holed by bullets and stained with blood, was torn down and desecrated.

Father Smyth moved into the stockade, ministering to the dying until he was dragged away by the troops intoxicated with their victory. The stockade was then set on fire, together with anyone who remained within the confines of the once proud rebel headquarters for an independent Australia.

The scene of carnage was recorded by Samuel Irwin of the *Geelong Advertiser*, who described the dead and wounded rebels being thrown onto military carts. "They all lay in a small space with their faces upward, looking like lead. Several of them were still breathing and at every rise of their breasts the blood spouted out of their wounds or just bubbled out and trickled away."[91]

In the action which lasted fifteen or twenty minutes at least fourteen diggers were killed and twenty wounded, of whom eight would later die. Others were gunned down by the troops and police as they rampaged through the surrounding camps. The wounded Lalor was hidden by one of his rebels until he was taken, unconscious, to the house of Father Smyth. The priest brought doctors Doyle, Stewart, Sutherland and

The Battle of Eureka Stockade, from the Picturesque Atlas of Australasia, 1886. NATIONAL LIBRARY OF AUSTRALIA

Gibson who amputated his left arm. Eventually he was smuggled out of Ballarat to the home of his fiancée in Geelong where he had to be operated on for another bullet in his side. Four of Thomas's men were killed and twelve wounded.

Hotham declared martial law on the diggings, although it was repealed on 5 December after only three days, and offered rewards for the capture of the surviving rebel leaders. The reaction in Melbourne to the news of the battle indicated what could have happened had the battle been lost. Chief Commissioner of Police Sadleir described "the extent and gravity of the feeling of the citizens of Melbourne in opposition to the Government of which Sir Charles Hotham was the head".[92] A public meeting called by the mayor of Melbourne at Hotham's instigation to support the British Crown was taken over by supporters of the rebellion and adopted a resolution against the government.

The shots fired at Eureka echoed around the world. Newspapers in London, Rome, Paris, Dublin, New York and San Francisco carried despatches of the strike for freedom. The Crimean War was in full swing but the front page of the *New York Times* on 24 March 1855 was occupied by the "rebellion of the Southern Cross". The report ended with a stirring tribute to the diggers and the hoisting of the Southern Cross – "Long may it wave".[93] In California, the leading daily of the time gave the banner headline to the Australian rebellion and declared "that as all men are born free and equal this meeting claims their right to a voice in the framing and passing of laws which they are called upon to obey".[94]

A report from Italy headed "Insurrection in Australia" reported: "In Australia the people hoisting the Southern Cross have just been engaged in a bloody struggle against the British troops and difficulties at the diggings are not likely to be put at end by the slaughter of some 20 stout diggers. So England may well tremble for their tenure in the land of gold".[95] Despatches published in Ceylon, as Sri Lanka was then known, announced that the people of Australia had risen and declared their independence and that troops had put down the insurrection in "sanguinary engagement".

At a time when Britain was engaged in a major war, six morning papers in England covered the drama; *The Times* gave the greatest coverage of events, a total of three columns. The accounts described the battle and the proclamation of martial law, and reported that 10,000 citizens of Melbourne had assembled to review events. The casualty lists at Eureka appeared side by side with those from the Crimea. The Irish journal *Nation* hailed the event as another of the disasters that "rapidly accumulate round that proud and cruel empire upon whose domains it has hitherto been boasted the sun never sets".[96]

In Paris *La Presse* reported that the "armed revolt was a protest against

V. R.

Colonial Secretary's Office,
Melbourne, 11th December, 1854.

£500

REWARD

FOR THE APPREHENSION

OF

Frederick Vern

WHEREAS

A Man known by the name of VERN, has unlawfully, rebelliously, and raitorously levied and arrayed Armed Men at Ballaarat, in the Colony of Victoria, with the view of making war against Our Sovereign Lady he QUEEN:

NOTICE IS HEREBY GIVEN

That whoever will give such information as may lead to the Apprehension of the said VERN, shall receive

A REWARD OF £500

being the Reward offered by SIR ROBERT NICKLE.

By His Excellency's Command,

JOHN FOSTER.

DESCRIPTION OF VERN.

Tall, about 5 feet 10½ inches, long light hair falling heavily on the Side of his head, ttle whisker, a large flat face, eyes light grey or green and very wide asunder. Speaks with a strong foreign accent. A Hanoverian by birth, about 26 years of age.

BY AUTHORITY: JOHN FERRES, GOVERNMENT PRINTER, MELBOURNE.

Substantial rewards were offered for the capture of the rebel leaders.
BEATTIE COLLECTION, NATIONAL LIBRARY OF AUSTRALIA

harsh regulations and a first step for the independence of Australia", following the example of her elder sister America.[97] Another weekly in Paris reported "Australia is in revolt".[98]

The alarm bells rang loud and clear in London, despite Hotham's report that the Battle of Eureka had been won, that Ballarat was no longer the democratic capital, that Lalor was wounded and in hiding with a price on his head and some 160 rebels were held prisoner. Most were released within a few days but several were held for months awaiting trial. Only one American, John Joseph, was arrested. He was to be the centrepiece of Hotham's treason trials. But they could find no jury to convict him, nor indeed anyone else.

Pressure from the United States, exerted through its consul general in Melbourne, made sure not one American rebel was prosecuted, while London, faced with unremitting hostility of the mass of the people in the colony, abruptly dropped all charges. Within three years universal manhood suffrage was introduced and property qualifications for members of the Legislative Assembly were abolished.

Lalor emerged with one arm and his sweetheart at his side to contest the first election under the new law that gave the diggers parliamentary representation. He was elected without opposition on 10 November 1855 to represent Ballarat in the Victorian Legislative Council. The following year he was elected to the newly created Legislative Assembly for North Grenville and in 1859 he transferred to South Grant; he was defeated in 1871 but regained his seat in 1875. During nearly twenty-five years in parliament he served as Postmaster General and Speaker of the Parliament.

The battle had been lost and the republic was long deferred, but many basic rights were won. The men at Eureka did not die in vain: they laid the foundations of democracy in an independent Australia. However he had to modify it later, Peter Lalor, when he was first elected provisional president and commander-in-chief and was asked his objective, replied simply "Independence".

The Southern Cross was retrieved by an English trooper, John King, who remained in Australia and founded a family. The flag was kept by the King family until it was obtained by the Ballarat Fine Art Gallery in 1895.[99] It was restored and in 1973 was unveiled by the then Prime Minister, Gough Whitlam, who saluted the men of Eureka with the words:

> *It is béyond question the events of December 3, 1854 persist in the memory and consciousness of our people—in the words of one writer—"the pioneer and supreme Australian event in the spectacular sense". Dr H. V. Evatt, a great statesman and perceptive historian, went so far as to declare that: "Australian democracy was born at Eureka".*[100]

9. *THE BATTLE OF BATTLE MOUNTAIN*

One of the last pitched battles of the Hundred Years War was fought in September 1884 at a place known today as Battle Mountain, eighty kilometres north-east of the mining city of Mount Isa in northern Queensland. It was the culmination of almost ten years of guerilla struggle by the powerful Kalkadoon people to prevent the taking of their land and the extirpation of their heritage and culture by European invaders moving north with their stock and possessions and superior firepower. The struggle had been so successful that a paramilitary force was assembled to try to break once and for all the fierce resistance of the Kalkadoons, which goes down in the annals of Australian history as the most dogged and bloody of all.

The battle was itself a prelude to another fought just thirty-one years later by sons of the same troops, who, under orders, charged up the cliffs at Gallipoli with much the same results as for the Kalkadoons who, just as inexplicably suicidal, charged down the mountain into the smoking mouths of the guns they had so long avoided.

The First Probes into North Queensland

The first shadow of the struggle to come was cast when Cristovão de Mendonça sailed along the east coast of Australia 250 years before Captain Cook,[1] who almost certainly used the maps made by this great Portuguese navigator. In 1521 Mendonça was appointed by Diego Lopes, the Portuguese governor of Goa in India (where the Catholic patron of Australia, Francis Xavier, is buried), to "search the Isles of Gold" for gold,[2] although the hidden agenda was also to find Magellan. In the service of Spain Magellan was the first man to circumnavigate the world; in doing so he was also invading Portuguese spheres of influence.

Mendonça sailed from Pedir with three caravels on 18 March 1521 on an epic voyage that took him through the Torres Strait, which Torres was not to see for another eighty-five years, and down the east coast of Australia. On Mendonça's map Princess Charlotte Bay, the landlocked harbour of Cooktown, Repulse Bay and the Great Barrier Reef are clearly indentifiable. He called the entire coast "Coste Dangereux", which it undoubtedly was for subsequent generations of sailers.[3] The expedition coasted south, charting Fraser Island and continuing on to what appears to be Botany Bay in an area Mendonça named "Coste des Herbaiges".[4] This first probe was, from all the evidence, peaceful.

The next probe came a lifetime later when Luis Vaez de Torres sailed through Torres Strait in 1606, after parting company with Pedro Fernandez de Quiros, who thought he had found the great southern continent. Although the people of the north apparently ignored the Portuguese, they repelled an attempted landing by Torres and it was left to the Dutch to commit the first act of aggression.

In the same year that Torres sailed through the strait—1606—the Dutchman Willem Jansz in the *Duyfken* probed the western side of Cape York. The result was bloody conflict. The Dutch East India Company had given instructions to Jansz—as it did to Carstensz who followed him in 1623 in the *Pera* and *Arnhem* and to Gonzal commanding the *Rijder* and *Buijs* in 1756—to kidnap "full grown persons or better still . . . boys and girls, to the end that the latter may be brought up here and be turned into useful purpose in the said quarters when occasion shall serve".[5] The Dutch all attempted to make friends when they first landed and then to carry out their instructions. The people of the north responded with sufficient strength to drive them back to the sea. The reports of Jansz and Carstensz particularly testified to the fighting prowess of the people of the north who had served fair warning that they would not surrender to any invader without a fight.

The Dutch incursions were the prelude to the arrival of the last of the great invaders, the English. They did not merely sail by or carry out random bloody probes, but mounted a full-scale invasion and eventually occupied the north. In less than a hundred years there were six major British naval surveying expeditions into north Queensland waters. Following Cook in the *Endeavour* in 1770 came Flinders in the *Investigator* in 1802, Phillip Parker King in 1818 and 1822 in the *Mermaid* and the *Bathurst*, Wickham and Stokes in the *Beagle* between 1838 and 1842, Blackwood with the naturalist Joseph Beete Jukes in the *Fly* between 1842 and 1846 and Owen Stanley with the *Rattlesnake* and the *Bramble* between 1846 and 1850.

The pattern of contact was the same. Cautious friendship failed when customs were misunderstood or violated or when it seemed that the invaders were intent on taking possession of land which was not theirs. One skirmish took place in 1848 at Cape Melville where the armed men of the *Bramble* drew up battle lines to repulse an attack by the Mutumui who rightly believed they were the advance party of an invasion. The people of the north sustained casualties in this first clash.[6]

Owen Stanley with naturalists John Macgillivray and Thomas Huxley made visits to Evans Bay on the tip of Cape York two years running and in 1849 stayed for two months. Macgillivray commented that the local people were attracted by the ship as "vultures by a carcass".[7] The English enlisted their help to find supplies of fish and turtle meat and to show them the country. In fact every sailor had a regular helper, paid with articles such as pipes, tobacco, biscuits, steel axes and knives.

Relations proceeded with such success that the English were invited to become part of the kinship system. Each regular helper became an Englishman's "younger brother", although some of the officers and men were thought to be the ghosts of returned dead relatives.[8] In the same way that the English later arbitrarily imposed English names on everything from hills and rivers to people, they were themselves renamed and treated as relations. Macgillivray recorded how his "younger brother"[9] protected him in an argument which broke out when, in rewarding some dancers for their performance, the English gave biscuits to the women to distribute instead of giving the gifts directly. In the misunderstanding it seemed the erstwhile relatives were about to fall out, but it did not happen. The contact was one of the few which stood the test of confrontation between a venerable and peaceful culture and one built on war and conquest of people and their lands.

The English naval probes were not the only incursions into north Queensland waters. From the 1840s merchant ships that ventured there often behaved as little more than pirates in their dealings with the northern peoples, sometimes paralleling the atrocities of the sealers in the south of the continent. One of the first was *Will o' the Wisp*, sent north by a Sydney merchant to look for sandalwood for the China trade. On the Palm Islands the master of the vessel and crewmen were wounded in an armed clash and an unrecorded number of Black Australians were killed by sword and swivel gun while trying to flee in the water.[10] In another fight the *Rattlesnake*'s guns were used to kill a number of local people at Goold Island in Rockingham Bay when an argument developed after peremptory demands by the English were met with opposition. Because of the extraordinary nature of this incident "Captain Stanley felt it his duty to report it to the Colonial Government" of the time.[11]

Battle lines were being drawn with a vengeance. It was becoming obvious that these latest invaders were intent on more than casual visits for trade and social intercourse.

Despite the bloody clashes and the toll exacted by cannon, gun and sword the people of the north continued to hold out a hand of friendship to those in need. Typical was the experience of James Morrill, an

Englishman from Essex who was shipwrecked on the Great Barrier Reef in 1846. With six other survivors he drifted on a raft for forty-two days before being washed ashore at Cape Cleveland near today's city of Townsville.[12] Three died after landing and Morrill and the remaining three were welcomed by the Bindal, who thought they were deceased relatives returned as whites. They later moved south to live with the people at Port Denison (now Bowen) for two years. His companions died of natural causes and Morrill returned to the Bindal people where he lived for thirteen years. The Englishman was totally absorbed into the culture and lifestyle of the people, learning the language and taking his place within the extended family structure. It was very likely a parting in affection when he decided to rejoin his own people who by 1859 had advanced as far north as the Burdekin River.

Following the naval probes spanning nearly ninety years and the activities of the many merchantmen, the tide of invasion was about to sweep in from the south. In 1843 the New South Wales Legislative Council sought the establishment of an overland route from the east coast to Port Essington on the Cobourg Peninsula, which would facilitate trade with Asia as well as opening up land for further conquest and acquisition. Ludwig Leichhardt, the German explorer, led the way on an epic journey in 1844–45, dramatically tearing down the veil of mystery and distance which had kept hidden from the English the potential of north Queensland and the rich well-watered lands of the Burdekin and its tributaries. His report was rhapsodic: "one of the finest [districts] we have seen . . . the most picturesque landscape we had yet met with . . . Finer stations for the squatter cannot exist".[13] This was indeed the clarion call for the invasion of the north.

The Leichhardt expedition was really a military probe, comprising as it did ten armed men, including two Black Australians from the south, seventeen horses and sixteen cattle. They moved in what Leichhardt described as "light marching order",[14] covering ten miles (sixteen kilometres) a day for twenty-three days, and reached the Valley of the Lagoons on the Burdekin on 4 May 1845. They made various accidental contacts with the people of the north along the way, using their black scouts to exchange greetings, but the military-like expedition served notice that the invaders were not to be trifled with. The people of the north did a little probing themselves and tried to cut out some of the bullocks; they were left in no doubt about the power of the guns.

As he moved steadily north Leichhardt believed that the show of force had frightened the people to such an extent that he even let the night watch lapse. In late June he and his party camped about forty-eight kilometres from today's town of Mitchell on a site surrounded by a narrow belt of tea-trees, providing ample cover for any attacking force. The two black scouts attempted to interfere with some local women and shot dead an old man who valiantly defended them.[15] The northern people decided that the invaders had to be halted and planned an attack on the encampment at night. John Gilbert, the naturalist with the expedition, was killed instantly in the attack and two others were wounded, but the guns proved more than a match for the raiders who were driven off, probably with casualties. Leichhardt was able to resume his push north and the next river he crossed was named Gilbert after the dead Englishman.

Three years later another quasi-military expedition led by Edmund Kennedy and comprising thirteen men, twenty-eight horses and 100 sheep, set out from Rockingham Bay (between today's Cairns and Townsville) to blaze a trail to Cape York. Closely observed by the local people, they had to proceed south-west before turning north and found the going so tough that they covered only thirty-two kilometres in six weeks. Kennedy was tired and frustrated when a group of northern people appeared to wave him and his companions back. When finally a spear was thrown he ordered his men to open fire, killing at least one and wounding three of the northerners.[16] Despite this skirmish a meeting a week later was friendly. It was obvious, however, that the expedition was determined to advance, and the English camp was attacked on the Walsh River and again on the Mitchell.[17] Once again there were probably black casualties.

When Kennedy and his force reached a point near Princess Charlotte Bay, the local people fired the grass to windward of the party, who narrowly escaped the flames. A week later in the same area they were again asked to retreat and instead launched an attack, firing into the war party.[18] It must have been apparent to the members of the expedition that they were unwelcome. Repeatedly they were exhorted to retreat with threats of action and frontal attacks. All failed before the guns of the invaders. When Kennedy missed his relief ship at Princess Charlotte Bay he decided to push on with a smaller party, leaving eight men under William Carron at Weymouth Bay. After only twelve days another three were left at Shelburne Bay while Kennedy and a black scout, Jacky Jacky (Galmarra), made desperately for Port Albany. A final attack killed Kennedy and wounded the scout.

The eight survivors of the once impressive invasion force left at Weymouth Bay were threatened by war parties time and time again, but were not attacked until the two survivors were actually being rescued. The last three at Shelburne Bay had died or been killed. The invasion force had been not only stopped but wiped out.

In 1856, following in Leichhardt's footsteps but from west to east, came A. C. Gregory's North Australian Exploring Expedition. The people of the north made a determined attempt to turn back the invaders. On 3 September 1856 between the Leichhardt and Albert Rivers Gregory found his expedition was under observation. Nine fighting men of the north came the next day to wave them back and then withdrew. A larger war party appeared on 5 September and unleashed a shower of spears, but Gregory was ready. He shot the leader and a horseback charge completed the rout.[19]

Gregory, who strongly supported the establishment of the paramilitary Native Police force in Queensland, noted that as a result of either direct or indirect contact with the Macassans the northern people had iron tools, tomahawks and axes. Although they had no guns, the very nature of their environment helped them to resist invading forces.[20]

The Kalkadoons and their Country

This north-west Queensland nation occupied the area surrounding the present day town of Mount Isa. Their lands extended east to Cloncurry, west to the Georgina River, north to the O'Shanassy and Seymour Rivers and south beyond the Selwyn Range and to Sulieman Creek.

The rugged terrain of the Cloncurry Pre-Cambrian belt formed a natural defensive environment for the Kalkadoons who were described by white recorders as a fierce, aggressive and independent people and proved to be formidable opponents. Aiding them in their ten years of guerilla war was the terrain which like the scarred face of the moon was crisscrossed by countless gullies, gorges and ravines, little changed to this day.

The survival of the people depended on the careful conservation of water supplies. Other nations in more abundant and verdant locations could afford to lose a little land and water but the Kalkadoons could not. This lent an extra edge and determination to their struggle between 1874 and 1884.

There are only four perennial watercourses on Kalkadoon land. Smaller sources of water exist but may only flow for a few days or weeks each year; larger ones may flow for several months before drying up. The O'Shanassy and Widdallion Creeks flow partially underground in the limestone, but even they fade away as they get further from their sources.[21] The Kalkadoons supplemented their supplies from permanent natural dams of crystal clear water in the many gorges.

Despite the harsh environment the Kalkadoon lands were rich in food. Wild game—kangaroos, possums, echidnas, bandicoots, birds including emus, fish, reptiles, frogs, crayfish, ants, grubs and caterpillars—was plentiful and combined with various seeds, edible roots, fruits, berries, vines, capers and peas provided all the nutrients necessary for a well-balanced diet. Yet even now strangers to Kalkadoon country may face death, unable to find food or water.

The Kalkadoons lived in semi-permanent villages of beehive-like dwellings called *wulliberri*. Reminiscent of houses on the African veldt, they were constructed of wooden frames thatched by thick grasses that

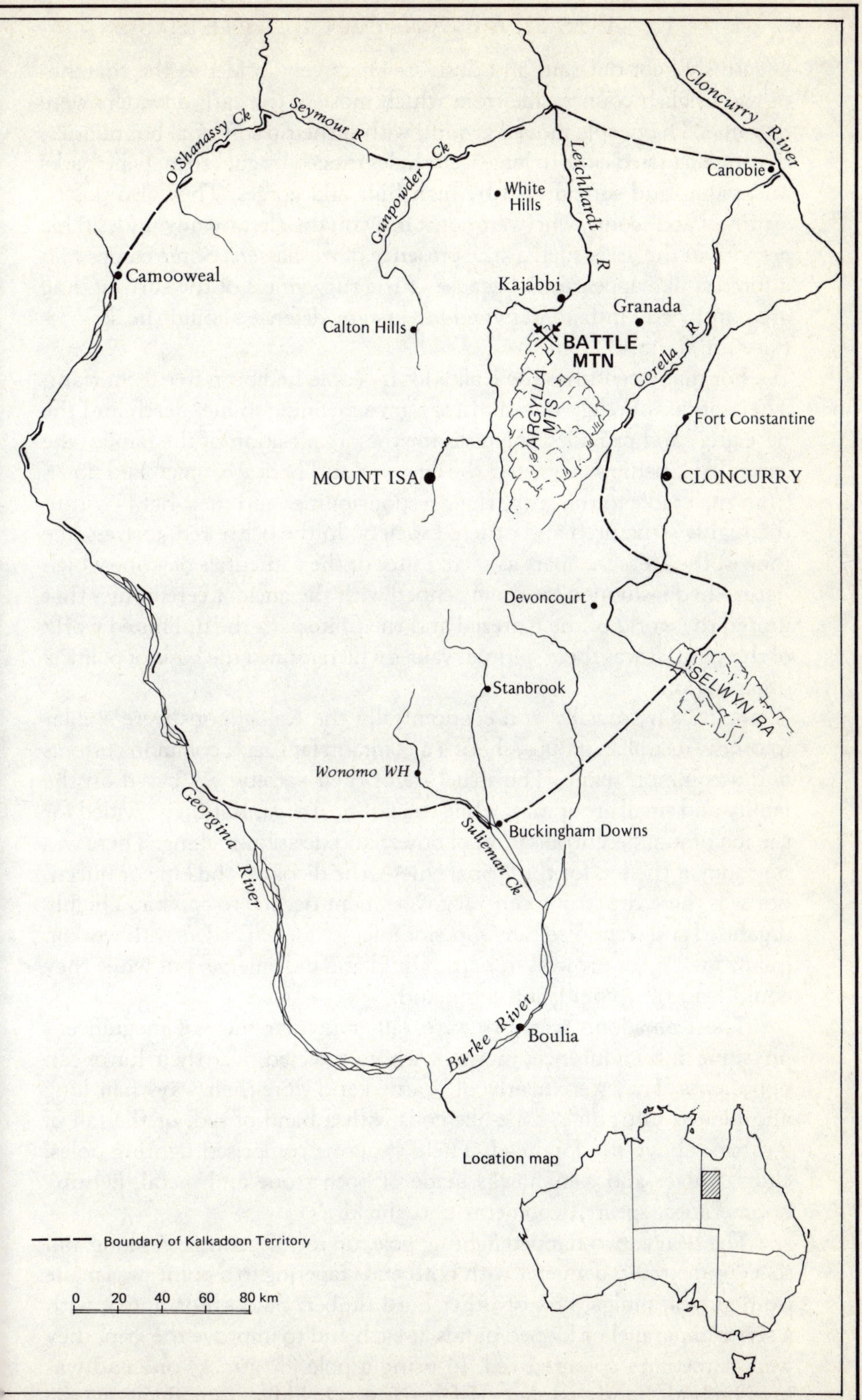

Cloncurry River
Seymour R
O'Shanassy Ck
Gunpowder Ck
Leichhardt R
Canobie
White Hills
Camooweal
Kajabbi
Granada
Calton Hills
BATTLE MTN
ARGYLLA MTS
Corella R
Fort Constantine
MOUNT ISA
CLONCURRY
Devoncourt
SELWYN RA
Stanbrook
Wonomo WH
Georgina River
Sulieman Ck
Buckingham Downs
Burke River
Boulia
Location map
Boundary of Kalkadoon Territory
0 20 40 60 80 km

effectively kept out rain and dust—as effectively in fact as the thatches of the English countryside from which most of the early invaders were to come. The people moved around within their traditional boundaries, to camps situated close to large waterholes fringed by gum trees, paperbarks and palms and surrounded by high hills and gorges. They also posted sentinels and scouts, who were constantly on the alert for any undesirable activity in the area, such as the presence of trespassers. Some camps had a fortress-like appearance because of the ruggedness of the surrounding area and were, in fact, designed for instant defence should the sentries raise an alarm.

For many centuries the Kalkadoon people had been free from want. Their rituals of religion and history gave meaning to life, death and the hereafter, and provided the basis for the organisation of the family, the extended kinship system and the customs and heritage which laid down from the cradle to the grave their responsibilities and their rights within the highly structured and ordered society. In the ochre-red, fortress-like ranges, the areas set apart as sacred sites or the cathedrals of stone which nature had fashioned for them echoed with the ancient ceremonies that united the world of the material and the finite with the unlimited world of the spirit. It was these spiritual values which formed the basis of political organisation.

Politically, socially and economically the Kalkadoons were similar to other Australian groups, sharing a common language, common customs and a common name. The structure of their society was based on the family and small groupings, while the political organisation provided for the maximum decentralisation of power and decision-making. There was no room at the top for the "tribal chief", the dictator, the king or queen, nor was there the strong central government needed to combat a highly organised and technologically superior military force. Leaders with wisdom in law making or prowess in battle could and did emerge, but while they could lead they could not command.

The Kalkadoon warriors were tall, muscular men of magnificent physique and endurance, many of whom towered over their European opponents. They were nearly all bearded and wore their wavy hair long and plaited into thick, rope-like coils with a band of red, or the tail of a dingo, above the forehead. Their weapons comprised fighting poles, clubs, knives and tomahawks made of both stone and metal, fighting boomerangs, spears, woomeras and shields.[22]

The heavy, two-handed fighting pole, up to 137 centimetres long and six centimetres in diameter with both ends tapering to a point, was made from gidyea, mulga, box or other hard timber. Smooth or fluted, with a series of parallel or looped bands at each end to improve the grip, they were sometimes coloured red. In using a pole for attack, one end was held by both hands, while in defence it was held horizontally above the

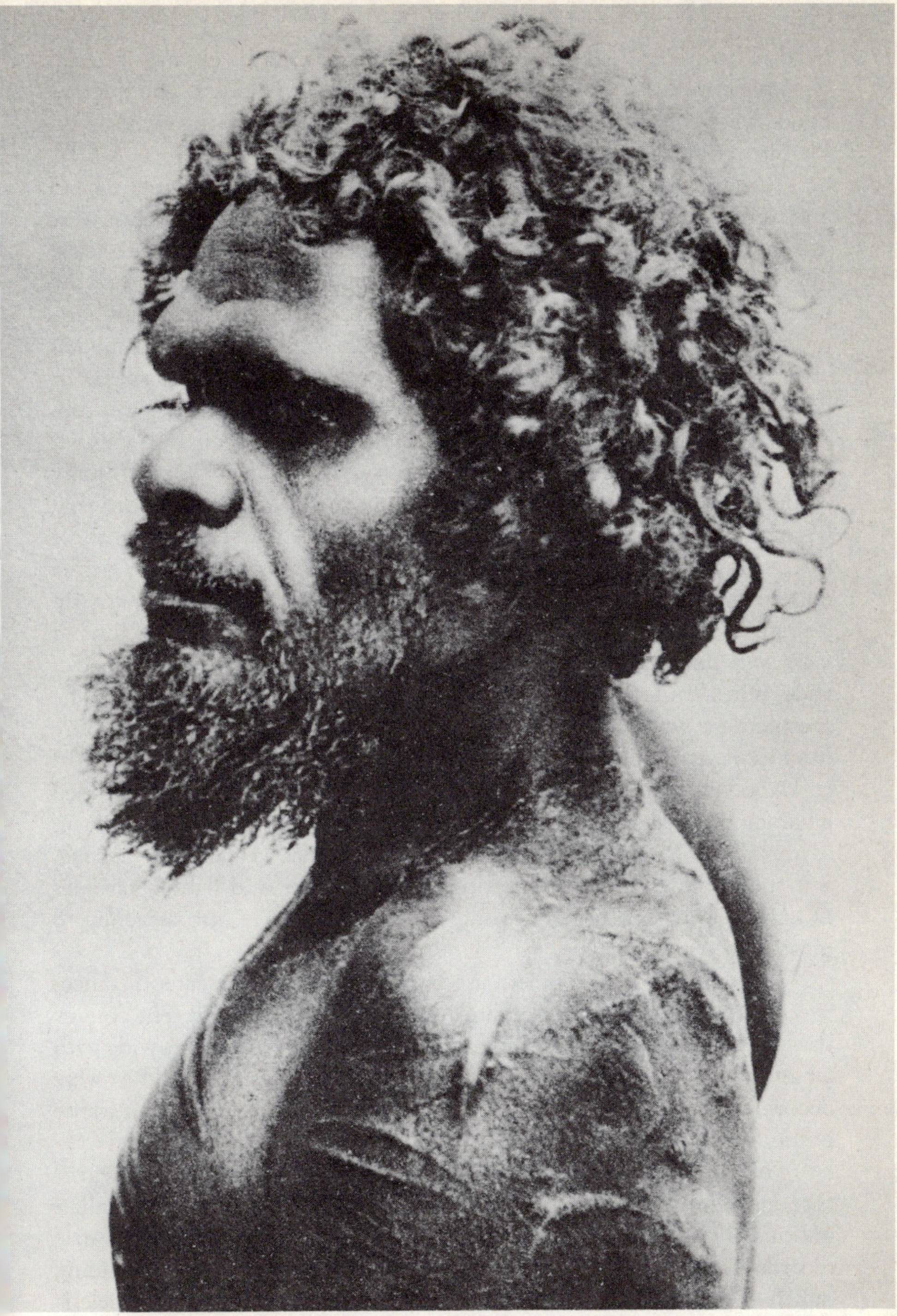

A Kalkadoon warrior.
PHOTOGRAPH BY CHARLES KERRY, NATIONAL LIBRARY OF AUSTRALIA

head. The clubs, made from gidyea, were coloured black and were up to sixty centimetres in length. The head tapered to a point, and circular bands were cut in the handle. They were used for throwing rather than for hitting at close quarters.

Tomahawks were up to twenty-three centimetres wide at the head and were attached to the wooden handle with possum sinew. Knives were fifteen centimetres long and the handles were often encased in the testical pouch removed from a kangaroo and, later, in a demonstration of the use of new technology, a sheep. Hardwood fighting boomerangs were meant to be thrown at comparatively close quarters. The hooked models were designed to counter defensive actions by poles, clubs, spears or boomerangs in hand to hand combat by catching the opponent's weapon.

While this range of weapons was undoubtedly effective in combat with people who had a similar armoury, it was totally and fatally inadequate against the weaponry of the invaders. The only weapons that were in any way effective in that situation were their spears. The three metre long hand spear known as the *mar-ri-mo* was made from gidyea or scrubwood such as rosewood. About sixty centimetres from the tip a ring was gummed onto the wood into which nails or pieces of flint or glass were fixed. The spatulate-tip hand spear was up to five centimetres wide but about thirty centimetres shorter than the *mar-ri-mo*. The spatulate-tip woomera spear was one of the heaviest spears. It was more than two metres long. The shaft was ornamented, the butt made of light corkwood and the spatulate tip up to forty-three centimetres long included a half-moon shaped wooden hook. The heavy 3.5 metre reed spear known as *libijara* was thrown with a woomera and a similar weapon, the *mabana*, was specially designed for spearing cattle. Smaller and lighter varieties of *libijara* were also used and one or two hooks were also attached to most of the reed spears.

The sophisticated woomera used to propel the spear greater distances was also used as a short single-handed sword in close fighting. The convex shields, sixty-six centimetres long and twenty-three centimetres wide with a handle cut at the back, completed the Kalkadoon armoury. They were decorated with red, black and yellow vertical lines, lending colour to the battle formation.

The tactics the Kalkadoons used against the invaders were learnt through long and bitter experience. Like most of the other Australian nations they greatly underestimated the power of firearms: the battle records show how many times gallant lines of attacking warriors, holding out their shields for protection, died with the bark shattered and useless. Warriors prepared for warfare with people beyond the frontier by painting three wide circular bands on the upper and lower limbs and a boomerang shape from each shoulder to the middle of the waist belt in front. A battle leader would be identified by a "thick opposum-string hanging from around the neck, hitched to another passing around the waist with a head dress of white feather down".[23]

The gathering of intelligence was one of the more successful aspects of Kalkadoon campaigns. They carefully monitored the enemy, often sending women, children and old people to observe them. Their other great advantage was the knowledge of their own country, the knowledge of fords, passes, tracks and caves that helped them to communicate, move rapidly and escape from pursuit. The balance of power lay with the Kalkadoons for a short time, when their frontier bushcraft, local knowledge, physical courage and determination equalled the limited firepower of the guns and the speed and endurance of the enemy's horses. But as the invaders gathered their forces for the last battle the scales had tipped dramatically against them; they faced vastly improved weapons, men with knowledge of the country and above all the ruthlessly drilled detachments of the Native Police.

The population of the Kalkadoon people has been estimated at about 2000 at the time of the English invasion,[24] a formidable force like the Nyungar people of Western Australia and like them one which formed the spearhead of resistance. The people challenging the rule of the Kalkadoons could not have provided a more vivid contrast in their way of life and their political and social organisation.

The Colony of Queensland

In 1859 the northern half of New South Wales became a separate colony, and was named Queensland as a compliment to the then Queen of England, Victoria Saxe-Coburg-Gotha. Through the patronage of the English prime minister, William George Gladstone, Irish-born George Ferguson Bowen was appointed the first governor, and Robert Wyndam Herbert was sent out with him as colonial secretary. Governor Bowen gave his name to the town of Bowen, his secretary lent his middle and last names to other locations in the colony, while Bowen's wife, a cultured young Greek woman, gave her names to the town of Roma and the Diamantina River.

Bowen stood at the apex of a highly structured society in which each hierarchy exercised authority over another until the lowest level was reached. Here life was dedicated to obeying other people's orders without question. The lash and the hangman's rope were constant reminders to would-be transgressors. Moreton Bay, the first permanent English settlement in Queensland, was founded in 1824 at the Brisbane River and rapidly gained the reputation of being the worst prison in the Pacific. It is symptomatic of the period that the commandant, Patrick Logan, a Scot in the English service, was killed in 1830 by a Black Australian who was probably the only one of his people hailed by the prisoners of the time as a hero. Although the penal colony was closed in 1839, the restless drive of the new people could not be resisted. By the 1840s they had overrun the Darling Downs region west of Brisbane and by the time the new colony was established the outriders of occupation were moving steadily north. There were to be no more friendly warnings to retreat, for now the English expeditions shot first. In the south a quasi-military unit, the Corps of Native Police, was raised as early as 1848 and despatched to the Macintyre River under the command of Frederick Walker.

This unit, which survived in Queensland until 1909, developed the reputation of being "callous butchers".[25] It engaged in the systematic killing of Black Australians, not only warriors but women and children of all ages. Often the only survivors were women, captured and retained for the purposes of prostitution. In 1861 the colonial legislature set up a select committee, made up of landowners, to inquire into the police and the Native Police. It whitewashed the atrocities of the corps and described the people of the land as "being sunk in the lowest depths of barbarism". The official view of those who were seeking to take by force the land and water was that the people were a "race of subhumans beyond help or redemption".[26] This was taken as complete justification for a policy of genocide. The corps would have as many notches on their guns for the killing of mothers, grandmothers and children as they would for warriors killed in action.

The corps grew in strength to more than 200 by the mid-1870s and its upkeep represented five per cent of the colony's budget—compared to Australia's current expenditure on defence of ten per cent of the national budget. Governor Bowen complained that the Imperial Government maintained more troops in New Zealand and South Africa than in Australia and that the colonists in Queensland were more heavily taxed for defence in proportion to their numbers than the people of the United Kingdom.[27]

Each detachment consisted of a senior European officer, usually from one of the British regiments, called at first lieutenants and after 1864, sub-inspectors, sometimes a subordinate European officer with the rank of acting sub-inspector, a camp sergeant and up to six troopers.[28] The non-commissioned officer drilled the troopers when they were in camp, was responsible for supervising stores and remained in charge when the commanding officer and the detachment went out on punitive patrols.

It was the duty of the detachments to respond to any calls for help by the occupiers of the land, the squatters, and in effect to join their armed posses in any operation. Any meeting of local people was to be broken up; any attacks were to be followed up by "retributive justice",[29] which to some commanders meant killing large numbers of Black Australians in retaliation for any trooper or squatter killed. The technique was intimidation by constant patrolling. Sometimes patrols were on the move for a month at a time travelling forty to fifty kilometres a day, opening fire at any people they encountered.

The officers in charge of the patrols had unchecked power. It was only when massacres were publicised that action was taken, and then the officers concerned were simply dismissed. The names of the slain men, women and children were not recorded. Lieutenant Frederick Wheeler, who had shot dead a ten-year-old child in a peaceful location with white witnesses, told the 1861 Select Committee, "I act on my own discretion, and on my own responsibility".[30] He was actually charged, but left the area without the charge being heard. The commanders also had power of life and death over their own troops; in the case of insubordination the death penalty was often applied. Prisoners taken in action were normally summarily executed rather than escorted to headquarters. The troopers were allowed to keep women for their own purposes.

The Native Police were thus soldier, police, prosecuter, judge, jury and executioner. Their excesses often provoked even fiercer resistance, setting in train even bloodier reprisals.

The troopers wore caps variously described as white drill with a peak, black or dark green with a red band,[31] and dark blue with a white calico sun-flap that covered the back of the neck. The jacket was dark blue with red facings. Full dress uniform trousers were dark blue or dark green with a red stripe,[32] but on duty white moleskin trousers were worn with leggings, boots and spurs and a red Garibaldi shirt. On patrol the troopers often discarded most of their uniforms. They were armed with Snider carbines, the bullets from which exploded on entering the body, leaving gaping wounds similar to those caused by dum dum bullets two generations later.

As in other parts of Australia the landowners and their hired hands formed armed auxiliary units. They wore broad-brimmed hats, Garibaldi shirts, trousers or moleskin breeches often with a red silk sash around the waist, perhaps a tie, and heavy boots and jingling spurs. They were often even more heavily armed than the troopers, who were not trusted to carry revolvers; they carried the same carbines, but also shotguns and .45 Colts.

By the 1880s the tactics of both groups had come a long way since the English infantry in their red coats marched out to fife and drum after elusive guerilla fighters. The invaders had 100 years' experience behind them, were able to match the Kalkadoons, among the best warriors in the continent, in bushcraft, and knew the value of a surprise attack. The Native Police and the auxiliary unit of squatters who faced the Kalkadoons in the Battle of Battle Mountain exceeded in number a British infantry company of 200 men.[33]

The years from 1861 to 1897 saw wave after wave of invaders throughout Queensland, not only English but Irish, Scots, Germans, Scandinavians,

Italians and Chinese. Strong lines of communications were established to the bases in the south and the face of the countryside was changed by new patterns of land usage and new technologies. The railway from Ipswich to Brisbane (built in 1865–75), the discovery of gold at Gympie in 1867 and the expansion of the sugar industry along the coast and the pastoral industry inland saw the white population swell, increasing pressures on the beleaguered Australians.

The land of the people was appropriated under alien laws based on the myth that the almost one million Australian inhabitants in 1788 had never existed. That they did was paradoxically admitted by the English authorities then proclaiming them to be British subjects and as such subject to "British law". This denied them title to their own land, and when they resisted its appropriation described them as "outlaws". Their resistance was thus labelled criminal, to be punished either by the people who took their land or by the troops or by both.

"British law" conferred quite different privileges upon the people who acquired the land. Some land was given away as grants but there also developed about 1825 in New South Wales tenure by occupation,[34] that is, by squatting. In an effort to control the occupation of land outside the bounds of settlement squatters were given licences under a new system administered by Crown Lands commissioners. In Queensland Governor Bowen initially confined the settled districts to a very limited area within ten miles (sixteen kilometres) of Ipswich on the Darling Downs and elsewhere to within three miles of the coast. He had the power, however, to proclaim any place in the state an intermediate district where leases could be sold to the highest bidder; the rent was based on the carrying capacity of the land for sheep or cattle. The limited involvement permitted white Queenslanders in the government of the colony was restricted to wealthy landholders, and succeeding administrations brought in land bills designed to give them more liberal terms. The original owners of land were totally confused and horrified by this combination of military force, complicated bureaucratic carving up of territory and a body of law based on the quaint notion that a distant queen whom they had never seen or heard of owned everything in sight in the name of the "Crown".

Probing expeditions into north and west Queensland were followed by squatters with their flocks and herds and guns, by miners, and by the Native Police Corps. There was no negotiation. The guns spoke and whole communities were dispossessed, driven from their land, their food supplies destroyed and access to the food of the newcomers denied.

For a while Australians in Queensland held their frontiers, but inevitably were overcome by the invaders' superior firepower. The stand of the Kalkadoon people at Battle Mountain in 1884 marked the end of effective resistance in Queensland.

First White Contacts on Kalkadoon Land

The first contact the Kalkadoon people had with the invaders was in 1860 when the ill-fated expedition led by Robert O'Hara Burke and William John Wills set out from Melbourne to blaze a trail north to the Gulf of Carpentaria. The cumbersome expedition at first comprised fifteen men, twenty-one tonnes of supplies, camels, horses and stock. Through monumental inefficiency the entire operation suffered one disaster after another, and by the time they crossed the Kalkadoon's boundaries the party was reduced to only four. They passed through the Cloncurry Ranges following one of the tributaries of a river, thought to be either the Corella or the Dugald, to the west of the Cloncurry River. Without knowing it Burke and Wills had entered the territory of what would become the most feared nation of all time.

Wills wrote in his diary:

> *Saturday, 12 January, 1861: We then entered a series of slaty, low sandstone ranges . . . the more stony portions are, however, covered in porcupine grass and here and there with mallee . . . from the highest portion which we reached at a distance of about seven miles, we had a pretty good view of the country towards the north . . .* [35]

He reported that there was plenty of evidence of occupation. When they came in sight of the ranges they saw several columns of smoke to the east and west, which they thought were from cooking fires. They did not know that they were the signal fires of the Kalkadoons. It was obvious to the Kalkadoons that the party was moving on, so they simply watched to ensure they did not take possession of either the land or the precious water supplies which they were using without permission.

In 1861–62 three expeditions searching for survivors of Burke and Wills's party encroached on Kalkadoon land or on neighbouring territories. An expedition led by the former commandant of the quasi-military Native Police, Frederick Walker, left Rockhampton in September 1861 bound for the Albert River on the Gulf of Carpentaria. The force, comprising three Englishmen and five troopers, was ordered by a war party of thirty men to evacuate a waterhole north-east of where Hughendon now stands. Walker did not bother to reply to the charge of trespassing and led a charge which effectively wiped out the party, all of whom were either killed or wounded.[36] In another engagement near the site of Burketown Walker's party was attacked by Black Australians, who advanced in a half-moon formation which Walker said was favoured by those using the woomera. He ordered a cavalry charge in which more than a dozen men died immediately.

Following closely on Walker's heels came the Landsborough and McKinlay expeditions but the Kalkadoons watched them closely but avoided completely any confrontation. The concern of the people at these four heavily armed expeditions marching through their land in the short space of two years was to be multiplied a thousand-fold when the landseekers followed their trails.

The infant colony was created as a vast pastoral empire for landseekers intent on taking up more and more "virgin" land. There were tough adventurers from Victoria and New South Wales, some, not wealthy, seeking independence. There were younger sons of English and Scottish landed gentry and young owner-managers from English squatting families, who received financial backing to seek more land for their family's already vast empires. There were battlers from Ireland, England or Europe, trying to escape from the poverty of wage earning or unemployment in their native countries. All were gambling their lives to find a fortune and were prepared for the hardships and dangers involved.

The Jardine expedition in 1864 found the resistance of the people on the western side of Cape York as strong as Kennedy had found on the eastern side. The English settlement of Somerset at the tip of Cape York Peninsula had been established in 1863 and it was intended it should become the "Singapore of the north", a fort from which the surrounding country and its people could be subdued.[37] The Jardine brothers, Frank and Alexander, set out from Rockhampton with ten men, forty-one horses and a mule to drove 250 head of cattle north to Somerset. The people of the north attacked no fewer than eleven times in a vain attempt to turn them back. When surprise failed, the northern men stood their ground against the guns only to be wiped out time and time again. It is estimated almost 100 were killed or wounded but the Jardines and their men escaped injury.[38]

The first to actually squat on the fringes of Kalkadoon land was Edward Palmer, who in 1864 drove cattle to the Cloncurry River and established Canobie Station at the infall of the Dugald River. Born in Wollongong in New South Wales, he was more in tune with the land of his birth, which he called "New Holland" in his writings, than were most European and Asian invaders, and he left a vivid account of the period from his people's point of view.[39] He described the invaders' diet as far inferior to that of Black Australians: flour, their staple, was made into thin Johnny cakes, which were cooked in ashes and eaten hot. Some flour was so old that the grubs and worms in it died and when it was thrown out dead dingoes and crows testified to its fatal properties. Sugar came in casks and was like black treacle—spilt on the floor it left stains like blood. "Pig weed (portulaca) boiled or roasted on a shovel" was popular, tea was made from "marjoram bush" and coffee from the scrapings of the burnt edges of damper.

Palmer was one of the few to recognise that the lifestyle and customs of the people of the north were superior to those of the struggling poor of Europe and Asia. To him they were a happy people with plentiful food supplies, living healthy lives to a "good old age".[40] They followed the ancient laws and customs, observing marriage rules with great strictness, and kept within their boundaries, not trespassing on neighbouring lands without consent.

The opening of the port of Burketown on the Gulf of Carpentaria in 1865 strengthened not only the number of invaders but their stomachs as well with food imported from the south. The town was a magnet for outlaws from the south, and had no police and only three women. Once it was established, however, it facilitated the invasion of Kalkadoon territory and Palmer recognised that war was inevitable. Squatting on the fringe of their territory, he maintained good relations with them; he came to recognise their laws and strove, successfully, to reach an accommodation with them, studying their language so that he could better understand his neighbours. He was to write in his old age that "the white race were the aggressors, as they were the invaders of the black's hunting territory . . . Whenever new districts were settled, the blacks had to move on to make room. The result was war between the races".[41] But his belief in the ultimate victory of the invaders was absolute—"Nothing can avert the doom that is written as plainly as was the writing on the wall at Belshazzar's feast".[42]

The pressure on the Kalkadoons was maintained not only by the grazing kings but by mining interests as well. The great mineral wealth on their land was discovered by Ernest Henry, the son of a Scottish soldier, who migrated from Harrington in the English county of Cumberland to Melbourne in 1857.[43] Failing to make his fortune on the Victorian goldfields, he headed north where in 1859 he joined one of the quasi-military expeditions made up of southern squatters seeking land. This expedition led by George Elphinstone Dalrymple skirted Kalkadoon country. The vast land caught the imagination of the twenty-three-year-old immigrant boy and his father gave him money to buy land on the Upper Dawson. He could have passed into obscurity but he was still young and restless.

In 1863 Henry went north again. He took up Hughenden Station and developed other properties, but the pastoral bubble burst leaving him well nigh broke. Deciding to head west for the heart of the Kalkadoon country to start all over again, he was joined by a friend, Roger Sheaffe. Both sons of English Army officers, they were the same age and had much in common. They reached the Cloncurry River, 400 kilometres from Hughenden, and following it downstream discovered an isolated rocky peak just outside the Kalkadoon border. Henry called it Fort Constantine because it reminded him of a Crimean fort. In 1867 he found a copper lode near Fort Constantine, which subsequently came to be known as the Great Australian Copper Mine. He had his samples tested and sailed for England to raise money to begin mining. He returned the following year with thirty Cornish miners and a lease which said he was entitled to 2500 acres (1011 hectares) including some Kalkadoon land, and mined and exported the ore to England for six years.

In 1882 Henry began exploring in Kalkadoon territory. The Kalkadoons greeted him if not as a friend then at least as a friendly foreigner. When he explained his quest for copper ore they took him to an imposing outcrop of ore, which rose to a height of fifteen metres in a gully beside a quartz reef, some eighty kilometres west of Cloncurry. He called the site Argylla, an adaptation of the Kalkadoon name.

Henry indicated to the Kalkadoons that he was not one of the robber invaders who took everything and gave nothing; he was generous in his gifts of flour and corned beef. Some thirty Kalkadoons—men, women and children—joined him in working the mine and he became almost one of their clan. Later in 1882 he discovered a deposit that became the Mount Oxide mine, 130 kilometres north-west of Cloncurry, with the assistance of three Kalkadoons and one of the neighbouring Workoboongo people. Apart from his part in the Dalrymple expedition, he usually travelled on his own or in the company of two trusted Kalkadoon men with whom he had formed a friendship. This relationship led them to invite him into their camps to meet their families.

In an atmosphere of escalating tension, however, even Henry could not escape, particularly when he became associated with a man named Alexander Kennedy, who was to assist in leading the forces against the Kalkadoons for a final solution.

By the mid-1870s it was obvious that the Kalkadoons were under siege. The invaders with their goods and chattels and herds were growing daily in strength and numbers, not only on the fringes of Kalkadoon land but deep within their territory. Backup communications behind the frontiers were improving rapidly. Burketown was a centre for bringing in arms and supplies. Telegraphic communication was established with Townsville from Brisbane in 1869 and three years later the line was extended to the mouth of the Norman River.

Every white invader carried guns. Kennedy, for example, always carried a .45 Colt revolver and a carbine, and for good measure a shotgun as well. His bullets were made on his station, which held enough gunpowder for six months. In every homestead loaded weapons were always within easy reach in bedrooms, kitchens, even dining rooms. When the squatters and their men went calling socially they carried little revolvers in their belts, whether they were eating, drinking or relieving themselves. The women who joined them as wives or servants also carried guns. Mrs Robert Gray of Hughenden had her own gun and it is recorded that a Mrs Scott practised every day with her revolver, which she always carried, cocked and ready, in her belt.[44]

Moving from one fortified homestead to another, the squatter rode fully armed with a brace of pistols and a rifle "slung in light cavalry fashion".[45] Farmers and miners carried guns by day and kept them loaded and ready by their beds at night. The miners coming fresh from Europe and Asia were shocked to find that it was compulsory to hump a heavy revolver in case of attack by the people on whose land they were working.

The Guerilla War 1877–84

The region was a powder keg but there was no general outbreak of hostilities until Alexander Kennedy took up Buckingham Downs in 1877. Until then the Kalkadoons had had to deal with the various transient expeditions, with the gentle Palmer and Henry whom they had befriended, and with some settlers who tried but failed to establish themselves in this harsh country. Among the last were the Brown brothers, who founded Bridgewater Station just inside the Kalkadoons' boundary in 1874. They unwittingly selected land without permanent water. Wisely the Kalkadoons did not interfere, but watched and waited while the brothers and their cattle went thirsty and eventually gave up.

Kennedy, however, began his life in Kalkadoon country like a latter-day Ghengis Khan. Born in 1837 at Dunkeld in the Scottish county of Perthshire, he migrated to Australia in 1861, attracted by a placard on a house in the nearby town of Ayr, "Wanted, Young Men for Queensland".[46] He became overseer on Rio Station on the lower Dawson River, moved on to the Springsure district, and when the sheep industry fell on hard times decided to grow sugar cane near Rockhampton. He failed at this enterprise. After he married he borrowed £12,000 from the bank and in 1877 secured a property, which he named Buckingham Downs, on Sulieman Creek on the southern border of Kalkadoon country. He later took over another tract of Kalkadoon land, which he called Noarnside, but his most direct challenge to the Kalkadoons came in 1881 when he took up Calton Hills in their very heartland, 160 kilometres north-west of Cloncurry.

From the outset Kennedy indulged in no discussion, no negotiation. He took possession of the land and the water, drove off the game and destroyed the natural food supplies. Anyone who attempted to take a share of the cattle that had replaced the native animals faced death by shooting. Sacred sites which had been kept inviolate for centuries were trampled by men and animals alike and those who would worship became trespassers. He seemed to have declared a personal war that at times took

---

OVERLEAF:
Defeated in battle, Black Australians were dispossessed of their land, their homes and their livelihood. This illustration, titled "Queensland squatters 'dispersing' Aborigines", appeared as the frontispiece in A. J. Vogan's The Black Police, *published in 1890.* NATIONAL LIBRARY OF AUSTRALIA

on all the marks of a vendetta. "They're all scorpions, and who wants to be stung with one of those poisonous things," he wrote.[47] He had arrived in Queensland at a time when killings on the frontiers were commonplace. For instance, his arrival in the Springsure district coincided with the massacre of the Wills family, which became the talk of the district and revived the story of the Fraser massacre of 1857. The bloody cycle of killing and reprisal seemed doomed to go on forever, or at least until one of the protagonists was wiped out.

Within a year of Kennedy's arrival in the Kalkadoons' territory guerilla war began. Drays were ambushed, bullocks and horses driven off, although the Kalkadoons still hesitated to begin the killing. Then in December 1878 they made a stand at Wonomo Waterhole.

With three stockmen and a mob of cattle a man named Molvo crossed into Kalkadoon territory from Boulia intending to occupy land on Sulieman Creek. When he decided to camp at the waterhole, the Kalkadoons, who had been monitoring the incursion, challenged their occupation of such an important watering place that was probably also a sacred site. First they sent emissaries to open dialogue, but when it became obvious that Molvo and his party were there to stay, the signal for attack was given. All four intruders were killed and the cattle were either speared for food or driven off.

A council of war determined to maintain the momentum by attacking the nearby white bridgeheads at Stanbrook Station and Sulieman Creek. When the alarm was raised at Stanbrook every armed man was mustered to repel the attack and the war party retreated.

Next to come under fire was the Sulieman Creek homestead held by Alexander Kennedy. He was away in Cloncurry and his brother-in-law, Robert Currie, was in charge. His wife, who had proved her marksmanship against dingoes and birds, was ready to defend the homestead but the women and children were evacuated to Buckingham Downs, the capital of the Kennedy principality. As the Kalkadoons gathered in some hundreds a message was sent to the district police headquarters near Boulia, about 100 kilometres to the south. A strong force of troopers, mainly Native Police, commanded by Sub-Inspector Eglington, reached the homestead before the Kalkadoons launched a frontal attack. For the Kalkadoons this was the bloodiest episode of the entire guerilla war. It is estimated that 300 were killed,[48] but not until the dead and wounded lay in mounds did they withdraw.

As they retreated the victorious whites were further reinforced by the return of Kennedy, who asked Eglington, "Did you get the piebald black?" When Eglington replied in the negative, Kennedy urged pursuit, saying, "Well, come along. That fellow is one of a mob that I have had my eye on for a long time—a cheeky trouble-making chap".[49] They caught up with part of the war party who had taken up a commanding position in rugged hilly country. It was a useless last stand for them and many were wiped out. As Kennedy and the troopers walked among the bodies he pointed out the corpse of his brave "piebald black". A man with a fine physique and distinctive pinkish white patches of skin, he had argued with Kennedy about the rights of his people against the demands of the invaders. Kennedy admitted his intelligence but was content to see him dead.

From this encounter the Kalkadoons learned that they could not carry out a massed attack against guns, and that even in their own rough terrain they could not withstand a charge by mounted invaders: they did not mass for battle again until their famous last stand in 1884. Instead, they swooped down from the hills in small parties, hitting the invaders where it hurt them most by attacking the cattle that represented their capital. Many cattle took off and became wild, others died in the swampy valley flats. And whenever an invader could be challenged, he was.

The Kalkadoons rightly saw Kennedy as their most powerful opponent, the bulwark of the invaders—if he retreated it would mean freedom from the landseekers. The continual guerilla war did keep many from entering Kalkadoon land, but Kennedy stayed on. He placed on record his view that the "inferior race" must go and was fixed in his belief "that the only way to survive in this wild country was to show conclusively who was master".[50] Always in the lead of the invaders involved in armed clashes, he was renowned for the grim satisfaction he took in hunting down and killing any Kalkadoons who could be found after an engagement. He was "a man who was uncompromising in his dealings with the Kalkadoons".[51] He had many narrow escapes from death—individual warriors even sought to kill him in single combat—and those who were his friends were also endangered.

The miner Ernest Henry had travelled with the Kalkadoons as friends, learned much of their language and customs and shown them respect. But he had also been cultivated by Alexander Kennedy and was often seen out riding with him. On one occasion, when Kennedy was riding over to Argylla to visit Henry, he received a warning. A Kalkadoon woman ran forward with an excuse he should look at his horse's foot, and as Kennedy bent down, whispered that Henry was in danger. Kennedy ignored her and Henry was nearly killed.

A young Kalkadoon man, convinced that Henry was part of the invasion force which would dispossess his people, decided to challenge him. His young friends, to even the contest, took Henry's firearms and left them to joust. If this had happened in medieval Europe the story would have found its way into the poems of the troubadours. The challenger confronted Henry, speared him in the upper part of his body, and then closed with him in a fight to the death. They wrestled, each striving for a stranglehold, watched by other warriors and two local women who had been with Henry for some time. At last Henry's opponent broke off and conceded defeat. The warriors left Henry in the care of his Kalkadoon friends who took him to his hut. The two women applied poultices of oatmeal to his spear wound before taking him to Cloncurry to his own people.

Even the powerful, single-minded Kennedy, however, is known to have had at least one moment, if not of doubt about his bloody actions, at least of apprehension or fear. Shortly after the group led by Molvo had been wiped out, a man named Russell told Kennedy that Molvo had appeared to him in a dream, shivering and saying, "I have come for my blankets, I am cold".[52] Kennedy was amazed at Russell's description of the dead man, whom he had never seen, and went to the creek where Molvo and his companions were buried. Dingoes had dug up the bodies, which were scattered around the creek. Kennedy reburied them and as it was close to sundown decided to make camp for the night. Despite the noise of howling dingoes, crying curlews and other creatures of the night he slept well, but in the middle of the night he was awakened by a terrible commotion. Whether or not he thought the ghosts of the dead had returned to haunt him he did not record but admitted later to his terror, and to his relief in finding that a dingo had caused the noise by jumping into an old salted beef cask.[53]

During the early 1880s the guerilla war intensified and Kennedy was involved in many incidents. His servant, and spy, was a young Kalkadoon man he called Sandy. According to Kennedy, an old woman who had fallen behind in one of the bloody actions, unable to feed the boy because of her age and infirmity, had begged Kennedy to take him. It is not recorded what happened to his mother. A war party of about forty, planning to attack Kennedy's main homestead while he and his men were out mustering, were surprised when Kennedy and his servant Sandy returned. Alone, Kennedy charged the raiding party which retreated rapidly into the bush. Next day, Kennedy attempted, unsuccessfully, to hunt down his adversaries. He then persuaded Sandy to play traitor and to act as his spy. Sandy, a renegade and an uninitiated man, knew the terrain and proved adept in the role of intelligence gatherer.[54]

On one occasion, hearing the noise of a Kalkadoon ceremony near the fortified homestead at Calton Hills, Kennedy sent Sandy to spy on the gathering. The information he brought back was indeed a surprise. A new song was sung that night, dedicated to Kennedy himself:

We kill Kennedy in the morning,
We kill Kennedy in the morning.
We of the Kalkadoon tribe; have our glory and prowess departed?
Our hunting grounds are ravished,
Our water is taken by the cattle,

But bullock is good
Kill and we shall have beef for ever!
Kill the white man,
Kill the white man!
Do not our women deride us?
We are many and can conquer the white man's magic.
We kill Kennedy in the morning,
We kill Kennedy in the morning![55]

It was the highlight of the ceremony. As the women provided the accompaniment of tapping boomerangs and clapping, the men danced, depicting grazing animals and the hunt of the warriors.

Sandy went running back to the homestead. Kennedy saddled his horse and, riding at full gallop, fired into the gathering, scattering the singers and dancers. One or two women failed to escape. Kennedy refrained from killing them and instead used them to send a menacing message to the warriors, warning them of the dire consequences that would follow if they should reappear.[56]

Kennedy was not losing the war but he was not winning either. He could hold his own but only by keeping all his properties on a war footing. He decided to go to Brisbane to seek help for a final solution. He rode into Cloncurry, then north to Normanton, unimpeded—the Kalkadoons did not have the strength to cut communications—and sailed south on a coastal boat to Brisbane.

At a conference with Commissioner D. T. Seymour, head of both the police department and the paramilitary forces, and other officers, Kennedy announced that if the government did not move against the Kalkadoons he would organise his own military force and finish the war himself. Seymour warned him that if he attempted to follow this course of action he would be arrested. Kennedy left in disgust, but had not gone far before Seymour overtook him. "Look here," Seymour said, "I could not tell you what to do in there. We shall do what we can to increase the number of police patrols in the bad area; meanwhile, if you have trouble, you know what to do."[57]

In effect Kennedy had been given a blank cheque to raise his own forces and proceed with open warfare.[58]

In the 1880s Cloncurry was a strategic outpost on a hostile frontier. Marcus de la Poer Beresford was the officer-in-charge of the Native Police force stationed there when the war was at its height. In January 1883 he and a detachment of four troopers were attacked by Kalkadoons as they camped on a spur of the McKinlay Ranges at the head of Fullarton River near Farleigh Station. They took several prisoners and held them under guard. During the night the prisoners escaped and armed themselves from one of the secret caches of weapons which the Kalkadoons had established in nearly every gorge in the area. Consequently, Beresford's unit was wiped out, he himself being fatally wounded.[59] Reinforcements were rushed from Boulia but thrashed around fruitlessly before retreating back to their base.

Now the Kalkadoons gained the upper hand. During the rest of the year they sent defiant messages to the people of Cloncurry, warning them to stay away from Kalkadoon territory. It is likely that even Kennedy kept to his fringe territory. The invaders' cattle were taken as needed by the Kalkadoons, who feasted and sang as in days gone when they acknowledged no man king. Squatters rode out from their fortress homesteads only in armed parties, moving rapidly through Kalkadoon country and conscious that they were under constant observation. The dreaded Native Police, on the verge of mutiny, cowered in their barracks in Cloncurry as the Kalkadoons drove off their entire complement of horses.[60] Cloncurry itself was virtually under siege. The people locked up in the town showed little inclination to challenge the Kalkadoon fighting men and in fact never did. The Kalkadoons let them skulk in the town and ignored their old enemies the troopers.

It seemed that the Kalkadoons had won, that the invaders would fold their tents and go. Certainly the dawning of 1884 was "the highwater mark of Kalkadoon resistance",[61] their finest hour in the ten years since the arrival of the invaders. Before the year was out victory would be turned into bitter and final defeat at Battle Mountain. The immediate events which led to the final act began in far away Brisbane.

The premier of Queensland from 1879 until late in 1883 was Sir Thomas McIlwraith, another Scottish immigrant from Ayr. At first a civil engineer, in the 1860s he acquired pastoral interests in the Maranoa district of Queensland and entered Queensland politics a decade later. In 1879 he married Harriette Ann Mosman, a sister of A. F. Mosman who had taken up land he called White Hills in the very heart of Kalkadoon country. As a besieged pastoralist, and brother-in-law of the premier, Mosman knew where the power was.[62] In 1883 McIlwraith appointed as commanding officer of the beleaguered Cloncurry Native Police Detachment a man who was to play a key role at Battle Mountain. Frederick Charles Urquhart, the son of an English Army officer, was born in England and arrived in Australia as a migrant in 1875.

Drilling his troopers with what has been described as the "vehemence of a Prussian Sergeant-Major",[63] Urquhart set out to rebuild the force. He rounded up the scattered horses, bought or commandeered more and steadily built up some of the lost confidence of the whites. The Kalkadoon warriors watched with more than passing interest. They could see that a new leader had arrived, someone for whom perhaps they could have respect. A message was brought from the hills challenging Urquhart to single combat. Mahoni, from whom the challenge is believed to have come and who may have been a Kalkadoon leader, promised that if Urquhart rose to the challenge, he would end up as dead as the previous commander of the garrison.[64] Urquhart replied that unless the Kalkadoons ceased fighting they would be wiped out. He followed up this defiance with a surprise patrol, the first since the Kalkadoon victories. Training and firepower combined with his own leadership forced the Kalkadoons to retreat. From a new and stronger camp forty kilometres out of Cloncurry he initiated regular patrols, which brought a new insecurity to the Kalkadoons. Though preoccupied with this new enemy on their eastern frontier they resumed their pressure on their other principal enemy, Kennedy, in the centre of their lands and to the south.

In mid-1884 they killed Kennedy's partner, James White Powell, while he was camped on Mistake Creek some ninety-five kilometres from Calton Hills.[65] There was jubilation that one of Kennedy's deputies had been despatched and that night a feast in a gorge celebrated the event. Photographs of Powell's family were taken from his wallet and used as targets for spears. With his customary dash, Kennedy rode eighty kilometres non-stop to meet Urquhart and his men. Pausing only to bury Powell, they combined forces and trapped the war party in a gorge. The Kalkadoons fought with spears and boomerangs, but the carbines caused many casualties. Mosman was also present and his daughter, Mrs Burke, later gave a detailed account of the reprisal.[66] Mosman told his daughter that the squatters and troopers killed "men, women and children . . . but mainly men".[67]

Urquhart did not believe in an "eye for an eye and a tooth for a tooth" but, as he said in one of his own verses, that "For every one of these poor bones, A Kalkadoon shall die". For nine weeks posses of armed squatters and troopers combined to "clear up" the district. Casualties from this operation have been estimated at between 500 and 700: the human body contains 500 bones.[68]

September 1884

The immediate prelude to the last battle came in September 1884 when a Kalkadoon war party decided to raid Hopkins' Granada Station on the Dugald River. By this time the English penetration of north Queensland had opened the way for people from the rest of the world, including 20,000 Chinese, who had come from the great provinces of Canton, Hokkien, and Fukien mainly to work on the land, toil on the wharves and dig for gold. One of these immigrants was employed by Hopkins to man a lonely outstation and to care for his sheep. The raiding party burnt the outpost and killed the shepherd.[69]

Hopkins called for maximum reprisals and so put in train the chain of events that led to the battle. While Hopkins gathered all the men who could be raised in the neighbourhood, Urquhart and his troopers made

Men of the paramilitary Native Police with their British commander.
JOHN OXLEY LIBRARY

their way to Granada where the largest armed force in the war with the Kalkadoons began to assemble.

Although there is no evidence that he was present, one can only assume that Alexander Kennedy, like the other squatters and their hired hands, rallied to the cause. Kennedy, who was forty-seven years old at the time, was known as "Old Man Kennedy" to the younger Urquhart, whom he had joined on many patrols and with whom he shared the view that the Kalkadoons had to be wiped out.

By the time Urquhart gave the order to move out after the raiding party, his combined force of troopers and auxiliaries numbered about 200. From the hills the Kalkadoons watched as the small army assembled and rode out from Granada, following the trails from one Kalkadoon dwelling place to another – after the years of guerilla warfare the area held few secret places in which the Australians could hide. The Kalkadoons must have recognised the strength and purpose of the force and sent out messages for warriors to assemble, since estimates of their army are as high as 1000, although the fighting men probably numbered no more than 600.[70] It was traditional for the Kalkadoons to have a battle leader wearing the possum-tail insignia, and the leader on this fateful day followed this great tradition. In other parts of the world the English knew by name the war leaders they were fighting, such as the Zulu leader, Chaka, and the Maori Hone Heke, but the name of the Kalkadoon leader at Battle Mountain was never recorded.

In the hilly country at the head of Prospector Creek the Kalkadoons made a stand on the boulder-studded peak of Battle Mountain, eighty kilometres north-east of Mount Isa. They had assembled a huge stock of spears, boomerangs and other weapons and as the warriors arrived they began stockpiling rocks and boulders. By the time Urquhart's army came into view through the droopy-leafed trees on the plain below, the greatest gathering of the Kalkadoons for a decade was quiet and ready. Among the giant anthills and isolated boulders Urquhart mustered his forces in full view of the Kalkadoons but beyond spear range. When all was ready he rode out in front of his troops and shouted up the mountain, "Stand in the Queen's name",[71] an invocation to the distant Queen-Empress Victoria to whom the Kalkadoons were supposed to look for protection.

The reply was a shower of missiles. Urquhart raised his arm and the 200 mounted men in broad-brimmed hats, military caps and everything from Garibaldi shirts to uniforms of blue and green began the only cavalry-style charge in the history of Australia. They were at full gallop when they reached the lower slopes of the mountain and began firing carbines and Colts, shotguns and revolvers in a deafening cacophony which Urquhart hoped would panic the Kalkadoons.

Their bullets pinged harmlessly against the rocks and after covering no more than thirty metres of open ground the horses found the slope too steep. The attackers were forced to dismount within range of the warriors' spears. A shower of spears and missiles descended on men and horses alike. Horses scattered as the men who had charged so confidently scurried for cover among the rocks. As their fire died away the warriors above them yelled in derision and defiance.

Urquhart did not find it easy to rally either the troopers or the auxiliaries to advance on foot up the slope. Each time they moved, awkwardly, slowly, from the cover of one rock to another, the deadly spears of the Kalkadoons and their seemingly inexhaustible store of missiles found their mark. Then a huge Kalkadoon warrior picked out Urquhart as he clambered over a steep, open patch and brought him down with a lump of cement-hard anthill.[72] He tumbled over backwards with a wound to his face, knocked out cold. The warrior reached for a spear leaning against the rock he was sheltering behind and swung it up for the death stroke. As he did so one of the troopers shot him dead.

Covering fire from the rest of the force enabled troopers to carry Urquhart down the mountain and out of range of the spears. A general retreat was ordered and the attackers temporarily abandoned their injured on the mountainside.[73] Their numbers were equalled if not exceeded by the Kalkadoon dead. While Urquhart lay unconscious for several hours his army milled around, leaderless and dispirited. They could offer little fight. Whenever they ventured within range an explosion of missiles as if from a small volcano descended upon them, and they retrieved the injured with great difficulty.

For a while it seemed that the battle was over, that the warriors could celebrate one of the major victories of the Hundred Years War, but Urquhart regained consciousness and despite his wound once again took command. He called a council of war and decided on a new strategy.[74] Dividing his forces, he sent a strong detachment of troopers and auxiliaries to attack from the other side of the mountain, while he continued the main frontal assault. The tactics were effective in confusing the Kalkadoons, who did not seem able to decide which slope they should defend. In moving from one side to the other they made easy targets and suffered heavy casualties.

It was at this stage that the Kalkadoon battle leader gave an order which can be likened to the one that led to the famous charge by the Light Brigade against the Russian artillery at Balaclava during the Crimean War.[75] The Kalkadoon warriors formed into ranks and carrying their heavy fighting spears before them like lances charged straight down the slopes into the blazing muzzles of the guns. As a French observer had commented of the charge at Balaclava, it was magnificent but it was not war. Under sustained and intensive fire the line wavered, then retreated, leaving the slope covered with dead and wounded. Again the line reformed, again they charged down the hill only to be mown down by steady fire. Some warriors with an apparent disregard for danger and death reached the invaders' line, where they fought desperately with spear and shield before the bullets stopped them.

This last charge saw the bravest perish: the remaining warriors turned away, leaving about 200 dead on the battlefield. In their last stand on Battle Mountain victory only just eluded the Kalkadoons. They came close, because of sheer courage, to achieving the greatest triumph in the history of the Australian Hundred Years War.

The victorious invaders treated their wounded and made camp as night fell. The next day the dingoes and crows had a feast on the bodies of the slain. Those among Urquhart's force who had escaped unwounded pursued the remnants of the Kalkadoons for several days. Unsung by their conquerors, the dead lay scattered on the hillside, whitening bones testifying for years afterwards to the scale of the slaughter.[76]

It is estimated that in the period 1878 to 1884 between 500 and 900 Kalkadoons were killed; 277 Australians were killed in the Korean War, 518 during the Boer War and 414 in the Vietnam War.[77]

Aftermath

Urquhart went on to become commissioner of police for Queensland and was later administrator of the Northern Territory. He married seven years after the battle, and made a triumphant visit to his native England where he was hailed as one of the conquerors in a distant bastion of Empire, although at a tea-party one woman accused him of "murdering a lot of poor defenceless blacks in Australia".[78] He died, an honoured and respected citizen, in Brisbane in December 1935.

Alexander Kennedy went on to amass more land and wealth. With Roger Sheaffe he took over another vast slice of Kalkadoon land, which they called Devoncourt, where ironically the Kalkadoon remnant, now reduced to 500, survived under the ever-watchful eye of the conqueror and his guns. On reaching seventy years of age Kennedy moved to a comfortable home in Cloncurry and in 1908 he too returned to his native country to be applauded for his efforts for Empire. He retired to the Brisbane suburb of Auchenflower where he died at the age of ninety-eight in 1936.[79]

Thomas McIlwraith, whose appointment of Urquhart led to the battle, was knighted in 1882 and was in England in 1884. He returned after the defeat of the Kalkadoons and served again as premier in 1888 and 1893. But his business dealings went awry and with debts of £250,000 he was forced to resign from politics in 1897 amid allegations of corruption and mismanagement on a grand scale. He died in London in 1900.

The shadows of time obscure the Kalkadoon leaders. The warrior Mahoni, who sent the challenge to combat to the young commander

Urquhart when he arrived in Cloncurry, vanished without trace.

The unnamed battle leader of the Kalkadoons is credited with a son who survived the slaughter on Battle Mountain. Tubbie Terrier,[80] an English distortion of his Kalkadoon name, was tall, well built and handsome and had fought until a bullet had creased his skull and knocked him unconscious. On regaining consciousness he found the battle over and the victors removing their wounded and counting the dead. He lay still, pretending to be dead, until darkness fell and the troopers withdrew and he could crawl away to safety.

About six months after the battle he arrived at Glenroy Station on the Leichhardt River with his wife and the widow of a slain warrior. Neil Macdonald, the manager, recognised his courage and perhaps his status, and hid him from the troopers. Tubbie Terrier formed a great attachment to the Macdonald children and would take the youngest, aged three, into the bush to look for bees' nests, the child sitting on his shoulders holding onto his mop of wavy black hair. Neil Macdonald later said he trusted the lives of his family to the Kalkadoon warrior who would have defended them to the death.

The last known Kalkadoon survivor of the battle, Tubbie Terrier died in Cloncurry Hospital in 1930 aged about seventy-two years, a refugee in his own country.[81]

The passing of the years has healed the scars. The Kalkadoons today are rebuilding their numbers, reviving their language, their heritage and pride. In 1984 the centenary of the battle was marked by a Kalkadoon Cultural Festival in Mount Isa and on 21 October more than 100 people gathered at Kajabbi, which is only twenty kilometres from Battle Mountain, for the unveiling of a memorial to the gallant Kalkadoons who fell in battle. The twentieth of October has been proclaimed Memorial Day by the Kalkadoon Tribal Council and 100 years after the battle the Kalkadoon people are resolved never to forget the heroism of those who fought so long and so well.

On 7 October 1972 the Hon. R. Katter, then Minister for the Army, named an American-built helicopter *Kalkadoon* in a ceremony at Kalkadoon Park in Mount Isa. In his speech the Minister said:

> *It is fitting that the Army's new helicopter should be named after the Kalkadoon tribe, which lived and hunted in the Mount Isa and Cloncurry area. The Kalkadoons have gone down in history as one of the few . . . tribes in Australia that has stood up to the whites in open battle.*[82]

10. *PILGRIMAGES*

During the course of researching *Six Australian Battlefields* we visited all the battle sites. At each one the shadows of the past seemed to become more substantial and our visit became a pilgrimage.

Of them all only Eureka can claim an impressive man-made memorial, although in the land of the Kalkadoons Battle Mountain rears up from the red plain as it has for thousands of years, a natural monument to the last pitched battle of the Hundred Years War. In contrast, the sites of the first battles against the invaders have been swamped by the twentieth-century development of Sydney. The city of Parramatta has spread far beyond the battlefield by the river, where not even a sign recalls the event. The last stand of the Dharuk people is difficult even to find since the name Richmond Hill no longer appears on the map.

Yet our pilgrimages to all these sites evoked the sights and sounds of the redcoats locked in combat with their opponents so vividly it was as if we had gone back in time.

Australians of all colours and generations can salute the heroes of the past who defended their country for so long and so well. There is no disgrace in their defeat, and only generosity and maturity in acknowledging their strength.

Three Sydney Battlefields

Symbolically, a pilgrimage to the battlefields of Parramatta, Vinegar Hill and the Hawkesbury can conveniently begin at Brickfield Hill at the southern end of George Street, one of Sydney's main canyons of commerce. Brickfield Hill marked the outskirts of early Sydney and it was to there that the Eora guerilla forces under Pemulwuy penetrated during their twelve years of resistance to the invaders. As one continues west past Central Station, dominated by its tall clock tower, George Street

TOP: *The modern city now overlooks the site of the Battle of Parramatta.*

BOTTOM: *Vinegar Hill today.*

PHOTOGRAPHS BY MARJI HILL

becomes first Broadway and then Parramatta Road. Once out of the city itself the road passes through the suburb of Annandale, although Major George Johnston's Annandale House has long since been demolished.

Parramatta Road follows substantially the same route traversed by British regiments as they marched to Parramatta to battle the Eora and Dharuk peoples and to confront the Irish rebels at Vinegar Hill, although it now passes not open, grassy country and isolated wagon stops but an unbroken line of stores, car yards, factories and, for the thirsty, occasional pubs, until it finally takes a turn into Church Street, Parramatta.

Searching for George Street, which leads to the site of the Battle of Parramatta, we turned into Macquarie Street, where the two-storey Houison House built in the 1840s stands on land where in a little shack the founder of Melbourne, John Batman, was born in 1800. George Street, named after George III, was the first planned thoroughfare in Australia. It ran from Queens Wharf on the south bank of the Parramatta River west to Government House on a rise overlooking the town. The first lath and plaster house was built for Governor Phillip in 1790. Governor Hunter built on the same site in 1799 a more luxurious house in which he reigned in splendour. Enlarged by Macquarie in 1815, the mansion ran down, becoming a boarding house and then part of the King's School until its restoration as a museum.

At the eastern end of George Street close to the river's edge were the Marine Barracks and gardens and, a little further on, Queens Wharf. It was in this area that the Battle of Parramatta took place, although the marines had gone by the time of the battle in 1797 and it was the New South Wales Corps which faced the Eora war party led by Pemulwuy. The barracks were used as a store after the marines left and were pulled down in 1830. The wharf has disappeared too but the site is marked by a memorial to the men who served in the four ships of the Australian Navy called HMAS *Parramatta*. Clay Cliffe Creek, which Pemulwuy and his warriors would have crossed without difficulty as they advanced on Parramatta from Toongabbie, is still there but encased in a drainage pipe.

The whole area today is a sylvan setting for picnics and lazy afternoons in the summer sun. The quick-running brown stream is flanked on one side by gentle grassy banks, on the other by thick trees, and the only battle sounds to be heard are the click of bowls from the greens of the Parramatta Masonic Club across the way. Alongside the HMAS *Parramatta* memorial is a perpetually flying national flag. It would be appropriate if the Battle of Parramatta and the great Pemulwuy were also commemorated and the flag of black Australia could fly alongside as a symbol of new peace.

We set out from Parramatta for the battlefield at Vinegar Hill along O'Connell Street, perhaps a tribute to O'Connell the Irish Liberator, past

Parramatta Gaol, a grim stone structure built in 1842 to replace the original log gaol on what is now Prince Alfred Park, and onto Windsor Road. On our thirty kilometre drive north west to Windsor we passed first the turnoff to Old Toongabbie—a vivid reminder of Pemulwuy's one triumph—and then the Old Northern Road to Castle Hill where the Irish Rebellion began. Once through Kellyville (named after an Irish settler, not the famous Ned Kelly) we crossed Smalls Creek (which the Irish Ambassador to Australia until 1986, Joseph Small, claimed for his ancestors) and Caddies Creek before turning left to Vinegar Hill, now a national heritage site.

At the end of Vinegar Hill Road—so named by Blacktown City Council—the hilltop site is on land generously set aside by the Castlebrook Lawn Cemetery. Through the scattered gum trees planted in 1983 when the council organised the first commemoration of the battle, it is possible to see west to the Blue Mountains, north-west across the still open country to Windsor and the Hawkesbury River and south-east towards Parramatta and Sydney. Only a gentle breeze and one's own imagination whisper reminders of the death and deceit that marked the battle.

It is only twelve kilometres from Vinegar Hill to the site of the Battle of the Hawkesbury. Windsor Road runs through gentle hills, now grazing land, small orchards and plant nurseries, past the little townships of Rouse Hill, Vineyard and McGraths Hill to the neat Macquarie town of Windsor. The whole town, including its main street, is a memorial to the ubiquitous governor. Past Richmond Airforce Base and through Richmond, the road crosses the rich flats of the Hawkesbury River. Here signs warn of flooding and icy roads, testimony to the hazards of the land of the Dharuk people. Across the broad Hawkesbury River through North Richmond we headed for Bell's Line Road and Richmond Hill. This country is dominated by the memory of Major Francis Grose, the military commander who succeeded Governor Phillip and who gave enormous amounts of land to his fellows in the New South Wales Corps. The small settlements of Grose Vale and Grose Wold were named after him, as was the Grose River, a nearby tributary of the Hawkesbury, which rises in the deep gorges of the Blue Mountains. Here Major Grose built a magnificent baronial mansion on one of the grants he allocated to himself; it is now the St John of God Hospital and on its gate are the words "God is Love". History truly belongs to the victors.

A gentle climb up Grose Vale Road brought us to the crest of Richmond Hill. In the distance were the Blue Mountains, forever misty and blue, and all around were rolling green hills. As the long day's shadows lengthened, kookaburras and bellbirds called as they had done for the generations of the Dharuk on the site of a running battle which today is neither known nor commemorated.

The site of the Battle of the Hawkesbury. PHOTOGRAPH BY MARJI HILL

Bathurst Remembers

Few heroes of the 200 years of black resistance in Australia have been honoured by the people or the authorities in the areas in which they fought. Bathurst, however, has immortalised Windradyne in the name of a new suburb, Windradyne Heights, and his grave is not far away on the property of one of the outstanding white families to settle in Australia in colonial days.

After a half-hour flight from Sydney we landed at the neat little airport eight kilometres out of town. We drove along an avenue of tall trees to Bathurst's older sister, the town of Kelso, where Macquarie secured the loyalty of his first military garrison and their auxiliaries by giving them ten blocks of fifty acres to be cultivated, over the sleepy Macquarie River and into Bathurst itself.

Every corner of the town is full of history. In George Street, near the square that has replaced the old produce markets, is Macquarie's Old Government House where the governor stayed during his second visit to Bathurst in 1821. Ribbon Gang Lane, off William Street, marks the spot where Ralph Entwistle and the nine rebels who joined him in his wild bid for freedom in 1829 were publicly hanged. In these streets the bushranger Ben Hall once ruled for a day and Cobb & Co., the legendary stage coach service, had their headquarters. There is also the cottage of one of Australia's greatest prime ministers, Ben Chifley, who was born and buried in Bathurst.

The motel we stayed at, the Governor Macquarie Motor Inn, was guarded by British soldiers, their rifles at the ready—fortunately they were only lifesize murals. In the bar was a photograph of the sketch by John Lewin believed to be a portrait of Windradyne. One wall was covered with a mural depicting the exploits of Ralph Entwistle, and another with the episodes from the life of Ned Kelly.

To reach Windradyne's grave, we drove back through Kelso—where at the oldest church in the district, the Anglican Church of the Holy Trinity, his enemy Major James Morisset is buried—and turned off onto Sofala Road. For a couple of kilometres it was lined with trees and flanked by neat suburban houses, then the open countryside took over. Wide grazing lands stretched to the horizon, and beyond the roadside edged with the vivid purple flowers known variously as Riverina Bluebell, Patterson's Curse or Salvation Jane, mobs of sheep and fat beef cattle stood in green growth belly high after the flood rains. About a kilometre past the fast-running Winburndale Rivulet we reached a gate marked by three poplars, the entrance to the Suttor property of Brucedale, once the historic heart of the Wiradjuri's land and the site of one of their sacred burial grounds.

At the top of a steep slope we could see Brucedale homestead, a long house with an elegant verandah and an imposing Georgian door which could have graced a Dublin or London terrace. Tall gum trees shaded the house and the green lawn in front where a group of English elms reminded us that the founder of Brucedale, George Suttor, came from Chelsea in London in 1800.

The Suttor family was Scottish but George had gone to London to work in the Chelsea market gardens. Joseph Banks is said to have encouraged him to take cuttings to breed in Australia. On his arrival in New South Wales George was given a property at Baulkham Hills to do just that and he became a significant figure in the colony. In the Bligh Rebellion of 1808, however, when ordered by Macarthur and the rebels to muster at Parramatta and march with them, he refused and was jailed for six months. He was called to England in 1810 to give evidence on Bligh's behalf. But the military clique never forgot and never forgave. Even twelve years later when settlers were being given 2000 acres on the other side of the Blue Mountains Suttor received only 320, for as he said he was not the governor's pet. He chose a spot on the creek, brought his precious fruit trees from Baulkham Hills and planted them around a modest house dominated by a giant oak tree. The house, the oak tree and some of the fruit trees survive but the Suttors moved up the hill to the present house in 1837. Building the house and the property was the work of George's son, William Henry I, who was followed by William Henry II, his son Roy, and then John, whose own family represents the sixth generation.

Windradyne's resting place can just be seen from the house, two kilometres away as the crow flies but twice that distance to drive. It is as beautiful a place now as it must have been in 1829. Backed by stringybarks and yellow box, the cemetery lies on the edge of a small plain which slopes slightly upwards and westwards to the foot of the rocky Pine Range. Below, the tree-lined Winburndale Rivulet wanders away to disappear through a valley to the north. Here, in a traditional Wiradjuri burial place always respected by the Suttor family, a stone memorial topped with an axe was unveiled by Mrs Roy Suttor on 25 April 1954. A bronze plaque reads:

> *Last resting place of Windradyne, alias Saturday*
> *Last chief of the Aborigines.*
> *First a terror but later a friend of the settlers*
> *Died of wounds received in a tribal encounter 1835.*
> *A true patriot.*

Standing in that place with John Suttor, recalling a family who made peace with the Wiradjuri, whom Windradyne regarded as friends and who learned his language as he learned theirs, we also remembered the bloody battles that had taken place in the surrounding countryside. The memorial at Brucedale commemorates them all.

John Suttor with Al Grassby at the Windradyne memorial.
PHOTOGRAPH BY MARJI HILL

Ballarat—Democratic Capital of Australia

On the eve of the 132nd anniversary of the Battle of Eureka Stockade we set off by car for Ballarat from Melbourne's Tullamarine Airport. We sped through the outskirts of Melbourne, across flat brown country with clumps of gum trees on the horizon and heavily timbered areas where the trees fell in like soldiers in a line on both sides of the road, past a signpost pointing the way to historic Creswick, from where the Creswick Volunteers set out to support the cause of independence and freedom, to Ballarat, now a town of 70,000 people. A huge Southern Cross flag flying gloriously in the breeze from a tall flagpole on Bakery Hill welcomed us to the spot where this first Australian flag was hoisted on 29 November 1854.

For a century the only public recognition of this major event in Australian history was a small weatherworn notice on the back of St Paul's Church Hall. On 2 December 1973 the Premier of Victoria, Rupert Hamer, in the presence of a great crowd watched Peter Lalor III, in the uniform of the Victorian Police Force, hoist the flag once again. This time it would never be taken down. Lalor declared that, in the circumstances of the time, he would have fought alongside his grandfather.

Stawell Street led us to the site of the battle, where there is an imposing monument, a column set on a high square platform with a cannon at each corner. A plaque on the column dedicates the monument to "the heroic pioneers who fought and fell on this sacred spot in the cause of liberty and the soldiers who fell at duty's call". It stands amidst gently sloping lawns dotted with trees that provide welcome shade from the hot summer sun. There was not a sound save the constant click of a sprinkler and the rumble of distant traffic reminiscent of gunfire. The guns of 1854 gave way to the guns of an Australian Army platoon in 1973, when they fired a volley of honour at the first ever commemoration of Eureka by an Australian Government.

In the early 1980s Jack Ginifer, Victorian Minister for Immigration and Ethnic Affairs, supported the efforts to properly recognise Eureka and began a Eureka celebration which was continued in his name for some years, organised by his chairman of the Victorian Ethnic Affairs Commission, Gary Shepherd. For ten years Eureka Day, 3 December, was also observed nationally by the annual Lalor Address on Community Relations in Canberra, which was inaugurated by the then Commissioner for Community Relations Al Grassby in 1975 when the Southern Cross flew officially for the first time in the national capital.

We climbed the steps of the memorial once again in 1986 to salute the fallen and their cause. As we stood in silent tribute it was a bitter thought that although the anniversary was being celebrated in Ballarat, elsewhere in Australia it was being almost totally ignored. Only one writer, John Lahy, cared to pay homage to the dead, writing a remembrance

The memorial plaque at the flagpole on Bakery Hill, Ballarat.
PHOTOGRAPH BY MARJI HILL

The monument at Eureka salutes both diggers and soldiers.
BAYLEY COLLECTION, NATIONAL LIBRARY OF AUSTRALIA

in the Melbourne *Age* of 3 December. It was sad to reflect that today's Australians, who have reaped the rewards the rebels fought for, have again forgotten them. One day 3 December will be nationally observed, and the Southern Cross will be recognised by the Australian nation as its first flag.

Pinjarra Today

The site of the Battle of Pinjarra lies on the outskirts of the small Western Australian town of the same name, some eighty-six kilometres south of Perth. From Perth, the South Western Highway runs long and straight like a spear, rising and falling with each kilometre. The towering plateau to the east at the beginning of the run south falls away to gentle green hills, then rises again near Pinjarra.

The first glimpse of the town is the nineteenth-century facade of the Premier Hotel standing guard near the bridge spanning the Murray River, which was named after a long-dead English colonial secretary. Across the bridge, in the main street of Pinjarra, is the venerable St John's Church of England, the fifth oldest church in use in the state. Built in 1847, it replaced the original wattle-and-daub church which was destroyed by floods. Its graveyard is the resting place of many men and women who were alive at the time of the Battle of Pinjarra—William Beacham, who arrived on the ship *Loftus* in 1829, Mary Batesman who died in 1878 aged sixty-one years, Jane Thorpe who died in 1867 at sixty-two years. The oldest tombstone is that of Jane Pollard, a fourteen-year-old girl who died in 1844; she would have been four years old at the time of the battle. These were people who followed the Army into the Murray River district, part of the wave of settlement made possible by the defeat of the Nyungar people at Pinjarra.

Just two kilometres down the main street, past the standard gaggle of stores and service stations, past the old court house with its English coat of arms, a reminder of the Imperial past, and the quaintly named "Cornish Way", where a group of Nyungar families have made their home, is the gnarled old jarrah which marks the site of the Battle of Pinjarra. In days past a brass plate set into a recess cut in the trunk commemorated the battle. According to Oscar Little of Pinjarra, the plaque was stolen one night by white vandals who also attempted to burn down the jarrah. When this was unsuccessful they brought in a bulldozer to push it over. This attempt failed too, and the tree still stands strong and firm, although bearing the marks of the fire.

It is only one tree among the many hugging the banks of the river and after the plaque was stolen its identity was in doubt. The honour of identifying it again went to Oscar Little, who was encouraged in his search by Ken Colbung, who today presides over the Nyungar organisation which passes on to the young the timeless heritage of a great people. Oscar Little and Ken Colbung have explored every inch of the battle site and conserve the verbal history of their people and of the battle and the killings that followed.

Walking along the high banks of the Murray River where the Nyungar fished for maron and trapped possums, still much in evidence, and avoided, as one should today, a savage-looking species of lizard, it is easy to reconstruct the story of the battle. Here the Nyungar people were trapped in their village, there the ambush caught them in a deadly crossfire as they attempted to cross the river only to find a line of redcoats barring their retreat. And there, when the numbers of dead and dying made it clear the fight was lost, some of the spearmen attempted to escape downriver. Local people point to a site near the present saleyards where they were killed and their bodies abandoned to be buried in the sandy soil later by their countrymen.

Local history also holds that there were further killings at the camp site at the end of what is today known as Camp Road, which is accessible from the main street near the senior high school. This was a major river crossing in the past and Oscar Little remembers an old white settler, born last century, who lived in the big colonial house which today prevents access to the river and who recalled the past troubles. Downstream from the battle site the ford used by Stirling and his fusiliers is now a favourite place for children to play and a bus load of Nyungar, including a daughter of Ken Colbung, gambolled there on our visit.

Despite its proximity to the town, the battle site has an air of peace and tranquillity. The sunlight plays hide and seek among the tall trees and the calls of birds mingle with the murmur of the water. There is no sign of death or killing, but the memories of yesteryear live on in the hearts and minds of the people who carry the sorrow of brave men fallen in battle, of women and children extirpated, and of a land lost.

Battle Mountain

Our pilgrimage to Battle Mountain began in the mining town of Mount Isa, two and a half hours flying time north-west of Brisbane. Now a neat cluster of shops, offices, hotels and houses around the base of a 270 metre high chimney stack, Mount Isa did not exist at the time of the battle. Today, it has become the capital of the Kalkadoon people.

The Kalkadoon Tribal Council has its headquarters there, the Baiame Health Centre administered by the Kalkadoons for Kalkadoons functions in a fine new building and the Kalkadoon Cultural Centre has a permanent exhibition in the Frank Aston Rotary Underground Museum. The respect of the people of Mount Isa for the Kalkadoons is illustrated by the number of facilities which proudly bear their name—Kalkadoon Park, Kalkadoon High School, Kalkadoon Indoor Soccer Club, and the Kalkadoon Sobriety House.

Fire-blackened but still alive, this jarrah tree once bore a brass plate commemorating the Battle of Pinjarra. PHOTOGRAPH BY MARJI HILL

TOP: *The site of the Battle of Pinjarra.*

BOTTOM: *Battle Mountain looms above the surrounding plain.*

PHOTOGRAPHS BY MARJI HILL

We were welcomed by Sister Angela of the Franciscan Missionaries of Mary. A daughter of Dublin, she arrived in Australia at the end of World War II. Together with sisters from Sydney, Brisbane, Portugal and another Irish woman from Cashel, Sr Angela became the point of contact between the Kalkadoons and the rest of the community. From 1975 to 1982 the sisters worked with the Office of Community Relations and its team to help settle complaints of racial discrimination, and sometimes to convince the conquerors that the war was over.

That the guerilla war waged by the Kalkadoons was successful for almost ten years was due in large measure to the fact they were fighting in their own country. At the Kalkadoon Cultural Centre we were able to see something of the life the people had developed before the invasion. While the invaders relied on imported foodstuffs of desperately poor quality the Kalkadoons had a choice of 300 different fruits and vegetables, supplemented by a wide range of game and fish. More than seventy-five per cent of their diet consisted of foods collected by the women. The Kalkadoon demonstrators pointed out that the bloodwood, a species of eucalypt, grows everywhere in the area. What are often thought to be its fruits are actually galls formed by an insect. The tree provides sweet water, while the insects supply a feast of proteins from an early larval stage, which tastes like a layer of coconut, and later Kalkadoon caviar, myriads of little tasty brown balls. The Kalkadoon pharmacoepia was extensive—examples include medicinal gums for muscle aches, and a plant known locally as caustic bush used to make bandaids to dress wounds and sores, which acted as a germicide but also had healing properties.

Today the secrets of the food and water supplies are taught by the Kalkadoons to school children from Mount Isa and the surrounding countryside so that they can survive if they are lost in the bush. Tragically, people lost in this district still die of hunger and thirst within easy reach of both food and water, if only they knew where to look. The ignorance of Burke and Wills unfortunately lives on.

For the trip to Battle Mountain we set off in a four-wheel-drive, driven by Margaret Major, Director of the Kalkadoon Cultural Centre, and accompanied by Arthur Peterson. Along the straight bitumen road that darts 120 kilometres across the open bushland to Cloncurry, we passed scatterings of ironbark and bloodwood trees, odd clumps of mallee and groups of tall anthills glowing blood red in the late afternoon sun. Suddenly we came to a row of ghost gums standing like sentinels along the banks of a dry creek bed, the first of many such creeks in a dry countryside that had nevertheless a kind of stark beauty. We passed a huge stone mountain, looking like a smaller Uluru transported from Central Australia, a clear area of red soil at the end of a range of peaks, more scarred creeks and dry gullies. The soil changed suddenly from bright red to grey black, then back to red again.

As we continued to eat up the miles Margaret told us how a Kalkadoon came to be called Major. Her father worked as a stockman and sat so tall and straight in the saddle that the white owner of the property christened him "The Major". Overnight he became an Anglo-Australian, at least in name.

Less than a half an hour out of Mount Isa we took a sudden turn off the highway onto a rocky dirt road. A few bumpy kilometres on we turned left again to follow a rugged bush track over creeks and river beds. At last we had our first glimpse of Battle Mountain through the trees. The bush track ended and we abandoned our vehicle about half a kilometre from the foot of the mountain and walked the rest of the way.

The main peak of Battle Mountain loomed, flanked on the right by a lesser hill falling away to the flats and on the left by a gently rising series of hillocks which met the main slope less than a third of the way up. The scene of the battle lay before us. The terrain remains unchanged, the only mark of invaders at the time of our visit in 1985 an iron wagon-wheel track made a generation before by an overlander from Cloncurry. The shadows were lengthening as the sun began to sink behind the mountain. We stood looking up, trying to imagine the gallant Kalkadoons forming on the peak in line of battle to charge down the mountain. The red anthills seemed to be marching towards the slope, and the eerie stillness of the place, without so much as a bird's cry, evoked the ghosts of the past.

The sun was sinking fast as we turned away to walk back to the four-wheel-drive. To our consternation it had disappeared. We felt a shiver of panic as the shadows deepened and the ranks of anthills took on a new menace. "I can't see it," Margaret Major said casually, "but I know where it is." The rugged terrain had hidden the vehicle completely, but she had marked the spot by nearby trees and bushes. As we clambered aboard and headed for the track to take us back it was as though we had stepped back in time. The spirits of the Kalkadoons brooding on Battle Mountain seemed to watch us leave.

EPILOGUE

No nation can truly come of age unless it is mature enough to know its past as a means of understanding the present and planning for the future. If the people of the United States of America were taught their history as Australians are taught what purports to be their history, all mention of the War of Independence would be excised, the Civil War would become a misunderstanding and the Indian Wars would be suppressed altogether.

Australia has an exciting history and every one of its people from any of 140 ethnic backgrounds, speaking 240 languages including those of the first Australians, and practising eighty different religions, can be proud of the fact that the continent of Australia is at this time the only one on earth on which a shooting war is not being fought.

But we will not be at peace until we make peace with the Australians who held and conserved the land for over 40,000 years.

The original Australians are in the process of capturing the hearts and minds of the world—they are the oldest continuing civilisation on earth and the world wants to know about it. The world will quickly find, however, that after 200 years of paternal colonial rule the original Australians die twenty years earlier than their conquerors, their children die at birth at three times the rate of white children, more than eighty per cent are without work or hope of work, and they are still the most racially discriminated against group in their own country. Australia can begin to atone for all of this by achieving an accord with the original Australians similar to those which other migrant nations have been able to reach with their original people. In Papua New Guinea, New Zealand, the United States of America and Canada treaties have been made with the founding people in an attempt to give them dignity and to recognise their rights. In many cases these agreements are now being challenged as inadequate, but at least they provide a starting point for an update.

Australia lags more than 100 years behind these nations—we have no treaty at all. The legal basis for the existence of our nation is the doctrine of *terra nullius*, a land without people, the evil fiction that no one lived here when Captain James Cook arrived.

As a first step to healing the rift between black and white Australia, it must be declared—by Act of Parliament, by treaty, by constitutional amendment—that this doctrine is wrong. It must be acknowledged that the traditional people occupied, cared for and identified with the land that is now Australia for at least 40,000 years, that they have traditional rights to land, culture and heritage, and that as the founding people they are the base of today's multicultural society.

Once this is recognised, all Australians, whether they came themselves from, or can trace their roots to, the United Kingdom or Ireland, Africa, Asia, the Middle East, the Americas, India, the Pacific or Europe, can be equally recognised as contributors to our society.

As long as Australia fails to reach such an accord our credibility in the world is at risk. To make judgments abroad while we are being judged by world opinion for our failures at home is to invite a charge of hypocrisy, or worse. As the then Prime Minister Gough Whitlam so eloquently put it: "Our treatment of the Aboriginal people of Australia is the litmus test of our dedication to justice, peace and equality in the world. By our conduct in this area the world will judge us".

No clearer warning could have been given than that by Pope John Paul II, addressing a gathering of Black Australians at Alice Springs on 29 November 1986:

> *Let it not be said that the fair and equitable recognition of Aborigines' rights to land is discrimination.*
>
> *To call for the acknowledgement of the land rights of the people who have never surrendered those rights is not discrimination. Certainly what has been done cannot be undone. But what can now be done to remedy the deeds of yesterday must not be put off until tomorrow.*

Australia must awaken to the truth and the facts.

The Australian War Memorial in Canberra contains records of Australians killed in what were mostly other people's wars in places such as Sudan, South Africa, Russia and China, but there is not one reference to the Hundred Years War at home or to those who fought and died in it.

Australia is dotted with more war memorials per head of population than any other country on earth; those commemorating the battles at home number less than the fingers of one hand.

Australian children know the names of Geronimo, Chief Sitting Bull and Chaka the Zulu, but few could name even one hero of the black and white resistance to tyranny. Until now, Australian history has been written so that it reads, as Mark Twain so accurately observed, like a fairy story, in which there is no conflict, no bloodshed, and in which the lies of *terra nullius* and the myth of homogeneity are presented as truths.

After 200 years it is time for a new start.

NOTES AND BIBLIOGRAPHIES

1. *Invasion*

NOTES

1. M. F. Christie, *Aborigines in Colonial Victoria 1835–86* Sydney: Sydney University Press, 1979, p.12

2. N. Peterson, *Change and the Aboriginal: a Traditional Life, a Conservative History* Canberra: AGPS, 1975, (unpaged); M. Sahlins, *Stone Age Economics* London: Tavistock, 1974, pp.1–39

3. D. Horton, "Prehistory" in M. Hill and A. Barlow, *Black Australia* Canberra: AIAS, 1978, p.21

4. R. M. and C. H. Berndt, *Arnhem Land: its History and People* Melbourne: Cheshire, 1954, pp.34–5

5. J. Isaacs (comp.), *Australian Dreaming* Sydney: Lansdowne Press, 1980, pp.261–3

6. C. C. Macknight, *The Voyage to Marege* Carlton, Vic.: Melbourne University Press, 1976, p.2

7. Macknight, p.51

8. Isaacs, p.266

9. ibid.

10. Macknight, p.90

11. Isaacs, pp.269–72

12. Macknight, p.86

13. Macknight, p.3

14. D. J. Mulvaney, *The Prehistory of Australia* rev. edn, Harmondsworth: Penguin, 1975, p.42

15. ibid.

16. D. J. Mulvaney, "Australian Aborigines 1606–1929: opinion and fieldwork" in *Historical Studies* 8, 30, 1958, p.132

17. ibid., p.131

18. ibid., p.132

19. quoted in Mulvaney, p.133

20. ibid., p.133

21. ibid.

22. K. G. McIntyre, *The Secret Discovery of Australia* Adelaide: Souvenir Press, 1977, p.248

23. C. M. H. Clark, *A History of Australia* vol.1, Parkville, Vic.: Melbourne University Press, 1962, p.49

24. Clark, p.50

25. A. Grassby, *The Spanish in Australia* Melbourne: AE Press, 1983, pp.20–1

26. Grassby, p.21

27. Clark, p.51

28. L. R. Marchant (comp.), *A List of French Naval Records and Illustrations Relating to Australian and Tasmanian Aborigines* Canberra: AIAS, 1969, p.3

29. J. Arundel, "The military history of Parramatta" in *Parramatta and District Historical Society Journal* 2, 1921, p.11

30. quoted in C. G. Weeramantry, Cultural and ideological pluralism and contemporary public international law, unpublished paper given at International Academy of Comparative Law, XVth Congress, Australia, 18 August 1986, p.47

31. Henry Reynolds, Professor of History, James Cook University (pers comm.)

32. quoted in Weeramantry, p.30

33. ibid.

BIBLIOGRAPHY

Arundel, J., "The military history of Parramatta" in *Parramatta and District Historical Society Journal* 2, 1921, pp.8–13

Berndt, R. M., and C. H., *Arnhem Land: its History and People* Melbourne: Cheshire, 1954

Black, Paul, "Introduction to languages" pp.20–2 in M. Hill and A. Barlow *Black Australia; an Annotated Bibliography and Teacher's Guide to Resources on Aborigines and Torres Strait Islanders, 1977–82* Canberra: AIAS, 1985

Charlesworth, Max, *The Aboriginal Land Rights Movement* [Geelong]: Deakin University, 1983 (Contemporary Australia Unit B Module 3)

Christie, M. F., *Aborigines in Colonial Victoria 1835–86* Sydney: Sydney University Press, 1979

Clark, C. M. H., *A History of Australia: I: From the Earliest Times to the Age of Macquarie* Parkville, Vic.: Melbourne University Press, 1962

Flood, Josephine, *Archaeology of the Dreamtime* Sydney: Collins, 1983

Grassby, A. J., *The Spanish in Australia* Melbourne: AE Press, 1983

Hill, Marji, "Of the lives and deeds of the immortal beings, Aboriginal stories: a cultural perspective" in *Orana* 19, 2, 1983, pp.109–12

Hill, Marji, and McLeod, Neil, *From the Ochres of Mungo: Aboriginal Art Today* Melbourne: Dorr-McLeod, 1984

Horton, David, "Prehistory" pp. 19–23 in M. Hill and A. Barlow, *Black Australia: an Annotated Bibliography and Teacher's Guide to Resources on Aborigines and Torres*

Strait Islanders Canberra: AIAS, 1978

Isaacs, Jennifer (comp.), *Australian Dreaming: 40,000 Years of Aboriginal History* Sydney: Lansdowne Press, 1980

McIntyre, Kenneth Gordon, *The Secret Discovery of Australia: Portuguese Ventures 200 Years before Captain Cook* Adelaide: Souvenir Press, 1977

Macknight, C. C., *The Voyage to Marege: Macassan Trepangers in Northern Australia* Carlton, Vic.: Melbourne University Press, 1976

Maddock, Kenneth, *The Australian Aborigines* Harmondsworth: Penguin, 1974

Marchant, Leslie R. (comp.), *A List of French Naval Records and Illustrations Relating to Australian and Tasmanian Aborigines, 1771 to 1828* Canberra: AIAS, 1969

Mulvaney, D. J., "Australian Aborigines 1606–1929: opinion and fieldwork" in *Historical Studies* 8, 30, 1958

——, *The Prehistory of Australia* rev. edn, Harmondsworth: Penguin, 1975.

Peterson, Nicolas, *Change and the Aboriginal: a Traditional Life, a Conservative History* Canberra: AGPS, 1975

Sahlins, Marshall, *Stone Age Economics* London: Tavistock, 1974

Weeramantry, C. G., Cultural and ideological pluralism and contemporary public international law, International Academy of Comparative Law XVth Congress, Australia, 18 August 1986

2. *The Army of Occupation*

NOTES

1. H. Reynolds, *The Other Side of the Frontier* Townsville: History Department, James Cook University, 1981, p.165

2. ibid.

3. P. Stanley, "While acting under orders": the Slaughterhouse Creek massacre of 1838. Unpublished paper, n.d., p.2

4. *Historical Records of Australia* I, IV, p.364

5. *Australian Encyclopaedia* Sydney, Grolier, vol.6, p.74

6. D. Collins, *An Account of the English Colony in New South Wales . . .* Sydney: Reed, 1975, p.159

7. J. Bonwick, *First Twenty Years of Australia* London: Sampson Low, Marston, Searle & Rivington, 1882, p.34

8. ibid.

9. Bonwick, p.35

10. Bonwick, p.36

11. ibid.

12. Bonwick, p.37

13. Bonwick, p.50

14. M. H. Ellis, "British military regiments in Australia" in *R.A.H.S. Journal & Proceedings* 7, 6, 1951, p.313

15. P. Stanley, *The Remote Garrison* Kenthurst, NSW: Kangaroo Press, 1986, p.8

16. Ellis, p.322

17. Ellis, p.314

18. Ellis, p.318

19. quoted in M. Higgins, "Deservedly respected: a first look at the 11th Regiment in Australia", *Journal of the Australian War Memorial* 6, April 1985, p.15

20. ibid.

21. *Australian Encyclopaedia* vol.6, pp.76–7

22. quoted in P. Stanley, " 'Oh!, the sufferings of my men'; the 80th regiment in New South Wales in 1838" in *The Push from the Bush* 11, 1981, p.2

23. ibid., p.1

24. ibid., p.8

25. ibid., quoted, p.14

26. ibid., p.15

27. *Australian Encyclopaedia*, vol.5, p.382

28. J. Arundel, "The military history of Parramatta" in *Parramatta and District Historical Society Journal* 2, 1921, p.9

29. B. Bridges, "The Mounted Police (1826–1850)" in *R.A.H.S. Newsletter* 1969, p.6

30. ibid.

31. Bridges, p.7

32. M. F. Christie, *Aborigines in Colonial Victoria 1835–86*, Sydney: Sydney University Press, 1979, p.74

33. Christie, p.74

34. Christie, p.77

35. Christie, p.69

36. Christie, p.40

37. M. Austin, "The early defences of Australia" in *R.A.H.S. Journal* 49, 3, 1963, p.191

38. Austin, p.194

39. Austin, p.201

40. *Australian Encyclopaedia* vol.6, p.75

41. ibid.

BIBLIOGRAPHY

Arundel, J., "The military history of Parramatta" in *Parramatta and District Historical Society Journal* 2, 1921, pp.8–13

Austin, M., *The Army in Australia 1840–50: Prelude to the Golden Years* Canberra: AGPS, 1979

——, "The early defences of Australia" in *R.A.H.S. Journal* 49, 3, 1963, pp.189–204

Australia. *Commonwealth Historical Records of Australia.* Series 1, vols 1, 3 and 4. Library Committee of the Commonwealth Parliament, 1914–

The Australian Encyclopaedia, 10 vols, Sydney: Grolier, 1962

Barnett, Correlli, *Britain and Her Army 1509–1970: a Military, Political and Social Survey* Harmondsworth: Penguin, 1974

Barthorp, Michael, *British Infantry Uniforms since 1660* Poole: Blandford Press, 1982

Bonwick, James, *First Twenty Years of Australia* London: Sampson Low, Marston, Searle & Rivington, 1882

Bowling, A. H., *British Infantry Regiments 1660–1914* London: Almark, 1970

Bridges, Barry, "The Mounted Police (1826–1850)" in *R.A.H.S. Newsletter* 1969, pp.6–7

Christie, M. F., *Aborigines in Colonial Victoria 1835–86* Sydney: Sydney University Press, 1979

Collins, David, *An Account of the English Colony in New South Wales . . .* 2 vols (first published 1789 and 1802) Sydney: Reed, 1975

Ellis, M. H., "British military regiments in Australia" in *R.A.H.S. Journal & Proceedings* 7, 6, 1951, pp.313–43

Featherstone, Donald, *Weapons and Equipment of the Victorian Soldier* Poole: Blandford Press, 1978

Higgins, Matthew, "Deservedly respected: a first look at the 11th Regiment in Australia" in *Journal of the Australian War Memorial* 6, April 1985

Myatt, Frederick, *The British Infantry 1660–1945: the Evolution of a Fighting Force* Poole: Blandford Press, 1983

Reynolds, Henry, *The Other Side of the Frontier: an Interpretation of the Aboriginal Resistance to the Invasion and Settlement of Australia* Townsville: History Department, James Cook University, 1981

Sheppherd, Alan, *The King's Regiment* Reading, Berks.: Osprey, 1973

Stanley, Peter, " 'Oh!, the sufferings of my men'; the 80th regiment in New South Wales in 1838" in *The Push from the Bush* 11, 1981, pp.1–22

——, "While acting under orders": the Slaughterhouse Creek massacre of 1838. Unpublished paper, n.d.

——, *The Remote Garrison: the British Army in Australia 1788–1870* Kenthurst, NSW: Kangaroo Press, 1986

Taylor, Arthur, *Discovering British Military Uniforms* Tring, Herts.: Shire, 1972

3. The Hundred Years War

NOTES

1. H. Reynolds, "The other side of the frontier . . . " pp.1–20 in H. Reynolds (ed.), *Race Relations in North Queensland* Townsville: James Cook University, 1978

2. H. Reynolds, "The unrecorded battlefields of Queensland" pp. 23–52 in Reynolds, *Race Relations in North Queensland*

3. N. A. Loos, "The pragmatic racism of the frontier" pp.279–301 in Reynolds, *Race Relations in North Queensland*

4. Loos, p.283

5. Loos, p.286
6. Loos, p.292
7. H. Reynolds, *The Other Side of the Frontier* Townsville: History Department, James Cook University, 1981
8. ibid., p.82
9. ibid., p.87
10. ibid., p.88
11. ibid., p.87
12. P. Stanley, "While acting under orders": the Slaughterhouse Creek massacre of 1838. Unpublished paper, n.d., p.2
13. ibid.
14. *Blossom Magazine* 1, 1828, p.64
15. G. N. Stewart, "Convict rebel: Ralph Entwistle" pp.27–36 in E. Fry (ed.), *Rebels and Radicals* Sydney: Allen & Unwin, 1983
16. Stanley, p.5
17. Stanley, p.6
18. Stanley, p.8
19. ibid.
20. Stanley, p.9
21. B. Gammage, " The Wiradjuri war 1838–40" in *The Push from the Bush* 16, 1983, p.4
22. Gammage, p.5
23. ibid.
24. Gammage, pp.6–7
25. Gammage, p.10
26. ibid.
27. Gammage, p.12
28. Gammage, p.15
29. Gammage, p.14
30. ibid.
31. ibid.
32. M. Gilmore, *More Recollections* Sydney: Angus & Robertson, 1935, p.245
33. G. Blomfield, *Baal Belbora* Chippendale, NSW: Apcol, 1981, pp.4–6
34. D. L. Carrington, "Riots at Lambing Flat, 1860–1861" in *R.A.H.S. Journal* 46, 4, 1960, p.230
35. Carrington, p.236
36. D. Porter, "Explorer's slaughter of Aborigines recalled", *Sydney Morning Herald* 26 June 1986
37. M. F. Christie, *Aborigines in Colonial Victoria 1835–86* Sydney: Sydney University Press, 1979, p.57
38. ibid.
39. Christie, p.59
40. ibid.

41. Christie, p.60

42. Christie, p.61

43. Christie, p.63

44. Christie, p.64

45. Christie, p.65

46. Christie, p.66

47. Gammage, p.3

48. L. Ryan, *The Aboriginal Tasmanians* St Lucia, Qld: University of Queensland Press, 1981, pp.3–4

49. C. Wise, "Black rebel: Musquito" pp.1–7 in E. Fry (ed.), *Rebels and Radicals* Sydney: Allen & Unwin, 1983, p.3

50. Ryan, p.4

51. Ryan, p.97

52. Ryan, p.99

53. quoted in Ryan, p.104

54. Ryan, p.110

55. Ryan, p.112

56. ibid.

57. S. D. Lendrum, " The 'Coorong Massacre': martial law and the Aborigines at first settlement" in *Adelaide Law Review* 6, Sept. 1977, p.26

58. F. Robinson and B. York, *The Black Resistance* Camberwell: Widescope, 1977

59. Robinson and York, p.66

60. Robinson and York, p.94

61. quoted in A. Markus, *From the Barrel of a Gun* West Melbourne: Victorian Historical Association, 1974

62. B. Cummins, " The Black War" in *Walkabout* 1973, pp.40–3

63. Robinson and York, p.42

64. Robinson and York, p.80

65. Robinson and York, p.81

66. Robinson and York, p.83

67. H. Pedersen, "Pigeon: an Australian Aboriginal rebel" pp.7–15 in Bob Reece and Tom Stannage (eds), *European–Aboriginal Relations in Western Australian History* Nedlands: University of Western Australia Press, 1984, p.7

68. Pedersen, p.9

69. Pedersen, p.10

70. Pedersen, p.11

71. Pedersen, p.13

BIBLIOGRAPHY

Blomfield, Geoffrey, *Baal Belbora: the End of the Dreaming* Chippendale, NSW: Apcol, 1981

Carrington, D. L., "Riots at Lambing Flat, 1860–1861" in *R.A.H.S. Journal* 46, 4, 1960, pp.223–43

Christie, M. F., *Aborigines in Colonial Victoria 1835–86* Sydney: Sydney University Press, 1979

Cummins, Bob, "The Black War" in *Walkabout* 1973, pp.40–3

Fitzgerald, Brian, " 'Blood on the saddle': the Forrest River Massacres, 1926" pp.16–25 in Bob Reece and Tom Stannage (eds), *European–Aboriginal Relations in Western Australian History* Nedlands: University of Western Australia Press, 1984

Gammage, Bill, " The Wiradjuri war 1838–40" in *The Push from the Bush* 16, 1983, pp.3–17

Gilmore, Mary, *More Recollections* Sydney: Angus & Robertson, 1935

Hercus, Luise and Sutton, Peter (eds), *This is What Happened: Historical Narratives by Aborigines* Canberra: AIAS, 1986

Johnston, William Ross, A study of the relationship between the law, the State and the community in Colonial Queensland. MA thesis, University of Queensland, 1985

Lendrum, S. D., "The 'Coorong Massacre': martial law and the Aborigines at first settlement" in *Adelaide Law Review* 6, Sept. 1977, pp.26–43

Loos, N. A., " The pragmatic racism of the frontier" pp. 279–301 in H. Reynolds (ed.), *Race Relations in North Queensland* Townsville: James Cook University of North Queensland, 1978

Markus, Andrew, *From the Barrel of a Gun: the Oppression of the Aborigines 1860–1900* West Melbourne: Victorian Historical Association, 1974

Pedersen, Howard, "Pigeon: an Australian Aboriginal rebel" pp.7–15 in Bob Reece and Tom Stannage (eds), *European–Aboriginal Relations in Western Australian History* Nedlands: University of Western Australia Press, 1984

Porter, David, "Explorer's slaughter of Aborigines recalled" *Sydney Morning Herald* 26 June 1986

Quanchi, Max, "Violence darkens pages of our past" *Age* 1 October 1985

"Rebellion at the Female Factory" in *Blossom Magazine* 1, 1828

Reynolds, Henry, *The Other Side of the Frontier* Townsville: History Department, James Cook University, 1981

——, " The other side of the frontier: early Aboriginal reactions to pastoral settlement in Queensland and northern New South Wales" pp.1–20 in H. Reynolds (ed.), *Race Relations in North Queensland* Townsville: James Cook University, 1978

——, " The unrecorded battlefields of Queensland" pp.23–52 in H. Reynolds (ed.), *Race Relations in North Queensland* Townsville: James Cook University, 1978

Robinson, Fergus, and York, Barry, *The Black Resistance: an Introduction to the History of the Aborigines Struggle Against British Colonialism* Camberwell, Vic.: Widescope, 1977

Ryan, Lyndall, *The Aboriginal Tasmanians* St Lucia, Qld.: University of Queensland Press, 1981

Stanley, Peter, "While acting under orders": the Slaughterhouse Creek massacre of 1838. Unpublished paper, n.d.

Stewart, Gordon Neil, "Convict rebel: Ralph Entwistle" pp.27–36 in E. Fry (ed.), *Rebels and Radicals* Sydney: Allen & Unwin, 1883

Wise, Christine, "Black rebel: Musquito" pp.1–7 in Eric Fry (ed.), *Rebels and Radicals* Sydney: Allen & Unwin, 1983

4. *The Twin Battles of Sydney*

NOTES

1. W. E. H. Stanner, "The history of indifference thus begins" in *Aboriginal History* 1, 1, 1977, p.4
2. D. Collins, *An Account of the English Colony in New South Wales* 2 vols, Sydney: Reed, 1975, vol.1, p.460
3. C. M. H. Clark, *A History of Australia* vol.1, Parkville, Vic: Melbourne University Press, 1962, p.73
4. Clark, p.77
5. ibid.
6. Clark, p.78
7. Clark, p.76
8. Stanner, p.5
9. *Historical Records of Australia* I, I, pp.1–8
10. Clark, p.86
11. Stanner, p.5
12. ibid.
13. Stanner, p.6
14. Stanner, pp.8–9
15. Stanner, p.9
16. Clark, p.114
17. Stanner, p.7
18. Stanner, p.11
19. Stanner, p.10
20. J. Bonwick, *First Twenty Years of Australia* London: Sampson Low, 1882, p.181
21. Stanner, p.11
22. Stanner, p.12
23. Clark, p.116
24. Stanner, p.11
25. Stanner, p.13
26. Clark, p.117
27. *Historical Records of New South Wales* 1, Part 2, p.191
28. ibid., p.192
30. Stanner, p.15
31. Bonwick, p.181
32. Stanner, p.15

33. *HRNSW* 1, 2, p.214
34. Stanner, p.16
35. Stanner, pp.6–7
36. Clark, p.121
37. ibid.
38. *HRNSW*, 1, 2, p.308
39. Clark, p.122
40. Clark, p.123
41. W. Tench, *Sydney's First Four Years* Sydney: Angus & Robertson, 1961, p.205
42. Tench, p.206
43. Tench, p.207
44. Collins, p.118
45. Collins, p.122
46. Collins, p.146
47. Collins, p.168
48. Clark, p.128
49. Clark, p.132
50. Tench, p.205
51. J. E. Ellis, A "Troublesome Savage": the Story of Pemulwuy. Unpublished CCAE assignment in Aboriginal Studies, p.25
52. Ellis, p.26
53. Bonwick, p.179
54. Collins, p.275
55. Clark, p.134
56. Clark, p.142
57. J. L. Kohen, *Aborigines in the West: Prehistory to Present* Sydney: The Western Sydney Project, 1985 (pages unnumbered)
58. Collins, pp.326–9
59. Kohen
60. Collins, p.339
61. Collins, p.466
62. Collins, p.348
63. ibid.
64. ibid.
65. Collins, p.349
66. *HRNSW*, 3, p.65
67. *HRNSW*, 2, p.307
68. ibid.
69. *HRA* I, I, p.499
70. *HRA* I, I, p.500
71. Pilger, John, *Heroes* London: Cape, 1986, p.39

72. Kohen
73. quoted in Pilger, p.39
74. Pilger, p.39
75. Clark, p.143
76. *Illustrated History of Australia* Sydney: Hamlyn, 1974, p.70
77. *Illustrated History of Australia*, p.71
78. *HRA* I, I, p.689
79. B. Bridges, "Pemulwuy: a 'noble savage' " in *Newsletter of the R.A.H.S.* 1970, p.3
80. Collins, vol.2, p.20
81. ibid.
82. ibid.
83. ibid.
84. J. H. Heaton, *Australian Dictionary of Dates and Men of the Time . . .* Sydney: Robertson, 1879, p.3
85. Collins, vol.2, p.24
86. ibid.
87. Collins, vol.2, p.26
88. *HRA* I, II, p.24
89. Clark, p.160
90. Clark, p.161
91. ibid.
92. *HRA* I, III, pp.466–7
93. ibid.
94. ibid.
95. *HRA* I, III, p.467
96. *HRA* I, III, p.582
97. ibid.
98. *HRA* I, III, pp.582–3
99. K. Willey, *When the Sky Fell Down: the Destruction of the Tribes of the Sydney Region 1788–1850s* Sydney: Collins, 1979, p.167
100. Willey, p.170

BIBLIOGRAPHY

Arundel, J., "The military history of Parramatta" in *Parramatta and District Historical Society Journal* 2, 1921, pp.8–13

Australia. *Commonwealth Historical Records of Australia*, Series 1, Vols 1, 2 & 3 Library Committee of the Commonwealth Parliament

Barlow, Alex, and, Hill, Marji, *Heroes of the Aboriginal Struggle* South Melbourne, Vic.: Macmillan, 1987

Barrington, George, *The History of New South Wales . . .* London: Jones, 1810

——, *A Sequel to Barrington's Voyage to New South Wales . . .* London: Lowndes, 1801

Bonwick, J., *First Twenty Years of Australia* London: Sampson Low, Marston, Searle & Rivington, 1882

Bridges, Barry, "Pemulwuy: a 'noble savage'" in *Newsletter of the R.A.H.S.* 1970, pp.3–4

Clark, C. M. H., *A History of Australia: I: From the Earliest Times to the Age of Macquarie* Parkville, Vic.: Melbourne University Press, 1962

Collins, David, *An Account of the English Colony in New South Wales . . .*, 2 vols (first published 1798 and 1802), Sydney: Reed, 1975

Ellis, Jane E., A "Troublesome Savage": the Story of Pemulwuy, Unpublished Canberra CAE assignment in Aboriginal Studies, 1980

Heaton, J. H., *Australian Dictionary of Dates and Men of the Time . . .* Sydney: Robertson, 1879

Illustrated History of Australia Sydney: Hamlyn, 1974

Kohen, J. L., *Aborigines in the West: Prehistory to Present* Sydney: The Western Sydney Project, 1985

McQueen, Humphrey, "Defending Australia" in *Identity* 2, 4, 1975

NSW Government *Historical Records of New South Wales*, vols 1–3, Sydney: Potter, 1892

Pilger, John, *Heroes*, London: Cape, 1986

Stanner, W. E. H., "The history of indifference thus begins" in *Aboriginal History* 1, 1, 1977, pp.3–26

Tench, Watkin, *Sydney's First Four Years . . .* Sydney: Angus & Robertson, 1961

Willey, Keith, *When the Sky Fell Down: the Destruction of the Tribes of the Sydney Region 1788–1850s* Sydney: Collins, 1979

5. *The Battle of Vinegar Hill*

NOTES

1. C. M. H. Clark, *A History of Australia* vol.1, Parkville, Vic.: Melbourne University Press, 1962, p.90

2. quoted in Clark, p.70

3. Clark, p.92

4. Clark, p.94

5. P. O'Farrell, *The Irish in Australia* Kensington, NSW: NSW University Press, 1987, p.25

6. Clark, p.103

7. Clark, p.104

8. Clark, p.156

9. quoted in Clark, p.155

10. Clark, p.156

11. ibid.

12. ibid.

13. Clark, p.164

14. T. Pakenham, *The Year of Liberty: the Story of the Great Irish Rebellion of 1798* London: Hodder & Stoughton, 1969, p.26

15. Clark, p.170

16. ibid.

17. ibid.

18. ibid.

19. Clark, p.169

20. Clark, p.171

21. ibid.

22. Pakenham, p.18

23. Pakenham, p.13

24. quoted in Pakenham, p.13

25. Pakenham, p.188

26. Pakenham, p.289

27. Pakenham, p.256

28. G. O'Tuathaigh, *Ireland Before the Famine 1798–1848* Dublin: Gill & Macmillan, 1972, p.29

29. quoted in Pakenham, p.137

30. Pakenham, p.329

31. J. G. Symes, *The Castle Hill Rebellion of 1804* n.p.: Hills District Historical Society, 1979, p.5

32. Symes, p.6

33. Symes, p.5

34. J. Holt, *Memoires of Joseph Holt: General of the Irish Rebels 1798* 2 vols, London: Colburn, 1838, p.195

35. Holt, p.194

36. Holt, p.195

37. *HRA* I, IV, p.566

38. Symes, p.8

39. quoted in Symes, p.8

40. Holt, p.196

41. Symes, p.8

42. Symes, p.11

43. Symes, p.12

44. Symes, p.9

45. Symes, p.12–13

46. Symes, p.10

47. Symes, p.13

48. Symes, p.9

49. Symes, p.16

50. *Historical Records of New South Wales* vol.5, Sydney: Government Printer, 1897, p.345

51. quoted in Symes, p.16

52. Symes, p.16

53. Symes, p.18

54. ibid.

55. C. Oman, *The Great Revolt of 1381* Oxford: Clarendon Press, 1906, p.51

56. Oman, p.75

57. Oman, p.78

58. Symes, p.19

59. *HRNSW* 5, p.349

60. ibid.

61. *HRA* I, IV, p.570

62. Holt, p.201

63. Symes, p.23

64. Symes, p.24

65. Symes, p.25

66. Symes, p.26

67. Holt, p.201

68. J. G. Murtagh, *Australia: the Catholic Chapter* Melbourne: Polding Press, 1969, p.11

69. P. O'Farrell, *The Catholic Church and Community in Australia: A History* West Melbourne, Vic.: Nelson, 1977, p.6

70. O'Farrell, p.7

71. ibid.

72. F. W. Faber, "Faith of Our Fathers", in J. A. De Luca (comp.), *The New Living Parish Hymn Book* Sydney: Dwyer, 1986

73. Symes, p.25

74. Symes, p.26

BIBLIOGRAPHY

Bonwick. J., *First Twenty Years of Australia* London: Sampson Low, Marston, Searle & Rivington, 1882

Clark, C. M. H., *A History of Australia: I: From Earliest Times to the Age of Macquarie* Parkville, Vic.: Melbourne University Press, 1962

Cobley, John (comp.), *The Crimes of the First Fleet Convicts* Sydney: Angus & Robertson, 1970

Dolan, C. P., "Australia's first battle" in *The Navy, Army & Airforce Journal* 1935, pp.7–8

Froude, James Anthony, *The English in Ireland in the Eighteenth Century* London: Longmans, Green, 1884

Historical Records of Australia I, IV, Library Committee of the Commonwealth Parliament, 1914

Holt, Joseph, *Memoirs of Joseph Holt: General of the Irish Rebels 1798* 2 vols, London: Colburn, 1838

Levi, J. S., *The Forefathers: a Dictionary of Biography of the Jews of Australia 1788–1830* Sydney: Australian Jewish Historical Society, 1976

McDowell, R. B., *Ireland in the Age of Imperialism and Revolution 1760–1801* Oxford: Clarendon Press, 1979

Murtagh, James G., *Australia: the Catholic Chapter* Melbourne: Polding Press, 1969

NSW. *Government Historical Records of New South Wales* vol.5, Sydney: Government Printer, 1897

O'Farrell, Patrick, *The Catholic Church and Community in Australia: a History* West Melbourne, Vic.: Nelson, 1977

——, *The Irish in Australia* Kensington, NSW: NSW University Press, 1987

Oman, Charles, *The Great Revolt of 1381* Oxford: Clarendon Press, 1906

O'Tuathaigh, Gearoid, *Ireland Before the Famine 1798–1848* Dublin: Gill & Macmillan, 1972

Pakenham, Thomas, *The Year of Liberty: the Story of the Great Irish Rebellion of 1798* London: Hodder & Stoughton, 1969

Symes, James G., *The Castle Hill Rebellion of 1804* n.p.: Hills District Historical Society, 1979

Teeling, Charles Hamilton, *History of the Irish Rebellion of 1798 and Sequel to the History of the Irish Rebellion of 1798* Shannon: Irish University Press, 1972

6. *The Battle of Bathurst*

NOTES

1. T. Salisbury and P. J. Gresser, *Windradyne of the Wiradjuri: Martial Law at Bathurst* Sydney: Wentworth, 1971, p.11

2. Salisbury and Gresser, p.11

3. C. M. H. Clark, *A History of Australia: I: From Earliest Times to the Age of Macquarie* Melbourne: Melbourne University Press, 1962, p.282

4. Clark, p.266

5. Clark, p.267

6. T. M. Perry, *Australia's First Frontier: The Spread of Settlement in New South Wales 1788–1829* London: Melbourne University Press, 1963, p.271

7. quoted in Perry, p.26

8. Perry, pp.26–8

9. Salisbury and Gresser, p.11

10. Salisbury and Gresser, p.12

11. ibid.

12. ibid.

13. quoted in Perry, p.30

14. Salisbury and Gresser, p.13

15. ibid.
16. ibid.
17. quoted in Salisbury and Gresser, p.13
18. Salisbury and Gresser, p.15
19. Salisbury and Gresser, p.14
20. ibid.
21. ibid.
22. ibid.
23. ibid.
24. Salisbury and Gresser, p.15
25. ibid.
26. Perry, p.30
27. Clark, p.280
28. ibid.
29. *Historical Records of Australia* I, IX, pp.141–5
30. *HRA* I, IX, p.141
31. *HRA* I, IX, p.142
32. Clark, p.315
33. *Australian Encyclopaedia*, vol.5, p.453
34. C. Liston, "Sir Thomas Brisbane in New South Wales" *Royal Australian Historical Society Journal* 71, 2, 1985, p.91
35. Liston, p.92
36. Salisbury and Gresser, p.18
37. Liston, p.94
38. ibid.
39. Liston, p.95
40. *Australian Encyclopaedia*, vol.2, 127
41. Mundy quoted in P. J. Gresser, The Aborigines of the Bathurst District: Historical Sketch. Unpublished manuscript, 1964
42. ibid.
43. ibid.
44. Gresser, p.7
45. ibid.
46. ibid.
47. P. J. Read, A History of the Wiradjuri people of New South Wales 1883–1969. PhD thesis, Canberra: ANU, 1983, p.3
48. Read, p.6
49. Read, p.8
50. C. Cooper, "Art of Temperate Southeast Australia" pp. 28–41 in *Aboriginal Australia* Sydney: AGDC, 1981, p.32
51. Read, p.14

52. Cooper, p.35

53. Cooper, p.29

54. ibid.

55. L. Black, *The Bora Ground*, n.p., 1944, p.12

56. Black, p.16

57. Black, p.17

58. Cooper, p.36

59. Cooper, p.34

60. Cooper, p.32

61. Clark, p.382

62. Salisbury and Gresser, p.20

63. Salisbury and Gresser, p.19

64. ibid.

65. ibid.

66. Salisbury and Gresser, p.20

67. Salisbury and Gresser, p.22

68. ibid.

69. Salisbury and Gresser, p.23

70. ibid.

71. Salisbury and Gresser, p.24

72. Salisbury and Gresser, p.25

73. Salisbury and Gresser, p.26

74. Extract from Bonwick Transcripts p.1433 in P. J. Gresser, Articles and Extracts Relating to the Aborigines of the Bathurst District . . . Sydney, Mitchell Library (unpublished manuscripts)

75. *Sydney Gazette* 19 August 1824

76. *Sydney Gazette* 5 August 1824

77. ibid.

78. Salisbury and Gresser, p.27

79. quoted in Salisbury and Gresser, p.33

80. quoted in Salisbury and Gresser, p.30

81. ibid.

82. M. Barthrop, *British Infantry Uniforms Since 1660* Poole: Blandford Press, 1982, p.64

83. Barthrop, p.65

84. ibid.

85. Salisbury and Gresser, p.31

86. Salisbury and Gresser, p.31–2

87. quoted in Salisbury and Gresser, p.34

88. *Sydney Gazette* 30 September 1824

89. ibid.

90. ibid.
91. ibid.
92. Gresser, p.11
93. *Sydney Gazette* 14 October 1824
94. Gresser, p.11
95. ibid.
96. *Sydney Gazette* 21 October 1824
97. *Sydney Gazette* 28 October 1824
98. Salisbury and Gresser, p.33
99. Gresser, p.11
100. Salisbury and Gresser, p.35
101. Read, p.28, referring to M. Pearson estimates
102. Salisbury and Gresser, pp. 37–8
103. Salisbury and Gresser, p.36
104. ibid.
105. Salisbury and Gresser, p.37
106. ibid.
107. Salisbury and Gresser, p.39
108. ibid.
109. Salisbury and Gresser, p.40
110. Salisbury and Gresser, p.41
111. Salisbury and Gresser, pp.42–3
112. Salisbury and Gresser, p.38

BIBLIOGRAPHY

Australian Encyclopaedia 10 vols, Sydney: Grolier, 1962

Barthrop, Michael, *British Infantry Uniforms Since 1660* Poole: Blandford Press, 1982

Black, Lindsay, *The Bora Ground* n.p., 1944

"The Black War" in *The Living Australia* 40, pp.19–21

Clark, C. M. H., *A History of Australia: I: From Earliest Times to the Age of Macquarie* Melbourne: Melbourne University Press, 1962

Coe, Mary, *Windradyne: a Wiradjuri Koorie* Glebe, NSW: Blackbooks, 1986

Cooper, Carol, "Art of Temperate Southeast Australia" pp.28–41 in *Aboriginal Australia* Sydney: AGDC, 1981

Greaves, Bernard, *The Story of Bathurst* Sydney: Angus & Robertson, 1961

Gresser, P. J., The Aborigines of the Bathurst District: Historical Sketch. Unpublished manuscript held in AIAS Library

——, Articles and extracts relating to the Aborigines of the Bathurst District, principally from the *Sydney Gazette* of 1824. Mitchell Library (from unpublished manuscripts held in AIAS Library)

Historical Records of Australia Series I, vols IX and XI, Library Committee of the Commonwealth Parliament, 1917

Kohen, J. L., *Aborigines in the West: Prehistory to Present* Sydney: Western Sydney Project

Liston, Carol, "Sir Thomas Brisbane in New South Wales in *Royal Australian Historical Society Journal* 71, 2, 1985, pp.91–106

Perry, T. M., *Australia's First Frontier: The Spread of Settlement in New South Wales 1788–1829* London: Melbourne University Press, 1963

Read, Peter John, A History of the Wiradjuri People of New South Wales 1883–1969. PhD thesis, Canberra: ANU, 1983

Salisbury, T., and Gresser, P. J., *Windradyne of the Wiradjuri: Martial Law at Bathurst* Sydney: Wentworth, 1971 (Studies in Australian Pacific History 4)

Whyman, Kevin, Morgan, Les, and Hepworth, Tony, *The Wiradjuri* Wagga Wagga, NSW: Riverina CAE, 1981

7. *The Battle of Pinjarra*

NOTES

1. N. Green, *Broken Spears: Aborigines and Europeans in the Southwest of Australia* Perth: Focus Education, 1984, p.28

2. Green, p.30

3. W. Dampier, *A Voyage to New Holland* London, 1703

4. Green, p.27

5. Green, p.33

6. Green, p.34

7. Green, p.37

8. *HRA* III, VI, pp.468–75

9. *Historical Records of Australia* III, VI, pp.551–84

10. *HRA* III, VI, pp.600–2

11. Green, p.48

12. M. C. Howard, "Aboriginal society in south-western Australia"in R. M. and C. H. Berndt (eds), *Aborigines of the West: Their Past and Their Present* Nedlands: University of Western Australia Press, 1979, p.90

13. Howard, p.91

14. Green, p.49

15. quoted in Green, p.51

16. Green, p.16

17. A. Hasluck, *Thomas Peel of Swan River* Melbourne: Oxford University Press, 1965, p.9

18. Hasluck, p.11

19. Hasluck, p.22

20. Green, p.75

21. Green, p.77

22. quoted in Green, p.76

23. *Perth Gazette* 9 March 1833
24. Hasluck, p.145
25. Hasluck, p.144
26. Green, p.95
27. quoted in Green, p.96
28. quoted in Green, p.97
29. ibid.
30. Green, p.98
31. Green, p.93
32. ibid.
33. Green, p.94
34. Hasluck, p.149
35. Hasluck, p.150
36. ibid.
37. quoted in Hasluck, p.151
38. ibid.
39. Hasluck, p.151
40. Green, p.99
41. Green, p.101
42. Green, p.102
43. ibid.
44. G. F. Moore, *Diary of Ten Years Eventful Life of an Early Settler in Western Australia*, Nedlands: University of Western Australia Press, 1979
45. Green, p.104
46. ibid.
47. Green, p.104–5
48. Green, p.105
49. Moore, op.cit.
50. quoted in Green, p.105
51. Green, p.106
52. ibid.
53. ibid.
54. quoted in Green, p.97

BIBLIOGRAPHY

Berndt, R. M., "Aborigines of the South-west", pp. 81–9 in R. M. and C. H. Berndt (eds), *Aborigines of the West: Their Past and Their Present* Nedlands: University of Western Australia Press for the Education Committee of the 150th Anniversary Celebration, 1979

Crowley, Frank, *A Documentary History of Australia: Vol.I: Colonial Australia 1788–1840* Melbourne: Nelson, 1980

Dampier, W., *A Voyage to New Holland* London, 1703

Fletcher, Christine, "The Battle of Pinjarra: a revisionist view" pp.1–6 in Bob Reece and Tom Stannage (eds), *European–Aboriginal Relations in Western Australian History* Nedlands: University of Western Australia Press, 1984

Goldsmith, Frank H., "The Battle of Pinjarra" in *Journal & Proceedings of R.A.H.S.* 37, 6, 1951, pp.344–50

Green, Neville, "Aboriginal and settler conflict in Western Australia 1826–1852" in *The Push from the Bush* 3, 1979, pp.68–94

——, *Broken Spears: Aborigines and Europeans in the Southwest of Australia* Perth: Focus Education, 1984

——, *Nyungar Past and Present* Perth: Focus Education, 1983

Hancock, D., "The battle of Pinjarra" in *Parade* 246, 1971

Hasluck, Alexandra, *Thomas Peel of Swan River* Melbourne: Oxford University Press, 1965

Historical Records of Australia III, VI, Library Committee of the Commonwealth Parliament, 1923

Howard, Michael C., "Aboriginal society in south-western Australia" pp.90–9 in R. M. and C. H. Berndt (eds), *Aborigines of the West: Their Past and Their Present* Nedlands: University of Western Australia Press for the Education Committee of the 150th Anniversary Celebration, 1979

Ilbery, E. S., Grose, J. E. and Battye, J. S., "The battle of Pinjarra, 1834" in *The Western Australian Historical Society Journal and Proceedings* I, 1927, pp.24–37

Illustrated History of Australia Sydney: Hamlyn, 1974

Irwin, F. C., *The State and Position of Western Australia* London: Simpkin, Marshall, 1835

Moore, G. F., *Diary of Ten Years Eventful Life of an Early Settler in Western Australia . . .* First published 1884. Facsimile edn, Nedlands: University of Western Australia Press, 1978

Terry, Peter, "The battle of Pinjarra" *Sunday Times* 27 October 1985

——, "Slaughter a skeleton in our cupboard", *Sunday Telegraph* 27 October 1985

8. *The Battle of Eureka Stockade*

NOTES

1. J. Flood, *Archaeology of the Dreamtime* Sydney: Collins, 1983, pp.205–6
2. K. G. McIntyre, *The Secret Discovery of Australia* Medindie, SA: Souvenir Press, 1977, p.263
3. M. Christie, *Aborigines in Colonial Victoria 1835–86* Sydney: Sydney University Press, 1979, p.50
4. Christie, p.7
5. Christie, p.29
6. Christie, p.136
7. Based on figures in Christie, p.207
8. Christie, p.136

9. A. L. Haydon, *The Trooper Police of Australia* London: Melrose, 1911

10. *Australian Encyclopaedia* Sydney: Grolier, 1962, vol.9, p.119

11. J. Bauer, California and Australia: Coincidences, Contacts and Connections. MA thesis, California State University, 1974, p.20

12. Bauer, p.21

13. ibid.

14. ibid.

15. Bauer, p.19

16. Bauer, p.23

17. Bauer, p.24

18. Bauer, p.26

19. ibid.

20. ibid.

21. Bauer, p.28

22. Bauer, p.30

23. Haydon, p.80

24. Bauer, p.32

25. ibid.

26. Haydon, p.81

27. S. Korzelinski, *Memoirs of Gold-digging in Australia* St Lucia, Qld: University of Queensland Press, 1979, p.42

28. Korzelinski, p.44

29. Korzelinski, p.55

30. Korzelinski, p.56

31. Korzelinski, p.59

32. Korzelinski, p.64

33. T. Dare, *Australians: Making a Great Nation* Brookvale, NSW: Child & Henry, 1985, p.68

34. Dare, pp.67–8

35. quoted in Dare, p.69

36. Dare, p.69

37. ibid.

38. Dare, p.73

39. G. M. Gold, "The search for gold" pp.9–23 in G. M. Gold (ed.), *Eureka: Rebellion Beneath the Southern Cross* Adelaide: Rigby, 1977, p.13

40. Dare, p.66

41. quoted in Gold, p.13

42. Gold, p.14

43. quoted in Gold, p.16

44. G. M. Gold, "The rebellion" pp.25–49 in G. M. Gold (ed.), *Eureka: Rebellion Beneath the Southern Cross* Adelaide: Rigby, 1977, p.25

45. G. Serle, "The causes of Eureka" pp.42–54 in *Historical Studies: Eureka*

Supplement London: Melbourne University Press, 1965, p.42

46. H. D. McQueen, "Causes of Eureka" pp.51–61 in G. M. Gold (ed.), *Eureka: Rebellion Beneath the Southern Cross* Adelaide: Rigby, 1977, p.59

47. ibid.

48. Gold, "The rebellion", p.25

49. Serle, p.44

50. ibid.

51. Serle, p.46

52. Gold, p.25

53. ibid.

54. ibid.

55. quoted in Serle, p.49

56. quoted in Gold, p.26

57. ibid.

58. ibid.

59. ibid.

60. Gold, p.26

61. ibid.

62. quoted in Gold, p.29

63. ibid.

64. ibid.

65. ibid.

66. quoted in Gold, p.30

67. quoted in Gold, p.32

68. quoted in Gold, p.34

69. quoted in A. J. Grassby, "Shots that echoed around the world" pp.9–13 in Department of Immigration *Eureka: a Saga of Australian History* 1973, p.10

70. R. Carboni, *The Eureka Stockade* Melbourne: Dolphin, 1947, p.83

71. Gold, p.29

72. quoted in Gold, p.30

73. ibid.

74. A. J. Grassby, "Echoes of Eureka" pp.81–9 in G. M. Gold (ed.), *Eureka: Rebellion Beneath the Southern Cross* Adelaide: Rigby, 1977, p.86

75. Carboni, p.72

76. quoted in Gold, p.32

77. quoted in Serle, p.52

78. quoted in Serle, p.53

79. quoted in Gold, p.32

80. ibid.

81. quoted in Carboni, pp.88–9

82. quoted in Gold, p.32

83. quoted in Gold, p.37

84. quoted in Gold, p.34
85. Carboni, p.103
86. Carboni, p.96
87. Dare, p.72–3
88. Carboni, p.104
89. Gold, p.40
90. quoted in Gold, p.40
91. quoted in Gold, p.45
92. quoted in Gold, p.46
93. A. J. Grassby, "Shots that echoed around the world", p.10
94. ibid.
95. ibid.
96. Grassby, "Shots that echoed around the world", p.11
97. ibid.
98. ibid.
99. M. Willis and G. M. Gold, "Eureka our heritage" pp.91–109 in G. M. Gold (ed.), *Eureka: Rebellion Beneath the Southern Cross* Adelaide: Rigby, 1977, p.91
100. A. J. Grassby, Battle of the Eureka Stockade. Unpublished paper, p.3

BIBLIOGRAPHY

Australian Encyclopaedia, 10 vols, Sydney: Grolier, 1962

Bauer, June, California and Australia: Coincidences, Contacts and Connections. MA thesis, California State University, 1974

Carboni, Raffaello, *The Eureka Stockade* Melbourne: Dolphin, 1947. (First published 1855)

Christie, M. F., *Aborigines in Colonial Victoria 1835–86* Sydney: Sydney University Press, 1979

Dare, Tim, *Australians: Making a Great Nation* Brookvale, NSW: Child & Henry, 1985

Dunn, Michael and Robert Darby, "The aftermath" pp.63–79 in G. M. Gold (ed.), *Eureka: Rebellion Beneath the Southern Cross* Adelaide: Rigby, 1977

Flood, Josephine, *Archaeology of the Dreamtime* Sydney: Collins, 1983

Gibson, Tom, "The Eureka Stockade" *Canberra Times* 7 December 1985

Gold, Geoffrey, "The rebellion" pp.25–49 in G. M. Gold (ed.), *Eureka: Rebellion Beneath the Southern Cross* Adelaide: Rigby, 1977

——, "The search for gold" pp.9–23 in G. M. Gold (ed.), *Eureka: Rebellion Beneath the Southern Cross* Adelaide: Rigby, 1977

——*(ed.), Eureka: Rebellion Beneath the Southern Cross* Adelaide: Rigby, 1977

Grant, James, *The Narrative of a Voyage of Discovery* . . . London: Egerton/Military Library, 1803

Grassby, A. J., Battle of the Eureka Stockade. Unpublished paper

——, "Echoes of Eureka" pp.81–9 in G. M. Gold (ed.), *Eureka: Rebellion Beneath the Southern Cross* Adelaide: Rigby, 1977

——, "Eureka: a saga" pp.14–19 in Department of Immigration *Eureka: a Saga of Australian History*, 1973

——, "Shots that echoed around the world" pp.9–13 in Department of Immigration *Eureka: a Saga of Australian History*, 1973

Haydon, A. L., *The Trooper Police of Australia* . . . London: Melrose, 1911

Korzelinski, Seweryn, *Memoirs of Gold-digging in Australia* St Lucia, Qld: University of Queensland Press, 1979

McIntyre, Kenneth Gordon, *The Secret Discovery of Australia: Portuguese Ventures 200 Years Before Captain Cook* Medindie, SA: Souvenir Press, 1977

McQueen, H. D., "Causes of Eureka" pp.51–61 in G. M. Gold (ed.), *Eureka: Rebellion Beneath the Southern Cross* Adelaide: Rigby, 1977

Molony, John, *Eureka* Ringwood, Vic.: Viking, 1984

Serle, Geoffrey, "The causes of Eureka" pp.42–54 in *Historical Studies: Eureka Supplement* 2nd edn, London: Melbourne University Press, 1965

Turner, Henry Gyles, *Our Own Little Rebellion: the Story of the Eureka Stockade* Melbourne: Whitcombe & Tombs, n.d.

Whitlam, E. G., "Eureka: the birth of Australian democracy" pp.3–8 in Department of Immigration *Eureka: a Saga of Australian History*, 1973

Willis, Michael, and Gold, Geoffrey, "Eureka our heritage" pp.91–109 in G. M. Gold (ed.), *Eureka: Rebellion Beneath the Southern Cross* Adelaide: Rigby, 1977

9. *The Battle of Battle Mountain*

NOTES

1. K. G. McIntyre, *The Secret Discovery of Australia: Portuguese Ventures 200 Years Before Captain Cook*, Adelaide: Souvenir Press, 1977, p.246

2. McIntyre, p.243

3. McIntyre, p.247

4. McIntyre, p.248

5. J. E. Heeres quoted in N. Loos, *Invasion and Resistance: Aboriginal–European Relations on the North Queensland Frontier 1861–1897* Canberra: ANU Press, 1982, p.8

6. Loos, p.9

7. Macgillivray quoted in Loos, p.9

8. Loos, p.9

9. ibid.

10. Loos, p.10

11. J. Macgillivray, *Narrative of the Voyage of HMS Rattlesnake* . . . London: Boone, 1852, p.99

12. Loos, p.12

13. L. Leichhardt quoted in Loos, pp.12–13

14. Loos, p.14

15. Loos, p.15
16. Loos, p.17
17. ibid.
18. Loos, p.18
19. Loos, p.16
20. ibid.
21. R. E. M. Armstrong, *The Kalkadoons: a Study of an Aboriginal Tribe on the Queensland Frontier* Brisbane: Brooks, p.42
22. W. E. Roth, *Ethnological Studies among the North-west-central Queensland Aborigines* Brisbane: Government Printer, 1897, pp.142–51
23. Roth, p.142
24. Armstrong, p.49
25. B. Bridges, "The Mounted Police" in *Royal Australian Historical Society Newsletter* 83, p.7
26. Loos, p.23
27. H. Reynolds, "The unrecorded battlefields of Queensland" in H. Reynolds (ed.), *Race Relations in North Queensland* Townsville: James Cook University, 1978, p.38
28. Loos, p.25
29. ibid.
30. F. Wheeler quoted in Loos, p.26
31. A. L. Haydon, *The Trooper Police of Australia* London: Melrose, 1911, p.372
32. H. G. Lamond, "Native Mounted Police" *Walkabout*, Nov. 1949, p.32
33. Armstrong, p.140
34. E. Palmer, *Early Days in North Queensland* Sydney: Angus & Robertson, 1903, p.15
35. T. Bergin, *In the Steps of Burke and Wills* Sydney: ABC, 1981, pp.88–9
36. Loos, p.20
37. Loos, p.21
38. ibid.
39. Palmer, *Early Days in North Queensland*
40. Palmer, p.211
41. Palmer, p.213
42. Palmer, p.209
43. G. Phillips, "Ernest Henry . . . " in *Historical Society of Queensland Journal* 2, 1923, pp.97–120
44. Reynolds, "The unrecorded battlefields of Queensland", p.35
45. Reynolds, p.26
46. H. Fysh, *Taming the North* Sydney: Angus & Robertson, 1950, p.3
47. quoted in Fysh, p.114
48. Armstrong, p.128
49. Fysh, p.96

50. quoted in Fysh, p.113
51. Armstrong, p.88
52. Fysh, p.97
53. Fysh, p.98
54. Fysh, p.122
55. Fysh, p.124
56. ibid.
57. Fysh, p.139
58. Armstrong, p.130
59. Armstrong, p.132
60. ibid.
61. ibid.
62. Armstrong, p.134
63. ibid.
64. Mention of the name Mahoni is the only reference in the white literature to a possible Kalkadoon leader, Fysh, p.142
65. Armstrong, p.136
66. ibid.
67. Armstrong, p.138
68. ibid.
69. Armstrong, p.140
70. Armstrong, p.142
71. ibid.
72. ibid.
73. Armstrong, p.144
74. ibid.
75. ibid.
76. Armstrong, p.145
77. Armstrong, p.172
78. Fysh, p.186
79. Fysh, p.251
80. H. Holthouse, *Up Rode the Squatter* Adelaide: Rigby, 1974, p.120
81. Holthouse, p.121
82. Armstrong, p.144

BIBLIOGRAPHY

Aplin, Bill, *The History of the Exciting North West* n.p., n.d.

Armstrong, R. E. M., *The Kalkadoons: a Study of an Aboriginal Tribe on the Queensland Frontier* Brisbane: Brooks, n.d.

Barnett, Susan, A study of the Queensland Native Mounted Police Force in the 1870s, BA Hons. thesis in History, University of Queensland, 1975

Bergin, Tom, *In the Steps of Burke and Wills* Sydney: ABC, 1981

Blake, Barry J., *The Kalkatungu Language: a Brief Description* Canberra: AIAS, 1969

Bridges, Barry, "The Mounted Police (1826–1850)" *Royal Australian Historical Society Newsletter* 83, 1969, pp.6–7

Cilento, Raphael, and Lack, Clem, *Triumph in the Tropics: an Historical Sketch of Queensland* Brisbane: Smith & Paterson, 1959

Dent, M. K., "The Kalkadoons, 1: Artefacts" *Mimag*, 1973, pp.9–11

Eussen, R. V., "The Kalkadoons, 2: Rock Canvas" *Mimag*, 1973, pp.12–15

Farnfield, D. J., "Problems of Early Queensland 1859–1870" pp.9–18 in *Lectures on North Queensland History* Townsville: History Department, James Cook University, 1974

Fysh, Hudson, *Taming the North* rev. edn, Sydney: Angus & Robertson, 1950

Haydon, A. L., *The Trooper Police of Australia* London: Melrose, 1911

Holthouse, Hector, *Up Rode the Squatter* Adelaide: Rigby, 1974

Kennedy, K. H., "The Profits of Boom: a Short History of the Cloncurry Copper Field" pp.1–34 in *Lectures on North Queensland History: Third Series* Townsville: History Department, James Cook University, 1978

Lack, Clem, and Stafford, Harry, *The Rifle and the Spear* Brisbane: Fortitude Press, n.d.

Lamond, Henry G., "Native Mounted Police" *Walkabout* Nov. 1949, pp.31–2

Laurie, Arthur, "The Black War in Queensland" in *The Royal Historical Society of Queensland Special Journal to Mark the Centenary of Queensland 1859–1959* 6, 1, 1959, pp.155–73

Loos, N. A., "Aboriginal–Dutch Relations in North Queensland, 1606–1756" *Queensland Heritage* 3, 1, 1974, pp.3–8

——, Aboriginal–European Relations in North Queensland 1861–1897 PhD thesis, Department of History, James Cook University, 1976

——, "Aboriginal resistance in North Queensland" pp.233–45 in *Lectures on North Queensland History: Third Series* Townsville: History Department, James Cook University, 1978

——, "Aboriginal resistance on the mining, rainforest, and fishing frontiers" pp.163–75 in *Lectures on North Queensland History* Townsville: History Department, James Cook University, 1974

——, *Invasion and Resistance: Aboriginal–European Relations on the North Queensland Frontier 1861–1897* Canberra: ANU Press, 1982

——, "The pragmatic racism of the frontier" pp.279–301 in H. Reynolds (ed.), *Race Relations in North Queensland* Townsville: James Cook University, 1978

Macgillivray, John, *Narrative of the Voyage of HMS Rattlesnake . . .* London: Boone, 1852

McIntyre, Kenneth Gordon, *The Secret Discovery of Australia: Portuguese Ventures 200 Years Before Captain Cook* Adelaide: Souvenir Press, 1977

Palmer, Edward, *Early Days in North Queensland* Sydney: Angus & Robertson, 1903

Pearson, S. E., "Beresford and the Kalkadoons" pp.33–5 in Glenville Pike (ed.), *Campfire Tales: an Anthology of True Stories* Mareeba: Pinevale, 1981

Phillips, George, "Ernest Henry: the Discoverer and Principal Prospector of the Cloncurry Mineral District of North-west Queensland" in *Historical Society of Queensland Journal* 2, 2, 1923, pp.97–120

Reynolds, H., " The Other Side of the Frontier: Early Aboriginal Reactions to Pastoral Settlement in Queensland and Northern New South Wales" pp.1–20 in H. Reynolds (ed.), *Race Relations in North Queensland* Townsville: James Cook University, 1978

——, *The Other Side of the Frontier: An Interpretation of the Aboriginal Response to the Invasion and Settlement of Australia* Townsville: History Department, James Cook University, 1981

——, "Settlers and Aborigines on the Pastoral Frontier" pp.153–61 in *Lectures on North Queensland History* Townsville: History Department, James Cook University, 1974

——, " The unrecorded battlefields of Queensland" pp.23–52 in H. Reynolds (ed.), *Race Relations in North Queensland* Townsville: James Cook University, 1978

Robinson, Fergus, and York, Barry, *The Black Resistance: an Introduction to the History of the Aborigines Struggle against British Colonialism* Camberwell, Vic.: Widescope, 1977

Roth, Walter E., *Ethnological Studies Among the North-west-central Queensland Aborigines* Brisbane: Government Printer, 1897

Skinner, L. E., *Police of the Pastoral Frontier: Native Police 1849–59* St Lucia, Qld: University of Queensland Press, 1975

Truscott, C., "A Pastoralist's Paradise among the Ferocious Kalkadoons" *Parade* 309, n.d.

INDEX